The Civil-Military Fabric of WEIMAR
FOREIGN
POLICY

GAINES POST, JR.

The Civil-Military Fabric of **Weimar**

Foreign

Policy

PRINCETON
UNIVERSITY PRESS

LCC Card: 72-7799
ISBN: 0-691-05211-5

This book has been composed in
Linotype Times Roman.
Printed in the United States of America
by Princeton University Press,
Princeton, New Jersey

To my Mother and Father

I BEGAN the research on this book like a novice backpacker about to hike into a wilderness area. I thought I knew the general terrain and techniques; I assumed that the trail would be easy to follow. After some time in the documentary wilderness of German foreign policy and military planning, I realized, however, that some of its contours had been charted poorly or not at all by early surveyors; I also discovered that the marked trail ended rather abruptly. I went on, not expecting to tame this fascinating wild area, but hoping to come to terms with it in a way which made sense to me, fulfilled my urge to explore, and gave me an appreciation of its dimensions.

Preface

I have tried to provide a more accurate map and break a new trail for others. If I have indeed succeeded, it has not been without support. I wish to thank the following for their kind assistance in the search for unpublished documents and other sources and in the use of them: the staff of the Politisches Archiv of the Auswärtiges Amt, Bonn; Dr. Wolfgang Mommsen and the staff of the Bundesarchiv, Koblenz; the staff of the document section of the Militärgeschichtliches Forschungsamt (now part of the Bundesarchiv-Militärarchiv), Freiburg; Dr. Thilo Vogelsang and the staff of the Institut für Zeitgeschichte, Munich; Dr. Jürgen Rohwer and the staff of the Bibliothek für Zeitgeschichte (Weltkriegsbücherei), Stuttgart; Dr. Helmut Schnitter of the Deutsche Akademie der Wissenschaften zu Berlin, Institut für Geschichte; R.R.A. Wheatley and K. Hiscock of the Foreign Office Library,

London; Lieutenant Commander P. K. Kemp and J. D. Lawson of the Naval Historical Branch, Ministry of Defence, London; the Public Record Office; the British Museum; the Hoover Institution, Stanford, California, especially Mrs. Agnes Peterson; and the Libraries of Stanford University and the University of Texas at Austin. My thanks also go to the Deutscher Akademischer Austauschdienst and Stanford University for research and travel grants; and to the University Research Institute and Graduate School of the University of Texas at Austin for financial aid during the last stages of preparing the manuscript.

I am grateful to the former officers of the Reichswehr and to others who freely answered my questions and provided valuable information through interviews and correspondence; their names can be found in the bibliography. Here I want particularly to thank Lieutenant General Hermann Flörke and his family for their hospitality, their candor, and their friendship, all of which began when I was stationed in Giessen as a lieutenant in the United States Army.

Of the many persons who have encouraged my interest in history, I wish to mention the late scholars Theodor E. Mommsen of Cornell University, Fritz Ernst of the University of Heidelberg, and H. E. Bell of New College, Oxford. In no small sense is this book written in their memory. Professor Gordon A. Craig directed my dissertation (on which this work expands) at Stanford University, and I am indebted to him for his critical counsel. Others who assisted me over rough spots in the manuscript in its various stages are Professor John C. Cairns, Professor Jon Jacobson, Professor Henry A. Turner, Jr., Donald Alexander, and Thomas Sullivan. Susan J. Sherrill typed the final manuscript.

I thank my wife Jeanie, who read the manuscript more carefully than I wrote it. She is an enthusiastic backpacker, and believes that historians should activate their verbs and recognize a chiasmus when they see one.

Haskell, Texas
June 4, 1972

Contents

CONTENTS

LIST OF ABBREVIATIONS

AA   Files of the German Foreign Office (*Auswärtiges Amt*). See bibliography for complete listing.
DBFP *Documents on British Foreign Policy 1919-39.*
RK   Files of the German Reich Chancery (*Reichskanzlei*).
RWM   Files of the German Defense Ministry (*Reichswehrministerium*).

The Civil-Military Fabric of WEIMAR
FOREIGN
POLICY

In the historiographic debate over Germany's responsibility for the outbreak of the two world wars, scant attention has been given to German politico-military activity in the Weimar Republic. This lacuna should be filled; in foreign policy and military planning, the Weimar Republic was not simply an interregnum between Wilhelmian Germany and the Third Reich. The following analysis has two purposes. In the first place it will attempt to integrate German foreign policy and military planning, for, whereas Weimar diplomats and military leaders emphasized the interconnection and developed ideas and procedures for joint planning, historians have usually treated the foreign and military affairs of the republic separately. Diplomatic histories recount the problems of German foreign policy stemming from Germany's isolated and militarily weak position without examining, beyond such well-known episodes as General Hans von Seeckt's opposition to Gustav Stresemann's Locarno policy, relations among the Foreign Office and the Defense Ministry and the two service commands. And studies of the Reichswehr—the Army and the Navy—dwell upon the internal political role of professions whose primary responsibility, at least in the period 1924-29, was the security of the Reich against foreign attack. Second, this inquiry into joint planning will try to chart directions and changes in the evolution of civil-military relations in the republic, in the hope of shedding some light on the general problem of modern civil-military relations.

Introduction

3

In the chapters that follow, "foreign policy" and "policy" will be used not only in the narrow sense to indicate national goals, but also more broadly to include the means by which these objectives are pursued. There are two different categories of means: 1) intermediate goals that might be viewed as steps toward attaining long-range goals; and 2) diplomacy, which is not restricted to negotiation but encompasses all the methods of implementing national policy in an international system, including the application or threat of military force.

The term "politico-military" will refer to those activities belonging to both foreign policy and military planning: the security of national political and territorial integrity, and— seldom divorced from national security—the attainment of national goals in an international setting. Of fundamental importance in both areas of activity are considerations that can be defined as strategic, in the sense that they affect the ratio of the nation's own military strength to that of other nations:[1] national boundaries and internal routes of communication; international alignments and pledges of foreign assistance; the material resources, size, and capability of the armed forces; and the most likely combat theaters in the event of war. Politico-military activity and strategy are, therefore, confined neither to the military profession nor to wartime planning.

The fact that politico-military activity occurs while a nation is at peace raises the question of how political and military influences interact to determine the goals and means of national policy. Civil-military relations, or the peculiar relationship between a nation's military organization and its political institutions and social values, is thus an underlying theme in politico-military history. The emphasis below is on the distri-

[1] See Edward Hallett Carr's broad definition of strategy in *The Twenty Years' Crisis, 1919-1939: An Introduction to the Study of International Relations* (2d ed., New York, 1946), p. 110; also the discussion of policy, strategy, and diplomacy in Alfred Vagts, *Defense and Diplomacy: The Soldier and the Conduct of Foreign Relations* (New York, 1956), pp. 453-55, 462-65.

bution of authority in the institutional sector of civil-military relations, and on the tension between military and civilian norms insofar as they challenge or confirm that distribution.[2]

The dimensions and the problems of institutional civil-military relations have changed since the early nineteenth century, when Karl von Clausewitz wrote that the military point of view should always be subordinate to the political. The industrial revolution and the attendant increase in the power and administrative complexity of the modern nation state have blurred any distinction between a purely military sphere of activity and a purely political or civilian one. During the First World War, Georges Clemenceau and David Lloyd George belatedly acknowledged that war had become too serious a matter to be left to the generals, whereas Field Marshal Paul von Hindenburg and General Erich Ludendorff concluded that war was too serious to be left to the politicians. But neither the civilian control of the Allied Prime Ministers nor the military control of the German High Command, both examples of emergency rule in the last two years of the war, solved the problem of defining—much less achieving—a tolerable civil-military equilibrium in highly industrialized societies containing numerous bureaucratic agencies

[2] For the history of German civil-military relations and definitions of German militarism, see Gerhard Ritter, *Staatskunst und Kriegshandwerk* (4 vols.; Munich, 1954-68), and his "Das Problem des Militarismus in Deutschland," *Historische Zeitschrift*, CLXXVII (1954), 21-48; Hans Herzfeld, "Zur neueren Literatur über das Heeresproblem in der deutschen Geschichte," *Vierteljahrshefte für Zeitgeschichte*, IV (1956), 361-86. See also the general accounts of modern civil-military relations in Michael Howard, "The Armed Forces as a Political Problem," *Soldiers and Governments: Nine Studies in Civil-Military Relations* (London, 1957); Alfred Vagts, *A History of Militarism: Civilian and Military* (rev. ed., New York, 1959), as well as his *Defense and Diplomacy*. Useful conceptual models are presented by Samuel P. Huntington, *The Soldier and the State: The Theory and Politics of Civil-Military Relations* (Cambridge, Mass., 1957); Morris Janowitz, *The Professional Soldier: A Social and Political Portrait* (Glencoe, Ill., 1960).

and parliamentary bodies more or less representative of mass electorates.

The civilian and military leadership in the Weimar Republic attempted to solve that problem. Unlike Britain, France, and the United States, where readjustments in civil-military relations also occurred in the postwar years, Weimar Germany had a new constitution. Its leaders were, therefore, the more conscious of arguments for adjusting civil-military relations within a malleable political system. The Weimar constitution contained a number of institutional levels where this adjustment might take place: the executive level, where a distinction was made between the presidency and the government (Chancellor and Reich ministers), each of which had its respective responsibilities and powers; the departmental or bureaucratic level, where cabinet ministers, responsible to the Reichstag, headed offices of professional experts not politically responsible; the parliamentary level, where deputies in the Reichstag represented the public will, possessed the sovereign power over legislation, and could force the resignation of the Chancellor and heads of department by votes of no confidence; and the federal level, where Prussia, more than any other state (*Land*), retained geographic size and regional power great enough to challenge the Reich in national defense, although the constitution entrusted that function exclusively to the Reich.

Because of the default of the Reichstag, the refractory attitude of the Prussian government, and the preference of the departments and the executive for adjustments above party politics in the Reichstag, the most concerted attempt to clarify civil-military relations was made on the departmental level. Two departments viewed as their own almost exclusive province of mutual or collegial responsibility that area of civil-military intercourse defined above as politico-military.[3] Al-

---

[3] As one kind of "institutional solution" to the problem of uniting policy and strategy, Vagts names "collegial arrangements between military and civilian officials who are to prepare or wage war together." *Defense and Diplomacy*, p. 467.

6

though intradepartmental differences arose for each, neither the Foreign Office nor the Defense Ministry welcomed close parliamentary scrutiny of deliberations that they considered vital to Germany's national security, and that they believed must be kept out of the ill-informed and unstable grasp of public opinion. They saw civil-military relations as essentially interdepartmental and executive-departmental. Therefore they tried to define and preserve their respective goals and areas of professional competence, to develop the proper relationship between themselves and the executive, to exclude the Reichstag from their definitions of the "political arm" and "political control," and to encourage and adopt joint planning procedures in the interests of interdepartmental understanding.

The long-range goal of German foreign policy after the First World War was not international solidarity, but the reestablishment of full sovereignty and the position and attributes of a Great Power. Standing between defeated Germany and its restoration to sovereign and Great Power status was the Treaty of Versailles, and the Foreign Office (*Auswärtiges Amt*) in Berlin's Wilhelmstrasse considered revision of that treaty an article of faith. For German politico-military activity, revision of the military clauses and of the eastern borders with Poland was the major concern. That area of German foreign policy and military planning—notably the Polish question—is the core of this study.

Although diplomats in the Wilhelmstrasse differed over which configuration of European alignments would be the best for territorial revision in the east, they agreed that Germany must regain the Corridor and Danzig. They were more preoccupied with the strategic implications of the Corridor for German security than with the fate of the German minority there. They preferred peaceful revision, but some conceded that revision depended ultimately on the use of force in favorable international circumstances. This appreciation of the value of military power as an instrument of foreign policy—not merely to defend recognized German territory,

7

but to attain an external territorial objective—helps to explain the Wilhelmstrasse's support of secret rearmament and collaboration between the German and Soviet Armies, as well as the cooperation between the Foreign Office and Defense Ministry.

In the opinion of the service commands and other offices in the Defense Ministry (*Reichswehrministerium*), including that of the civilian Defense Minister, the Treaty of Versailles placed Germany in a strategically intolerable position. The Army and Navy viewed national security as their first duty, and deplored Germany's vulnerability to invasion. Yet, in spite of inter-service differences over the organization and operational employment of the armed forces, both services were strongly inclined to think beyond immediate strategic necessity to future strategic advantage, beyond current strengths to projected mobilizations, beyond border defense to forceful border revision, and, especially the Navy, beyond a war in the east to a two-front "war of liberation."

During the years 1924-29, a period of relative domestic stability and continuity of leadership in the Foreign Office, civilian and military leaders developed the Weimar system of civil-military relations, one which seemed capable of resolving most politico-military differences at the departmental level. Although this system rejected parliamentary control over foreign policy and military planning, it was compatible with the principle of civilian or political control when defined in interdepartmental and executive-departmental terms. After Seeckt's dismissal in 1926, cooperation between the Foreign Office and Defense Ministry increased markedly in assessing Germany's territorial aims in the current international situation, and in planning for rearmament and operational contingencies. Wilhelm Groener, Kurt von Schleicher, and Wilhelm Heye, unlike Seeckt, admitted in practice as well as theory the primacy of the Foreign Office in foreign affairs, an attitude that, when coupled with their policy of collaboration with the Wilhelmstrasse, augmented the Clausewitzean renaissance which had already begun in military training under Seeckt.

The Defense Minister, Army Command, and Naval Command lamented Germany's divergence from the teachings of Clausewitz in World War I and, with the Foreign Office, vowed never again to allow foreign policy and military planning to follow independent paths nor to permit the military arm to become ascendant over the Foreign Office and the executive. Finally, the Defense Minister and both services concurred with the Foreign Office that the armed forces would not remain forever a strictly defensive weapon, but would eventually expand and enable Germany to pursue a *Machtpolitik* that would be based on interdepartmental collaboration and civilian control and might exploit a favorable international situation.

During the years of crisis, 1930-33, German foreign policy and military planning pursued the same goals as before, but the Weimar system of civil-military relations broke down. In an attempt to restore internal order and increase Germany's military power, the military leadership intervened more and more in Weimar politics. This intervention, as well as other institutional pressures and changes, upset the pattern of inter-departmental and executive-departmental planning peculiar to the late 1920s. Both service commands continued to study Clausewitz, encourage joint planning with the Foreign Office independent of the Reichstag, and share with the diplomats the belief in the efficacy of force as a means of policy. After 1930, however, the resolution of conflicts in politico-military activity would no longer depend chiefly on steady interde-partmental interaction, but on the unstable relationship between the departments and an increasingly powerful executive.

THE YEARS OF STABILITY, 1924-29: POLICY IN THE FOREIGN OFFICE

There is an idea in London that the German
proposals for security on the West are only
made with a view to rendering the position
more favourable for war in the East. There
is no foundation for this suspicion. . . .
> Lord D'Abernon, March 1925

The Corridor question cannot be resolved
except by force, together with numerous
favorable circumstances.
> Karl von Schubert, November 1925

Part I

CHAPTER I

Eastern Europe

REVISION AND THE WILHELMSTRASSE

THE THIRTEENTH of President Woodrow Wilson's Fourteen Points called for the erection of "an independent Polish state . . . which should be assured free and secure access to the sea. . . ." To achieve this, the terms of the Treaty of Versailles required Germany to cede to the new Poland a "Corridor" through West Prussia along the valley of the lower Vistula River up to the Baltic Sea, and the province of Posen. Germany also gave up Danzig, which became a self-governing free city under the supervision of a League of Nations commissioner, and there Poland was granted free access to the Baltic. Plebiscites in East Prussia and Upper Silesia would determine whether Germany was to lose still more of its eastern land. The overwhelmingly pro-German vote of 11 July 1920 in Allenstein and Marienwerder assured the retention of these districts by East Prussia. In Upper Silesia, however, the plebiscite of 20 March 1921 did not restore that area in its entirety to Germany. The League of Nations Council, to which the question was referred in the confusion that followed the vote, decided against the German argument that Silesia was an indivisible economic whole, and granted Poland a valuable industrial portion of Upper Silesia.

By these territorial provisions, the Treaty of Versailles put to trial a hypothesis of Otto von Bismarck. In 1854 Bismarck had observed that "an independent Poland might cease being Prussia's determined enemy only if we handed over territories without which we cannot exist, territories such as the lower Vistula, all of Posen, and the Polish-speaking area of Silesia."[1]

[1] Bismarck to Otto von Manteuffel, 23 February 1854; in Otto

13

The recovery of most of these same territories was a consistent and outspoken objective of every government of the Weimar Republic, and was supported by an overwhelming majority of the German electorate, including those who voted on the Left.[2] After 1923 territorial revision remained a major goal of German foreign policy during Gustav Stresemann's six-year tenure as Foreign Minister.

Weimar foreign policy under Stresemann was very much the province of the Foreign Office: the Foreign Minister, the permanent officials in Berlin, and the envoys at Germany's missions in the field.[3] The Foreign Office did not attain this preeminence without effort, however, for it confronted the consequences of the New Diplomacy which had emerged during the First World War. The New Diplomacy threatened a revolutionary change in the formulation and execution of foreign policy. No longer was it simply taken for granted that policy was the private domain of specialists negotiating secretly, responsible only to the heads of state. Foreign policy must be brought within the ambit of public politics, deter-

---

von Bismarck, *Die gesammelten Werke* (15 vols. in 19; Berlin, 1924ff.), I, 430.

[2] Martin Broszat, *Zweihundert Jahre deutsche Polenpolitik* (Munich, 1963), pp. 166-67; Erich Matthias, *Die deutsche Sozialdemokratie und der Osten 1914-1945* (Tübingen, 1954), pp. 49ff., 65f.

[3] Although the Foreign Minister was not a career diplomat, Stresemann's powerful departmental position and long period of office identified him in German and European eyes as a foreign policy expert and negotiator as much as a party man; many members of the foreign service served at one time or another both in Berlin and abroad; the minister, officials in the Wilhelmstrasse, and envoys all contributed to the formulation and implementation of foreign policy. Because of this blurring of distinctions between the three official roles, the terms "Foreign Office" and "diplomats" usually refer below to all three as a collective group, unless specific intradepartmental contrasts are made. Perhaps this meets Leonidas E. Hill's criticism of the confusion of roles in Gordon A. Craig and Felix Gilbert (eds.), *The Diplomats 1919-1939* (Princeton, N.J., 1953); Hill, "The Wilhelmstrasse in the Nazi Era," *Political Science Quarterly*, LXXXII (1967), 550n.

14

mined by national opinion through parties and representatives in parliament, and executed openly through "diplomacy by conference" by cabinet ministers responsible to parliament and professionals subject to their ministers.[4] Like an exclusive club forced to lower its criteria for membership, the German diplomats grudgingly gave way to a democratizing of the policy-making process, for they realized that foreign policy was closely tied to domestic politics, and that public opinion could not be ignored.[5]

In adjusting to the demands of democratization, however, diplomats in Germany, as elsewhere, did not permit a total eclipse of traditional diplomacy. They believed that the idealism of the New Diplomacy had not altered the real substance of foreign policy (*Politik*), the definition and pursuit of national interests: the nation (rather than individuals or interest groups or mankind) has a set of clearly definable goals that it tries to attain in an international system characterized by the competition among interests of its component sovereign parts.[6] The men in the Wilhelmstrasse remained confident

[4] Craig and Gilbert, *Diplomats*, pp. 3-11; Harold Nicolson, *Diplomacy* (3d ed., London, 1963), chaps. 3, 4; Arno J. Mayer, *Political Origins of the New Diplomacy, 1917-1918* (New Haven, Conn., 1959), pp. 1-8, 53-58.

[5] See Ludwig Zimmermann, *Deutsche Aussenpolitik in der Ära der Weimarer Republik* (Göttingen, 1958), pp. 14ff.; Hajo Holborn, "Diplomats and Diplomacy in the Early Weimar Republic," in Craig and Gilbert, *Diplomats*, p. 171; Annelise Thimme, *Gustav Stresemann* (Hanover & Frankfurt, 1957), p. 125.

[6] For the prevailing attitude in the Wilhelmstrasse, Germany, and Europe, see Erich Kordt, *Nicht aus den Akten* (Stuttgart, 1950), pp. 36-37. The assumption that national interest is a fundamental guiding principle in both the study and conduct of foreign policy rests on epistemological and ontological presuppositions that frequently are not explicitly defined. National interest implies empirical goals and rational behavior by the political actors. Yet national interest is a variable that cannot be measured empirically; it is often based on value rather than quantifiable, rational considerations; political actors often behave irrationally, influenced by presumptions about the nature of the international environment, by "images" of the goals and be-

15

that they were the Germans most qualified to articulate these goals and reach them.

The Weimar constitution supported the diplomats by designating the Foreign Office as "the sole agency for the administration of German foreign interests."[7] But the constitution also gave the public a voice in the determination of these interests, by plebiscite and through the Reichstag. Parties opposing a policy of the government could, if they obtained enough signatures, demand a special referendum to try to defeat that policy. On a regular basis, policy was exposed to public scrutiny and debate in the Reichstag. By such powers

---

havior of foreign leaders, and by deep "collective forces" in history. See Raymond Aron, *Peace and War: A Theory of International Relations*, trans. R. Howard and A. B. Fox (New York, 1966), pp. 89-92; Carr, *Twenty Years' Crisis*, pp. 75-88; Joseph Frankel, *National Interest* (London, 1970), especially chaps. 7, 9; Stanley Hoffmann, *The State of War: Essays on the Theory and Practice of International Politics* (New York, 1965), chaps. 1, 9; Robert Jervis, *The Logic of Images in International Relations* (Princeton, N.J., 1970); Pierre Renouvin and Jean-Baptiste Duroselle, *Introduction to the History of International Relations*, trans. Mary Ilford (New York, 1967), chap. 10; Arnold Wolfers, *Discord and Collaboration: Essays on International Politics* (Baltimore, 1962), chap. 3 and pp. 147-49. The examination of German foreign policy and military planning below dwells upon empirical reasons and attempts to improve Germany's strategic situation, but also considers less tangible German conceptions of power, freedom, prestige, and the like.

[7] Holborn, "Diplomats and Diplomacy," in Craig and Gilbert, *Diplomats*, p. 148. The following discussion of the constitution and foreign policy is based on the accounts in Holborn, pp. 148-50, and Zimmermann, *Deutsche Aussenpolitik*, pp. 22-34. As Holborn points out, other agencies—like the Finance Ministry and Economics Ministry—"were officially charged with foreign policy, or could unofficially concern themselves with it." Some helpful definitions of the wider range of the groups and actors within foreign policy elites: Joseph Frankel, *The Making of Foreign Policy: An Analysis of Decision-Making* (London, 1963), chaps. 2, 3; Donald C. Watt, *Personalities and Policies: Studies in the Formulation of British Foreign Policy in the Twentieth Century* (Notre Dame, Ind., 1965), chap. 1; Wolfers, *Discord and Collaboration*, chap. 1.

16

as interpellation, vote of no confidence, and ratification of treaties the Reichstag could influence the course of foreign policy.

The degree of influence was limited by the Reichstag's inability to reconcile its internal differences. Although the political parties concurred on certain objectives—for example, revision of the German-Polish border—they could not agree on the means best suited to accomplish them. The Reichstag Foreign Affairs Committee was not immune to party differences, nor did its members always keep detailed reports from the Foreign Minister confidential. In the opinion of the diplomats, therefore, this committee of politicians proved to be an unsatisfactory link between the Foreign Office and the public. In its stead, the Foreign Minister and his subordinates preferred to confer personally with responsible party leaders, foreign affairs experts, and journalists, all of whom they could count on to keep the public less confused and more informed.

The Foreign Minister performed the indispensable task of liaison between Foreign Office and public. As a party member and minister responsible to the Reichstag, and as the head of an office of experts, he personified the partial democratization of foreign policy. The efficient conduct of policy also required smooth relations between the minister, President, and Chancellor, for the President was empowered to conclude treaties and alliances, accredit envoys, and call special policy meetings in his office; and the Chancellor, to determine the general lines of policy.[8]

[8] Stresemann cited this constitutional fact in the summer of 1925 in an argument with the Nationalist Party over the proposed western security pact. The Nationalists contended that Stresemann's policy had been initiated without their knowledge. Stresemann replied that the Chancellor, Hans Luther, had approved sending feelers for such a pact to London and Paris, that it was therefore the policy of the government (not merely the Wilhelmstrasse, as the Nationalists alleged), and that as a minister he was not bound by the constitution to report to anyone but the Chancellor while executing the government's policy. In a rare but nearly disastrous collision between the two men, Luther did not immediately accept Stresemann's contention

Gustav Stresemann excelled as Foreign Minister. He explained policies forcefully and convincingly in the Reichstag, and he won the esteem and confidence of the statesmen under whom he served, Presidents Friedrich Ebert (1919-25), and Paul von Hindenburg (1925-34), Chancellors Wilhelm Marx (Center Party), Hans Luther (nonpartisan), and Hermann Müller (Social Democrat). Stresemann managed with equal success his important relationship to his staff of bureaucrats in the Foreign Office. Although he never felt at home with bureaucratic routine, which he left to his willing Secretary of State, Karl von Schubert, he was, as one of his subordinates recalls, exceptionally adept at "grasping political ideas and adapting them to the domestic and foreign problems in any particular situation."[9] A mutual trust and respect grew between Stresemann and the officials in the Wilhelmstrasse, an atmosphere in which the Foreign Office could confidently revise its procedures.

The Foreign Office had been reorganized immediately after the war in an attempt to adjust to the forces of democratization.[10] The so-called Schüler reforms had abolished the old "Political Department," combined the diplomatic and con-

---

that cabinet ministers were required to report only to the Chancellor when carrying out the government's policy, for, "although Stresemann's constitutional argument was unassailable, it had long been common practice in the Republic's cabinets for the ministers to consult with the representatives of the various participating parties before taking important steps." Henry Ashby Turner, Jr., *Stresemann and the Politics of the Weimar Republic* (Princeton, N.J., 1963), pp. 205ff. See also Zimmermann, *Deutsche Aussenpolitik*, pp. 265-66.

[9] Herbert von Dirksen, *Moscow, Tokyo, London: Twenty Years of German Foreign Policy* (Norman, Okla., 1952), p. 46. See also the sketches of Stresemann in Gordon A. Craig, *From Bismarck to Adenauer: Aspects of German Statecraft* (Baltimore, 1958), pp. 70-83; and Lutz Graf Schwerin von Krosigk, *Es Geschah in Deutschland* (Tübingen & Stuttgart, 1951), pp. 70-77.

[10] On the organization of the Foreign Office, see Zimmermann, *Deutsche Aussenpolitik*, pp. 34-40; Holborn, "Diplomats and Diplomacy," in Craig and Gilbert, *Diplomats*, p. 150; Kordt, *Nicht aus den Akten*, pp. 32, 40.

sular services as well as the political and economic divisions, and divided them into three regional groups. A major purpose of these reforms had been to dislodge the aristocracy, which had dominated diplomatic posts and political desks, and to allow new blood to reach the upper regions of the foreign service. In 1924-25, however, a new procedure began when veteran diplomats were named deputies to the chiefs of department. These deputies, known as directors (*Dirigenten*), met frequently with the Foreign Minister and Secretary of State, and often did not divulge secret matters discussed at these meetings to their chiefs, some of whom were new men. This select group of directors was very similar to the "Political Department" of the old Foreign Office, and in it survived an important remnant of secret diplomacy.[11]

The Schüler reform had been carried out in the interests of conforming an inherited bureaucratic ministry to the newborn republic. On the other hand, the Foreign Office undertook the reform of 1924-25 in its own interest as an independent bureaucratic entity.[12] The Foreign Office enjoyed so much autonomy within a few years of the founding of the republic partly because the diplomats took advantage of the change in the political regime to preserve many of their prerogatives, an opportunity always open to bureaucrats in similar unstable circumstances. But this autonomy was also a result of the weakness of Germany's parliamentary institutions. Beset by the divisive effects of including too many splinter parties, some of them avowedly opposed to the republic, the Reichstag was unable to cope with the internal political and

[11] Dirksen, *Moscow, Tokyo, London*, p. 42; Zimmermann, *Deutsche Aussenpolitik*, p. 39. The opposition of career diplomats to the disintegrating effects of the Schüler reform is evident in Rudolf Nadolny, *Mein Beitrag* (Wiesbaden, 1955), p. 80.

[12] Both of these reforms were evidence of what a contemporary called "structural disharmonies" between the bureaucracy and the other elements of the Weimar state, which groped for a modern bureaucratic system in place of the old system based on class distinctions. Arnold Köttgen, *Das deutsche Berufsbeamtentum und die parlamentarische Demokratie* (Berlin & Leipzig, 1928), pp. 85-90.

19

economic crisis caused by the French occupation of the Ruhr early in 1923. By default, the Reichstag left the government and its agencies to search for solutions to the problems: inflation, payment of reparations to the Allies, and insurrection by Communists and National Socialists. By the end of 1923 the government had restored order, and the bureaucratic departments had strengthened their position in directing the affairs of state.

When Stresemann resigned as Chancellor at the end of November 1923, to remain Foreign Minister until his death in October 1929, he headed a Foreign Office that had reasserted its independence from control by parties and interest groups. Although susceptible to movements of public opinion, Weimar foreign policy after 1923 was usually framed and executed by the Foreign Minister and his department of professionals.[13]

While the electorate and successive Chancellors prescribed the general objective of revision in the east, the men who formulated and implemented Germany's Polish policy were Stresemann, Count Ulrich von Brockdorff-Rantzau, Baron Ago von Maltzan, Karl von Schubert, Erich Wallroth, Herbert von Dirksen, Erich Zechlin, and Ulrich Rauscher. They expressed in memoranda and messages various motives for revision. Wallroth, Chief of the Eastern Department (IV) from 1923 to 1928, viewed the border situation as harmful to German economy and culture. Revision was not only "ethi-

[13] Harold Nicolson distinguishes between foreign policy, which is the "legislative" or "deliberative" responsibility of the cabinet and parliament, and diplomacy (or negotiation), the execution of policy, which "should generally be left to professionals of experience and discretion." *Diplomacy*, pp. 3-5. Perhaps, as Nicolson warns, ignoring this distinction can be detrimental "to any sound democratic control of foreign policy"; yet making it implies a clear separation of powers which neither the Weimar Republic nor any other democracy has achieved. In fact, "autocracy, at least in the handling of foreign affairs, has been the prevailing constitutional form" in the modern era; Quincy Wright, *A Study of War* (abridged ed., Chicago, 1964), p. 158.

cally right," but also "politically wise." The borders should be changed "in our favor . . . , in accordance with historical, ethnographic, cultural and economic considerations."[14] To Zechlin, who headed the Polish Section (IVPo) in the Eastern Department from 1923 to 1928, the borders in the east were "open wounds." The Polish policy of de-Germanization in the lost territories further inhibited friendly relations between the two countries.[15] The Minister to Warsaw, Rauscher, a Social Democrat, charged that the Allies had made the new Poland a "permanent enemy of Germany" by granting it the Corridor and Upper Silesia.[16]

Like the others, Stresemann was concerned about the fate of the German minority in Poland. Although this solicitude for Germans abroad was genuine, the Foreign Office could and did use the current argument of self-determination as a political trump for the restoration of lost territories whose importance was primarily strategic. For, as Zechlin noted, "the weaker the German minority is in the lost territories, the poorer the chances are of restoring a territorial connection between East Prussia and the Reich."[17] The Corridor isolated East Prussia. It was a "wound," a painful incision in the organic Reich that Bismarck had built. The metaphor was common in the Wilhelmstrasse. The pain was still keener because of the diplomats' awareness of the vulnerability of East Prussia and the need for a secure bridge of communications to that province similar to that which had existed prior to the Treaty of Versailles.[18] Strategic, more than ethnographic or

[14] Foreign Office (hereafter *AA*, for *Auswärtiges Amt*), Wallroth to Stresemann, 19 November 1926, 2945/D572447-52. (See bibliography for list of Foreign Office files consulted, and corresponding microfilm numbers.)

[15] *AA*, Zechlin memorandum, 8 September 1926, 4556/E150079-87.

[16] *AA*, Rauscher memorandum, 25 July 1924, 7127/H147628.

[17] *AA*, Zechlin to Maltzan, 6 November 1923, 3241/D704692.

[18] Stresemann, for example, in a directive to German chiefs of mission, 30 June 1925, stressed the communications to and vulnerability of East Prussia; *AA*, 4556/E149428-9. The Foreign Office con-

cultural, reasons explain why the irreducible core of German territorial aims included the Corridor and Danzig.

On occasion, German political leaders and diplomats spoke of revision in terms that suggested more than the readjustments demanded in official German policy,[19] but by and large the men responsible for Germany's eastern policy concurred in limiting the extent of Germany's territorial demands. In 1925, while Stresemann's negotiations for a western security pact were returning Germany to the center of the stage in European diplomacy, the Eastern Department summarized German territorial interests along the frontier with Poland. Herbert von Dirksen, who had recently become the director of that department, wrote that the Corridor and Netze-Gau—to points south of Thorn (Toruń)-Bromberg (Bydgoszcz)—must be returned to Germany. "This would at the same time guarantee the return of the following important railroad lines: Danzig-Neustadt (Weyherowo)-Lauenburg; Schneidemühl-Konitz-Dirschau-Marienburg-Elbing; Thorn-Bromberg-Schneidemühl; Danzig-Dirschau-Bromberg." Danzig must be included in this settlement, Dirksen continued, not simply because it was settled by Germans, but because

---

sidered insufficient the mere rights of transit provided Germany in the Corridor Transit Treaty of 1921. For the details of that agreement, which Poland honored right up to the outbreak of war in 1939, see Harald Von Riekhoff, *German-Polish Relations, 1918-1933* (Baltimore, 1971), p. 38.

[19] In a conversation with Brockdorff-Rantzau in July 1922, Chancellor and Foreign Minister Joseph Wirth said " 'Poland must be destroyed.' " Herbert Helbig, *Die Träger der Rapallo-Politik* (Göttingen, 1958), p. 119. The Foreign Office weighed the possibility of combining with the Soviet Union to force Poland back to its "ethnographic frontiers"; see below. Such statements would seem to substantiate the conclusion that German diplomats "looked upon an independent Poland as a disastrous obstacle to German expansion to the east," the view of Roman Debicki, *Foreign Policy of Poland 1919-39: from the Rebirth of the Polish Republic to World War II* (New York, 1962), p. 47. But most of the documentary evidence indicates that the Foreign Office accepted Poland's existence, however reluctantly, and concentrated on a limited program of revision.

it was indispensable for the security of communications between Germany and East Prussia.[20]

Relying on such geographic and ethnographic studies as Dirksen's, Stresemann defined the limits of the Corridor in an instruction to the chiefs of German missions abroad. In German diplomatic parlance, he noted, the Corridor included Danzig, "what is now the Polish part of West Prussia, except for Strasburg and Löbau, which were already predominantly Polish in 1914," and the Netze region around Bromberg. The Corridor's southern border "would run south of the Netze river, approximately along the line Filehne-Czarnikau-Kolmar, south of Bromberg to Thorn, encompass that city [Thorn] and then follow the railroad line Thorn-Deutsch Eylau, so that this important route—Schneidemühl-Bromberg-Thorn-Deutsch Eylau—would again be in German hands." Turning his attention to Posen, Stresemann advised that Germany, in its own best interests, should renounce any claim to an area that was "undoubtedly Polish ethnographically," for doing so would improve Germany's chances of gaining its main objectives—the Corridor and Upper Silesia.[21] Dirksen, however, though admitting that Posen was not so pressing a problem as Danzig and the Corridor, thought that the German-Polish border in Posen should be "rounded off" farther east.[22]

After Locarno, Stresemann continued to think in terms of Danzig, the Corridor, and Upper Silesia when discussing territorial revision.[23] In 1928, Secretary of State Karl von Schu-

[20] *AA*, Dirksen to Schubert, 21 March 1925, 4569/E168384-5.

[21] *AA*, Stresemann to chiefs of mission, 30 June 1925, 4556/E149417; also Stresemann to Crown Prince William, 7 September 1925, 7318/H159871-2 (also printed in Stresemann's *Vermächtnis*, ed. Henry Bernhard [3 vols.; Berlin, 1932-33], II, 553-55).

[22] *AA*, Dirksen memorandum, 16 November 1925, 4569/E168406-15; attached to the memorandum is a map of Posen and the Corridor, with railroad lines and boundaries (current and proposed), not filmed. Dirksen to Wallroth and Schubert, 29 December, *ibid.*, E168456-65.

[23] *AA*, Stresemann to Friedrich Sthamer (Ambassador to London), 19 April 1926, *ibid.*, E168665-71; Stresemann conversation

bert cautioned against defining the Corridor's southern limits:

> It is dangerous and can cause damage, unforeseeable today yet irreparable later, if one confines the Corridor to the lost areas of West Prussia and Pomerania. The Netze region . . . does not by the slightest title belong to the Corridor, even if one views this problem in terms of communications, as is frequently done in Germany. . . .
>
> Whoever limits the Corridor to West Prussia and Pomerania surrenders the important Netze region, in which, before the separation and even today after hundreds of thousands have emigrated, the strongest German element is to be found. Through the Netze region runs the Bromberg Canal in the direction east-west, but also the second main railroad line, Insterburg-Thorn-Bromberg-Schneidemühl-Berlin, which is no less vital for communications between East Prussia and the Reich than the northern lines, Marienburg-Dirschau-Neuenburg-Stettin as well as Marienburg-Dirschau-Konitz-Schneidemühl-Berlin. Bromberg is—with at least as good reason as Danzig—the center of the Corridor.

Schubert also advised against neglecting Posen in any solution of the Corridor question. Because of its importance for communications and its German majority, the western part of Posen should revert to German ownership.[24]

The preceding résumé of German territorial interests enables us to correlate the reasons for and extent of German revisionism in the east. In each of these memoranda, Stresemann and his subordinates in the Foreign Office referred to

---

with August Zaleski (Polish Foreign Minister) at Geneva, 10 December 1926, *ibid.*, E168905-9. See also Zygmunt Gasiorowski, "Stresemann and Poland after Locarno," *Journal of Central European Affairs*, xviii (1958-59), 299, 305.

[24] *AA,* Schubert memorandum (unsigned, but almost certainly his—he rarely signed his own private notations), 11 August 1928, 4569/E169175-9.

the German minority in Poland, sometimes alluding to the Wilsonian principle of self-determination of peoples, one of a number of the Fourteen Points on which the Germans felt betrayed. But the Foreign Office placed still greater emphasis on strategic factors. Bromberg and Thorn were important rail centers, at a time when railroads were still the major arteries of economic sustenance and military movement. "Rounding off" the border with Posen would restore the railroad line Breslau-Bentschen-Schwerin to Germany, shortening the distance between Silesian industry and East Prussia. According to the Foreign Office's ethnographic map of the Corridor, most of the area northeast of Thorn and east of the Vistula contained a Polish majority. And Stresemann's " 'German bridge,' which joined East Prussia ethnographically with the rest of Germany," and which Stresemann used to justify drawing the boundary so far south, ran through the Netze region and then turned northward to follow the Vistula valley.[25] Yet the desired boundary conformed to the railroad line Thorn-Deutsch Eylau, and was itself a kind of "rounding off" of Polish territory between Thorn and East Prussia.

Thus, primarily strategic considerations determined Germany's eastern territorial aims: Danzig and the Corridor (and Netze region) secured communications with East Prussia; Upper Silesia was the industrial supplement to Lower Silesia; and western Posen, of secondary importance and renounced by Stresemann in 1925, was worth regaining if possible because it would improve German communications in the area. These were specific and limited objectives, which the Foreign Office conceived to be in the interests of national security. What means did Germany employ in pursuing territorial revision; that is, which intermediate goals appeared advantageous; which diplomatic methods, peaceful or forcible, were chosen?[26]

[25] *AA*, Stresemann to chiefs of mission, 30 June 1925, 4556/E149417; attached to this instruction was an ethnographic map (not filmed).

[26] The contrast between goals and means of policy cannot be

25

POLAND

Germany's Polish policy was bound in a deadlock not uncommon in international affairs after World War I: how one state bent on changing the territorial status quo could coexist with a neighboring state equally adamant that the existing boundaries must be preserved.[27] Poland insisted that Germany's revisionist aims were a threat to the European peace established by the Treaty of Versailles, whereas Germany argued that the treaty must be revised if justice were to be served and peace secured for all time. In such a confrontation, coexistence connoted tension—latent or overt—not cooperation. For the consensus in the Foreign Office was that pressure would be required to induce Poland to assent to revision, in international circumstances favorable to Germany.[28] This assumption was reflected in the way in which the Foreign Office dealt with matters like the recognition of borders,

---

sharp, for "all means can be said to constitute intermediary or proximate goals, and few goals if any can be considered ultimate, in the sense of being sought as ends in themselves." Wolfers, *Discord and Collaboration*, p. 68. To German diplomats, territorial revision was both a means toward restoring Great Power status and a goal whose attainment would probably require the prior restoration of many of the internal attributes of a Great Power. For different classifications of goals, see Wolfers, chap. 5; Aron, *Peace and War*, chap. 3; Frankel, *National Interest*, chaps. 4, 5. Regaining the lost eastern territories constituted, to borrow terms from Wolfers and Aron, a "possession goal" or a "space" goal rather (or more) than a "milieu goal" or a demographic or ideological one. On national security as a conception of national interest, see Wolfers, chap. 10; Renouvin and Duroselle, *Introduction to International Relations*, pp. 268-71: "the search for security may be active or passive," and one active example is the attempt "to conquer an advanced line of defense, a strategic frontier."

[27] For comprehensive treatments of Germany's Polish policy, see Christian Höltje, *Die Weimarer Republik und das Ostlocarno-Problem 1919-1934* (Würzburg, 1958); Josef Korbel, *Poland between East and West: Soviet and German Diplomacy toward Poland, 1919-1933* (Princeton, N.J., 1963); Von Riekhoff, *German-Polish Relations*.

[28] Kordt, *Nicht aus den Akten*, pp. 39-40.

the signing of a treaty with Poland, and the improvement of relations, particularly in the economic sphere.

Germany's refusal to recognize the postwar borders with Poland determined the kind of treaty—if any—that Germany might sign with its eastern neighbor. In 1924 Stresemann suggested that an arbitration treaty with Poland might assuage French anxiety about evacuating the Rhineland and thereby leaving its Polish ally in an unfavorable strategic position. Germany should, on its own volition and not under Allied pressure, offer to sign with Poland an arbitration treaty similar to that between Germany and Switzerland, except that the German draft must omit that part of the preamble that mentioned recognition of territorial integrity.[29] Rauscher, to whom Stresemann addressed this proposal, replied from Warsaw that Poland was then in no mood to accept such a treaty, and would view it as an ineffectual substitute for a general security pact including France.[30] In a subsequent message to Stresemann, Rauscher made very clear his own opposition to any treaty that would recognize the territorial status quo. Such a treaty would demoralize the Germans in the lost territories, and would make Germany appear as "half sovereign" and the defeated state, whereas Poland would appear the victorious state and "fully sovereign."[31]

Negotiations in 1925 for a western security pact raised again the question of a treaty between Germany and Poland. Stresemann assured Brockdorff-Rantzau, the Ambassador to Moscow, that the arbitration treaties that Germany was will-

[29] *AA*, Stresemann to Rauscher, 8 March 1924, 4556/E148361-8. See also Zygmunt Gasiorowski, "Stresemann and Poland before Locarno," *Journal of Central European Affairs*, XVIII (1958-59), 28-29.

[30] *AA*, Rauscher to Stresemann, 11 March 1924, *ibid.*, E148354-7.

[31] *AA*, Rauscher to Stresemann, 25 July 1924, 7127/H147628-35. Stresemann, whose respect for Rauscher grew over the years, and who was later to cite his ability and record in reply to anti-Socialist bias among high-placed conservatives (see chap. 2, n. 46), wrote "very good analyses" in the margin of Rauscher's message.

ing to sign with Poland and Czechoslovakia would, however much they signified Germany's peaceful intentions, not be a "real obstacle" to Germany's political objective of border revision.[32] Exactly what an arbitration treaty might embody was the subject of a number of dispatches between Berlin and the German missions in Paris and London. Schubert instructed the Ambassador to Paris, Leopold von Hoesch, to reiterate Germany's opposition to a nonaggression pact with Poland, which would be "nothing other than a form of recognizing the borders." Such an agreement simply and ineffectually forbade war; in contrast, an arbitration treaty allowed for the "practical removal of the possible causes of war." French and Polish criticisms of Germany's proposed treaty—that it went too far by giving Germany a means of revising the borders peacefully; and that it did not go far enough "because we still formally retain the final resort to war"—showed that what they in fact wanted was "a formal recognition or guarantee of the Polish borders."[33] Up to this point it would appear that the Wilhelmstrasse's interest in the arbitration treaty was a positive one in the sense that such a treaty would be the best guarantee of a peaceful revision, for the arbitration board would provide a means of redress and the span of its deliberations would constitute a cooling-off period, during which an armed attack by one signatory against the other would be an open breach of the treaty.

The attitude of the Wilhelmstrasse on this issue was noteworthy, however, for its reserve, not its positive commitment. Stresemann's willingness to sign an arbitration treaty with Poland stemmed chiefly from his desire to reach a settlement with the western powers rather than with Poland. Having

[32] *AA*, Stresemann to Brockdorff-Rantzau, 19 March 1925, 4562/E155072. The same opinion appeared in a memorandum by Zechlin on "the effects of the security pact on Germany's eastern policy," 25 August 1925, *ibid.*, E155863-6.

[33] *AA*, Schubert to Hoesch, 21 March 1925, 2945/D571572-4. See also Stresemann's memorandum of 1 July 1925 in *Vermächtnis*, II, 115ff.

agreed to sign, Germany kept a wild card in its hand, the technical legal point that an arbitration treaty did not absolutely rule out military conflict. When the British Foreign Secretary, Austen Chamberlain, announced before the House of Commons late in March that Germany was ready to renounce any military solution to the border question, the German Ambassador, Friedrich Sthamer, hastened to restate his government's position. He felt that Chamberlain's statement did not take everything into account. In particular he reminded Chamberlain that "if an arbitral judgment is not complied with, the possibility of an armed conflict exists, even though practically it is as good as impossible." Chamberlain, hardly the most self-controlled of the diplomats who collaborated on the preliminaries to the Treaty of Locarno, lost his temper at this, for it seemed to him that Germany was trying to back out of the negotiations for an arbitration treaty, a reversal which he did not want to have to reveal to the Commons. Sthamer reassured him that this was not Germany's intention, and that a report to the Commons was out of the question, since he merely wanted to call Chamberlain's attention to certain ramifications of arbitration treaties of the type that Germany had declared its readiness to sign. Sthamer left this conference unconvinced that Chamberlain knew such treaties in detail or had "weighed their consequences."[34]

In Berlin, Secretary of State Schubert handed to Lord D'Abernon, the British Ambassador, a statement of policy in which the Foreign Office emphasized that, although Germany regarded an arbitration treaty as a means of preventing

[34] *AA*, Sthamer to Schubert, 25 March 1925, 3241/D706241-2; Erich Eyck, *A History of the Weimar Republic*, trans. H. P. Hanson and R.G.L. Waite (2 vols.; New York, 1962-63), II, 7-8. See also Chamberlain's statement to the Imperial Conference, 20 October 1926, in E. L. Woodward and Rohan Butler (eds.), *Documents on British Foreign Policy 1919-1939* [hereafter cited as *DBFP*] (London, 1946 and continuing), Series IA, II, 922-23. For Chamberlain's personal qualities as a diplomat, see Gordon A. Craig, "The British Foreign Office from Grey to Austen Chamberlain," in Craig and Gilbert, *Diplomats*, pp. 42ff.

a German-Polish war, it was "not willing to renounce the possibility of war *expressis verbis* in a treaty."[35] D'Abernon, an astute observer of German politics as well as skillful diplomat, could be expected to report Germany's case to London clearly and with an understanding of some of the Wilhelmstrasse's legalistic niceties which Chamberlain had neither the patience nor firsthand knowledge to match.[36] Meanwhile, the lesson Schubert drew from the Sthamer-Chamberlain conversation was that German diplomats must steer carefully between appearing too noncommital and giving in on points essential to German policy. Sthamer, too, was concerned lest the British misinterpret Germany's position in a way that placed Germany at a disadvantage then and in the future.[37]

Whether Germany's Polish policy during the security pact negotiations was fully understood in all European capitals is questionable. The conciliatory "spirit of Locarno" tended to obscure the technicality Chamberlain had not comprehended: in concluding an arbitration treaty with Poland in 1925, and in joining the League a year later, Germany had not ruled out the possibility of war with Poland over the border question.[38]

[35] *AA*, Schubert to Sthamer, 29 March 1925, 2945/D571620-1.

[36] German reservations confirmed Lord D'Abernon's observation that "it is difficult to get [German statesmen] to make a positive affirmation or take a definite engagement." *Lord D'Abernon's Diary* (3 vols.; London, 1929-30), II, 287; also p. 211.

[37] *AA*, Schubert to Sthamer, 29 March 1925, 2945/D571620-1; Sthamer to Schubert, 1 April, 3241/D706249-50.

[38] Stresemann pointed this out in a speech to the central committee of his own party, the German People's Party (DVP), 22 November 1925; Henry Ashby Turner, Jr., "Eine Rede Stresemanns über seine Locarnopolitik," *Vierteljahrshefte für Zeitgeschichte*, XV (1967), 423-25. Stresemann mentioned the work done by Friedrich Gaus, the chief legal expert in the Wilhelmstrasse, in drafting the arbitration treaty. For its text, see William J. Newman, *The Balance of Power in the Interwar Years, 1919-1939* (New York, 1968), pp. 218-24. On Gaus and the treaty: Zimmermann, *Deutsche Aussenpolitik*, pp. 268-69; Höltje, *Weimarer Republik und Ostlocarno-Problem*, pp. 80-82; Jürgen Spenz, *Die diplomatische Vorgeschichte des Beitritts Deutschlands zum Völkerbund 1924-1926* (Göttingen, 1966), pp. 104-105; Dirksen, *Moscow, Tokyo, London*, pp. 44, 60. One of Chamberlain's

Foreign diplomats might have grasped this point had they witnessed the operational exercises conducted jointly by the Army and Foreign Office in the late 1920s, for these dealt with more contingencies than mere self-defense against Polish (and French) aggression.[39]

In view of their respective attitudes toward the Treaty of Versailles and revision, the prospects of friendly relations between Germany and Poland were slim indeed. Each side accused the other of subverting international attempts to evolve a scheme for European security. The "In" baskets in the Wilhelmstrasse frequently contained reports from civilians and public officials in East Prussia, Danzig, Pomerania, and Silesia, predicting an imminent Polish invasion. The Poles, they alleged, were motivated by a "Drang nach Westen," and coveted East Prussia, Danzig, Pomerania, and the rest of Silesia.[40] Moreover, Poland was tightening an economic noose around East Prussia and Danzig, and, according to Danzig officials and statistical studies in Berlin, the Polish Baltic port of Gdynia was growing at an alarming rate. To Heinrich Sahm, President of the Danzig Senate from 1919 to 1931, Gdynia was part of the entire Danzig question and must be included in any discussions at Geneva about the fate of that city. Threatened economically by Gdynia and politically by Polish annexationist aspirations, Danzig was also "a fateful issue for Germany."[41]

---

subordinates understood at least the spirit if not the letter of Germany's attitude toward the arbitration treaty; memorandum by Mr. Gregory, 10 April 1925, *DBFP*, Ser. IA, I, 857; see also Addison (Berlin) to Chamberlain, 10 December, *ibid.*, pp. 241ff.

[39] See below, chap. 6.

[40] For example, the booklet "Polens Drang nach dem Westen," by Ernst Hansen; copy in *AA*, Abteilung IVPo, Akten betr. Politische Beziehungen Polens zu Deutschland, Band 24 (not filmed).

[41] Heinrich Sahm, *Erinnerungen aus meinen Danziger Jahren, 1919-1930* (Marburg, 1955), pp. 138, 155. See also Ernst Ziehm, *Aus meiner politischen Arbeit in Danzig, 1914-1939* (Marburg, 1957), p. 158. A Polish writer rejects the statement that Gdynia threatened Danzig's existence; Debicki, *Foreign Policy of Poland*, pp. 49f. For

The Wilhelmstrasse was not blind to the difference between legitimate requests from the border areas and Danzig for economic aid, and alarmist rumors that Polish military forces were massing for an attack. The diplomats did not exclude the possibility of forceful measures by Poland or ignore the strategically vulnerable positions of German Silesia, Danzig, and East Prussia.[42] From 1924 to 1929, however, they privately discounted the likelihood of a Polish invasion, while they tried to damage Poland's international reputation by calling attention to press releases about ominous Polish troop movements—even when they were based on rumor—and dwelling on "Polish chauvinism and racial hatred."[43]

The cardinal rule in the German Foreign Office was that there could be no lasting rapprochement between Germany and Poland unless and until Poland agreed to a settlement of the Corridor question. The arbitration treaty of 1925 was not an attempt to improve relations with Poland; rather it was a concession to the western powers. The Treaty of Locarno, signed on 16 October, did not soothe anti-German feeling in Warsaw, and Germany's economic policy was conspicuously anti-Polish. In February and March 1926 German diplomats tried to persuade France and Britain to reject Polish efforts to obtain a permanent seat on the League of Nations Council. Foreign capitals were notified that Marshal Jozef Pilsudski's coup in May 1926 did not change the temperature of German-Polish relations, for the anti-German clique in Warsaw was still strong.[44] In January 1927 the Polish For-

---

an excellent account of the Danzig question and its effects on German policy, see Christoph M. Kimmich, *The Free City: Danzig and German Foreign Policy, 1919-1934* (New Haven, Conn., 1968).

[42] *AA*, note to the attention of Dirksen, Wallroth, and Schubert, 28 March 1925, K190/K035671.

[43] *AA*, Wallroth to the German embassy in Washington, 27 January 1925, 2945/D571441; Stresemann to chiefs of mission, 7 August 1925, *ibid.*, D571878-9.

[44] *AA*, Gerhard Köpke to German missions, 15 May 1926, and Wallroth to missions, 14 June 1926, *ibid.*, D572212, 272; Wallroth

eign Minister, August Zaleski, told the Sejm (Assembly) that Poland would of course refuse to pay the territorial price that Germany continued to fix for friendly relations.[45]

The conviction of many German diplomats that Poland would consent to revision only out of weakness was temporarily reflected and assimilated in Germany's economic policy toward Poland.[46] In 1922 Chancellor (and Foreign Minister) Joseph Wirth had set the tone in the economic sphere, at least implicitly, when he declared that he would " 'conclude no treaties through which the Poles might be strengthened.' "[47] This attitude, coupled with the demand for political concessions in return for any economic aid, characterized Stresemann's policy until late 1926. Supporting this policy in the Wilhelmstrasse were Wallroth, Dirksen, and Zechlin, and echoing it in high international financial circles was Hjalmar Schacht, President of the *Reichsbank*. Schubert and Rauscher opposed it.

Early in 1925 Dirksen noted that a settlement of the Corridor question favorable to Germany would be possible only if Poland's position were very weak, weaker than it currently was. But soon, Stresemann suggested, perhaps Germany, along with the "Anglo-Saxon powers," could take advantage of Poland's languishing economy by refusing loans until Poland agreed to make territorial sacrifices. Germany would join Britain and the United States in a loan only if it could thereby pursue its political objectives. Economic pressure would also be useful in forcing Poland to reduce the size of its Army. Meanwhile, Dirksen counselled in November, Germany must

---

memorandum on post-Locarno German-Polish relations, April 1926, 5265/E321229-35. See also Korbel, *Poland between East and West*, p. 205.

[45] See Höltje, *Weimarer Republik und Ostlocarno-Problem*, p. 188.

[46] On Germany's anti-Polish economic policy, see Korbel, *Poland between East and West*, pp. 197ff.; Gasiorowski, "Stresemann and Poland after Locarno," pp. 294ff.

[47] Wirth to Brockdorff-Rantzau, 24 July 1922; in Helbig, *Träger der Rapallo-Politik*, p. 119.

wait, for Poland's economic plight was not yet serious enough.[48]

Schubert stated the minority opinion. Making loans conditional on the return of territories was bound to fail, for financial pressure had never in history forced a country to give up territory. There was, Schubert believed, no way to resolve the Corridor question except "by force, together with numerous favorable circumstances." Since that was not practicable "in the foreseeable future," Germany should take part in the international effort to make Poland financially stable. This would give Germany the chance to constrain Poland to lower its military budget (as a condition of loans), thereby reducing Poland militarily to middling importance. Only then, Schubert concluded, would its "territorial reduction" be possible. Dirksen disagreed. Weakening Poland militarily, which was in any event a necessary policy, could be accomplished without simultaneously bolstering its economy. Regaining the Corridor was "also conceivable without force," as before in the three partitions of Poland. Thus, Germany must delay Poland's economic rehabilitation.[49]

The Stresemann-Dirksen economic policy gave way slowly and reluctantly. Stresemann continued to tie political conditions to economic aid in a message to Sthamer in London, where the Governor of the Bank of England, Montagu Norman, concurred with German economic policy toward Poland.[50] And even after the British Foreign Office insured that no political strings were to be attached to any eventual international loan, the Wilhelmstrasse clung to the hope that it could still affix them to a commercial treaty between the two countries. In October 1926, for example, Wallroth advised

[48] *AA*, Dirksen to Schubert, 21 March 1925, 4569/E168384-5; Stresemann to chiefs of mission, 30 June, 4556/E149433; Dirksen memoranda of 16 November and 29 December, 4569/E168406-15, 456-65.

[49] *AA*, Schubert memorandum, late November 1925, 4569/E168400-4; Dirksen's handwritten comment at the end of his copy of Schubert's memorandum, 5462/E369906.

[50] *AA*, Stresemann to Sthamer, 19 April 1926, 4569/E168665-71.

Stresemann that revision of the borders could not be omitted from consideration of any policy toward Poland. Although Germany needed the market that a commercial treaty promised, the Foreign Office would not be sorry if no treaty were signed, for Poland's economic recovery would make it all the more unwilling to consider German proposals for revision. On the other hand, Wallroth admitted, Germany must not risk international disapprobation by obviously thwarting such a treaty.[51]

International opinion was but one of Ulrich Rauscher's reasons for advocating serious attempts to reach an economic agreement with Poland. Rauscher certainly deserved much of the credit for the amelioration of German-Polish relations in the late 1920s.[52] He was a conscientious and level-headed diplomat whose dispatches to Berlin were antidotal during periods of heightened tension, informative when Germany's political education in the affairs of the new eastern Europe was essential, and constructive when the Wilhelmstrasse sought a *modus vivendi*. He consistently urged that accepting a favorable treaty made good economic and political sense. Moreover, even offering economic concessions to Poland was justifiable if by doing so Germany could procure better treatment for the German minority in Poland. Like Schubert, Rauscher denied the assumption "that territorial questions can be resolved in conjunction with financial ones." By June 1926 Dirksen and Zechlin were less sanguine on this point than they had been late in the previous year. According to

[51] *AA*, Wallroth to Stresemann, 5 October, 2945/D572394-8.

[52] In November 1927, a representative of the Polish Foreign Office told Stresemann that Rauscher had been of "great influence" in Warsaw in encouraging Pilsudski to try to reach an economic agreement with Germany; *Vermächtnis*, III, 233. See also Dirksen, *Moscow, Tokyo, London*, p. 31: "Rauscher was one of the few outsiders who turned out to be a success. He developed into a most successful representative of his country in a difficult and thankless post. . . . We became very good friends"; Jules Laroche, *La Pologne de Pilsudski: Souvenirs d'une ambassade, 1926-1935* (Paris, 1953), p. 67; Von Riekhoff, *German-Polish Relations*, pp. 311-17; above, n. 31.

Rauscher, the three were now in agreement that although German representatives should continue to inject revisionist propaganda into international economic discussions they should not expect thereby to gain their political objective.[53]

By the end of 1926 circumstances dictated a shift in German policy. Pilsudski's coup had been followed by greater internal stability and the beginnings of economic recovery. Stresemann therefore had to write off one of his preconditions for territorial revision, Poland's economic collapse, which he had hoped would precipitate a peaceful resolution of the Polish question.[54] In December, Stresemann and Zaleski agreed that the time was not favorable for resolving the border question.[55] With both sides agreeing to abate that most divisive of issues, it became possible for them to seek a *modus vivendi* of mutual benefit. A growing number of groups inside Germany called for rapprochement—among them the German-Polish Committee, which gained new members from the ranks of those industrialists who—like Rauscher—believed that the German-Polish tariff war, far from forcing Poland to make political concessions, was in fact injuring the German economy.[56] The tariff war had begun in the summer of 1925 (after

[53] *AA*, Rauscher to Dirksen, 11 and 17 June 1926, 4569/E168771-8, 781-4; Rauscher to Schubert, 23 October 1927, 7370/H166490-3 (Rauscher thanked Schubert for having supported his views in the past and asked him to continue doing so); Rauscher to Stresemann, 25 October 1928, 7149/H151256-7.

[54] See Harvey Leonard Dyck, *Weimar Germany and Soviet Russia, 1926-1933: A Study in Diplomatic Instability* (New York, 1966), p. 38; also *Vermächtnis*, III, 235-39, 244. Werner Freiherr von Rheinbaben, a foreign affairs expert in the German People's Party (DVP), acknowledged the current stalemate over the border question, and called for German-Polish cooperation in other areas, such as minorities; see his article "Deutschland und Polen," *Europäische Gespräche*, VI (1928), 17-21.

[55] *AA*, Stresemann notes of conversation, 10 December 1926, 4569/E168905-9.

[56] The chairman of the Committee, Prof. Julius Wolf, was received by Dirksen and Zechlin on 9 February 1927; *AA, ibid.*, E168957-61.

the expiration of the commercial regulations set by the Treaty of Versailles and of a short-lived provisional trade agreement); it had halted bilateral negotiations. Talks were resumed late in 1927 and though frequently interrupted, they led to the signing of a commercial treaty in March 1930.[57] And the year ended on a conciliatory note in a private conversation between Stresemann and Pilsudski in Geneva. Pilsudski scoffed at any suspicion that Poland intended to seize East Prussia and according to Stresemann expressed a genuine desire to reach a friendly understanding with Germany.[58] But territorial revision—a subject Pilsudski had not alluded to in the Geneva talk—remained an objective of German policy, and any compromise short of that goal was necessarily tenuous. After 1926 revision was pushed farther into the future, and it was in Berlin's best interests, having distinguished between economic policy and political objectives, to improve relations with Poland while giving more patient attention to Germany's international position.

Failing Poland's internal collapse and a bilateral agreement with it, the Wilhelmstrasse maintained that a successful resolution of the border question ultimately depended on a "favorable international constellation." Stresemann's dictum, which sometimes caused frustration in the Wilhelmstrasse, was that Germany must remain flexible in European affairs. Lacking military strength and political prestige, it could ill afford to single out an "eastern" or a "western" policy, or to commit itself to a specifically British or French policy. In-

[57] On the tariff conflict and trade negotiations, see Charles Kruszewski, "The German-Polish Tariff War (1925-1934) and Its Aftermath," *Journal of Central European Affairs*, III (1943), 294-315; Von Riekhoff, *German-Polish Relations*, chap. 7; for an East German view, Berthold Puchert, *Der Wirtschaftskrieg des deutschen Imperialismus gegen Polen 1925-1934* ([East] Berlin, 1963).

[58] *AA*, Stresemann minute of their talk, 9 December 1927, 2945/ D573408-10; Korbel, *Poland between East and West*, p. 241; Gasiorowski, "Stresemann and Poland after Locarno," pp. 310-11. Stresemann reiterated Pilsudski's remarks to East Prussian officials in Königsberg a few weeks later; *Vermächtnis*, III, 247.

stead, Germany's best means of attaining its objectives was to use "finesse," to align with that power or bloc of states whose policy was—actually or potentially—compatible with German interests.[59] But in what alignment would Germany have the best chance of defending itself effectively and regaining its lost territories? This was the central question which guided the Foreign Office in its evaluation of Lithuania, the Soviet Union, Czechoslovakia, Rumania, and the West.

LITHUANIA

Germany's Lithuanian policy was dictated by three major considerations.[60] First, Lithuania—and the other Baltic States, Latvia and Estonia—formed "a bridge to Russia," and it served the interests of both Germany and the Soviet Union to maintain this bridge.[61] Second, Lithuania and Poland, in a state of war since 1920, would remain enemies so long as Poland held Vilna.[62] Finally, Lithuania exercised virtually complete sovereignty over the former German town and territory of Memel, which the German government included among its goals for territorial revision. Although German-Lithuanian relations underwent fluctuations, the effect of this third consideration was to keep the status quo of friendly association well short of an alliance against Poland.

Preserving the bridge of communications between Germany and the Soviet Union was necessary to the successful

[59] *AA*, Stresemann memorandum, 22 August 1923, "Grundzüge unserer Aussenpolitik," 3241/D704486-7; letter to Crown Prince William, 7 September 1925, 7318/H159875 (also in *Vermächtnis*, II, 554-55).

[60] For Lithuania and German-Soviet relations, see especially Dyck, *Weimar Germany and Soviet Russia*, pp. 36-46; Korbel, *Poland between East and West*, pp. 223-39.

[61] *AA*, Stresemann memorandum, 22 August 1923, 3241/D704488.

[62] That was likely to be a long time, for Poland's claim to Vilna was not only ethnographic, but also strategic because Vilna provided "defense against attacks from the east and . . . direct connection between Poland and Latvia." Debicki, *Foreign Policy of Poland*, p. 41.

implementation of the policy of economic intercourse laid down in the treaties of Rapallo and Berlin, and to possible combined military planning in the event of a war in East Europe. At times Germany seemed to be less fully committed than was the Soviet Union to the maintenance of this bridge. During and after the negotiations for a western security pact in 1925, the idea of compensating Poland with a corridor through Lithuania in return for Poland's cession of territories to Germany was discussed in European capitals with an earnestness that deeply troubled Moscow.[63] For Polish gains in Lithuania would extend Polish hegemony in the Baltic region while simultaneously severing the Baltic land connection between the Soviet Union and its lone western sympathizer. This was the crux of a Foreign Office memorandum of November 1926 rejecting the compensation plan, and of a Soviet protest to Stresemann in December.[64] Early in 1927, in a clear statement of the value to Germany of maintaining good relations with the Soviet Union, Stresemann reaffirmed Germany's opposition to the erection of a "political barrier between Germany and Russia."[65]

Polish-Lithuanian tension was a mixed blessing to Germany. On the advantageous side, it thwarted Polish efforts to construct an eastern security pact analogous to Locarno, and kept Lithuania dependent on the support of both Germany and the Soviet Union. After Pilsudski's coup, when they were disillusioned because of Poland's refusal to collapse internally, officials in the Eastern Department flirted briefly

[63] *AA*, Stresemann to chiefs of mission, 30 June 1925, 4556/ E149432; Zechlin memorandum, 19 November 1926, "Bemerkungen über die Lösung der östlichen Grenzfragen," 4569/E168868-78.

[64] *AA*, Wallroth's reply to Zechlin's memorandum of the same day (n. 63), *ibid.*, E168879-82. For the Soviet protest, in a talk between Georgi Chicherin (Soviet Peoples Commissar for Foreign Affairs) and Stresemann, see Korbel, *Poland between East and West*, pp. 228-29.

[65] *AA*, Stresemann to Hoesch, 3 February 1927, 2945/D572562-3; Stresemann note of talk with President Thomas Masaryk of Czechoslovakia, 13 March, *ibid.*, D572731.

with the idea of encouraging Poland to attack Lithuania. Germany (and the Soviet Union) would then have been able to exploit Poland's international disrepute by demanding territorial revision.[66] But just as Stresemann decided to stabilize Germany's Polish policy, so he declared Germany's interest in dampening the conflict between Lithuania and Poland, which was again reaching the kindling-point following the coup in Lithuania by A. Voldemaras on 17 December 1926. A Polish-Lithuanian war brought with it the disadvantage of threatening "to open the entire eastern question." Stresemann was anxious to prevent such an untimely international debate, although he did not intend to help bring about the opposite extreme, a Polish-Lithuanian rapprochement, which would be tantamount to Polish hegemony over the Baltic States.[67]

Lithuania's possession of Memel formed a persistent obstacle to close German-Lithuanian relations. Although strategically not so critical as the Corridor and Danzig, Memel contained a German population that the Weimar Republic had pledged to protect and recover. The explicit reservation in the Wilhelmstrasse's policy was that Germany must in no way compromise its claim to Memel by offering Lithuania too much support against Poland. Furthermore, the Memel question affected Germany's relations with the Soviet Union. Moscow wanted neither to foster German hegemony along the Baltic coast, nor to risk estranging Germany by guaranteeing Memel to Lithuania. Thus, the Soviet-Lithuanian nonaggression agreement of September 1926 did not mention Memel, an omission of which German diplomats approved.[68]

[66] *AA*, Wallroth's reply to Zechlin's memorandum of 19 November 1926 (notes 63, 64); Dyck, *Weimar Germany and Soviet Russia*, pp. 44-45.

[67] *AA*, Stresemann to London embassy, 12 January 1927, and Stresemann to Hoesch, 3 February, 2945/D572513-15, 562-3.

[68] See Dyck, *Weimar Germany and Soviet Russia*, pp. 36-37, 40; ". . . the fleeting intrusion of the Memel question in the negotiations on the Polish problem only served to confuse them, ultimately frustrating German attempts to incorporate in the Berlin understanding

Germany's Lithuanian policy after 1926 continued to be one of economic and political support without entering into binding agreements. Stresemann wanted above all to avoid a premature "opening of the entire eastern question." Thus, he worked for peaceful mitigation of the Polish-Lithuanian conflict. But he also adapted German policy to the exigencies of the Rapallo partnership, which he believed must be preserved.

THE SOVIET UNION

In international politics, Germany and Soviet Russia had much in common. Both had fallen from diplomatic grace as Great Powers, both harbored grievances toward and mistrust of the western Allies, and both rejected the territorial settlement in eastern Europe. These powers of attraction outweighed ideological polarity and the mutual political hostility involved in the war and the Treaty of Brest-Litovsk. Yet any study of German-Soviet relations during the Weimar period must be careful to distinguish between the actual details and the potential in agreements between the two states. It is perhaps because of the latter, and the enigmatic visage of Soviet foreign policy, that this area of Weimar policy has attracted so much attention.[69]

[of April 1926] an iron-clad Soviet pledge not to bargain with Poland."

[69] Works already cited are Helbig, *Träger der Rapallo-Politik*; Korbel, *Poland between East and West*; Dyck's thorough and incisive *Weimar Germany and Soviet Russia*. See also Edward Hallett Carr, *German-Soviet Relations between the Two World Wars, 1919-1939* (Baltimore, 1951); Karl Dietrich Erdmann, "Deutschland, Rapallo und der Westen," *Vierteljahrshefte für Zeitgeschichte*, XI (1963), 105-65; Gerald Freund, *Unholy Alliance: Russian-German Relations from the Treaty of Brest-Litovsk to the Treaty of Berlin* (New York, 1957); Zygmunt Gasiorowski, "The Russian Overture to Germany of December 1924," *Journal of Modern History*, XXX (June 1958), 99-117; Hans W. Gatzke, "Von Rapallo nach Berlin: Stresemann

When he assumed office in August 1923, Stresemann inherited secret military collaboration between the German and Soviet Armies (see chapter three), and the Treaty of Rapallo (16 April 1922), in which the German and Soviet governments agreed to resume diplomatic relations, waive mutual claims for reparations and indemnities, and establish closer commercial relations on a most-favored-nation basis. The new Foreign Minister wanted to maintain good relations with the Soviet Union because it was vital to prevent the erection of a hostile "barrier" in the east, which would lead to a Franco-Soviet bloc against Germany, because it was important to provide markets for Germany's "intellectual and economic products," and because only the Soviet Union had strongly backed Germany over the French occupation of the Ruhr and the question of revision in the east.[70] Whether Rapallo should be expanded into a political and military alliance directed against Poland was a question never ignored, yet never answered affirmatively in the Wilhelmstrasse.

The chances of an anti-Polish alliance seem to have been greatest in 1924, although Stresemann had already stated his policy of "finesse." Brockdorff-Rantzau had left for his ambassadorial post in Moscow late in 1922 convinced that an

---

und die deutsche Russlandpolitik," *Vierteljahrshefte für Zeitgeschichte*, IV (1956), 1-29; Herbert Helbig, "Die Moskauer Mission des Grafen Brockdorff-Rantzau," *Forschungen zur Osteuropäischen Geschichte*, II (Berlin, 1955); Gustav Hilger and Alfred G. Meyer, *The Incompatible Allies: A Memoir-History of German-Soviet Relations, 1918-1941* (New York, 1953); Fritz Klein, *Die Diplomatischen Beziehungen Deutschlands zur Sowjetunion, 1917-1932* (Berlin, 1952); Paul Kluke, "Deutschland und Russland zwischen den Weltkriegen," *Historische Zeitschrift*, CLXXI (1951), 519-52; Lionel Kochan, *Russia and the Weimar Republic* (Cambridge, 1954); Kurt Rosenbaum, *Community of Fate: German-Soviet Diplomatic Relations 1922-1928* (Syracuse, 1965); Theodor Schieder, *Die Probleme des Rapallo-Vertrags: Eine Studie über die deutsch-russische Beziehungen 1922-1926* (Cologne, 1956).

[70] *AA*, Stresemann memorandum, 22 August 1923, "Grundzüge unserer Aussenpolitik," 3241/D704490-1.

alliance with the Soviet Union would prevent German rapprochement with the West and fatally embroil Germany in a war between the Soviet Union and Poland, or between the Soviet Union and the West.[71] But after two years in Moscow Brockdorff-Rantzau had assumed Secretary of State von Maltzan's pro-Soviet position, and he began to wonder whether the German-Soviet "community of fate" might not yield territorial rewards. The conclusion that neither he nor others in the Foreign Office seriously entertained the idea of an alliance with the Soviet Union for a fourth partition of Poland[72] must be qualified by the correspondence of December 1924. In talks in Moscow between Brockdorff-Rantzau and Soviet representatives, and in dispatches and memoranda signed by Maltzan and his successor, Schubert, the phrase "pushing Poland back to her ethnographic frontiers" was repeatedly used.[73] If, at the time, these officials "pursued no aggressive military designs,"[74] they certainly spoke of an objective that might eventually require military means, a possibility Schubert implied in his message to Brockdorff-Rantzau of 29 December.[75] This episode should not be dismissed lightly as

[71] On Brockdorff-Rantzau's "Promemoria" of 15 August 1922 on German policy, see below, chap. 3, n. 87. Extracts from other memoranda by Brockdorff-Rantzau in 1922 in Helbig, "Die Moskauer Mission," pp. 300ff., and *Träger der Rapallo-Politik*, pp. 102ff.

[72] As examples, Helbig, *Träger der Rapallo-Politik*, pp. 5ff., 130-48, 204ff.; Höltje, *Weimarer Republik und Ostlocarno-Problem*, pp. 55-56, 62.

[73] *AA*, Brockdorff-Rantzau to Foreign Office, 5 December 1924, 4562/E154862-5; Maltzan to Brockdorff-Rantzau, 13 December, 2945/D571338-40; Schubert to Brockdorff-Rantzau, 29 December, 2860/D554677-8. Schubert's message was taken almost word for word from Bernhard W. von Bülow's note to Zechlin of 23 December, which recommended how to reply to Brockdorff-Rantzau's recent reports, 4562/E154910-12. (Bülow then occupied the League of Nations desk in the Foreign Office.) See also Gasiorowski, "Russian Overture to Germany of December 1924"; Korbel, *Poland between East and West*, pp. 153-59.

[74] Helbig, *Träger der Rapallo-Politik*, p. 166.

[75] *AA*, Schubert to Brockdorff-Rantzau, 29 December, 2860/

43

Soviet-inspired, nor constituting no actual offer of an alliance, nor a means of keeping Moscow in the Rapallo partnership while Germany courted the capitalistic West, nor an illusory departure from Stresemann's declared policy of steering non-commitally between east and west.[76] Whatever the truth in these protestations, a deeper significance should be noted: that Rapallo might culminate in a military alliance, although rejected for the present, was considered a future possibility.

Although the Wilhelmstrasse assured Moscow that replacing Maltzan with Schubert as Secretary of State in mid-December 1924 signified no change in Germany's eastern policy,[77] German diplomacy in 1925 assumed a sense of direction and confidence that it had lacked at the end of 1924. The Soviet government was not insensitive to this and throughout the Locarno negotiations sought reassurances that Germany was neither joining a western alliance against the Soviet Union nor renouncing its revisionist aims in the east.[78] The Soviets were particularly concerned about Germany's intention to enter the League of Nations. Would this not, Moscow asked, close the matter of a German-Soviet agreement to resolve the Polish question?

D554677-8. In Schubert's words, "Die Wahl der Mittel muss natürlich je nach Lage der Dinge vorbehalten werden."

[76] *AA*, Stresemann notes of conversations with Chicherin in Berlin on 30 September and 1 October 1925, 7129/H147979-91, 992-8; Spenz, *Vorgeschichte*, p. 49. Contrast Gasiorowski, "Stresemann and Poland before Locarno," p. 45; Korbel, *Poland between East and West*, pp. 175-78; Eyck, *Weimar Republic*, II, 25-27.

[77] *AA*, Zechlin to Brockdorff-Rantzau, 19 December, 4556/E148612.

[78] Spenz, *Vorgeschichte*, chap. 4; Edward Hallett Carr, *A History of Soviet Russia: Socialism in One Country 1924-1926* (3 vols.; New York, 1958-64), III, 248-82. For a post-World War II Soviet interpretation of Locarno—the West obliged Germany's militaristic-monopolistic aspirations in East Europe and opened the door to the invasion of the Soviet Union—see V. B. Ushakov, *Deutschlands Aussenpolitik 1917-1945*, trans. E. Wurl ([East] Berlin, 1964), pp. 103ff.

44

Stresemann admitted that joining the League could hinder Germany's active intervention on the side of the Soviet Union "should circumstances arise which brought a reduction of Poland to its ethnographic frontiers definitely into the realm of the possible." On the other hand, even if Germany were not a member, "it would have to count on the opposition of the Entente powers, at least France, Belgium and Czechoslovakia," and this would hinder German action anyway, at least for the foreseeable future. Things would be different "if Germany and Russia were strong enough and resolved to oppose any coalition with an armed hand." But in the current situation Germany could not regard a military alliance with the Soviet Union—whether open or secret—as a practicable political objective. Germany could, however, insist that its western policy did not contradict its eastern, and that Germany indeed had every intention of "continuing and deepening" its relations with the Soviet Union.[79]

In the summer of 1925 Stresemann observed that a solution of the Corridor question was "hardly conceivable without the cooperation of Russia and Germany,"[80] and he continued to mend fences with the Soviet Union. He had to placate not only Georgi Chicherin—the Soviet Peoples Commissar for Foreign Affairs—but also Brockdorff-Rantzau, who had opposed the Locarno policy from its inception, and who, in December 1925, complained to Stresemann "that the Russian proposal of December last year had never been answered and that he had been left completely in the dark concerning negotiations for a western pact."[81] In talks with Chicherin in

[79] *AA*, Stresemann to Brockdorff-Rantzau, 19 March 1925, 4562/ E155084-5. The ambassador conveyed Stresemann's views to Maxim Litvinov, Vice-Commissar for Foreign Affairs, on 7 April, *ibid.*, E155229-42; Brockdorff-Rantzau to Stresemann, 8 April, *ibid.*, E155178-81; Stresemann notes of talk with Litvinov in Berlin, 13 June, 7129/H147855-65 (also in *Vermächtnis*, II, 516-18).

[80] *AA*, Stresemann to chiefs of mission, 30 June, 4556/E149432.

[81] *AA*, Stresemann note of conversation (14 December) with Brockdorff-Rantzau, 15 December, 7129/H148099 (also in *Vermächtnis*, II, 534-35). In Berlin the preceding June, Brockdorff-Rant-

45

Berlin late in December, Stresemann was eager to show skeptics in Moscow and Berlin that Germany would not repudiate its relations with the Soviet Union. Having already signed a trade agreement with Soviet representatives on 12 October, Germany was prepared to discuss a treaty of neutrality.

Before negotiations bore fruit in the Treaty of Berlin, 24 April 1926, a considerable amount of diplomatic maneuvering was necessary. Berlin notified Paris and London that a treaty with the Soviet Union, by preventing a Polish-Soviet agreement, would keep open the door to peaceful revision of the German-Polish border. And Moscow had to be warned that the Polish-Soviet nonaggression treaty Chicherin had suggested during his visit to Warsaw in September 1925, which would give Poland security on its eastern borders, would end any chances for a German-Soviet treaty. For Soviet recognition of Poland's boundaries, even if only its eastern boundaries, would strengthen Poland's position against Germany.

The way to Polish-Soviet rapprochement was blocked by mutual hostility, Polish efforts to create an "eastern Locarno" of the Baltic States with or without the Soviet Union (the Soviet government was interested only in a bilateral agreement with Poland), and Poland's support of Rumania. The publication late in March of the renewed treaty of alliance between Poland and Rumania did not terminate Polish-Soviet talks, but helped induce Chicherin to accede to German conditions for a German-Soviet treaty.[82] In the Treaty of Berlin, each signatory reaffirmed Rapallo as the basis of continuing rela-

---

zau had voiced strong opposition to Stresemann's policy; 4562/E155427-32. In November President Hindenburg had persuaded an unrepentant Brockdorff-Rantzau not to resign. Hilger, *Incompatible Allies*, pp. 136-37.

[82] *AA*, Stresemann to Brockdorff-Rantzau, 24 February and 27 March 1926, 2945/D572083-5, 135-6; Gasiorowski, "Stresemann and Poland after Locarno," pp. 296-97; Korbel, *Poland between East and West*, pp. 189ff.; Hilger, *Incompatible Allies*, p. 154n.

tions, pledged to remain neutral should the other be the victim of unprovoked attack by one or more powers, and promised not to participate in any economic boycott of the other. Although not a formal declaration by the Soviet government on "the shape of its relations with Poland," the Berlin Treaty, in Stresemann's view, continued the valuable German-Soviet cooperation on matters in eastern Europe.[83]

The next three years, however, witnessed a gradual cooling in German-Soviet relations. There were a number of reasons for this. In the first place, Pilsudski's accession to power in May 1926 soon changed the dimensions of the Berlin-Moscow-Warsaw diplomatic triangle. His determination to free Poland from its dependence on France and to ennoble Poland's international image by taking the lead in East European affairs resulted in fewer communications along the Berlin-Moscow line concerning the Polish question, and a corresponding increase in direct contacts between Warsaw and the two neighboring capitals on questions of mutual interest. The Wilhelmstrasse remained apprehensive about Polish-Soviet talks for a nonaggression pact, which were continued in spite of Pilsudski's hostility toward the Soviet Union. But the diplomats could no longer politically afford to oppose such a pact (unless, of course, the Soviet government recognized Poland's border with Germany) or a similar agreement between the Soviet Union and France, for Germany must not appear contentious to western capitals if it depended upon their support for revision at some time in the future. Thus, in the summer of 1927, at the request of Austen Chamberlain and the League Six, Stresemann tried to dissuade Moscow from going to war against Poland following the assassination of the Soviet Minister to Poland, P. N. Voikov, on 7 June. It seemed to Chicherin that Stresemann, whom he accused of siding with Poland, was violating an axiom

[83] *AA*, Stresemann to Brockdorff-Rantzau, 30 April 1926, 2945/ D572193; also Schubert to Brockdorff-Rantzau, 3 April, 4564/ E162703-8.

47

of German-Soviet relations, namely, mutual hostility toward Poland.[84]

Second, Germany's relationship with Britain continued to improve after Locarno, while Anglo-Soviet altercations goaded Britain into breaking off diplomatic relations with the Soviet Union in May 1927. This breach reinforced the Kremlin's fears of a gigantic western offensive against the Soviet Union, and the amity between Germany and Britain looked like collusion in this alleged enterprise, in spite of reassurances that Germany would not side with Britain in the event of conflict.[85]

Germany's position between Britain and the Soviet Union became more awkward with the revelation of its secret military activities in the Soviet Union. In February 1927, two months after the *Manchester Guardian* had made common knowledge of German military installations on Soviet territory, Maxim Litvinov, Vice-Commissar for Foreign Affairs, came to Brockdorff-Rantzau in a state of some agitation and asked him about reports that the German government would soon expose the full nature of these secret relations. The ambassador in turn warned Berlin that if this indeed happened, the consequences would prove fatal to German-Soviet cooperation. Schubert instructed Brockdorff-Rantzau to reassure Moscow that although some kind of explanation was neces-

[84] See Dyck, *Weimar Germany and Soviet Russia*, pp. 92-96, 101. Dyck notes (p. 42) that German and Soviet policy in fact "threatened to cross on the Polish question," for Germany wanted Soviet support for revision, while the Soviet Union was preoccupied with the problem of security on its western borders.

[85] *AA*, Schubert to Brockdorff-Rantzau, 19 February 1927, 2945/ D572595-600. According to Hilger, "this fundamental difference of attitudes constituted the prime obstacle to a real Soviet-German friendship. In this lay the reason why the *Schicksalgemeinschaft* of which both Rantzau and Chicherin dreamed never became more than a *Zweckgemeinschaft* (community of purpose)." *Incompatible Allies*, pp. 130-31. For detailed accounts of the repercussions of the Anglo-Soviet break on German-Soviet relations, see Dyck, *Weimar Germany and Soviet Russia*, pp. 66-107; Rosenbaum, *Community of Fate*, pp. 242ff.

sary Germany would limit it as much as possible.[86] The Wilhelmstrasse skillfully maintained friendly relations with Britain while salvaging those with the Soviet Union, and it continued to sanction secret military cooperation after weathering a brief international and domestic storm. But these successes did not erase the mutual skepticism that had arisen in 1927 about the value of the German-Soviet tie.

The duality of policy emanating from Moscow was a third source of uneasiness in German-Soviet relations. The diplomacy of the Commissariat for Foreign Affairs and the revolutionary activity of the Comintern were sometimes contradictory, and foreign capitals could not always easily determine which of the two was ascendant at a given time.[87] The Communist risings of October 1923 in Saxony and Hamburg were planned in Moscow, yet the Soviet government had backed Germany during the Ruhr crisis earlier in the year. In spite of Chicherin's denials, German diplomats in Moscow and Berlin discerned that the Comintern performed the decisive role in Soviet policy toward the end of 1923. After the failure of the revolution in Germany, the Commissariat for Foreign Affairs regained its predominance, and Soviet policy toward Germany followed the more diplomatically orthodox perambulations of Chicherin. The lesson of October 1923, however, was an indelible one. The Wilhelmstrasse, sometimes prodded by the Defense Ministry, remained suspicious of the Comintern's subversive designs, and periodically introduced this divisive note into talks with Soviet diplomats.[88] Predictably, then, German anti-Bolshevik sensibilities were irritated when

[86] *AA*, Brockdorff-Rantzau to Schubert, 18 February 1927, and Schubert to Brockdorff-Rantzau, 20 February, 4564/E163491-3, 496-7.

[87] Carr, *Socialism in One Country*, III, 3-20; Theodore H. von Laue, "Soviet Diplomacy: G. V. Chicherin, Peoples Commissar for Foreign Affairs, 1918-1930," in Craig and Gilbert, *Diplomats*, chap. 8.

[88] For example, *AA*, Wallroth to Schubert and Gaus, 20 April 1927, 4562/E158700. For the apprehensions of "Easterners" in the Wilhelmstrasse, see Dyck, *Weimar Germany and Soviet Russia*, pp. 102-103, 108-109.

the Comintern stepped up its activities with the onset of economic depression in 1929.

Finally, the energy expended in Germany's western policy and Stalin's radical new course in domestic and foreign policy left the spirit of Rapallo debilitated. Harried by failures at home, in the west, and in the Far East, Stalin in 1927 began "to withdraw from the effort to conduct an active foreign policy. . . ."[89] Not the least cause for his disillusionment was Germany's strong economic and diplomatic ties with the western powers, policies which seemed to lead Germany away from the brink of proletarian revolution and into the armed camp Stalin believed to be virulently anti-Soviet. The view from the Kremlin was not entirely myopic. Germany's entry into the League of Nations, Stresemann's Thoiry conference in September 1926 with the French Foreign Minister, Aristide Briand, and Germany's stand in the Polish-Soviet confrontation of 1927, though not consummating an anti-Soviet cabal, evidenced Stresemann's inclination to tidy up Germany's relations with the West as a necessary precondition for accomplishing Germany's tasks in East Europe.[90]

A comparison of two studies prepared by Zechlin reveals the change in the thinking of the Foreign Office from 1925 to 1926. In August 1925 Zechlin regarded a war between the Soviet Union and Poland opportunistically. It was a "practical possibility," which Zechlin believed should not be forfeited in the forthcoming security pact and arbitration treaty, and it would provide Germany with the earliest opportunity to regain the Corridor and Upper Silesia. Germany would find it difficult "to remain passive," particularly if Soviet forces gained the advantage and compelled the Polish government

[89] George Kennan, *Russia and the West under Lenin and Stalin* (Boston, 1960), p. 279.

[90] Stresemann wanted no misunderstanding among German Nationalists (DNVP) that, although a new cabinet was to be formed early in 1927, he would continue his western policy and not entertain thoughts of a military alliance with the Soviet Union or an alignment with Italy; *AA*, Stresemann to Chancellor (Marx), 14 January 1927, 7338/H163564.

50

to withdraw to southern Poland. Zechlin's major reservation was that German intervention to regain the lost territories would still be an act of aggression and thus provoke French reaction according to the terms of the Franco-Polish alliance, or, if Germany were a member of the League, collective action pursuant to Article 16 of the Covenant. In the international circumstances of August 1925, he concluded, "a German attack against Poland would be feasible only in the exceptionally favorable situation that, at the same time Poland fell in a Russo-Polish conflict, France were internally or externally paralyzed."[91]

By November 1926 both the actual and potential international configuration had changed. Germany was a Locarno signatory and a League member. Poland was stronger internally. Two months after Thoiry, Zechlin wrote that even if the Soviet Union were victorious in a war with Poland and friendly toward Germany the Polish question probably could not be solved according to German wishes unless Germany and France shared a close and full understanding. To pursue a policy of closer relations with the Soviet Union would not bring Germany "any closer to a solution of the Corridor question," for the Soviet government was currently hostile toward the League and Britain.[92]

Zechlin's conclusion—that perhaps it was high time for Germany to adopt "a definite line" of policy, i.e., a western line—was not shared by Stresemann, Schubert, Wallroth, Dirksen, Rauscher, or Moritz Schlesinger, an economic expert in the Wilhelmstrasse who had considerable influence on Germany's eastern policy. Too many economic and, Wallroth averred, strategic advantages were at stake to risk alienating Moscow.[93] But this did not align the Wilhelmstrasse with

[91] *AA,* Zechlin memorandum, 25 August, 4562/E155860-3.

[92] *AA,* Zechlin memorandum, 19 November, "Bemerkungen über die Lösung der östlichen Grenzfragen," 4569/E168868-78.

[93] *AA,* Wallroth's reply to Zechlin's memorandum (n. 92), 19 November, *ibid.,* E168879-82. For Schlesinger's views, see Dyck, *Weimar Germany and Soviet Russia,* pp. 50-63. Dirksen writes that Schubert, although a "Westerner," was not blind to Germany's need

51

Brockdorff-Rantzau, who at the time of his death in September 1928 was the lone important proponent of a strongly pro-Soviet policy. More significant than Moscow's esteem for his successor, Dirksen,[94] was the unprecedented fact that tension between the Soviet Union and Poland—only temporarily alleviated by the signing of the Litvinov Protocol in February 1929—no longer brought Moscow and Berlin closer together. The promise of territorial revision, latent in the early years of the Rapallo affair, continued to justify maintaining the tie with the Soviet Union, and reappeared in Army war games—and Foreign Office critiques—of the late 1920s.[95] But it remained a promise unfulfilled. German-Soviet agreements included no concrete provisions for "pushing Poland back to her ethnographic frontiers," a suggestion which the Wilhelmstrasse had ceased to make. By 1929, the conduct of German-Soviet relations had declined into a "marriage of convenience."[96]

CZECHOSLOVAKIA AND RUMANIA

The highest priorities at the eastern desks of the Foreign Office were Germany's policies toward Poland and the Soviet Union. Of tangential concern were Poland's relations with

---

"to counterbalance the Western influences by a good understanding with Russia." *Moscow, Tokyo, London*, p. 43.

[94] At Brockdorff-Rantzau's funeral, a Soviet diplomat told Gustav Hilger that the Kremlin would welcome Dirksen as the next ambassador, for he " 'was trained in the school of von Maltzan and represents the spirit of Rantzau.' " Hilger concludes a very complimentary sketch of Dirksen with the judgment that "he was the most suitable man to represent German interests in Moscow at a time when the maintenance of German-Soviet relations demanded not only consistency and dogged persistence but also wise moderation in striving for realistic aims." *Incompatible Allies*, pp. 223-24.

[95] See below, chap. 6.

[96] Carr, *German-Soviet Relations*, p. 101. See also Dyck, *Weimar Germany and Soviet Russia*, pp. 141ff., 151; Korbel, *Poland between East and West*, pp. 254-55; Dirksen, *Moscow, Tokyo, London*, pp. 66ff., 83ff.

other states, above all Czechoslovakia and Rumania. A hostile Czechoslovakia on Germany's southeastern flank would pose a strategic threat to Germany. If allied with both France and Poland, Czechoslovakia practically completed Germany's encirclement. While borderland Germans on both sides of the new boundary inclined toward alarmism, the Foreign Office was generally circumspect in its appraisal of relations among Czechoslovakia, France, and Poland.[97] Caution prevailed after the signing of the Franco-Czechoslovak Mutual Assistance Pact on 25 January 1924, in spite of some anxiety among German diplomats that a secret military agreement had also been concluded.[98] The French had in fact wanted one, but the Czechoslovak Foreign Minister, Eduard Beneš, refused to commit his country to anything more than the political alliance, which was, as he described it, " 'a very pliable instrument calling for frequent conferences on a basis of mutual equality but reserving complete liberty of action to both partners.' "[99]

Retaining "liberty of action" was a consistent principle of Beneš' foreign policy.[100] In 1925 the prospect of Germany's achieving a security pact in the west gave Warsaw and Prague a sense of solidarity, for the Poles wanted support against German revisionism, and the Czechoslovaks, fearing a German-Austrian *Anschluss* and possible encirclement by

[97] As an example, the Wilhelmstrasse questioned the reliability of hundreds of reports received by the Prague consulate from Czech-Germans alleging Czechoslovak preparations to combine with France for an attack against Germany. *AA*, May-June 1922, K94/K009972ff.

[98] *AA*, Foreign Office to London and Rome embassies, 7 February 1924, *ibid.*, K010056-7. Hoesch, with his usual perception, did not believe the rumors; Hoesch to Foreign Office, 27 March, K16/K002553-8. See also Piotr S. Wandycz, *France and Her Eastern Allies, 1919-1925: French-Czechoslovak-Polish Relations from the Paris Peace Conference to Locarno* (Minneapolis, Minn., 1962), pp. 303-304.

[99] In Wandycz, *France and Her Eastern Allies*, p. 300; the full text of the pact (in French), pp. 398-99.

[100] See Paul E. Zinner, "Czechoslovakia: The Diplomacy of Eduard Beneš," in Craig and Gilbert, *Diplomats*, chap. 4.

Germany, Austria and Hungary (all revisionist states which coveted portions of Czechoslovakia), needed a friendly border and outlet to the Baltic. But at talks in Warsaw late in April and in subsequent negotiations prior to Locarno, Beneš refused to sign a military agreement with Poland, accepted Locarno as a necessary, if inferior, alternative to the Geneva Protocol which he had helped to construct, and agreed to an arbitration treaty with Germany, in spite of Germany's refusal to recognize the German-Czechoslovak border; all three decisions disappointed Warsaw.[101] Czechoslovakia stood beside Poland in opposition to territorial revision although the Czechoslovaks would not commit themselves to a military alliance with Poland. They had nothing to gain and a trade agreement to lose by fighting at Poland's side against the Soviet Union. And, as President Thomas Masaryk remarked to Stresemann at Geneva in March 1927, he had no intention of developing relations with Poland to such an extent that he would have "to pull the chestnuts from the fire for Poland in the event of a conflict with Germany."[102] Moreover, the mutual mistrust between the two nations dating from the Peace Conference, the scene of acrimonious debate over Teschen, had not yet been dispelled. For these reasons, the Wilhelmstrasse did not view Czechoslovakia as an unqualified supporter of Poland.

The Foreign Office was not always sure that Poland, in its relations with Rumania, "only considered the threat from Russia."[103] The Polish-Rumanian alliance of 3 March 1921 provided for mutual defense to protect "their present eastern frontiers" against unprovoked Soviet aggression.[104] But its renewal five years later aroused suspicions in the Wilhelm-

[101] *AA*, Warsaw mission to Foreign Office, 22 September 1925, 2945/D571923. See also Wandycz, *France and Her Eastern Allies*, p. 306.

[102] *AA*, Stresemann note of conversation, 13 March, *ibid.*, D572732.

[103] Jozef Beck, *Final Report* (New York, 1957), p. 4.

[104] Text of the treaty in Stephan Horak, *Poland's International Affairs 1919-1960* (Bloomington, Ind., 1964), pp. 150-52.

strasse, because the new treaty of 26 March 1926 was no longer a defensive alliance directed specifically against the Soviet Union, a change that reflected Poland's concurrent attempts to reach some kind of understanding with Moscow in a nonaggression pact. The pact of 1926 pledged mutual assistance to preserve the political independence and territorial integrity of the signatories against any foreign aggressor. A Foreign Office memorandum on the new agreement observed that "Poland's reluctance to commit itself in the question of Bessarabia seems to have been overcome by Rumania's pledge to assume the guarantee for the western borders of Poland."[105] If this latter guarantee should be supplemented by a secret military convention, then the Polish-Rumanian alliance would take an even more ominous anti-German turn.

After receiving from the Bucharest mission a copy of military arrangements signed by Polish and Rumanian military representatives in Paris on 14 May, the Foreign Office may have regarded this as confirmation of Rumanian complicity in the encirclement of Germany. A report in the Polish Section stressed Poland's strategic advantage in Rumania's obligation to help guard Poland's frontier with the Soviet Union in the event of a German-Polish war. It was clear, the report continued, that Rumania had been forced to sign this agreement by France, whose aim was obviously to strengthen Poland as much as possible. Thus, in spite of its military weakness and its peaceful affirmations at Locarno, Germany was "to have the sword of Damocles over its head permanently."[106] Moreover, Wallroth informed German missions in Europe and Washington, the Defense Ministry's evaluation of the convention corroborated the judgment of the Foreign Office.[107]

[105] *AA*, Köpke memorandum, 16 April 1926, K178/K030602-3.

[106] *AA*, Schellhorn memorandum, 14 July, *ibid.*, K030705-10; the terms of the convention and " 'technical arrangements' " in messages from Bucharest to Foreign Office, 15 and 21 June, *ibid.*, K030679-80, 688-97.

[107] *AA*, Wallroth to missions, 24 September, *ibid.*, K030784, 787-8.

If the Foreign Office was convinced of the authenticity of the document and the practicability of its guarantees[108] (the Wilhelmstrasse's awareness of Rumania's weak politico-military posture and of possible changes in Polish policy following Pilsudski's coup in May might be mentioned here), this was only temporary. The Bucharest mission notified Berlin in July that the military convention had been changed, replacing the articles that mentioned a German-Polish war with a general reference to League measures in cases of conflict.[109] After July there can be no doubt that Germany exploited the secret convention of 14 May for propaganda purposes. Schubert's file contained a copy of it, along with an embellishing memorandum by Zechlin, for use against Poland in Geneva after Germany became a member of the League in September.[110] Wallroth instructed Hoesch to discuss it as if it were authentic, although the ambassador privately denied its validity and compared it to the alleged Franco-Czechoslovak secret military treaty of 1924.[111] And there is strong evidence that the Foreign Office was responsible for its publication in the United States by the Hearst press early in September.[112]

[108] Lord D'Abernon observed: "What added to German suspicion and resentment [of the amended Polish-Rumanian treaty] was the subsequent publication of a series of documents constituting a very plausible annexe to the main Polish-Roumanian Treaty." *Diary*, III, 247n.

[109] *AA*, H. Freytag to Foreign Office, 15 and 22 July, K178/K030736, 745.

[110] *AA*, copy of the convention and of a report by the Rumanian General Petala, 4556/E150092-9; Zechlin memorandum, September, *ibid.*, E150088-91. Dirksen notified the Bucharest mission on 14 July that the Foreign Office intended to use its copy of the secret convention for propaganda purposes, K178/K030703.

[111] *AA*, Hoesch to Foreign Office, 7 August, and Wallroth to Hoesch, 24 September, K178/K030750-3, 793.

[112] *AA*, *ibid.*, K030797ff. The Bucharest mission reported that Rumanian denials of the secret convention following its publication in September were weak, that the Rumanians were very angry at this news leak, and that there were different ideas in Bucharest as to who had been responsible (Germany, the Soviet Union, or a member of

In October the Bucharest mission reiterated that under the revised military convention, Rumania had "no commitments of a military nature except those directed against Russia."[113] Nor did this change in the next few years, and the Foreign Office did not believe periodic rumors that Polish-Rumanian military planning was turning against Germany or evolving into an offensive alliance against the Soviet Union.[114] Rumania and Poland were allied militarily against Soviet aggression and against any third power that joined with the Soviet Union in the conflict. They were allied politically against German aggression. But the Foreign Office could afford some degree of confidence that Rumania would be of negligible significance in a German-Polish conflict. Even if Germany were the aggressor, which Rumania and the League might have difficulty proving, Rumania was pledged to nothing more than benevolent neutrality toward Poland.[115]

In spite of bilateral agreements between Poland and the members of the Little Entente—political with Rumania, economic and cultural with Czechoslovakia and Yugoslavia—Poland would not be likely to enter a club that preserved its anti-Hungarian birthright, for Poland enjoyed friendly relations with Hungary.[116] The Little Entente did no more for

---

the former Crown Prince's entourage in Paris); 12 October, *ibid.*, K030836.

[113] *AA*, Bucharest mission to Foreign Office, 12 October, *ibid.*, K030832.

[114] *AA*, documents of June-December 1928, *ibid.*, K030881-2, 908ff., and 30 October 1929, *ibid.*, K030999-1002. On 5 December 1928, Krestinski told Stresemann that Pilsudski was planning a Polish-Rumanian attack against the Soviet Union to annex the Ukraine before turning against East Prussia, 2945/D573766-8. Rauscher discounted reports of such a Polish-Rumanian offensive; 6 December 1928, K178/K030939-42, and 26 February 1929, 4569/E169196-7.

[115] *AA*, Bucharest mission to Foreign Office, 24 November 1926, K178/K030852-4.

[116] *AA*, reports from German missions in Prague, Belgrade, Bucharest, and Warsaw, 1924-1929, 6192/E465396-570, *passim*. See also Bernadotte Schmitt (ed.), *Poland* (Berkeley, Calif., 1945), pp. 384-85.

the French alliance system than sign bilateral mutual assistance treaties with France. Polish relations with the Little Entente and France, countries that were apprehensive about the revisionism in Mussolini's foreign policy, helped deter Italy from interfering in the German-Polish border question.[117] In sum, Poland's position in eastern Europe was not a formidable one. Germany faced an antirevisionist conglomerate in that quarter—one whose cohesion, however, was strained by the particular interests of its parts.

[117] *AA*, reports from Ambassador Constantin Freiherr von Neurath in Rome to Foreign Office, 4 May 1926, 4569/E168694; 15 May, 2945/D572210; 19 April 1928, 4569/E169094-100. On Neurath's balanced assessment of German-Italian relations in the 1920s, see John L. Heineman, "Constantin Freiherr von Neurath as Foreign Minister, 1932-1935" (unpublished Ph.D. dissertation, Cornell University, 1965), pp. 64-70.

CHAPTER II

The West:
Force and Foreign Policy

THE WEST

WITH German-Soviet relations slipping into a "marriage of convenience," perhaps a more productive relationship lay to the west. Stresemann's policy of establishing an understanding with Britain and France had a number of immediate objectives: thwarting a bilateral Anglo-French defensive alliance, which Chamberlain was rumored to favor in the winter of 1924-25; early evacuation of Allied troops from the Rhineland; and a more conciliatory atmosphere for settling Allied-German disputes over other questions, such as military surveillance, disarmament, and reparations. But Stresemann's long-range goal was revision in the east. In pre-Locarno instructions and private correspondence, in speeches before his own party, the Reichstag Foreign Affairs Committee, and East Prussian dignitaries, and in talks with British and French statesmen, he was usually explicit about priorities and fundamentals: Germany's western policy was inextricably linked to its eastern policy, and was requisite to a satisfactory resolution of the Corridor question. Schubert, Wallroth, Dirksen, and Zechlin in Berlin, Sthamer in London, Hoesch in Paris, and Rauscher in Warsaw supported Stresemann's policy. All agreed on a sequence something like the following: conciliation and a relaxation of tension in the west, resulting in the willingness of London and Paris to cooperate or acquiesce in revision in the east. In the negotiations with Britain and France surrounding Locarno, Thoiry, and entry into the League of Nations, Germany neither recognized its eastern borders nor sacrificed its relations with the Soviet Union.[1]

[1] Stresemann to Maltzan (then Ambassador to Washington), 7

In his instruction of 30 June 1925, Stresemann asserted that economic pressure might be brought to bear on Poland by the "Anglo-Saxon powers," if they could be convinced of the injustice of the eastern border situation.[2] From Warsaw, Rauscher confirmed that Poland depended on Britain for financial aid and inclusion in the security pact.[3] Through Britain, therefore, Germany enjoyed a degree of political and economic leverage against Poland. Chamberlain's sympathetic attitude toward Germany during the Locarno prelude —when he unequivocally refused to guarantee or recognize as permanent the German-Polish borders—and Montagu Norman's temporary concurrence with Stresemann and Dirk-

---

April 1925, *Vermächtnis*, ii, 281-82; Stresemann speech to central committee of the DVP, 22 November, in Turner, "Rede Stresemanns"; *AA*, Stresemann before Reichstag Foreign Affairs Committee, 7 October 1926, 7333/H162672-3 (also in *Vermächtnis*, iii, 38); before closed meeting in Königsberg, 16 December 1927, 7372/ H166871 (*Vermächtnis*, iii, 248). See also Karl Dietrich Erdmann, "Das Problem der Ost- oder Westorientierung in der Locarno-Politik Stresemanns," *Geschichte in Wissenschaft und Unterricht*, vi (1955), 133-62; Jacques Bariéty, "Der Versuch einer europäischen Befriedung: Von Locarno bis Thoiry," in Hellmuth Rössler (ed.), *Locarno und die Weltpolitik 1924-1932* (Göttingen, 1969), pp. 42-43. All Reichstag parties agreed that Germany's western policy should not compromise the aim of border revision in the east; Höltje, *Weimarer Republik und Ostlocarno-Problem*, pp. 117ff.; Matthias, *Sozialdemokratie und der Osten*, pp. 66ff.

[2] *AA*, Stresemann to chiefs of mission, 4556/E149432-3. On Stresemann's economic and political motives for closer relations with the United States, see Bariéty, "Versuch," in Rössler, *Locarno und die Weltpolitik*, pp. 38-42. Maltzan opposed Germany's entry into the League in part because he believed that Germany would be in a better position in a future European war if on the side of the United States (the strongest world power) rather than any League state; Robert Gottwald, *Die deutsch-amerikanischen Beziehungen in der Ära Stresemann* (Berlin-Dahlem, 1965), pp. 121-22.

[3] Reich Chancery (hereafter *RK*, for *Reichskanzlei*), Rauscher to Foreign Office, 2 October 1925 (copy in Reich Chancery files), K1947/K506985. (See bibliography for list of Reich Chancery files consulted, and corresponding microfilm serial numbers.)

sen in their anti-Polish economic policy of 1925-26 gave Germany good reason to endeavor to maintain Albion's trust. Furthermore, British friendship would improve chances of revising other terms of the Treaty of Versailles: German reparations payments, Allied military control, and the Allied occupation of the Rhineland.

In terms of international alignments, the Wilhelmstrasse was less optimistic than it had been in the immediate postwar years about splitting the Anglo-French Entente by winning London's support in continental affairs. Britain made no offer of territorial concessions to Germany in return for German assistance against the Soviet Union in 1927, a silence that Berlin correctly interpreted as proof of Britain's loyalty to France in spite of their differences.[4] Nevertheless, the arguments for friendly intercourse between Berlin and London proved decisive whenever events in other quarters, such as the Anglo-Soviet rupture of 1927, embarrassed Anglo-German relations. Germany could still hope that Britain would accommodate itself to a peaceful revision of the Treaty of Versailles. And should the international situation one day permit a war between Germany and Poland, British neutrality was an absolute necessity for Germany.

For some of the same reasons, and to increase its security in the west, Germany could profit from good French relations. Without the cooperation of France, concessions over

[4] Dyck, *Weimar Germany and Soviet Russia*, pp. 106-107. For a statement of British policy toward France (one of "cooperation in settling post-war problems," for Britain, too, had "to reckon with a German revival and Italian ambitions"), see memorandum by Mr. Gregory, 10 April 1926, *DBFP*, Ser. IA, I, 850. An incisive and complete account of the persistence of the Anglo-French Entente after Locarno, and the corresponding disillusionment in the Wilhelmstrasse concerning revision through understanding, is Jon S. Jacobson's *Locarno Diplomacy: Germany and the West, 1925-1929* (Princeton, N.J., 1972). See also Holborn, "Diplomats and Diplomacy," in Craig and Gilbert, *Diplomats*, pp. 160ff.; Arnold Wolfers, *Britain and France between Two Wars: Conflicting Strategies of Peace from Versailles to World War II* (New York, 1940), chaps. 14-16, *passim*.

reparations, military surveillance, and occupation were out of the question. Franco-German understanding might also clear the way to a peaceful recovery of the lost territories. In fact, although it was not a topic at Thoiry, there were signs late in 1927 that the French—Briand, Philippe Berthelot (Secretary-General of the Ministry for Foreign Affairs), Henri Fromageot (a legal expert in the Foreign Ministry), and the military attaché in Berlin—were in favor of a revision of the German-Polish border.[5] Finally, the Wilhelmstrasse anticipated the possibility of strategic dividends from its investment in reconciliation with France: a weakening of the French alliance system that almost completely encircled Germany with vastly superior military forces.

French policy toward Poland in the immediate postwar years was determined by the supreme political objective of security. A strong Poland on Germany's eastern flank would reinforce France along the Rhine, and be the bastion of a *cordon sanitaire* against Bolshevism. Accordingly, France signed a political alliance with Poland on 19 February 1921. Article 3 provided for combined action in the event of unprovoked aggression against either of the two parties; the secret military convention signed two days later specified German aggression as the occasion for mutual aid, and in the case of a Polish-Soviet war appointed France to keep Germany's land and naval forces in check and send matériel to Poland.[6]

Although ignorant of the details of the secret convention

---

[5] Korbel, *Poland between East and West*, p. 242; also Richard Breyer, *Das Deutsche Reich und Polen 1932-1937: Aussenpolitik und Volksgruppenfragen* (Würzburg, 1955), p. 24. On the generally harmonious cooperation between Briand and Berthelot, see Richard D. Challener, "The French Foreign Office: The Era of Philippe Berthelot," in Craig and Gilbert, *Diplomats*, pp. 74ff. Berthelot had reservations, however, about Briand's optimistic attitude toward the League and rapprochement with Germany; Challener, pp. 74ff.; Zimmermann, *Deutsche Aussenpolitik*, p. 322.

[6] Wandycz, *France and Her Eastern Allies*, pp. 217-18; the full text of the convention (in French), pp. 394-95.

until the late 1920s, German diplomats realized the strategic significance of the Franco-Polish alliance. In June 1925 Stresemann argued that Poland had only one valid reason for retaining the Corridor: "the security of military communications with France." Poland would "scarcely still need the Corridor if German wishes [were] satisfied,"[7] that is, if Germany were granted its territorial objectives (including the Corridor) and thereupon became a satisfied and friendly neighbor. It is hard to believe that Stresemann hoped to sway Poland—and dissolve the Franco-Polish accord—with such ingenuous logic. To accomplish these objectives, the more realistic alternative was to weaken Poland's international position.

The Wilhelmstrasse disdained Poland's aspirations to be a Great Power.[8] Certainly German feelings of superiority had something to do with this attitude, but political expediency was the decisive motivation. The thwarting of Poland's campaign for a permanent seat on the League Council left Germany with more prestige and political leverage in that body. Forcing Poland to reduce the size of its Army, which Germany could try to accomplish through economic pressure and discussions for general disarmament, would lower Poland's power status, virtually eliminate its capability of fighting a two-front war, and thus tarnish its attractive image in Paris.[9] A simultaneous effort to reach an agreement with France would, it was hoped, loosen both the military and antirevisionist ties between France and Poland. This is precisely what vexed the Poles about Locarno. The Wilhelmstrasse accused

[7] *AA*, Stresemann to chiefs of mission, 30 June 1925, 4556/E149427-8.

[8] As an example, *AA*, Schubert memorandum, late November 1925, 4569/E168404. For German contempt during and after the Peace Conference, see H.W.V. Temperley (ed.), *A History of the Peace Conference of Paris* (6 vols.; London, 1920-24), II, 4; D'Abernon, *Diary*, III, 151; Dirksen, *Moscow, Tokyo, London*, p. 24. "Polnische Wirtschaft" is still a pejorative term in Germany.

[9] *AA*, Schubert memorandum, late November 1925, and Dirksen minute, 16 November, 4569/E168404, 406.

Poland of "bad faith" for discrediting German efforts to form a western security pact,[10] but, if we consider the strategic implications of Germany's western policy, we see that Polish fears were justified.

Locarno, Stresemann told the cabinet shortly after his return from that conference, had undermined the Franco-Polish alliance.[11] Before Locarno, France could have gone immediately to the aid of Poland if the latter had been attacked by Germany, but the security pact placed external restrictions on French action. By its terms, which were careful to show the pact's conformity with the League Covenant, France could intervene from the west in a German-Polish conflict if Germany, without provocation, remilitarized the Rhineland or attacked France, or if the League Council declared Germany the aggressor against Poland and ordered collective action according to Article 16 of the Covenant. Since the League lacked an international and legally binding definition of aggression, however, the consequent debate might give Germany time to advance into Poland before France could legally attack, assuming, that is, that Franco-German rapprochement were not firm enough to keep France out of the conflict.

Failing the League's unanimous decision, France could act unilaterally pursuant to Article 15, paragraph 7. But in this case (and in all other cases) France's legal right and political inclination to attack from the west were befogged by the security pact: France and Germany had renounced unprovoked

---

[10] *AA*, Schubert to Hoesch, 10 March 1925, 2945/D571519-20.

[11] *Vermächtnis*, II, 213. See also Stresemann's address to leaders of the DVP, 22 November 1925, in Turner, "Rede Stresemanns," pp. 429-30; Chamberlain's statement to the Imperial Conference, 20 October 1926, *DBFP*, Ser. IA, II, 921-23; Laroche, *La Pologne de Pilsudski*, p. 17; Josef Lipski, *Diplomat in Berlin 1933-1939*, ed. W. Jedrzejewicz (New York, 1968), pp. 9-11; F. S. Northedge, *The Troubled Giant: Britain Among the Great Powers 1916-1939* (New York, 1966), pp. 267, 270-71; Hans Roos, *Polen und Europa: Studien zur polnischen Aussenpolitik 1931-1939* (Tübingen, 1957), pp. 10-11; Von Riekhoff, *German-Polish Relations*, chap. 5.

acts of aggression; the Franco-German border was inviolate; the Rhineland could not be remilitarized by Germany or, following its evacuation, reoccupied unilaterally by any other power; and Britain and Italy were the guarantors of these provisions. In accordance with its alliance with Poland, reaffirmed at Locarno in a separate mutual assistance treaty,[12] France could legally invade Germany (across the Rhine or, after the evacuation of the Rhineland, across the Franco-German border) without British intervention only if Germany were the aggressor. Yet, again, who was to decide which party was the aggressor? Britain, by refusing to guarantee either the German-Polish arbitration treaty or the Franco-Polish alliance, had no obligation under Locarno to support France even if Germany were the aggressor against Poland. But Britain might disagree that Germany was in fact the culprit, in which event Britain was bound to uphold the security pact.[13] In short, Locarno introduced contingencies that might delay or even deter France from rushing to the assistance of its strongest eastern ally.

The Franco-Polish alliance suffered from internal attrition as well as external restrictions. The question of evacuation of the Rhineland caused sparks of friction between these two allies. The French regarded the Rhineland occupation, which

[12] The text in Horak, *Poland's International Affairs*, pp. 154-56.

[13] Having examined these and other possible conflict situations, the British Foreign Office gave the following answer to the crucial question "who decides who is the aggressor?" "Each party decides for itself. The fault in this case, if fault there be, is inherent in the Covenant and is one which Locarno has made neither better nor worse." Memorandum by the Central Department of the Foreign Office, 13 November 1925, "Cases in which Great Britain is bound to go to war" by the Locarno treaties, *DBFP*, Ser. IA, I, 146. In another study, a British official noted that Britain's course of action in the event of German aggression against Poland depended on its legal obligations but also, in the last analysis, on its national interests; memorandum by Mr. Gregory, 10 April 1926, *ibid.*, p. 857. For the British preference of a regional security pact to a reinforcing of the Covenant, see Wolfers, *Britain and France between Two Wars*, pp. 257ff., 325ff.

they tied to Germany's fulfillment of its reparations obligations, as part of their security system. After Locarno had guaranteed the Franco-German border and the demilitarization of the Rhineland (stipulated in Articles 42 and 43 of the Treaty of Versailles), and its spirit of conciliation had encouraged the Allies to evacuate the Cologne Zone in January 1926 (a year after the date designated by the treaty), Briand appeared willing to consider the early evacuation of the remaining two zones of occupation. Opposing this, however, French Army leaders and conservative politicians argued that early evacuation would expose France to a sudden German attack across the demilitarized buffer west of the Rhine before the French Army had had time to construct a strong defensive wall along the Franco-German border, or to reorganize in accordance with military legislation passed in 1927-28 that would reduce the size of its standing forces.

Because of this domestic pressure and his reluctance to grant such a major revision without some concession from Germany, Briand delayed in promising Stresemann early evacuation until August 1929 at the Hague Conference. There, where the two statesmen accepted the Young Plan for the regularization of reparations payments, Briand won a measure of financial security for his country in the form of provisions for the advance payment of reparations. In return, trusting in the protection afforded by the future Maginot Line and the British guarantee of a permanently demilitarized Rhineland, he agreed to end the occupation by 30 June 1930, five years ahead of schedule, and relinquished his proposal for permanent on-site inspection of the Rhineland by an international "commission of verification."[14]

Poland also viewed the occupation as strategically necessary for its own security, but Poland had no Locarno. In the spring of 1928 the campaign of the Polish Foreign Minister, August Zaleski, against an evacuation of the Rhineland without a compensatory eastern Locarno met with approval

[14] Jacobson, *Locarno Diplomacy*, parts 7, 8; Eyck, *Weimar Republic*, II, 204-10.

among Parisian conservatives, but parliamentary opposition to Briand's policy did not generate enough political power to remove him from office.[15] Germany fought any attempt to include the recognition and guarantee of its eastern borders in agreements with the West,[16] and Briand continued to seek a compromise with Germany while reassuring the Poles that although France could not produce an eastern Locarno it still took its obligations under the Franco-Polish alliance very seriously.[17]

In Warsaw, Pilsudski resented Locarno and Briand's policy of rapprochement, which he believed increased the imbalance between west and east and compounded Poland's problem of security.[18] But in the absence of German border concessions and an eastern Locarno, Pilsudski, in spite of his ambition to conduct policy independently, had to acknowledge the value of maintaining the military tie with France. He therefore welcomed frequent talks between French and

[15] Rauscher thought that Zaleski, while in Paris, was suffering from the "diplomatic sickness of frequenting preferably and sometimes exclusively the Faubourg St. Germain," where he came into contact with a conservative minority of Frenchmen; *AA*, Rauscher to Köpke, 28 June 1928, 4569/E169121-8. Briand remained Foreign Minister when Poincaré returned to power as head of a centrist ministry from 1926 to 1929, for the majority of the French public (and in the Chambers) favored Briand's foreign policy while demanding the conservative economic policy promised by Poincaré. Challener, "The French Foreign Office," in Craig and Gilbert, *Diplomats*, pp. 54-55. The two policies virtually merged in 1929, when Briand and Poincaré agreed that an early evacuation of the Rhineland promised financial compensation to France through the Young Plan; Jacobson, *Locarno Diplomacy*, pp. 356-61.

[16] Schubert asked Hoesch to remind Briand and Berthelot that German policy since Locarno gave sufficient evidence "that we do not contemplate warlike measures against Poland"; *AA*, Schubert to Hoesch, 16 June 1928, 2945/D573629-33.

[17] Polish representatives at the Hague Conference tried in vain to "restore the automatic action" the Franco-Polish alliance had lost with the signing of the Locarno agreements; Lipski, *Diplomat in Berlin*, pp. 14-19.

[18] Beck, *Final Report*, p. 3.

Polish military representatives, particularly regarding the matter of war supplies for Poland in the event of conflict with the Soviet Union or Germany.[19] The outcome of these talks was not always encouraging, however, and some of them must have confirmed the marshal's suspicion that his ally was pre-occupied with the security of the western half of their alliance.[20]

Joining the League of Nations, in conjunction with Locarno, afforded Germany a convenient means of refurbishing its international prestige and enlisting support for treaty revision. Stresemann suggested that Germany use the League as a forum to talk about peace and international reconciliation, rather than resort to the juristic pedantry which had in the past led people to think that Germany " 'did not want peace.' "[21] Of course German representatives, while extolling reconciliation, were not to lose sight of specifically national interests, a ground rule observed by all League members. Stresemann and the permanent German delegation frequently raised the issue of the German minority in Poland to confront Poland openly. But they also aimed the minority argument at the West, for, in point of fact, the Wilhelmstrasse believed that the gateway to peaceful territorial revision lay through friendly and direct negotiations with the Locarno powers rather than through Article 19 of the Covenant, an interpretation of internationalism that—like the Treaty of Locarno itself—implied that the Great Powers should dominate and guide European affairs.[22]

[19] *Ibid.*, p. 4.

[20] The chief of the French naval mission could not promise that France would be able to keep Poland's Baltic Sea communications open; *AA*, Rauscher to Foreign Office, 7 March 1929, K190/K036279-80.

[21] This in a letter to Count Stolberg-Wernigerade, in Thimme, *Gustav Stresemann*, p. 93.

[22] Stresemann speech to central committee of the DVP, 22 November 1925, in Turner, "Rede Stresemanns," pp. 429-30; Spenz, *Vorgeschichte*, pp. 172-75. For the attitude of Bernhard W. von Bülow (grandson of William II's Chancellor and head of the League

The strategic significance of the League for Germany was twofold. It offered the possibility of military support in the event of Polish aggression, although officials in the Foreign Office and Defense Ministry doubted whether the League's machinery—if indeed it could agree that Poland was the aggressor—would operate fast enough to save Germany from a Polish *fait accompli*.[23] On the other hand, Germany's membership did not completely rule out a forcible resolution of the Polish question.

The latter dimension of German membership took shape after months of deliberation in Berlin and consultation with the West, for the Wilhelmstrasse had reservations about joining the League. The Covenant would limit Germany's chances of taking direct advantage of a Polish-Soviet war, and might bind Germany to support League action against the Soviet Union, a commitment that Moscow viewed with alarm. But the German diplomats interpreted Articles 16 and 17, which outlined the obligations of League members against a member or nonmember state deemed guilty of aggression, in such a way that membership would block neither German revisionism nor German-Soviet cooperation.

A Foreign Office study of April 1925 conjectured that, in the event of a Polish-Soviet war, Germany could delay League action by refusing to view the Soviet Union as the aggressor and by upholding the Soviets during the complicated procedure that necessarily preceded any agreement to act collectively. Failing such an agreement, Germany as a League member might still "obtain freedom of action against Poland" if it brought a German-Polish dispute before the League for arbitration "and if then this proceeding did not lead to a unanimous decision by the remaining Council members."[24] Moreover, if the Soviet Union were finally declared

---

desk in the Wilhelmstrasse) toward Germany's membership in the League, see Zimmermann, *Deutsche Aussenpolitik*, p. 298.

[23] See below, chap. 6.

[24] According to Article 13 of the League Covenant, League mem-

the aggressor Germany could refuse to join in the economic sanctions, and could deny the passage of military aid from western powers through Germany.[25] This, the substance of Stresemann's assurances to the Soviet Ambassador, Nikolai Krestinski, on 25 April,[26] was also the condition of Germany's signing the Locarno Pact in October, the protocol of which limited a state's participation in League sanctions to a level commensurate with its geographic position and military situation.[27]

Germany's western policy was thoughtfully conceived and skillfully pursued. At its apex stood Locarno, affectionately

---

bers were to submit disputes to the Permanent Court of International Justice, or to "any tribunal agreed on by the parties to the dispute or stipulated in any convention existing between them" (para. 3). Article 15 allowed members to submit disputes "likely to lead to a rupture" directly to the League Council rather than to an arbitration tribunal (such as that provided for in the German-Polish arbitration treaty of 1925). Further (Article 15, para. 7), "if the Council fails to reach a report which is unanimously agreed to by the members thereof, other than the Representatives of one or more of the parties to the dispute, the Members of the League reserve to themselves the right to take such action as they shall consider necessary for the maintenance of right and justice." Text of the covenant in Chester V. Easum, *Half-Century of Conflict* (New York, 1952), pp. 853ff.

[25] *AA*, memorandum of April 1925 by Gaus and Bülow, "Die Bedeutung des Artikel 16 der Völkerbundssatzung für Deutschland," 7133/H148699-707; Schubert to Stresemann, 21 April, *ibid.*, H148697; *Vermächtnis*, II, 21-23. See also Eyck, *Weimar Republic*, II, 33-34; Gatzke, "Von Rapallo nach Berlin," pp. 9ff.; Korbel, *Poland between East and West*, p. 162; Rosenbaum, *Community of Fate*, pp. 113ff.; Spenz, *Vorgeschichte*, chap. 10.

[26] *AA*, Stresemann notes of conversation with Krestinski, 7129/H147795-801. A very much edited version of this conversation appears in *Vermächtnis*, II, 514-15; here (and elsewhere, e.g., II, 191) Stresemann admitted that it might be politically unwise, although legally possible, for Germany to hinder a unanimous decision by the League Council, if to do so would isolate Germany in world opinion.

[27] Stresemann speech to central committee of the DVP, 22 November 1925, in Turner, "Rede Stresemanns," pp. 420-23.

referred to as "das Kind" by Schubert and Lord D'Abernon while negotiations were in progress.[28] Subject to harsh attacks from German Nationalists and only grudgingly accepted by Poland, "the baby" was nevertheless well received in western European capitals. To one of its chief architects, Austen Chamberlain, it constituted " 'the real dividing line between the years of war and the years of peace.' "[29] Peace, as the Nobel peace prizes conferred on Chamberlain, Briand, and Stresemann attested, was the essential ingredient of the "spirit of Locarno." Just as significant to Berlin was the fact that Germany had reasserted at least its moral equality with other great nations.[30]

Although the Allies withdrew their Military Control Commission, their close—if not always harmonious—collaboration over the disarmament question and refusal to evacuate the Rhineland without German concessions to the West in the Young Plan dampened the spirit of Locarno. These developments, when added to the permanent demilitarization of the Rhineland, provided the Nationalists with a credible charge against Stresemann: his policy of understanding had failed

[28] D'Abernon, *Diary*, III, *passim*; F. G. Stambrook, " 'Das Kind'—Lord D'Abernon and the Origins of the Locarno Pact," *Central European History*, I (1968), 233-63.

[29] In G. M. Gathorne-Hardy, *A Short History of International Affairs 1920-1939* (4th ed., London, 1950), p. 76. See also the British Foreign Office "Memorandum respecting the Locarno Treaties," 10 January 1926, *DBFP*, Ser. IA, I, 16-17.

[30] For anecdotes concerning the Locarno negotiations and "spirit," see Paul Schmidt, *Statist auf diplomatischer Bühne 1923-45* (Bonn, 1949), chap. 4. Stresemann placed great value on the " 'psychological-political consequences' " of the treaty; Annelise Thimme, "Die Locarnopolitik im Lichte des Stresemann-Nachlasses," *Zeitschrift für Politik*, III (New Series, 1956), 53. See also George A. Grün, "Locarno: Idea and Reality," *International Affairs*, XXXI (1955), 477-85, a sobering reassessment of Locarno, which "was invested with a moral significance transcending the practical importance of the results." For an analysis of the changing meaning of "balance of power" and "brokerage" at Locarno, see Newman, *Balance of Power*, chaps. 1, 2.

either to divide the Entente or restore to Germany complete sovereignty and Great Power status. Yet, in a very real politico-military sense, his policy had succeeded. In spite of detours erected by the Allies, Stresemann had not only opened avenues to peaceful revision of the Treaty of Versailles but had also inserted a strategic wedge in the Franco-Polish alliance by placing legal barriers in the way of French intervention in an eastern European conflict. He thereby offered Germany the distant promise of deliverance from having to fight a war on two fronts.

FORCE AND FOREIGN POLICY

The Stresemann-Dirksen economic policy toward Poland in 1925-26 was predicated on the assumption that Germany might in fact attain territorial revision without the application or threat of force. The same postulate underlay the policy of rapprochement with the West and entry into the League of Nations. Yet also expressed in the Wilhelmstrasse was the opinion that Germany must ultimately use military force to resolve the Polish question.[31]

The arbitration treaty with Poland meant a renunciation of forcible means only "for the time being," in Dirksen's words; and even under the terms of the arbitration treaty and League Covenant it was possible for war to break out. Zechlin, an adherent to the Stresemann-Dirksen economic policy, avowed that in entering into a security pact and arbitration treaty Germany must not preclude "the practical possibilities that we still have against Poland," one of which was an "of-

---

[31] In this study, the application or threat of military force are considered diplomatic methods. Limiting the theory and content of diplomacy to negotiations runs these risks: one might ignore the reality of threats of force (as well as applications of force short of war, e.g., the Franco-Belgian occupation of the Ruhr) in conjunction with peacetime negotiations; one might imply that negotiations are not (or should not be) conducted in conjunction with wartime military operations. The German Foreign Office and Defense Ministry viewed both of these as pitfalls and hoped to avoid them.

fensive war," although it was "out of the question for the foreseeable future" in view of the current situation. Schubert and Rauscher believed that Poland would yield to no argument short of force. According to the former, Germany's Polish policy must aim at a future and final "power-political [*machtpolitische*] confrontation." "The Corridor and Upper Silesia," Rauscher wrote, "will return to Germany only as a result of a war and the related power-political convulsion of Poland. . . ."[32]

Obviously, then, important German policy-makers did envisage force as a legitimate means of policy if all other means failed, in spite of the reminiscence of a former German diplomat that "the Wilhelmstrasse rejected a forcible revision" of the Treaty of Versailles.[33] Did Stresemann himself contemplate the use of force to regain the lost territories? To consider his sentiments about force, without becoming embroiled in apologetics for Stresemann the German and Stresemann the European,[34] should be a pertinent preface to the examination of the place of force in Weimar foreign policy.

[32] *AA*, Dirksen minute, 16 November 1925, 4569/E168406; Zechlin memorandum, 25 August, 4562/E155860; Schubert memorandum, late November, 4569/E168400-4; Rauscher to Dirksen, 11 June 1926, *ibid.*, E168775. According to Kimmich, "Rauscher did not wish to suggest that Germany attack Poland." *Free City*, p. 164. Although this is true, Rauscher renounced neither the lost territories nor, apparently, the future war which he believed necessary for their return.

[33] Kordt, *Nicht aus den Akten*, p. 33.

[34] See Hans W. Gatzke's bibliographical article, "The Stresemann Papers," *Journal of Modern History*, XXVI (1954), 49-59. Among the warmest apologias for Stresemann the peaceful European are Henry Bretton, *Stresemann and the Revision of Versailles* (Stanford, Calif., 1953), and Martin Göhring, *Stresemann: Mensch, Staatsmann, Europäer* (Wiesbaden, 1956). Walter Görlitz has written a balanced biography, *Gustav Stresemann* (Heidelberg, 1947). The first significant revision of the view in Bretton and Göhring is Gatzke's *Stresemann and the Rearmament of Germany* (Baltimore, 1954). Of great insight in the study of his character and the aims and means of his policy are the works by Annelise Thimme cited above, *Gustav Stresemann*, and "Die Locarnopolitik." Scathing attacks against Stresemann as German expansionist are the rule behind the Iron

Stresemann's heroes were Frederick the Great, Baron vom Stein, Prince von Hardenberg, Prince von Metternich, and Bismarck—Frederick because of his skillful use of military force as an instrument of foreign policy, Stein and Hardenberg because they rallied the German people in the struggle against Napoleon, and Metternich and Bismarck because of their mastery of European politics. Not only for Stresemann were the ghosts of great Germans abroad, for, in a nation where measuring historical antecedents in terms of their contemporary relevance is an exceptionally widespread habit of mind, the parallel was frequently drawn between an outnumbered, surrounded, and conquered Prussia, and the subjugated and surrounded Germany of the 1920s. In the eyes of most Germans the Versailles settlement had been "dictated." It had deprived Germany of arms, sovereignty, and territory, "declassing" the nation to serfdom, a metaphor drawn from the German's recollection of his medieval predecessors. To recover pride and defend its "rights," Germany must regain the status and freedom of a sovereign and Great Power. If these psychological forces are kept in mind, then the recurrence of such words as *Freiheit, Recht, Schicksal, Kampf, Macht*, and *Volk* is less baffling to the student of politico-military history.

In speeches and private correspondence Stresemann named what he considered the three major wellsprings of power in a nation: armed forces, "united national will of the people," and economic strength. Which of these sources did the German Foreign Minister have at his disposal? In 1923 he had economic dislocation, but also the beginnings, in the *Rentenmark* introduced in November, of economic recovery and Germany's return to world economic significance. He had a people who were "politically immature, tossing to and fro between communism and right-radicalism." Recalling the lesson of Stein and Hardenberg, that there is more to national re-

---

Curtain; for example, Wolfgang Ruge, *Stresemann: Ein Lebensbild* ([East] Berlin, 1965).

74

vival than "saber-rattling without a saber," Stresemann lamented the political disunity within Germany. "If the German people were united," he wrote to the Crown Prince in October 1923, "much could be accomplished even now. But the German always views foreign policy only from the standpoint of internal party differences and thereupon loses sight of that which is necessary."[35] Stresemann hoped that his fellow Germans, realizing that "Leben ist Kampf," would "remain a Great Power as a people" by uniting "in the struggle for its rights."[36]

More detrimental to the conduct of foreign policy was Germany's lack of a powerful armed force. Stresemann drew the following connection between *Macht* and *Recht*: ". . . he who has the power to intercede for a right which is threatened defends his rights best, and the entire tragedy of German foreign policy consists in a struggle for right without having the power to back up this right at the necessary moment."[37] Unlike Frederick the Great, Stresemann could not say encouragingly to German diplomats about to leave for foreign posts, " 'when you enter the room, then remember that behind you stands the Prussian Army!' "[38] Because of its meager military resources and sequential loss of international authority, Germany had to seek *Recht* by means of shrewd negotiation without threatening to use force. Stresemann's policy of "finesse" was born of necessity; it was a form of *Realpolitik*, and he

[35] *AA*, Stresemann to Crown Prince William, 10 October 1923, 7118/H145901-4.

[36] *AA*, note in Stresemann's files for 1924, 7123/H146783. Also statements by President Hindenburg and Chancellor Hermann Müller concerning German unity and internal and external freedom in *Deutsche Einheit, Deutsche Freiheit: Gedenkbuch der Reichsregierung zum 10. Verfassungstag, 11. August 1929* (Berlin, 1929).

[37] *AA*, Stresemann speech before the "Arbeitsgemeinschaft deutscher Landsmannschaften in Gross-Berlin," 14 December 1925, 7131/H148396-7. This passage is omitted from the edited version in *Vermächtnis*, II, 231-44.

[38] *AA*, Stresemann notes for speech on 19 December 1925, 7131/H148356ff. The story also appeared in a letter to Father Vitus Langer of Vienna, 24 November 1927, 7143/H150284.

acknowledged Bismarck as its spiritual godfather.[39] This policy was based on an appreciation of the limitations imposed by want of power, but also the capabilities afforded by power, notably territorial revision. Alluding to the Polish question, Stresemann stated that war remained one means of procuring an adversary's "agreement" to modify its "rights."[40] The two largest political parties during the years of stability did not understand this particular synthesis of force and foreign policy, in which *Macht* meant not simply the application or threat of military force, but also the more intangible advantages derived from actual military strength—international prestige and "freedom." The Nationalists resolutely opposed reaching an understanding with the West at Locarno, and the Social Democratic Party officially rejected "the *Machtpolitik* of imperialistic and fascistic states."[41] Doctrinaires of both

[39] *Vermächtnis*, I, 375, 600-601. Stresemann borrowed the word "finassieren" from Heinrich von Srbik's *Metternich, der Staatsmann und der Mensch* (1925). Prof. Thimme has written a perceptive analysis of Stresemann's use of the term and his references to Metternich, Stein, and Hardenberg; "Die Locarnopolitik," pp. 55ff. See also Jean-Baptiste Duroselle, *Histoire diplomatique de 1919 à nos jours* (Paris, 1953), pp. 99-101; Eyck, *Weimar Republic*, II, 28-29; and, on Stresemann's skillful diplomacy without military power in 1925, Bernhard Knauss, "Politik ohne Waffen. Dargestellt an der Diplomatie Stresemanns," *Zeitschrift für Politik*, X (New Series, 1963), 249-56.

[40] Stresemann speech to DVP leaders, 22 November 1925, in which he referred to the preamble of the German-Polish arbitration treaty; Turner, "Rede Stresemanns," pp. 424-25; also above, chap. 1, n. 38. This address, according to Prof. Turner, is an unusually trustworthy source for Stresemann's foreign policy views. Stresemann frequently attuned his speeches to his particular audience; *ibid.*, pp. 412-15; Craig, *Bismarck to Adenauer*, pp. 82-83; Bariéty, "Versuch," in Rössler, *Locarno und die Weltpolitik*, pp. 34, 47.

[41] On the Nationalists and Stresemann's policy of rapprochement with the West, see Turner, *Stresemann and Politics*, chap. 6; Thimme, *Gustav Stresemann*, pp. 125-26. For the Socialist Party's military policy, at 1929 "party day" in Magdeburg, see Otto-Ernst Schüddekopf, *Das Heer und die Republik: Quellen zur Politik der Reichswehrführung, 1918 bis 1933* (Hanover & Frankfurt/Main, 1955), pp. 255-56.

Right and Left failed to realize that, although Bismarck's acuity as a negotiator was an inspiration to Stresemann, Frederick's lesson in the use of force was not forgotten.

The exercise of force to promote national interests was common in the years immediately following "the war to end all wars." A few examples may be recalled: Poland's seizure of Vilna in October 1920 after turning back the invading Red Army; the Polish rising in Upper Silesia led by W. Korfanty in May 1921; Lithuania's invasion of Memel in January 1923. Neither Allied nor League Commissions were able completely to reverse these accomplished facts, all of which affected German interests. With the possible exception of the incident in Upper Silesia, however, no single power-political event left such an imprint on the German mind as did the French occupation of the Ruhr in January 1923. It demonstrated what a superior power could do with impunity, and what a painful price Germany would have to pay so long as it lacked sovereignty and military strength. Traumatic effects cannot be measured, at least by the historian, but it would be hard to overestimate the effect that the above events had on German politico-military thinking. They offered dramatic proof that the New Diplomacy retained old undergarments.

As Maltzan's transfer indicated, there were differences of opinion in the Wilhelmstrasse over the appropriate policy for a powerless Germany. The only organizational tie between the Western and Eastern Departments was the Secretary of State, to whom the departmental heads were subordinate,[42] and perhaps in a structural way this contributed to the division between "Westerners" and "Easterners." This would help explain Brockdorff-Rantzau's sense of frustration when Maltzan was replaced by Schubert, who, according to one colleague, "never concealed his profound dislike of the Rus-

---

[42] Kordt, *Nicht aus den Akten*, p. 40. Dirksen recalls that "the Eastern Department enjoyed a special position within the Foreign Office. It was somewhat aloof, almost autonomous; a cloud of secrecy, amounting to magic, surrounded it." *Moscow, Tokyo, London*, p. 47.

sians."[43] Personal animosities were not absent in the higher echelons of the Foreign Office. Brockdorff-Rantzau's belief that Schubert was working against him, coupled with Stresemann's Locarno policy, almost led the sensitive ambassador to resign his post late in 1925.[44] The *Memoirs* of Ernst von Weizsäcker, who served in various diplomatic posts during the Weimar period and later became Secretary of State (1938-43), reveal the contempt felt by at least a few permanent officials in the Wilhelmstrasse for Stresemann,[45] and the split between the old guard of career diplomats and the new men like Stresemann, Hoesch, Rauscher, Sthamer, and Roland Köster.[46] And

[43] Hilger, *Incompatible Allies*, pp. 128-29.

[44] Schubert, according to Brockdorff-Rantzau, told the ambassador's brother that Brockdorff-Rantzau "treated him [Schubert] like a fool." *AA*, Stresemann note, 15 December 1925, 7129/H148100. See also Hilger, *Incompatible Allies*, p. 135.

[45] Although "Stresemann was indeed of a higher status than the general run of Foreign Minister, . . . in the Foreign Office he was held to be too trusting in international affairs, a field in which he was not fully at home." Ernst von Weizsäcker, *Memoirs of Ernst von Wiezsäcker*, trans. John Andrews (Chicago, 1951), p. 68. Judging from his *Memoirs*, which should be read very cautiously for the Nazi period, Weizsäcker was arrogant, scorned southern Europeans, and considered himself an expert in diplomacy, the art of which he believed politicians like Stresemann were incapable of mastering. Commenting on a large bust of Stresemann in the Wilhelmstrasse after 1929, "the only bust apart from a modest plaster one of Bismarck," Weizsäcker writes, "we in the Foreign Office thought the day would probably come when this Stresemann bust would be quietly removed." *Ibid.*, p. 69. (There is a Stresemann plaque in the foyer of today's *Auswärtiges Amt* in Bonn.) Contrast the charitable accounts of the diplomats' respect for Stresemann in Dirksen, *Moscow, Tokyo, London*, p. 46; Zimmermann, *Deutsche Aussenpolitik*, p. 37.

[46] Weizsäcker, *Memoirs*, pp. 51, 68; also Paul Seabury, *The Wilhelmstrasse: A Study of German Diplomats under the Nazi Regime* (Berkeley, Calif., 1954), pp. 15-18. For accounts that indicate less divisiveness and a recognition of the merits of some of the new men, see Kordt, *Nicht aus den Akten*, pp. 24-31; Dirksen, *Moscow, Tokyo, London*, pp. 42-46; Holborn, "Diplomats and Diplomacy," in Craig and Gilbert, *Diplomats*, pp. 150-54. In 1928 the

one student of the Wilhelmstrasse contends that this split extended into German policy, Stresemann working for reconciliation and the veteran diplomats attempting "to build a continental alliance [with the Soviet Union] which would restore German military and economic supremacy over Central Europe and enable her to rectify Versailles, not by patient negotiation and compromise, but by force."[47]

There is some validity in these views, for the directors sometimes withheld information from the new men who were their chiefs of department, and the diplomats themselves acknowledged the division between "Westerners" and "Easterners." But dichotomous classification is too facile and misleading. Stresemann, although against retaining Maltzan as Secretary of State and aware of the subversive threat of Bolshevism, never entirely embraced the West, but preserved economic and political intercourse with Moscow and promoted continued collaboration between the German and Red Armies.[48] Schubert, a strong supporter of Stresemann's policy of rapprochement with the West, had been a professional diplomat since 1906. Having joined the Eastern Department

---

Reich Minister of Justice, Oskar Hergt (formerly Chairman of the DNVP), opposed the Foreign Office's promotion of Roland Köster, according to the axiom that Socialists should not be allowed to advance in diplomatic rank. To Stresemann, Hergt's attitude was a regression to that of "the conservatives in the old empire. To this I can only say that the gentlemen have learned nothing. . . ." *AA,* Stresemann to Secretary of State Otto Meissner (in the President's office), 15 February 1928, 7147/H150846-7.

[47] Seabury, *The Wilhelmstrasse*, p. 23.

[48] Prof. Gatzke suggests "further investigation" into Stresemann's Soviet policy, "which may show that he did not differ as markedly from . . . Count Brockdorff-Rantzau as has been assumed by some writers." *Stresemann and Rearmament*, p. 79n. In reply, Prof. Thimme stresses the "middle way" of Stresemann's policy, balancing between east and west; *Gustav Stresemann*, pp. 110-11. In an article appearing in 1956, Gatzke's stance is closer to the "middle way"; "Von Rapallo nach Berlin," pp. 28-29. On Stresemann and Maltzan, see Lord D'Abernon, *Diary*, III, 120n.

while Maltzan was Secretary of State, Zechlin was worried about the harmful effects that the Locarno policy might have on Germany's eastern policy in 1925, but by November 1926 he had decided that Germany might benefit by adopting a clearly western policy. Wallroth, according to Gustav Hilger, "was one of those who tended to think that the Soviet regime could not last much longer and was therefore a negligible factor in world politics."[49] Yet in 1926 Wallroth reasoned that if Poland received Lithuania as compensation for the Corridor, the exchange would permanently alienate Germany from the Soviet Union, a serious disadvantage economically —and strategically—in the event of a war in Central Europe.[50] Dirksen, who was "rather enthusiastic" at the news from Rapallo in 1922, and who in retrospect believed that "the political expenses of Locarno and Geneva" were too high, was for a few years "a convinced supporter of Locarno."[51] Rauscher, a novice in the foreign service and a Social Democrat, cautioned against allowing Locarno and Germany's probable entry into the League to constitute a "break with Rapallo."[52] Even Brockdorff-Rantzau, the top "Easterner" after Maltzan's transfer to Washington, remained opposed to an irrevocable alignment with Moscow.[53]

In spite of the ominous overtones in the German-Soviet theme of "pushing Poland back to her ethnographic frontiers," it is doubtful that German policy went beyond the gen-

[49] Hilger, *Incompatible Allies*, p. 223.

[50] *AA*, Wallroth memorandum, 19 November 1926, 4569/E168879-82. For Wallroth's "western" preferences, which annoyed Brockdorff-Rantzau, see Dyck, *Weimar Germany and Soviet Russia*, pp. 48-50, 54-56, 85f., 102ff. Dirksen recollects that Wallroth "had a thorough knowledge of economic affairs, but lacked the gift for politics. He was an amiable, honest, and straightforward man, with whom I collaborated harmoniously," *Moscow, Tokyo, London*, p. 43.

[51] Dirksen, *Moscow, Tokyo, London*, pp. 31, 65.

[52] *RK*, Rauscher to Foreign Office, 2 October 1925 (copy in Reich Chancery files), K1947/K506984.

[53] See Hilger, *Incompatible Allies*, p. 129; Helbig, *Träger der Rapallo-Politik*, pp. 5ff., 130-48, 204ff.

eral declarations of good relations contained in the treaties of Rapallo and Berlin. If Germany had concluded a secret political or military agreement for the reduction of Poland, it would have been strategically suicidal before 1925 and would have jeopardized Germany's western policy after Locarno. Nevertheless, neither Stresemann nor the career diplomats shared the "nie wieder Krieg" sentiments of the Social Democratic Party. In 1925 and 1926, at the very time when Stresemann's policy of understanding was helping to spread the "spirit of Locarno," experts on the Polish question (Rauscher) and on the new western policy (Schubert) were concluding that the only solution to that question was by means of force in "favorable international circumstances." Since Germany had neither military power nor great diplomatic maneuverability, a forcible reconquest of the lost territories, whether alone or by intervening in a Polish-Soviet war, was out of the question. But was it out of the question permanently?

Since Stresemann's policy continued to promote peaceful change at a time when Germany lacked even the military capacity for self-defense, it would be incorrect to describe it as *Machtpolitik*. But it would also be wrong to assume that his policy of peaceful "finesse" stemmed from the conviction that Locarno and the Kellogg-Briand Pact represented a lasting departure from elemental facts of international life: the resort to war, or forcible acts without a formal declaration of war, or the threat of war, for external territorial goals that governments might determine to be in the interests of "national security."[54] In all the major policy decisions and mem-

[54] For the Wilhelmstrasse's attitude toward the Kellogg Pact (August 1928), see Robert H. Ferrell, *Peace in their Time: The Origins of the Kellogg-Briand Pact* (New Haven, Conn., 1952), pp. 175, 188-89. In spite of such attempts to prohibit aggression in international law, most world statesmen preserved the equation between military power and national prestige, and the willingness to use that power to protect or attain national interests. See Carr, *Twenty Years' Crisis*, chap. 8; Wright, *Study of War*, pp. 183-87; above, chap. 1, n. 26.

oranda touching on the Polish question and Germany's relations with the Soviet Union and the West, strategic considerations were of decisive influence. German policy after the German-Soviet talks of December 1924 did not reflect a fundamental shift away from the efficacy of *Machtpolitik*. Rather, Stresemann and the Wilhelmstrasse adopted a more mature and realistic appreciation of Germany's actual politico-military situation, and of the potential power of a re-armed Germany with greater freedom of movement in European affairs.

An observation by Lord D'Abernon provides a touchstone for Weimar foreign policy. "There is an idea in London," he wrote, "that the German proposals for security on the West are only made with a view to rendering the position more favorable for war in the East. There is no foundation for this suspicion, but it is essential that the German Government should go farther than it has done regarding good relations with Poland and security on the Polish frontier."[55] That the Weimar government refused to "go farther" toward security on the Polish border than an arbitration treaty, however, was entirely consistent with the principles underlying its acceptance of a security pact in the west. Any alteration of the European "power-constellation" must not merely help restore Germany's sovereignty and security, but should facilitate border revision in the east, an external national security objective in the judgment of the Foreign Office.

A summary of policy in the Wilhelmstrasse will recall that these politico-military objectives—sovereignty, security, and revision—were closely interwoven. Rapallo removed some of the stigma of international subjugation and checked any Polish designs of aggression against Germany; it also gave Germany support for peaceful revision and improved Germany's strategic position in Central and East Europe should Germany and the Soviet Union one day decide to put into actual practice their "silent maximal aim" of the ethnographic

[55] D'Abernon, *Diary*, III, 156-57 (entry of 26 March 1925).

82

reduction of Poland.[56] Rapprochement with the West offered Germany security on the western borders, a better chance of amending the economic and military clauses of the Treaty of Versailles, and the eventual restoration of full sovereignty and Great Power status; it also meant a more sympathetic ear for a settlement of the Polish question, financial allies for putting Poland in an economic vise, and, by weakening the mutual defensive ties between France and East Europe, some hope that a future war with Poland would not be on two fronts. Germany's membership in the League carried with it an increase in international prestige and the promise (however encumbered) of assistance against Polish aggression, and did not require Germany to expose itself to Soviet countermeasures by supporting any League action against the Soviet Union; it also gave Germany political and moral leverage against Poland in disputes over minorities and borders, and the opportunity to thwart League attempts to reverse a Soviet onslaught against Poland, and it did not preclude a German-Polish war. And, finally, Germany's more accommodating attitude toward Poland from the winter of 1926-27 decreased tension and thus diminished the obsession with the threat of Polish invasion which had gripped the Germans living near the eastern boundaries; it also, Rauscher noted, would dampen the French Right's powder in its attempt to defeat Briand's policy of keeping the Rhineland evacuation divorced from the Polish question.[57]

The time was not yet ripe for broaching the entire Polish question. Meanwhile, the diplomats agreed unanimously, as far as we can tell, that Germany must increase its military power. The German campaign for equality of armaments

[56] Hilger observes that this aim was "seldom mentioned, and it was not actively pursued between 1920 and 1939. It was the less ambitious aim of neutralizing the Polish state on which Berlin and Moscow were in agreement throughout the Rantzau era." *Incompatible Allies*, p. 154.

[57] *AA*, Rauscher to Köpke, 28 June 1928, 4569/E169121-8; Rauscher to Stresemann, 13 July, 7150/H151286-99.

(whatever the legal fine points might have been with reference to Part V of the Treaty of Versailles and Article 8 of the League Covenant) was based on national security and national interest.[58] An Army of 100,000 men was ludicrously small for self-defense in the middle of Europe; the size of the Army determined Germany's "alliance capability" (*Bündnisfähigkeit*) and freedom of unilateral action in a future conflict over the Polish question. The expansion and employment of the armed forces, the diplomats realized, affected German foreign policy and therefore required joint planning with the Defense Ministry.

[58] Thimme, *Gustav Stresemann*, p. 96. Contrast Bretton, *Stresemann and Revision*, p. 146: ". . . it is clear that [Stresemann] emphasized universal disarmament rather than increased reliance upon Germany's own potential strength." The German disarmament delegation at Geneva argued that disarmament was "in itself no guarantee of peace at all." Weizsäcker, *Memoirs*, pp. 63, 66ff. For feelings of military inferiority in the Foreign Office, see the memorandum of 21 June 1927 by D. Forster, *AA*, 3177/D683185-6.

THE YEARS OF
STABILITY, 1924-29:
THE MILITARY AND
JOINT PLANNING

A solution *must* be found which insures
cooperation between the Foreign Office
and the Army Command.
> *Truppenamt* memorandum, March 1920

. . . Apart from combatting internal disorder,
there are the following cases in which the . . .
employment of the armed forces comes under
consideration:
  a) self-defense,
  b) exploitation of a favorable political
     situation.
> Wilhelm Groener directive, April 1930

[The Navy manifests] a certain optimism about
the importance of Germany as a maritime
factor, . . . [and] a tendency . . . to consider
France as the given enemy.
> Dirk Forster, January 1928

Part II

CHAPTER III

Eastern Europe

Revision and the Bendlerstrasse

The Treaty of Versailles was also anathema to the Army.[1] To win freedom from the provisions of the *Diktat* and from the European "system" which it established was a national duty, for without this freedom no German could be secure against foreign attack or proud that his nation was denied the sovereignty and international status which it merited. The treaty imposed by the victors was unjust, and thus the vanquished felt a "moral responsibility" to circumvent it in the interests of national security.[2]

The terms of the Treaty of Versailles, which the remon-

---

[1] "Army," "Defense Ministry," "Bendlerstrasse," "military leadership," "the military": these terms will often be used interchangeably below to refer to the military arm as a departmental collective, unless intradepartmental distinctions are made among the Defense Minister, *Ministeramt*, Army Command, and other offices concerning specific issues. After the brief tenure of Gustav Noske, who fell from office in the aftermath of the Kapp *Putsch*, Weimar Defense Ministers (especially Groener and Schleicher) were experts in and advocates of departmental policies; they were not distinguished for a peculiarly "civilian" approach to politico-military affairs.

[2] See Erich von Manstein, *Aus einem Soldatenleben, 1887-1939* (Bonn, 1958), p. 115. Without exception, this view was shared by every officer whom the author interviewed (see bibliography), as well as by those whose recollections have been recorded in print, including Vincenz Müller, who was captured by the Soviets during the Second World War and subsequently helped organize the East German Army; see his *Ich fand das wahre Vaterland*, ed. Klaus Mammach ([East Berlin], 1963), p. 293. Müller's memoirs are a valuable source for defense policy in the Weimar Republic. The editor's ideological (anti-fascist) embellishments are few for the Weimar period.

strances of General Hans von Seeckt and Defense Minister Otto Gessler at the Spa conference of July 1920 had failed to mitigate, limited the German Army to 100,000 officers and men, with no reserves, and abolished universal conscription. Tanks, aircraft, and heavy artillery were forbidden; the General Staff, War Academy, cadet schools, and military missions abroad were banned. No fortifications nor troops were permitted in the Rhineland or west of a line running 50 kilometers east of the Rhine, and some of the fortifications along the eastern frontiers were to be dismantled. Allied troops occupied the Rhineland, and an Inter-Allied Control Commission regularly inspected Germany to insure the observance of these and other restrictions. In addition to these drastic reductions of Germany's capacity for self-defense, the treaty compounded its strategic problems by granting Poland the Corridor and other former German territories.

The Army and Foreign Office shared a common objective, revision of the Treaty of Versailles, but cooperation between the two developed slowly. One reason for this was that the Army, while severely reduced in size, retained traditions, professional pride, and the habit of independence from civilian control that antedated the rise of the diplomatic art in Prussia to a position of respect under Bismarck. This has led many authors to concentrate on the role of the Army in the internal politics of the Weimar Republic. They note that, under General von Seeckt, Chief of the Army Command (*Chef der Heeresleitung*) from March 1920 to October 1926, most officers thought in terms of serving the state, not the republic; they question the Army's loyalty in political crises such as the abortive Kapp *Putsch* of March 1920 and the Bavarian separatist drive in the autumn of 1923; and they conclude that the Army, anti-parliamentarian and aloof from party politics, remained a "state within the state."[3] What-

[3] F. L. Carsten, *The Reichswehr and Politics, 1918 to 1933* (Oxford, 1966), pp. 400ff. and *passim*; Gordon A. Craig, *The Politics of the Prussian Army, 1640-1945* (New York, 1956), pp. 387-89; Karl Demeter, *Das deutsche Offizierkorps in Gesellschaft und Staat,*

ever the validity of that thesis, it is true that during the
internal crisis of 1923 Stresemann doubted "the absolute
trustworthiness" of the Army in defending the constitution,
a reservation that stood in the way of closer cooperation between the Foreign Minister and the Chief of the Army
Command.[4]

1650-1945 (Frankfurt am Main, 1962), pp. 174-77; Hans Ebeling,
*The Caste: The Political Role of the German General Staff between
1918 and 1938* (London, 1945), p. 26; Herbert Rosinski, *The German
Army*, ed. and with introduction by Gordon A. Craig (New York,
1966), pp. 154, 171ff.; Wolfgang Sauer, "Die Reichswehr," in Karl
Dietrich Bracher, *Die Auflösung der Weimarer Republik* (2d ed.,
Stuttgart & Düsseldorf, 1957), pp. 237-38, 242, 260; Jürgen Schmädeke, *Militärische Kommandogewalt und parlamentarische De-
mokratie* (Lübeck & Hamburg, 1966), p. 187 and *passim*; John
W. Wheeler-Bennett, *The Nemesis of Power: The German Army in
Politics, 1918-1945* (London, 1953), pp. 76, 96. Other authors reject
this conclusion and contend that the Army, although never a warm
admirer of the republican form of government, served the republic
faithfully; Harold J. Gordon, Jr., *The Reichswehr and the German
Republic, 1919-1926* (Princeton, N.J., 1957), chap. 9; Wiegand
Schmidt-Richberg, *Die Generalstäbe in Deutschland 1871-1945; Aufgaben in der Armee und Stellung im Staate*, in *Beiträge zur Militär-
und Kriegsgeschichte*, III (Stuttgart, 1962), 63ff. Two recent works
fall somewhere between these two rather distinct categories; Klaus-
Jürgen Müller, *Das Heer und Hitler: Armee und nationalsozialistisches Regime 1933-1940* (Stuttgart, 1969), pp. 13-28; Rainer Wohlfeil, *Heer und Republik*, in *Handbuch zur deutschen Militärgeschichte*,
VI: *Reichswehr und Republik (1918-1933)* (Frankfurt am Main,
1970). The officers interviewed denied that they looked upon themselves as members of a "state within the state." They could not, however, define to the satisfaction of a foreigner the exact differences
among government, state, and Reich, a lack of clarity to which
Prof. Carsten correctly calls our atttention, but that does not necessarily lead to his conclusion that "Seeckt erred when he maintained
that the army was not a state within the state. The result of his
building a 'Chinese wall' round the army, of the rigid separation
from all new ideas and from the political parties, combined with
its great political influence, was that the Reichswehr did form a state
within the state." *Reichswehr and Politics*, p. 401.

[4] See Stresemann's letter to Crown Prince William, 23 July 1923,
in *Vermächtnis*, I, 218; on relations between Stresemann and Seeckt

Good relations between military and civilian officials were further discouraged, inadvertently, by the command structure as it developed under the new constitution. Amplifying the constitutional provision that the Reich had exclusive jurisdiction over national defense (Arts. 6.4 and 79), the *Wehrgesetz* (national defense regulations) of 23 March 1921 stated the following: " 'The president of the Reich is the commander-in-chief of the entire *Wehrmacht*. Under him the minister of defence exercises the power of issuing orders (*Befehlsgewalt*) to the entire *Wehrmacht*. At the head of the army stands a general as chief of the army command, at the head of the navy an admiral as chief of the naval command.' "[5] While Seeckt was Chief of the Army Command, this command structure was neither precisely defined nor consistently observed. Seeckt wielded more power than either the framers of the constitution or the Allies had ever envisioned. Loopholes in the *Wehrgesetz* itself allowed this to happen, for apparently the Chief of the Army Command retained the power of command over the troops (*Kommandogewalt*), as well as his position as the deputy to the Minister of Defense.[6] In the latter capacity, the Chief of the Army Command served as the authorized military representative of the Defense Minister for cabinet meetings and debates in the Reichstag. But Seeckt regarded himself as more than a subordinate in the chain of command or a deputy in cabinet deliberations. He enjoyed frequent and direct access to President Ebert, and often sent messages over the head of the Defense Minister to the President or Chancellor.[7] Furthermore, his protests in

---

in 1923, Hans Meier-Welcker, *Seeckt* (Frankfurt am Main, 1967), chap. 14.

[5] Carsten, *Reichswehr and Politics*, p. 111.

[6] *Ibid.*, pp. 108, 111.

[7] Otto Gessler, *Reichswehrpolitik in der Weimarer Zeit* (Stuttgart, 1958), p. 71 (from the introductory section by Kurt Sendtner). See also Sauer, "Die Reichswehr," in Bracher, *Auflösung*, pp. 248ff.; Friedrich Hossbach, *Die Entwicklung des Oberbefehls über das Heer*

cabinet meetings against Stresemann's Locarno policy rang with the certitude that he, not the Defense Minister, was the true spokesman for both the Army Command and the ministry. The frequent result was enmity between Seeckt and the civilian ministers in the Wilhelmstrasse and at the Defense Ministry in the Bendlerstrasse.[8]

Third, Seeckt's personal dislikes vitiated interdepartmental collaboration. He preferred the strategic conceptions of the military mind to those based on civilian judgment in the sphere of foreign policy. Seeckt disdained Stresemann, and he objected to " 'the narrow-mindedness of the Foreign Office which does not want generals to be active in politics. . . .' "[9] His own political activity brought him into conflict with the Foreign Office over personalities and policies: he criticized the appointment of Brockdorff-Rantzau as Ambassador to Moscow, resented civilian interference in the Army's clandestine enterprises in the Soviet Union, and categorically rejected the western policy of Stresemann.

In the early years of the republic, then, relations between the "frocks" and the "brass hats" were neither cordial nor trustful, and their respective leaders competed more than they

---

in Brandenburg, Preussen und im Deutschen Reich von 1655-1945 (Würzburg, 1957), pp. 85ff.

[8] Harold Gordon concludes that despite the friction between Gessler and Seeckt, "no definite choice was made during this period between the two alternative interpretations of the role of the Reichswehrminister—as civilian director of the Reichswehr or as the army's representative in the Cabinet. As a consequence, the power shifted between Chief of the Heeresleitung and Minister, depending to some extent upon which was the stronger personality and to some extent upon circumstances." *Reichswehr and Republic*, p. 327. For a somewhat exaggerated interpretation of the actual powers which Seeckt exercised, see Schmädeke, *Militärische Kommandogewalt*, chap. 3, *passim*.

[9] In Carsten, *Reischwehr and Politics*, p. 104. Lord D'Abernon attributed Seeckt's antipathy "to the fact that he thinks Stresemann too much of a politician, too much of a talker, and not sufficiently a man of action and decision." *Diary*, II, 271.

cooperated. Yet forces were at work against this painful reversion to the separation between civilian and military authorities of the prewar and wartime years, when policy had not been coordinated with military planning.

In the first place, under Seeckt's successor, General Wilhelm Heye, the Army Command adopted a "new course," one which accepted the republic (although not parliamentary sovereignty) and was willing to cooperate with its civilian officials. Colonel Kurt von Schleicher, head of the Armed Forces Department in the Bendlerstrasse, was an advocate of this "new course." " 'The question,' " he wrote late in 1926, " 'is not republic or monarchy, but what should this republic look like? And it is quite obvious that it can develop according to our wishes only if we cooperate in its construction cheerfully and tirelessly. Once we have acknowledged this idea, then we shall no longer evade the word "republic" so nervously or look around timidly [to see] whether anyone has heard it. . . .' "[10] The election of Hindenburg as President in April 1925, though not a victory for monarchism, encouraged Schleicher to anticipate a constitutional evolution in which the Army could cooperate. For Hindenburg personified military virtues and political authoritarianism, and this combination promised a new direction in Weimar politics: the development of a strong "presidential" regime sympathetic to the Army and able, if necessary, to govern without a majority in the Reichstag.[11]

[10] Memorandum of December 1926, in Thilo Vogelsang, *Reichswehr, Staat und NSDAP* (Stuttgart, 1962), no. 3, p. 410. General Otto Hasse compared the Army's relation to the republic to that of a man with his second wife. The Officer Corps must serve and honor the new spouse, and preserve the marriage against the disruptive influences of "Uncle Scheidemann" on the Left and retired generals and other monarchists of the Right; speech to local officers (retired, but still used to coordinate district recruiting and defensive measures) of Brandenburg and Silesia, 14 December 1928, *RK*, K953/K249639-41.

[11] On the constitutional implications of Hindenburg's election, see Andreas Dorpalen, *Hindenburg and the Weimar Republic* (Princeton,

Second, clarification of the lines of command and changes in personnel after 1925 helped to increase contacts and understanding between the Army and the Foreign Office. The professional ambit of the Chief of the Army Command was limited by a presidential decree of 2 February 1926, the response to the pressure placed on Stresemann by the Entente powers, who believed that Seeckt exercised too much authority. The decree defined the chief's powers as a " 'military adviser' " representing the Defense Minister " 'in military affairs of the Army,' " in contrast to " 'the responsible adviser of the Defense Minister in all areas of his official concern' " and " 'in the exercise of the power of issuing commands.' " This increased the authority of the Defense Minister since he or his staff could decide whether an issue was "military" and thus of legitimate interest to the Chief of the Army Command.[12]

N.J., 1964), pp. 44ff., 64-66, 83-86, 90-93; Peter Haungs, *Reichspräsident und parlamentarische Kabinettsregierung: Eine Studie zum Regierungssystem der Weimarer Republik in den Jahren 1924 bis 1929* (Cologne & Opladen, 1968), chap. 4, *passim*; also Josef Becker, "Zur Politik der Wehrmachtabteilung in der Regierungskrise 1926/27," *Vierteljahrshefte für Zeitgeschichte*, XIV (1966), 74; Schmidt-Richberg, *Generalstäbe*, p. 62; Gerhard Schulz, *Zwischen Demokratie und Diktatur: Verfassungspolitik und Reichsreform in der Weimarer Republik*, I (Berlin, 1963), p. 469; Wohlfeil, *Heer und Republik*, pp. 113-14.

[12] Gerhard Meinck, *Hitler und die Deutsche Aufrüstung, 1933-1937* (Wiesbaden, 1959), pp. 103-104; Schmädeke, *Militärische Kommandogewalt*, pp. 175-76; Schmidt-Richberg, *Generalstäbe*, p. 60; Wohlfeil, *Heer und Republik*, pp. 126-27. The decree did not in fact diminish Seeckt's authority over the Army; Carsten, *Reichswehr and Politics*, pp. 208-209; Gordon, *Reichswehr and Republic*, pp. 259f.; Meier-Welcker, *Seeckt*, pp. 482-84; Friedrich von Rabenau, *Seeckt: Aus seinem Leben, 1918-1936* (Leipzig, 1940), p. 422. As Meinck observes, however, these institutional checks would become effective if future chiefs were of weaker personality than Seeckt. Moreover, Hindenburg's election began to reduce Seeckt's influence over political issues. Hindenburg, unlike Ebert, took his constitutional role as Commander in Chief with literal seriousness, considered his own

Subsequent reorganization within the ministry under Wilhelm Groener added to the minister's powers at the expense of the Chief of the Army Command. The Armed Forces Department (*Wehrmachtsabteilung*), formerly in the *Truppenamt*, and the *Abwehr* (Intelligence) Department were placed directly under the Defense Minister. And in 1929 the creation of the *Ministeramt*, headed by Schleicher, integrating all offices subordinate to the Defense Minister except the Army and Navy budget sections, concentrated power in the hands of the minister and Schleicher in " 'all questions which the chiefs of the army and navy commands do not themselves want to represent, . . . in all questions which have no connection with military matters' and 'in military matters of a purely political nature.' "[13]

These measures and Seeckt's dismissal did not mark a victory for, in Seeckt's words, " 'the democratic, parliamentarian system' " in controlling the independent and powerful position which Seeckt had maintained against Dr. Gessler, Defense Minister from March 1920 to January 1928.[14] The

---

office competent in the military sphere, and asked the general's opinion only on military questions.

[13] From the decrees of 21 February and 8 October 1929; in Carsten, *Reichswehr and Politics*, p. 297. Schmädeke has published the earlier of the two documents in full; *Militärische Kommandogewalt*, pp. 210-11. Dorothea Groener-Geyer inaccurately states that Groener could not change the constitutional arrangement he had inherited, the Seecktian policy of complete authority of the Chief of the Army Command over personnel and disciplinary matters; *General Groener, Soldat und Staatsmann* (Frankfurt am Main, 1955), pp. 243-46.

[14] On the political background and significance of Seeckt's dismissal, see Carsten, *Reichswehr and Politics*, pp. 246-47; Craig, *Prussian Army*, pp. 383-85; Dorpalen, *Hindenburg*, pp. 111-13; Eyck, *Weimar Republic*, II, 85-91; Gatzke, *Stresemann and Rearmament*, pp. 60-61; Gessler, *Reichswehrpolitik*, pp. 301-11; Gordon, *Reichswehr and Republic*, pp. 357-58; Meier-Welcker, *Seeckt*, pp. 514-23; Meinck, *Deutsche Aufrüstung*, pp. 103ff.; Reginald H. Phelps, "Aus den Seeckt-Dokumenten, I," *Deutsche Rundschau*, LXXVIII (1952); Rabenau, *Seeckt*, p. 558; Schmidt-Richberg, *Generalstäbe*, p. 60;

Defense Minister never became an agent of parliamentary jurisdiction: the executive and Foreign Office, not the Reichstag, gained measurable civilian control over politico-military activity after Seeckt's release. After 1926 the Foreign Office could be reasonably sure that both the Chief of the Army Command and the Defense Minister recognized the primacy of the Wilhelmstrasse in foreign affairs, an important step toward joint planning. Although General Heye resented the encroachment of the *Ministeramt* on his own position, he did not challenge the authority of the Defense Minister as Seeckt had done. Moreover, Heye left foreign policy to the Foreign Office, where Stresemann demonstrated his longevity and success as a diplomat, to the approval of the Army, which was equally apprehensive about both ministerial and international instability. And Groener, Defense Minister after January 1928, actively encouraged cooperation between the two ministries in military intelligence, border defense, and war games.

A third factor was that Seeckt himself had a keen politico-military mind. During the war he had learned the disastrous effects of overestimating military power and the strategy of annihilation.[15] He had also observed how the best alternative —a strategy of attrition, in which the battle was subordinate to negotiation—had been made impossible by the dictatorial authority of the military arm under Hindenburg and Ludendorff. Seeckt believed that the Clausewitzean principle of political primacy must be revived. That his contempt for "politicians" led him to challenge that very dictum in certain political issues should not completely overshadow the fact that he emphasized it in his own writings and in his training policy.

Wheeler-Bennett, *Nemesis of Power*, pp. 151-53; Zimmermann, *Deutsche Aussenpolitik*, pp. 32-33.

[15] Shortly before the armistice he had written that Germany had overrated its strength, which "was not sufficient to force a decision in the west, at the same time supporting the other fronts and pursuing a policy of expansion in . . . the east." Letter to Arnold Rechberg, 3 October 1918, Seeckt Papers (microfilm), roll 19, Stück 89.

Finally, the facts of Germany's military weakness and geopolitical situation demanded cooperation between the Army and Foreign Office. Germany's "strategic fate," as a former officer puts it, was and is its position in the center of Europe.[16] The obsession with "encirclement" and "war on two fronts" was acute in this period. For both the Army and the Foreign Office, encirclement was a reality, not a paranoic delusion as many non-Germans contend. Germany's strategic "freedom of movement" in the event of another continental war had been seriously impaired by territorial losses and the military restrictions imposed by the Treaty of Versailles.[17] The restoration of that freedom and a more general freedom from the "chains" of Versailles was the common aim of civilians and generals alike, and both began to realize that such aims could best be pursued jointly.

This combination of influences was responsible for a maturation in civil-military relations at about the same time that German foreign policy reflected a more intelligent assessment of Germany's politico-military situation. The analysis that follows should help to demonstrate the shortcomings of propositions that the Army was a "state within the state," or a separate sociological entity that behaved like a "pressure group."[18] Neither of these theses, which refer chiefly to the parliamentary and societal dimensions of civil-military relations, devotes sufficient attention to the common departmental interests of the Army and the Foreign Office, or their efforts to clarify the decision-making process at the depart-

[16] Interviews with Generals Kurt Brennecke and Theodor Busse.

[17] *Bewegungsfreiheit* was the term used to denote this strategic requirement.

[18] Wolfgang Sauer argues that the Reichswehr was a "pressure group," or *Funktionärsschicht*, which arose in one specific political system and was transplanted into another." "Die Reichswehr," in Bracher, *Auflösung*, p. 242. On the Army and German society, see also Demeter, *Offizierkorps*, pp. 52-56, 224-26; Eckart Kehr, "Zur Soziologie der Reichswehr," in *Der Primat der Innenpolitik*, ed. Hans-Ulrich Wehler (Berlin, 1965), pp. 236, 239ff.; Ebeling, *The Caste*, pp. 3, 5; Wohlfeil, *Heer und Republik*, pp. 167-81.

mental and executive levels. Neither explains why Schleicher could write Stresemann that calumnious attacks against the Reichswehr in a pacifist periodical were also harmful to the affairs of the Foreign Office;[19] why in 1927 Stresemann welcomed Seeckt's advice on military questions such as disarmament and military attachés;[20] why Stresemann and Groener affirmed that interdepartmental loyalty should be strong;[21] and why the Armed Forces Department should have wanted to make sure that Stresemann knew that cooperation between the Chief of Protocol in the Foreign Office, Dr. Roland Köster (a Social Democrat), and the *Abwehr* Department had been smooth and should continue.[22]

Taken separately these are minor points. Furthermore, the various offices in the Defense Ministry, including the *Truppenamt* (in effect, the General Staff, subordinate to the Chief of the Army Command), devoted most of their energies to the everyday details of administering the Army, organizing the border defense, and planning maneuvers, not to the major questions of foreign policy.[23] Still, actual cooperation and a sense of common purpose existed with regard to Germany's territorial interests, its strategic situation, and the use of military force to defend the Reich and to attain foreign policy objectives. With respect to each of these topics of mutual concern, in which the Army's own views did not always coincide with those of the Foreign Office, the theory and latitude of joint planning at the departmental level must be examined.

[19] *AA*, Schleicher to Stresemann, 28 August 1927, 7346/H164878f.

[20] Seeckt sent his memorandum, "Militär-Attachés," to Stresemann on 18 July 1927; *AA*, 7414/H175326-30.

[21] *AA*, Stresemann to Groener, 29 February 1928; Groener to Stresemann, 7 March; 7375/H167415-17, 424.

[22] Minute for the chief of the *Wehrmachtsabteilung*, 7 January 1929, Nachlass Schleicher, no. 44, Bundesarchiv-Militärarchiv.

[23] Ambassador Eugen Ott criticizes Craig, *Prussian Army*, and Carsten, *Reichswehr and Politics*, for overlooking the role of "Kleinarbeit" or "Tagesarbeit," on which officials in the Defense Ministry spent far more time than on the questions of whether to be for or against the republic, or for or against Locarno. Interview.

In 1920, when Germany believed that it had been deceived and persecuted by the Allies at Versailles, when the Red Army threatened Poland, and when German regular troops and irregular free corps constituted a very substantial fighting force in the east, Seeckt wanted nothing less than a fourth partition of Poland, a return to the frontiers of 1914. His strategic reasons were broad in scope, for he viewed Poland as the cornerstone in Anglo-French plans to keep Germany separated from the Soviet Union and surrounded.[24] Similarly, the *Truppenamt* observed: " 'If Poland collapses the whole edifice of the Versailles Treaty totters. From this it follows clearly that Germany has no interest in rendering any help to Poland in her struggle with Russia. On the contrary, it can only be agreeable to us if Poland should cease to exist.' "[25]

But "back to 1914" became increasingly anachronistic as international order returned to Europe, and as Poland proved able to withstand the Red Army and survive its own growing pains. After 1925 the military leadership regarded foreign policy with greater circumspection, showed a willingness to give Stresemann's brand of *Realpolitik* a chance, and, while visiting the Red Army, seemed less inclined to talk promisingly of reducing Poland to ashes.

Instead of the restoration of the borders of 1914, more limited territorial goals were adopted, conforming on the whole with those set by the Foreign Office. Not surprisingly,

[24] See his memorandum of 4 February 1920, in Carsten, *Reichswehr and Politics*, p. 68, and his "Germany's Attitude to the Russian Problem," subtitled "Reply to a Pro Memoria from Count Br.-R. [Brockdorff-Rantzau] to the Reich Chancellor, dated September 11, 1922," in Freund, *Unholy Alliance*, pp. 136-37. Seeckt's reply, most of which appears in Rabenau, *Seeckt*, pp. 315-18, has been printed in full by Julius Epstein in *Der Monat* (November 1948) and, translated, by Wheeler-Bennett, *Nemesis of Power*, pp. 133-38. Seeckt again referred to the borders of 1914 as Germany's territorial goal in the east in a conversation with Soviet Ambassador Nicolai Krestinski in January 1925. Carsten, *Reichswehr and Politics*, pp. 235-36.

[25] *Ibid.*, p. 69, *Truppenamt* minute (probably by Colonel Otto Hasse) of 26 July 1920.

strong feelings of the superiority of *Deutschtum* colored the revisionist thinking of the Army, for many officers came from Pomerania and West and East Prussia, where their home towns or estates were threatened—if not occupied—by an aggressive and, to them, racially unsavory new Poland. Nevertheless, even more than in the Foreign Office, strategic considerations were of greater importance.[26] Of all the territories ceded to Poland, Upper Silesia was strategically the least significant, although the Army recognized its economic value. The province of Posen had before the war been the central sector of Germany's eastern defenses, a buffer against any Russian attack in the direction of Berlin, and a communications link between Silesia and East Prussia.[27] While it would have been advantageous to eliminate the Posen salient, or at least blunt it by transferring some of western Posen to Germany, this was not regarded a strategic necessity.[28]

[26] All former officers interviewed, including those who came from the eastern provinces, emphasized strategy.

[27] In 1920 a British study of the "Meaning, strategic and otherwise, of the loss to Germany of Polish Territory," observed that "perhaps the most important strategical effect of the Polish settlement and the cession of Germany's Polish possessions is the juxtaposition of two great salients—the Polish salient of Posnania, with its network of railways radiating from Posen, and the German salient of Middle Silesia, with a no less highly developed railway system radiating from Breslau. The narrowness of the latter salient constitutes a serious weakness from the military point of view." Temperley, *Peace Conference*, II, 210.

[28] Interviews with Generals Brennecke, Hermann Flörke, Paul Hausser, and Adolf Heusinger. In March 1919 Groener, concerned about possible territorial losses to Poland in the peace settlement and about resultant German-Polish tension, wrote that Germany must be allowed to retain its frontiers of 1914, including "'at least the *Warthelinie* with Posen.'" Only then, he believed, would Germany be strong enough to help defend Europe against Bolshevism. See Reginald H. Phelps, "Aus den Groener Dokumenten, II," *Deutsche Rundschau*, LXXVI (1950); Groener-Geyer, *General Groener*, p. 135. On 14 April 1919 Groener noted in a situation report (he was First Quartermaster General at the time) that, although the Supreme Command had been ready since March to launch an attack to re-

The loss of the Corridor and Danzig, on the other hand, was unanimously held to be one of the most invidious and unjust dictates of the Treaty of Versailles. The Corridor severed East Prussia from the Reich, leaving that province "encircled" by Poland and Lithuania. By sundering major rail arteries in eastern Germany, the Corridor limited Germany's "freedom of maneuver." In particular it frustrated the Army's desire to uphold the canon of envelopment, prescribed by Alfred Count von Schlieffen, Chief of the General Staff from 1891 to 1905, and practiced in August 1914 at the battle of Tannenberg and again in November when the German Ninth Army was transferred by rail from Silesia to Thorn for an attack against the Russian north flank. Envelopment and mobility, for which the German Army depended on railroads, continued to be fundamental operational doctrines in an officer corps that recalled with horror the static trench warfare on the western front and had too few forces to defend Germany's borders in depth.

The Army considered the Corridor vital to German security; regaining it, legitimate grounds for war.[29] The Army did not waver in this fateful verdict, but, like the Foreign Office, it had to adapt the goal of revision to the strategic realities of Germany's military weakness and the current international situation.

---

conquer Posen, the plan had been called off because of internal political unrest in Germany and because the Entente had effected a cease fire between Germany and Poland. Phelps, "Aus den Groener Dokumenten, II," p. 620. The importance of regaining Posen, however, was soon overshadowed when Germany had to give up the Corridor and Danzig, whose combined strategic value was much greater.

[29] Interviews (all). On Seeckt and the necessity of war against Poland, see Gordon, *Reichswehr and Republic*, p. 273. See also the testimony of Generals Werner von Blomberg and Johannes von Blaskowitz at Nürnberg, in *Nazi Conspiracy and Aggression* (8 vols. and 2 supplements; Washington, D.C., 1946ff.), VI, 414, 417.

Poland

The Army was especially sensitive to the danger of a Polish attack, although this uneasiness did not distress the Bendlerstrasse as much as it did the irregular border defense forces and some regular units stationed along the frontier. The Defense Ministry underwent periodic cases of the jitters during tense moments in German-Polish relations, when it recalled the Polish *fait accompli* in Vilna in 1920 and the incursion of Polish irregulars into Upper Silesia in 1921. But it did not expect large-scale aggression against German territory by Poland acting alone, for it knew that greater Polish military energy was directed against the Soviet Union.

After the Franco-Belgian occupation of the Ruhr, when the existence of the Franco-Polish alliance suggested the possibility of Polish action from the east, neither the Defense Ministry nor the Foreign Office believed that Polish intervention was imminent. Rauscher reported from Warsaw that, far from concentrating on the borders with Germany, Polish troops were in fact being shifted from western garrisons to the eastern front,[30] where Leon Trotsky, Soviet Commissar for War, had promised Soviet intervention on the side of Germany in the event of a Polish attack on Silesia. In 1925 Polish troop movements near Germany were interpreted as an attempt to exaggerate Germany's threat to Poland during the early stages of the security-pact negotiations, not as preparation for an invasion.[31] Pilsudski's coup on 12 May 1926 was followed by rumors that Poland might take this opportunity to seize Danzig, rumors that the Foreign Office doubted[32] and

---

[30] *AA*, 2945/D570836ff., for reports to and from the Foreign Office on Polish movements. Zechlin reassured Stresemann's private secretary that the Defense Ministry saw no evidence of aggressive designs by Poland, 7 February 1923, *ibid.*, D570844-7.

[31] *AA*, Hoesch (Paris) to Foreign Office, 6 January 1925; Foreign Office to Defense Ministry, 17 January; K190/K035619, 622-3. Schubert to Hoesch, 10 March, 2945/D571519-20.

[32] *AA*, Dirksen notes of conversation with Captain Reimer of the Naval Command, 18 May, 5462/E371066-7.

that the Army, too, would not trust. For the rest of the 1920s East Prussian officials and border intelligence posts continued to issue warnings about East Prussia's susceptibility to economic and military pressure from Poland,[33] but the détente between the two countries after Pilsudski's coup, and Poland's preoccupation with a flare-up in relations with Lithuania in 1926-27, minimized the threat of a Polish attack.

In its contingency planning, nonetheless, the Army tried to predict the probable avenues of a Polish offensive against Germany, with or without French support. The Germans surmised correctly that the Polish Army's first concern was to protect its flanks, although Berlin did not know the details of the so-called Foch Plan. In talks with the Polish General Staff in May 1923, Marshal Ferdinand Foch had argued that the main Polish effort in joint Franco-Polish operations in the event of war with Germany should be a direct advance against Berlin from Posen. Pilsudski, then Chief of the General Staff, had objected, for he thought that Poland must first secure its flanks and its communications outlet to the sea before essaying the more general offensive desired by the French. Pilsudski prevailed, and the Foch Plan that emerged from these deliberations included three offensive contingencies. "Plan Baltic Sea" provided for a Polish advance in Pomerania as far as the Oder; "Plan East Prussia," for the occupation of Danzig and parts of East Prussia; and "Plan Silesia," for the seizure of German Upper Silesia.[34]

[33] In a speech at Hanover on 20 October 1929, Dr. Ernst Siehr, *Oberpräsident* of East Prussia, obliquely chided west Germans for not fully appreciating the nature and extent of East Prussia's peril, although he realized that their attention was distracted by the occupation of the Rhineland; *AA*, L558/L161661ff. Reports from a border post in memorandum by Colonel Kühlenthal (T3 in the *Truppenamt*), 31 December 1929, *ibid.*, L161718.

[34] Roos, *Polen und Europa*, p. 6. For an earlier (British) opinion about the implications of the Corridor for Polish strategy, see Temperley, *Peace Conference*, II, 210: "Taking into consideration the range and power of modern artillery, it is unquestionably a fact that such a corridor is militarily indefensible except by offensive operations re-

Although unacquainted with the Foch Plan, the Foreign Office supplied the Defense Ministry with information about the Polish Army. German diplomats in Poland reported that the Polish Army had improved since 1920, that Pilsudski and the French military mission had no love for each other, and that Polish mobilization plans included provisions for civilian border security troops to hold the front lines until units of the regular Army arrived.[35] The first large-scale maneuver of the Polish Army, in 1925, tested its defensive capability against a joint German-Soviet invasion from East Prussia (toward Thorn) and the Ukraine (toward the Volhynia district of eastern Poland).[36] The Warsaw mission related in 1928 that, in addition to maneuvers open to foreign military attachés, the Poles conducted an annual secret war game on paper at Army headquarters in Warsaw; they did not invite even the French military mission.[37] The topic for this particular exercise in the spring of 1929 appears to have been a Polish attack against East Prussia. The Polish General Staff concluded that its forces were insufficient to overcome difficulties of terrain and penetrate deep into East Prussia, and "that a conquest of East Prussia was possible only with strong forces."[38]

On the basis of such information and its own intelligence activities, the German Army was able to cast an impression of its Polish counterpart. Captain Hubert Lanz, head of the

sulting in a great extension of the width of the corridor in the direction of one or both of its flanks."

[35] *AA*, K190/K035242-7088, *passim*.

[36] *AA*, Rauscher to Foreign Office, 22 August 1925, *ibid.*, K035800-3; German consulate in Thorn to Foreign Office, 28 August, Abteilung IVPo, Akten betr. Militärangelegenheiten, Band 8 (not filmed).

[37] *AA*, Warsaw mission to Foreign Office, 24 November, K190/K036221-2. According to this account, the situation in the war game of the preceding winter had been a conflict between Poland and Lithuania, in which Poland had also begun defensive preparations against the Soviet Union and Germany.

[38] *AA*, Emil von Rintelen (Warsaw) to Foreign Office, 7 November 1929, initialled by Schubert, and a transcript sent to the Defense Ministry (T3 of the *Truppenamt*) on 16 November, *ibid.*, K036387.

Polish division of the Statistical Section (T3) in the *Truppenamt*, provided Groener with the following estimate: the Polish officer corps was proud, nationalistic, pro-French, and anti-German; it emphasized cavalry and artillery, the latter attributed to French influence; leadership, troops, and training were all good, but the coordination between the combat branches—infantry, cavalry, and artillery—was not always satisfactory, and the offensive spirit appeared diminished.[39]

Shortly after succeeding Gessler as Defense Minister, Groener told Zechlin that the Defense Ministry would like to have a military attaché in Warsaw.[40] Stresemann approved of sending a military expert to Warsaw,[41] and, in view of the political difficulties involved in sending an active officer (this would have violated the Treaty of Versailles), the two ministries agreed to appoint the man recommended by Rauscher,

[39] Interview with General Lanz. Statistical Section (*Heeresstatistische Abteilung*) was a camouflage name for this successor to the Prussian General Staff's Foreign Armies Section (*Abteilung Fremde Heer*). On this, T3's duties, the close cooperation between T3 and the Foreign Office, and the indistinct connection between T3 and the other intelligence office (the *Abwehrgruppe* to 1928; thereafter, the *Abwehrabteilung*), see Manfred Kehrig, *Die Wiedereinrichtung des deutschen militärischen Attachédienstes nach dem Ersten Weltkrieg (1919-1933)* (Boppard, 1966), pp. 38-41; also Gert Buchheit, *Der deutsche Geheimdienst* (Munich, 1966), pp. 32-40.

[40] Apparently Groener was not satisfied with the military analyses from the regular officials of the Warsaw mission. Moreover, according to Zechlin, Groener saw "no value in military attachés except in Warsaw," for "Poland is the only country that interests us militarily." *AA*, Zechlin notes of conversation with Groener, 15 April 1928, 9182/E645778-9. See also Kehrig, *Wiedereinrichtung*, pp. 66-69.

[41] Stresemann and Forster favored the restoration of attachés because they appreciated the Army's need for information about foreign armies, but Köpke and Schubert advised postponing the matter until after the Rhineland had been evacuated; Kehrig, *Wiedereinrichtung*, pp. 97-106, 117-18. The Wilhelmstrasse gradually surrendered its objection to military attachés as Germany's international situation improved and as the diplomats became confident that the attachés would not play politics, independent of diplomatic missions, as the prewar naval attachés had done.

Count Richard Du Moulin, a former officer in the Prussian Army and currently an official in the Foreign Office. Dirksen willingly complied with the request of Colonel Kühlenthal, head of T3, that Du Moulin spend a few weeks at the Defense Ministry, observe military maneuvers at Döberitz, and visit installations in East Prussia before proceeding to Warsaw toward the end of 1928.[42]

A year later, the Foreign Office received from Du Moulin a long memorandum on Polish operation plans, and sent a transcript of it to Captain Lanz at the Defense Ministry. Du Moulin had difficulty in assembling evidence, for naturally the Poles did not share this information with anyone but their allies, and the Polish public was so uninterested in the possibility of war that no periodical literature or public utterances touched on the subject of military operations. Nevertheless he was able to give some impressions, with which foreign military attachés in Warsaw generally agreed.

The Polish Army thought itself incapable of confronting Germany alone, not only because of the superior strength of German industry but also because the Poles deemed the German Army, about which they were very well informed, superior to their own troops. Du Moulin certified that "this feeling of inferiority" was genuine, and observed that it

> undoubtedly makes it hard for the Polish military leadership to decide, in case of a war against Germany in which French intervention were not assured, to base its operation plan on the idea of a grand offensive in search of a deci-

[42] *AA*, memoranda by Zechlin, Köpke, and Dirksen of April and May 1928, *ibid.*, E645778-9, 785-8. In addition to Du Moulin, the Warsaw mission received Emil von Rintelen, who had been in the Paris embassy from 1923 to 1928. Rintelen's knowledge of military affairs won him the respect of Captain Lanz and other officers in the Defense Ministry. His sympathy for the military was in part familial —his father had been a general in the Kaiser's Army, and his brother was an officer who later became a general in the *Wehrmacht*. On " 'veiled military attachés' " in the late 1920s, of which Du Moulin and Rintelen were examples, see Kehrig, *Wiedereinrichtung*, pp. 42-69.

sion. Nor do the military attachés, with whom I could talk about this question, believe it likely that the Poles envision a large-scale offensive against us in a German-Polish war. In fact, the success of such an offensive would seem to be regarded by their Army command as way beyond the limits of the militarily attainable, so long as Poland cannot be certain that most of the German Army is detained on other fronts.

This did not mean, however, that the Polish Army was thoroughly preoccupied with the defense. Du Moulin noted the emphasis in Polish military circles on the idea of immediate successes in the field in order to bolster national morale for a longer struggle.

This notion, if one considers in this context the possibility of an attack against East Prussia, certainly cannot be labeled as too fantastic, and in fact one hears it stated repeatedly around here. It is hoped here that East Prussia will remain cut off from the rest of the Reich, and the conquest of East Prussia—of course reckoned only in military terms —is regarded here as possible, even if by no means easy. If reports about the last war game of the winter are correct, it produced, to be sure, no very encouraging result. . . . Nevertheless the possibility should be considered that from this failure, the necessity of abandoning the plan will not be inferred, but simply the lesson drawn that, in an attack against East Prussia, even larger numbers of troops must be employed.

Another possible offensive, Du Moulin continued, was against German Pomerania, a sensible tactical objective in a strategic defensive because it would increase the security of the rich grain-producing areas of Posen and the Vistula basin. Moreover, it would widen the Corridor, Poland's supply route to the sea, the barrier between the Reich and East Prussia.

In sum, all of these considerations lead to the conclusion that, while keeping the defensive as its main idea, minor tactical attacks by the Polish Army against East Prussia and possibly Pomerania are quite feasible. In the final analysis, fear of our superiority would therefore exert a determining influence on the Polish plan of operations in a German-Polish war insofar as successes against us are not sought at the most critical points, but at those where the least resistance is anticipated.[43]

Captain Lanz had reservations about some aspects of Du Moulin's report. He was not sure that the Polish Army "felt inferior" to the German Army; he thought that the Poles might rely so heavily on French intervention as to discourage even tactical offensive aspirations in Polish planning; and, if the Poles did decide on a tactical offensive, he believed that they would not regard Pomerania as a more important objective than Silesia, which Du Moulin did not mention. In general, however, the *Truppenamt* and Groener's office agreed with the purport of Du Moulin's memorandum, that, in the late 1920s, Poland had neither the desire nor the resources to invade Germany.[44] If Poland should nevertheless attack, German Army leaders were increasingly confident that they could successfully defend German soil.[45] At the same time they were certain that conducting an offensive war against

[43] *AA*, Du Moulin to Foreign Office, 27 December 1929, K190/K036418-23. Rintelen cited the American military attaché as his source that the tactical doctrine in the Polish Army was a war of movement (*Bewegungskrieg*), not of fixed positions. Rintelen to Foreign Office, 28 March 1929, *ibid.*, K036296-7.

[44] Interview with General Lanz, who recalls how Groener periodically summoned members of T3 to brief him. The peacetime size of the Polish Army around 1930 was approximately 265,000 officers and men in 30 infantry divisions, 4 cavalry divisions, and 6 cavalry brigades. It was expected to expand to two million in wartime. Meinck, *Deutsche Aufrüstung*, p. 2.

[45] Interviews with Generals Busse, Flörke, and Lanz. See also Gordon, *Reichswehr and Republic*, p. 215.

Poland was completely out of the question unless Germany found outside help and Poland had none.

LITHUANIA

Under the leadership of General von Seeckt, the Army Command developed a keen interest in both the current and the potential alignment of powers on which Germany's defense and national interests would depend. Of possible help to Germany in a war against Poland, Lithuania was shrewdly appraised for both political and military reasons: it possessed Memel, occupied a strategic position as a link in the Baltic "bridge" between Germany and the Soviet Union, and suffered from internal instability and military weakness. In foreign policy and military planning, Germany neither committed itself to unreserved support of Lithuania nor discounted that country's potential usefulness in the event of a German-Polish war.

In 1917, when the eastern policy of Hindenburg, Ludendorff, and General Max Hoffmann demanded annexations in the Baltic area, Seeckt wrote to a friend, " 'The difficulty lies in our wish to retain Courland and Lithuania. I have never been convinced of this necessity; on the contrary I consider it a worsening of our geographical position. . . .' "[46] After the war Seeckt's attitude toward Lithuania was determined by his Soviet policy. If the frontiers of 1914 were to be restored then of course Lithuania was another buffer state between Germany and the Soviet Union that would have to be eliminated. But Seeckt was not one to ignore the reality and strategic significance of Lithuania's existence. In 1923, when Military District I (East Prussia) headquarters told Seeckt that it had received feelers from certain Lithuanian sources for a military alliance between Germany (or East Prussia) and Lithuania, Seeckt replied that this was a matter for the government, not for East Prussian officials, and sent his own opinion to Stresemann:

[46] Letter of May 1917, in Carsten, *Reichswehr and Politics*, p. 105.

108

The possibility of a German-Lithuanian agreement will always have to be examined primarily with regard to our relations with Russia. In war and peacetime we have a vital interest in the routes that go through Lithuania, Latvia and Estonia, and secure communications with Russia. For its part Russia must attach the greatest importance to the security and preservation of these communications. For its conduct of a war against Poland, however, which would begin with a lengthy concentration of forces—lasting several weeks—with a strong right flank along and south of the Duna river, it will be of the greatest significance whether the Baltic States are its allies or at least benevolent neutrals, or whether they are under the political and military sway of Poland. Thus the interests of Germany and Russia in the Baltic run completely parallel: it is all the more important that discussions with Lithuania do not ensue without keeping in touch with Russia.

In any case, Seeckt concluded, in its relations with Lithuania Germany should not divulge "the strengths and weaknesses" of its defensive preparations in East Prussia, for Lithuania was a small state that might be attracted into the Franco-Polish bloc by promises of portions of East Prussia.[47]

On this question of German-Lithuanian relations there was cooperation and accord between the Foreign Office and Defense Ministry. Shortly after Seeckt's note to Stresemann, Secretary of State von Maltzan suggested to Lieutenant Colonel Friedrich von Bötticher from the Defense Ministry that he go in civilian clothes and under a pseudonym to the Lithuanian capital to study the situation. At a conference with Bötticher following his return from Kaunas, Maltzan and General Otto Hasse (then Chief of the *Truppenamt*) decided that the matter should be dropped, for Germany had no interest in committing itself to such a small and militarily weak state.[48]

---

[47] *AA*, Seeckt to Stresemann, 31 October, 3241/D704659-63.
[48] *AA*, notes (probably by Schubert) of talk with Defense Ministry about German-Lithuanian contacts in 1923, 10 January 1927, 4564/

Germany declined to offer Lithuania any pledges in a manner that was neither abrupt nor unfriendly, for neither ministry wanted the Army to lose touch with Lithuania. Nevertheless, this contact did not mature into a secret military agreement whereby German officers would have entered the Lithuanian Army in the event of a Polish-Lithuanian war. Early in 1927, when war between Poland and Lithuania seemed probable, the French Ambassador, M. Bruno Jacquin de Margerie, told Stresemann of reports that a German-Lithuanian agreement of this kind existed. The Defense Ministry denied it.[49] And in December 1927, Schubert informed Colonel Werner von Blomberg (recently appointed Chief of the *Truppenamt*) that, although the Foreign Office had not changed its position concerning the possibility of military talks with Lithuania, now was not the time to initiate them, for Lithuania was internally weak and its officer corps was showing signs of disintegration. On this the Foreign Office agreed with the Defense Ministry.[50]

THE SOVIET UNION

The Army saw in the Soviet Union a military counterweight to Poland and a haven for research, development, and training in forbidden weapons. The secret collaboration with the Red Army, by now a well-known but not always unbiased story, needs to be recast in a politico-military mold.[51] As in

---

E163477-8; General Hasse to Maltzan, 21 February 1924, *ibid.*, E162578. See also Meier-Welcker, *Seeckt*, p. 451. Bötticher was head of T3 at the time of his mission to Lithuania.

[49] *AA*, notes by Schubert (?), 10 January 1927, 4564/E163477-8; also Heye to Foreign Office, 6 January, 9481/H276456-7.

[50] *AA*, Schubert to Blomberg, 3 December, 9481/H276393.

[51] In addition to the works cited in chap. 1, n. 69, and above, n. 3, see Carr, *Socialism in One Country*, III, 47-56, 1010-17; Hans W. Gatzke, "Russo-German Military Collaboration during the Weimar Republic," *American Historical Review*, LXIII (1958); George W. F.

the case of policy at the Foreign Office, a distinction must be made between the actual substance of the Army's collaboration and the implicit promise of a military alliance. Three features of collaboration demand analysis: its role in interdepartmental civil-military relations; its repercussions for German diplomacy; and its military usefulness.

The Wilhelmstrasse was in an uncomfortable position, on the one hand in favor of secret collaboration, on the other fearful of too much independence in the Bendlerstrasse's conduct. By the end of 1922 the Army had clearly carved out its own private province of policy. Seeckt kept Chancellor Joseph Wirth informed of secret negotiations, but Wirth apparently thought better of passing this information on to President Friedrich Ebert. Nor did Wirth challenge Seeckt's opinion that " 'in all these measures . . . participation, and even official recognition, by the German Government would be absolutely out of the question. The detailed negotiations could only be conducted by military authorities.' "[52] Seeckt demanded military control partly because he did not want to risk seriously embarrassing the government should the secret collaboration be discovered.[53] Moreover, he did not claim the unreserved primacy of military officials, who would of course " 'make no agreements binding on the Reich without the knowledge of the political authorities.' "[54] But probably the

---

Hallgarten, "General Hans von Seeckt and Russia, 1920-1922," *Journal of Modern History*, xxi (1949); August Ernst Köstring, *General Ernst Köstring: Der militärische Mittler zwischen dem Deutschen Reich und der Sowjetunion 1921-1941*, ed. Hermann Teske (Frankfurt am Main, 1966), pp. 46-50; Helm Speidel, "Reichswehr und Rote Armee," *Vierteljahrshefte für Zeitgeschichte*, i (1953); especially John Erickson's thorough *The Soviet High Command: A Military-Political History, 1918-1941* (London, 1962), chaps. 6, 9, 11.

[52] Seeckt memorandum of 11 September 1922, in Freund, *Unholy Alliance*, p. 137.

[53] Hilger, *Incompatible Allies*, p. 199.

[54] Memorandum of 11 September 1922, in Freund, *Unholy Alliance*, p. 137.

main reason for Seeckt's insistence on independent military activity was his distrust of Brockdorff-Rantzau, whose appointment to Moscow he regarded as detrimental to an "active" German policy toward the Soviet Union.

Seeckt misjudged the Foreign Office. The Foreign Office was opposed not to secret collaboration, but to military independence, and it was able gradually to increase its knowledge of and assert its control over Germany's military relations with the Soviet Union.

Brockdorff-Rantzau continually pressed for civilian control, informing Berlin that the Army's activities in Moscow had gone much further than the Foreign Office realized, and that reckless statements by German officers in Moscow could only complicate the work of the Foreign Office.[55] Brockdorff-Rantzau's contacts with German military representatives in Moscow became closer, and even cordial in the case of Colonel (Ret.) von der Lieth-Thomsen, who commanded *Zentrale Moskau*, the recently established German military mission which controlled all secret military enterprises in the Soviet Union and was responsible directly to the *Truppenamt* in Berlin.[56] In spite of this improvement and the better understanding that developed between Seeckt and Brockdorff-Rantzau as the latter warmed toward Germany's eastern policy, the ambassador complained early in 1926 of the military's failure to observe the established rules governing

[55] *AA*, Brockdorff-Rantzau to Cuno, 29 July 1923, 4564/E162539-42. See also Carsten, *Reichswehr and Politics*, pp. 141f.; Hilger, *Incompatible Allies*, p. 200; Rosenbaum, *Community of Fate*, pp. 57-58.

[56] In November 1922 Gessler issued a directive to the Chiefs of the Army and Naval Commands, in which he named the Chief of the *Truppenamt* as the responsible officer for Germany's "military policy toward Russia." Defense Ministry (hereafter *RWM*, for *Reichswehrministerium*), 23 November, II M 62/1. In the *Truppenamt*, Major Herbert Fischer administered this area of planning. For a chart showing the ties between Defense Ministry, *Truppenamt*, *Zentrale Moskau*, and Foreign Office, see Speidel, "Reichswehr und Rote Armee," p. 43.

communication and cooperation with the civilian authorities regarding secret military relations.[57]

By 1926 Stresemann and the Foreign Office clearly dominated the field of foreign policy, and after Seeckt's dismissal it was probably only a matter of time before this control would extend to cover military collaboration with the Soviet Union. A single incident, however, precipitated the resolution in favor of the Foreign Office. On 3 December 1926 the *Manchester Guardian* published an article describing in detail some of the Reichswehr's secret activities. The Social Democratic Party, with Philipp Scheidemann its most outspokenly critical partisan, demanded a full explanation. As a result of this party's parliamentary pressure a special meeting of the Reichstag Foreign Affairs Committee was called, and a joint statement prepared by the Foreign Office and the Defense Ministry was read aloud. The ministries did not deny the recent allegations, but declared that the agreements mentioned in the *Guardian* article "had already been liquidated in full."[58] Neither department disclosed the full extent of the collaboration that had allegedly ceased, and the moral drawn from this episode by the Wilhelmstrasse was that civilian control must be increased over that which continued.

In a conference between Schubert and General Wilhelm Wetzell, Hasse's successor as Chief of the *Truppenamt*, Schubert asserted that in the past the Foreign Office "had wanted to know as little as possible of these matters so that it could say it was ignorant of them," but hereafter it "must be precisely informed about everything." Whether Germany could risk continuing the collaboration, Schubert said, depended on the decision of the Foreign Minister.[59] Since 1923 Strese-

---

[57] *AA*, Brockdorff-Rantzau memorandum, 18 January, 4564/E162667ff. See also Erickson, *Soviet High Command*, p. 249.

[58] Hilger, *Incompatible Allies*, p. 205. The protocol of 26 February 1927 (see n. 61) stated that the industrial enterprises begun after the military agreements of 1922 and 1923 had been "liquidated" by the end of 1926.

[59] *AA*, Dirksen notes of meeting with Schubert, Dirksen, Wetzell, and Major Fischer, 24 January 1927, 4564/E163480-4.

113

mann had known more of the details than Schubert's statement would indicate.[60] Probably Seeckt's dismissal removed an obstacle to civilian control that Stresemann had declined to challenge on this issue. In any case Stresemann stepped firmly into the imbroglio and set the pattern that existed for the next few years: closer cooperation between Foreign Office and Defense Ministry, and the ultimate responsibility for military relations with the Soviet Union in the hands of the government.

In May 1927 members of the Foreign Office (Stresemann, Schubert, and Köpke) and Defense Ministry (Gessler, Heye, and Blomberg) unanimously approved a joint protocol regulating secret military activities for the summer.[61] The preparations of the Defense Ministry pursuant to the protocol were subject to modification or even termination by the Foreign Office, a move Stresemann contemplated as Anglo-Soviet relations deteriorated in May and June.[62] Late in 1927 the Defense Ministry asked the Foreign Office to consent in sending a group of active officers to the flying school at Lipetsk in the coming year. The Defense Ministry overrode Stresemann's objections simply by sending them and then notifying the Chancellor and the Foreign Office. The Wilhelmstrasse was angered by this rude reversion to the independence the diplomats had determined to curtail.[63] But it appears to have

[60] At the latest, Stresemann knew of the collaboration shortly after becoming Chancellor in August 1923. On 18 June 1924, he sent copies to Gessler and Seeckt of a report from Brockdorff-Rantzau of the latter's conversation with Trotsky on 9 June. Stresemann called their attention to its details about secret military relations. *AA*, 7414/H175333-40.

[61] The protocol had been drafted by Dirksen and Major Fischer and dated 26 February 1927. *AA*, 4564/E163527-8. It was approved on 18 May; *ibid.*, E163880-4.

[62] For Stresemann's reconsideration of the protocol, see *AA*, note (by Wallroth?) to Schubert, 4 June 1927, 6698/H111735.

[63] Stresemann disapproved of sending active officers, but recommended sending young civilians "who would enter the Reichswehr after completing the course at Lipetsk." *AA*, Schubert notes, 6 February 1928, 9481/H276326-7. Evidence of pique in the Foreign

been an exception, for cooperation between the two ministries was usually smooth.

Beginning in 1927 the Defense Ministry submitted lists of the officers assigned annually to attend Red Army maneuvers to the Foreign Office for information and approval. In March 1928 Dirksen recommended that the Defense Ministry talk with Rudolf Hilferding, a prominent Social Democrat who had said before a meeting of the Foreign Affairs Committee that his party had information about continued secret collaboration, and assure him that his allegation had no foundation in fact.[64] Blomberg, who had replaced Wetzell as Chief of the *Truppenamt*, gave the Foreign Office a long written report of his inspection tour of German military installations in the Soviet Union and Red Army maneuvers during the summer of 1928. And in March 1929 Blomberg met with Groener and Stresemann to determine how many officers were to be sent to the Soviet Union for various kinds of training.[65]

On the surface, that the Army sent active officers to the Soviet Union in 1928 against Stresemann's objections substantiates the assertion of a former German diplomat: "It was clear . . . that the military would openly or secretly continue its military co-operation even if the political leadership were to break off all such relationships."[66] And perhaps Stresemann's power to cancel the protocol approved on 18 May 1927 was imagined; we do not know, for he did not exercise it. But to conclude that the Foreign Office "capitulated to the generals" is to suggest a submissiveness and de-

---

Office in Köpke memorandum of meeting with Dirksen, Blomberg, and Kühlenthal, 1 May 1928, *ibid.*, H276319-21. See also Carsten, *Reichswehr and Politics*, pp. 278-80.

[64] *AA*, Dirksen notes of conversation with Major Behschnitt, 21 March, 3177/D683217-18. Hilferding had been a member of the German delegation to the Genoa Conference in April 1922, and had welcomed the Rapallo Treaty for its economic promise.

[65] Carsten, *Reichswehr and Politics*, p. 280.

[66] Hilger, *Incompatible Allies*, pp. 205-206.

pendence that were not characteristic of the Wilhelmstrasse at the time.[67] Stresemann was willing to support the Army's illicit activities now that the Foreign Office had acquired greater control over them. And certainly his approval, which had led to the drafting of the protocol, was based on more than resignation to an existing state of affairs. He was not averse to any means of strengthening the Army short of disabling his western policy.

Secret collaboration caused headaches in the Wilhelmstrasse not only because of the question of control, but also because of the diplomatic repercussions. It was in violation of the Treaty of Versailles and thus ideal material for blackmail for the Soviets, who might have fatally injured Germany's relations with the West by revealing its existence. It was also the Army's elaboration of the "spirit of Rapallo," which had been initiated by politicians, not generals. In short, it both conformed to and threatened to destroy the policy of balance between east and west. Still, the cabinet and Foreign Office accepted military collaboration as part of general rapprochement with the Soviet Union.

This endorsement ensured politically awkward predicaments such as the Skoblevsky affair in 1926. Peter A. Skoblevsky, an agent of the Comintern, had been awaiting trial since his capture during the Communist-inspired rising of October 1923. He became the subject of heated debate between the Foreign Office and Defense Ministry when, in May

---

[67] *Ibid.*, p. 206. Hilger does add that they gave in "with the greatest of pleasure. All concerned, from Stresemann on down, were resolved not only to continue as before with military co-operation, but to intensify it, though with the greatest caution." This suggests that Hilger should have used a word other than "capitulate," which does not connote "the greatest of pleasure" or the willingness to "intensify" collaboration. Similarly, Kurt Rosenbaum refers to collaboration as a "Damoclean sword which forced the hand of the Germans" in 1926, and which could have been eliminated early in 1927 "despite military necessity." But then Rosenbaum, too, admits that Stresemann and the Foreign Office were in favor of continuing what was a militarily "profitable relationship." *Community of Fate*, pp. 225, 238, 261.

1926, Moscow asked for his release as part of an exchange for the return of over forty German citizens who were imprisoned in the Soviet Union. Brockdorff-Rantzau warned Stresemann that unless Germany released Skoblevsky Moscow would stab Germany in the back by revealing the secret collaboration in the trial of one of the German civilians, a Junkers engineer, and thereby ruin Germany's chances of being admitted to the League of Nations.[68]

On 14 July Schubert reiterated this warning at a conference with Gessler, Colonel Schleicher, and Major Herbert Fischer of the *Truppenamt*. In talks with General Hasse and Major Fischer early in the year he had found confirmation of his opinion that secret collaboration carried with it the risk of compromising the government, and General Hasse had stressed the need for friendly relations with the Soviet Union in order to obviate this danger. Gessler and Schleicher agreed that the danger existed, but Gessler doubted that Moscow would want to end collaboration, and believed that the interest of the western powers in Germany's entry into the League was "greater than their wish to catch us in some compromising position." The Defense Minister drew the line at allowing subversives to undermine national security, and insisted that Skoblevsky be tried. For Schubert, Germany's isolation—the likely outcome of Moscow's retaliation—was to be avoided at all costs; for Gessler, it was an unfortunate but necessary price to pay when internal security was at stake.[69] The Foreign Office prevailed, and in August it was announced that Skoblevsky would be released.

Even after clearing the hurdle of Germany's entry into the

---

[68] Rosenbaum, *Community of Fate*, pp. 220ff.

[69] *AA*, notes of Dirksen, who was present at the meeting, 14 July, 9481/H276477-90. Gessler himself appears to have been isolated, except for the support of Schleicher, whose preoccupation at the time was internal politics. The Defense Minister was unpopular in the Kremlin, and Brockdorff-Rantzau criticized his meddling in foreign policy and thereby threatening to upset the delicate balance between east and west effected by the diplomats. Rosenbaum, *Community of Fate*, pp. 222f.

League in September 1926, officials at the Foreign Office blanched when they imagined the effect that public revelations of secret collaboration might have on their western policy.[70] Stresemann was in Geneva when the *Manchester Guardian* article appeared, and he quickly formulated his answer to the inquisitive diplomats at the League. He could not refute the article completely, but would assure them that Germany had no secret military agreement with the Soviet Union; the German Army had merely made certain connections with German industrial representatives in the Soviet Union from whom it hoped to receive weapons in the event of an attack by Poland, for Germany was militarily weak in the face of the constant Polish threat. In any case these activities had almost come to an end, so that no one could attribute to them "any current importance of a military or political nature."[71]

Some of the activities continued, however, and the Foreign Office had to come to terms with that fact. Schubert advised that they be terminated as soon as possible without offending Moscow. He admitted to General Wetzell that he was not completely informed about the "military worth" of the tank and flying schools, but believed it could not be sufficient to "outweigh the political risk" of keeping them.[72] Strese-

[70] Moscow was also sensitive about the political repercussions of such disclosures. Soon after the revelations in the *Guardian*, Litvinov informed the Germans that his government could not afford to maintain ties with the German Army "if Gessler could not keep his mouth shut" and confessed the secret activities before a Reichstag committee. Stresemann planned to discuss the matter with General Heye; *AA*, Stresemann minute, no date, 7128/H147736.

[71] *AA*, Stresemann (Geneva) to Köpke, 5 December 1926, 4564/ E163419-21. Gessler, Heye, and the Chancellor, Wilhelm Marx, agreed to Stresemann's tactic; Köpke to Stresemann, 6 December, *ibid.*, E163422-3.

[72] *AA*, Dirksen notes of meeting with Schubert, Wetzell, and Major Fischer, 24 January 1927, 4564/E163483. Schubert had held the same opinion during the Skoblevsky affair; Rosenbaum, *Community of Fate*, p. 224.

118

mann, on the other hand, wanted these schools maintained[73] although he did not sanction them unconditionally, for he judged that the *Guardian*'s disclosures and the Anglo-Soviet conflict dictated caution. Thus, he asked that only civilians be sent to the secret schools and soon after the adoption of the protocol of May 1927 he wondered whether it should not be rescinded in view of the tension between London and Moscow.[74] But Stresemann's reservations diminished as cooperation between the Foreign Office and the Defense Ministry increased; as his Locarno policy survived the *Guardian* episode in good health; and as political incidents damaging to the Rapallo relationship did not lead to Soviet divulgence of secret collaboration.[75] In 1928 and 1929 he supported collaboration and refuted rumors that Germany still had secret military arrangements with the Soviet Union.[76]

Why, in view of these anxieties in the Wilhelmstrasse, did Stresemann endorse military collaboration? General Wetzell advised Schubert that the Soviets wanted and needed military contacts with Germany, without which "they would surely turn to France or another power." If that happened, Germany

[73] *AA*, Dirksen minutes of 9 and 19 February 1927, 4564/E163486, 494-5. Major Fischer told Dirksen that Stresemann, in talks with General Heye, was very interested in the continuation of the schools.

[74] Moreover, the Foreign Office opposed Seeckt's proposed trip to the Soviet Union in the spring of 1927 for fear that this would add to suspicions that secret military agreements existed. Seeckt was persuaded to cancel his plans; *AA*, Schubert to Neurath (Rome), 12 April; Neurath to Schubert, 17 April; 2860/D558595, 618.

[75] On the Hölz case (November-December 1927), see Dyck, *Weimar Germany and Soviet Russia*, pp. 116f.; Rosenbaum, *Community of Fate*, pp. 252-53. On the Shakhty affair (March-July 1928), Dyck, pp. 144-45; Rosenbaum, pp. 253ff.

[76] *AA,* Köpke to Stresemann and Stresemann to German embassy in London, 19 February 1929, K6/K000424-6. Nevertheless, Brockdorff-Rantzau and other German diplomats in the Soviet Union continued to warn of the possible political reverberations of both illegal activities and the legal presence of German officers at Soviet maneuvers. See Rosenbaum, *Community of Fate*, chap. 8, *passim; AA,* messages from Moscow and Kiev, 17 and 24 September 1928, 9524/E671684-90.

119

would lose the political and economic advantages that accompanied military cooperation.[77] Perhaps a cessation of collaboration after 1926 would have heightened feelings of Francophilia in Moscow, but its continuance did not prevent a meeting between Litvinov and Briand in September 1927, which prompted speculation that a Franco-Soviet understanding was near. In any case, Wetzell neglected to mention a reason that was almost as important to Stresemann as diplomatic considerations: the military value for Germany of collaboration.

The first few years of collaboration concentrated on German financial aid to the Soviet war industry and on the production of war materials—airplanes, shells, poison gas—and arrangements for their delivery to Germany. Offices were established in the *Truppenamt* (Sondergruppe *R*[ussland]) and in Moscow (*Gefu*, short for *Gesellschaft zur Förderung gewerblicher Unternehmungen*; it had an office in Berlin as well) to supervise the activities of military and industrial representatives, and to handle the complicated—and often strained—financial negotiations between the two countries. German and Soviet officers also exchanged visits, and in 1924-25 "a new emphasis was being laid on the testing of equipment and the training of personnel . . . rather than the actual production of war materials in factories located in the Soviet Union."[78] In 1924 a German air base was built at Lipetsk, and German officers reported there for training. By the end of 1926, General Wetzell reported, the delivery of shells had ceased, and Junkers had closed its two factories in the Soviet Union because of heavy financial loss; all that remained were negotiations to open a tank school at Kazan, experiments with poison gas, exchanges of officers for training and observing maneuvers, and the flying school at Lipetsk.[79]

[77] *AA*, Dirksen notes of conference with Schubert, Wetzell, and Fischer, 24 January 1927, 4564/E163483-4.

[78] Erickson, *Soviet High Command*, p. 248.

[79] *AA*, Dirksen notes of meeting with Schubert, Wetzell, and

These four areas of collaboration continued unabated, although the facilities and tanks required for the school at Kazan were not ready until the spring of 1929. In addition to regular visits to Red Army maneuvers, high-level inspection tours were scheduled. Beginning in 1928 the Chief of the *Truppenamt* made an annual trip to meet with the Soviet High Command.[80] In the spring of 1928 Colonel Hilmar Ritter von Mittelberger, head of the Organization Section (T2) of the *Truppenamt*, was in the Soviet Union. And General Hans Halm, an expert in the military use of railroads, spent nearly a year with the Soviet High Command, discussing problems of rail transport.[81]

The collaboration was beneficial to both Armies; the Soviets welcomed advice and the chance to observe German training techniques, and the Germans were grateful for war materials and training opportunities prohibited by the Treaty of Versailles. Moreover, the comprehensive reports of Mittelberger and Blomberg following their visits show "that the *Reichswehr* did obtain access to the inner ring of the Soviet command and acquired a not inconsiderable insight into Soviet military methods as a result of the collaboration."[82]

Although Germany's actual military ties with the Soviet Union were in themselves useful, military and civilian officials also appreciated the possibility of a German-Soviet al-

Fischer, 24 January 1927, 4564/E163480-2; Carsten, *Reichswehr and Politics*, pp. 234-35, 275-76. On German-Soviet collaboration in military aviation until 1933, see Karl-Heinz Völker, *Die Entwicklung der militärischen Luftfahrt in Deutschland 1920-1933*, in *Beiträge zur Militär- und Kriegsgeschichte*, III (Stuttgart, 1962), pp. 132, 140-42, 158-59; the same author's *Dokumente und Dokumentarfotos zur Geschichte der deutschen Luftwaffe* (Stuttgart, 1968), pp. 58-92.

[80] Erickson, *Soviet High Command*, pp. 271ff.

[81] Interview with General Hans von Donat. On Halm's mission, see below, chap. 9, n. 27.

[82] Erickson, *Soviet High Command*, p. 261. Erickson refutes Helm Speidel's contention that the German Army gave but did not receive. See Speidel, "Reichswehr und Rote Armee," pp. 35-36. For a summary of Mittelberger's report, see Erickson, pp. 261-63; for Blomberg's, see below, n. 100.

liance to smash the Versailles peace settlement and vanquish Poland. In November 1919 General Rüdiger Count von der Goltz, who earlier in the year had commanded German free corps against the Bolsheviks in the Baltic territories, regarded German-Soviet friendship as " 'simply natural,' " since both were " 'threatened by Britain.' "[83] The *Truppenamt* believed that Germany must " 'free herself from the chains of the Entente with the help of Soviet Russia, without falling victim to Bolshevism. . . .' "[84] In Seeckt's opinion the Soviet Union was Germany's most logical future ally, for it was the arch-enemy of Poland, whose existence was "intolerable," and whose destruction would be a death blow to French continental power.[85] Chancellor and Foreign Minister Wirth echoed Seeckt's hostility toward Poland, stating that " 'Poland must be destroyed,' " and suggesting that the Treaty of Rapallo should be enlarged following discussion with the Soviets of military problems, with special regard to Poland.[86]

At first, the policy of military cooperation initiated by Seeckt and Wirth alarmed Brockdorff-Rantzau, who viewed an exclusively eastern policy with military commitments as " 'dangerous' " and " 'hopeless,' " because it would bind Germany to the " 'unscrupulous Soviet Government' " and expose a weak Germany to French attack in the event of Soviet aggression against Poland.[87] But soon the occupation of the

[83] In Carsten, *Reichswehr and Politics*, p. 67. Von der Goltz, an ardent anti-Bolshevik, assumed that the Reds would not be " 'the Russia of the future.' "

[84] *Ibid.*, p. 69, *Truppenamt* minute (probably by Colonel Otto Hasse) of 26 July 1920.

[85] Seeckt memorandum of 11 September 1922, in Freund, *Unholy Alliance*, pp. 136-37. In a dinner conversation with Soviet Ambassador Krestinski in January 1925, Seeckt outlined his idea of the correct German policy: " 'Impossible to lean either on France or Britain. Therefore on Russia. Wait and exploit an Anglo-French conflict. Goal in the east: frontiers of 1914! . . . Germany cannot go against Russia.' " Carsten, *Reichswehr and Politics*, pp. 235-36.

[86] Conversations with Brockdorff-Rantzau, 24 July and 1 August 1922, in Helbig, *Träger der Rapallo-Politik*, pp. 119-20.

[87] From Brockdorff-Rantzau's "Promemoria" of 15 August 1922,

Ruhr and Germany's virtual isolation persuaded Brockdorff-Rantzau to adopt an eastern orientation of which Seeckt had thought him incapable in 1922.[88] In July 1923 the ambassador advised sustaining military collaboration, but subordinating it to "military-technical and political conditions." Under "political conditions" he underscored the Polish threat and the value of Soviet support in the event of a Polish attack, which would surely be actively supported by France. There could be "no question of a political or military alliance," but Germany should try to obtain a Soviet pledge of military aid against Poland; indeed "Russia itself has a vital interest in preventing the possibility of a successful Polish attack against Germany, which would strengthen Poland militarily and politically and thus threaten Russia."[89]

Although the allure of strategic collaboration was more tempting to the Army than to the Foreign Office, apparently neither Seeckt nor Heye took the final step of sealing a military pact for combined operations against Poland. During the Polish-Soviet war of 1920, Seeckt prepared contingency plans for a German attack against Poland, but German participation in the war did not go beyond sheltering numerous retreating Bolsheviks in East Prussia.[90] As secret cooperation

---

in Freund, *Unholy Alliance*, p. 133. For the complete document, see Helbig, "Die Moskauer Mission," pp. 331ff.; Schüddekopf, *Heer und Republik*, pp. 156ff.; *AA*, 4564/E162603-12. On Brockdorff-Rantzau's views in 1922, see Rosenbaum, *Community of Fate*, pp. 34ff.; on the misdating of the "Promemoria" by Julius Epstein—"Der Seeckt Plan," *Der Monat* (November 1948)—and others, *ibid.*, chap. 1, n. 39.

[88] Both men admired the *Realpolitik* of Bismarck, in which the isolating of France and courting of Russia had been complementary principles. For various views of the similarities and differences between Seeckt's policy and that of Brockdorff-Rantzau, see Helbig, *Träger der Rapallo-Politik*, pp. 118ff.; Hans Herzfeld, *Das Problem des Deutschen Heeres 1919-1945* (Laupheim, 1950?), pp. 10-11; Rosenbaum, *Community of Fate*, p. 62; Carl Severing, *Mein Lebensweg* (2 vols.; Cologne, 1950), II, 101.

[89] *AA*, Brockdorff-Rantzau to Cuno, 29 July 1923, 4564/E162543-5.
[90] On Seeckt's plan of 1920, see Rabenau, *Seeckt*, p. 297; Erickson,

gathered speed late in 1921 Seeckt met with Soviet military representatives in Berlin, and the course of action in the event of another war between Poland and the Soviet Union came up in the discussion. But no operational decisions were reached. Surveying Germany's surrounded position, Seeckt " 'recommended to the chancellor benevolent neutrality.' "[91] On the Soviet side, the Red Army High Command was probably not "seeking a military commitment, but rather making a test of *Reichswehr* intentions."[92] At a meeting on 10 February 1922 between Seeckt and Karl Radek, secretary of the Comintern, the general would not commit himself in the event of a future Polish-Soviet conflict.[93] In April, Otto Hasse represented the Army in the German delegation to the Genoa Conference, but the Treaty of Rapallo peripheral to that diplomatic summit included no secret military convention.[94]

Soviet High Command, p. 149; Gessler, *Reichswehrpolitik*, p. 198. Gessler insists that Seeckt drew up "a plan, a study," not an order, and that he (Gessler) never gave an order for combined operations. Captain Gotthard Heinrici, later commanding general in the Battle of Berlin against the Red Army in the spring of 1945, lodged about 30 Soviet soldiers in East Prussia; interview with General Heinrici.

[91] In Carsten, *Reichswehr and Politics*, p. 137. See also Rabenau, *Seeckt*, p. 309.

[92] Erickson, *Soviet High Command*, p. 152.

[93] *Ibid.*, p. 153 and n. See also Carr, *German-Soviet Relations*, p. 60; Carsten, *Reichswehr and Politics*, p. 138. Erickson discounts the likelihood that Radek's suggestion of a joint German-Soviet attack on Poland in the spring "embodied a serious Soviet military intention," and Carr believes that Radek was merely adhering to Lenin's tactic of " 'playing the Polish card' " in order to get German economic and military aid.

[94] Seeckt could not have been more pleased with Rapallo. In his opinion, it was " 'impossible to overestimate the advantage which would accrue to Germany if Poland knew that if she joined in a war of sanctions with France against Germany she would have Russia to contend with. . . . These matters must not be overlooked when considering a fresh strengthening of Russia with our assistance, and therefore at the same time a more active German policy. . . . Who, then, has concluded a written military agreement, binding us unilaterally, or who intends at present to do so? Certainly not the

In 1923, when Germany's politico-military weakness was magnified by the Franco-Belgian occupation of the Ruhr, the military leadership lost a degree of poise. As head of a German mission to Moscow in February, General Hasse talked irresponsibly of a German "war of liberation" in the near future, an utterance that dismayed Brockdorff-Rantzau and verified his low opinion of the military's prudence in foreign policy. Although the Soviets indicated that they would take action against any Polish aggression in Silesia or East Prussia, and although the German Army's feelings of encirclement and subjugation had reached a high point, almost certainly no agreements of an operational nature were made.[95] By the end of the year Soviet Russia's dynamic foreign policy had shifted from military adventure to revolutionary activity. As a result, the sparks for a military alliance or for a new Polish-Soviet war died down, although they were never extinguished.

In October 1923 Seeckt urged an " 'extension of the economic and military-political relations with Russia.' "[96] It was some time before the general, who made no secret of his antagonism toward Stresemann as a person and as Foreign Minister, realized that Stresemann's policy did not entail a suicidal rejection of " 'economic and military-political' " ties with the Soviet Union. Nor did that policy provoke crises in Franco-German relations or belligerence in eastern Europe, political configurations that might have roused unrestrained strategic expectations in the military. The relative international calm after Locarno; the closer interdepartmental cooperation between the Wilhelmstrasse and the Bendlerstrasse after Seeckt's dismissal (and after the disclosures in the *Manchester Guardian*); the anticipation that Stresemann's policy

---

responsible military authorities. . . . That the Treaty of Rapallo has brought upon us the suspicion that we could have achieved this increase of power *without* binding ourselves is the main advantage, scarcely to be overestimated, of this agreement.' " Memorandum of 11 September 1922, in Freund, *Unholy Alliance*, pp. 136-37.

[95] Erickson, *Soviet High Command*, pp. 159-60.

[96] Rabenau, *Seeckt*, p. 361.

would accelerate resolutions of the reparations and occupation questions: these conditions lent patience to the Army's daily activity, and responsibility to its assessment of and statements to the Red Army.

The Red Army's offensive capability had declined since 1920 because of the divisive effects of internal problems of reorganization and command.[97] German diplomats and military missions in the Soviet Union, who exchanged information on the preparedness and strategic posture of the Soviet Army, were aware of this decline. In February 1927 Brockdorff-Rantzau regarded as "completely credible" the declarations of the Soviet government that it had neither the intention nor the means to conduct an offensive war. In reply to a query from the Defense Ministry (T3 of the *Truppenamt*), Brockdorff-Rantzau and Rauscher surmised that reports of recent Soviet troop movements to the Polish border—if true —did not reflect a major foreign policy move, but were related to the reorganization of the Red Army.[98]

In the spring of 1928, T3 in turn corroborated Brockdorff-Rantzau's view that Moscow contemplated no offensive war and that rumors to the contrary were groundless. Colonel Kühlenthal, head of T3, observed that the Soviet Army was

[97] On these difficulties and their implications for the future of the Red Army, see Erickson, *Soviet High Command*, chap. 7.

[98] *AA*, Brockdorff-Rantzau to Foreign Office, 24 February (Foreign Office transcript to General Heye on 8 April), 9524/E671604-5; T3 to Foreign Office, 25 February; Brockdorff-Rantzau to Foreign Office, 26 March; Rauscher to Foreign Office, 12 May; K179/ K031138, 151-2, 186-7. Nevertheless, Soviet troop movements in late spring and summer were not unrelated to two events that "caused a war scare in Russia": Britain severed diplomatic relations with the Soviet Union in mid-May, and Voikov was assassinated in Warsaw on 7 June. See Korbel, *Poland between East and West*, pp. 217f. For reports to the Foreign Office and Defense Ministry concerning Soviet reactions, including troop movements, see Dyck, *Weimar Germany and Soviet Russia*, pp. 97-98; on the Soviet regime's use of the "artificial war scare" to divert public attention from internal hardships during the early stages of Stalin's economic program, Rosenbaum, *Community of Fate*, pp. 246f.

able to wage a successful defensive war against an army attacking from the west, especially if that invader were Poland, but "not yet capable of conducting a large offensive of its own into enemy territory." Concluding his report to the Foreign Office, he stressed "the fact that throughout the Red Army, Poland is considered *the* enemy, against whom all military preparations are directed," and that steps had been taken "to make popular a defensive war against Poland."[99]

In a full account of his trip to the Soviet Union in August and September 1928 General von Blomberg praised the Red Army, which was not "a sort of elite guard for an unpopular regime, but a people's army in the truest sense of the word." Under the leadership of General Shaposhnikov, Chief of the General Staff, the Red Army hoped to avoid a war with Poland for the present, and concentrated on improving its tactical efficiency. It was not "capable of a large-scale offensive," but was very impressive and improving steadily.[100]

When Blomberg talked with K. J. Voroshilov in 1928, the Soviet War Commissar pledged support in the event of a Polish attack on Germany, and asked whether the Soviet Union, if invaded by Poland, could "count on" Germany. Blomberg replied that such a decision rested with responsible political authorities.[101] Among those civilians in charge of Germany's foreign policy and military planning, Stresemann and Groener would neither dismiss the contingency of exploiting a Polish-Soviet war nor rely on the Soviet Union as a dependable future ally. The Foreign Minister asked East Prussians to think

[99] *AA*, Brockdorff-Rantzau to Foreign Office, 6 and 10 April; T3 to Foreign Office, 8 May; Kühlenthal to Hans Adolf von Moltke (director of the Eastern Department in the Foreign Office from 1928 to 1931), 6 July; 9524/E671649, 651, 663, 672-5.

[100] *AA*, Blomberg report, "Reise des Chefs des Truppenamts nach Russland," 17 November 1928, 9480/H276183-236. For its text, in German and with minor omissions, see F. L. Carsten, "Reports by Two German Officers on the Red Army," *The Slavonic and East European Review*, xli (1962), 218-41; Erickson summarizes the report in *Soviet High Command*, pp. 263-68.

[101] *AA*, Blomberg report, 17 November 1928, 9480/H276191.

twice before assuming that the Red Army was powerful enough to support Germany militarily, or apolitical enough to refrain from subversive activity.[102] And Groener, wary of the "Russian sphinx . . . with an Asiatic face," thought that Germany should maintain its economic relations with the Soviet Union, but watch developments there cautiously. To ally with the Soviet Union against France would be "madness."[103]

In view of these admonitions and the weighty western half of Stresemann's policy of balance, the political auguries were less and less favorable for a military pact with Moscow. Yet the tenor of German-Soviet military cooperation seemed to rest on a mutual understanding—without a definite agreement —concerning the common enemy, Poland.[104] Blomberg valued highly the German military ventures in the Soviet Union and the contacts between training schools and staffs, all of which he believed should be continued, divorced from ideological differences in internal politics. He laid stress on the "usefulness" of a strong Red Army, providing a formidable foe for Poland. It would be a mistake for Germany to make an enemy of such a worthwhile acquaintance.[105] In December 1929 General Heye told the French military attaché that, should the opportunity present itself, for example a war between the Soviet Union and Poland, the whole of Germany " 'would march against this neighbor that they hate.' "[106] It is, therefore, unwarranted either to conclude that the German

[102] *AA*, Stresemann speech before a closed meeting in Königsberg, 16 December 1927, 7372/H166873; this passage is omitted from the version in *Vermächtnis*, III, 247f.

[103] Groener article, "Einige Bemerkungen über die russische Sphinx," 3 October 1926, Nachlass Groener, no. 165, Bundesarchiv-Militärarchiv. An excerpt appears in Groener-Geyer, *General Groener*, pp. 231-32. In 1919 also, Groener had opposed the suicidal idea of a military alliance with the Soviet Union; *ibid.*, p. 145.

[104] See Erickson, *Soviet High Command*, pp. 277-78.

[105] *AA*, Blomberg report, 17 November 1928, 9480/H276235-6; also Moscow mission to Foreign Office on some of Blomberg's impressions, 24 September, 9524/E671684-5.

[106] Georges Castellan, *Le réarmement clandestin du Reich, 1930-1935* (Paris, 1954), p. 468.

Foreign Office and Army abandoned hope of an eventual military pact with the Soviet Union or to assert that they contracted an actual military commitment.

CZECHOSLOVAKIA AND RUMANIA

To the soldier as well as the diplomat, Czechoslovakia was an important piece on the chessboard of encirclement, a knight that might combine with the French queen and Polish rook to defeat Germany. The German Army was confident that it could defend against an attack from Czechoslovakia alone.[107] But it did not expect such a move; Czechoslovak military measures near the German border seemed natural for self-defense.[108] On the other hand, Czechoslovakia might use these preparations for a joint offensive with Poland and/or France against Germany. A Polish-Czechoslovak operation from Prague and Posen could sever the Silesian salient from the Reich. For a Franco-Czechoslovak military combination, the logical avenue of Czechoslovak attack would be through Bavaria, along the valley of the Main river, toward Frankfurt on the Main. The junction of Czechoslovak and French forces in the Main valley would isolate southern Germany.[109] Germany might with good reason expect Czech-

[107] Interviews with Generals Brennecke, Busse, Flörke, and Lanz. See also Gordon, *Reichswehr and Republic*, p. 215. In 1927 the peacetime size of the Czechoslovak Army was 100,000 in the summer half-year and 140,000 in the winter. Fully mobilized for war, it would have numbered 1,220,000, but there were weapons enough for only 400,000—or about 20 divisions—in wartime. Meinck, *Deutsche Aufrüstung*, p. 2.

[108] Interviews with Generals Brennecke and Flörke. Flörke participated in a war game near the Czechoslovak border in 1929, under the direction of Colonel Wilhelm List, during which Czechoslovak supply depots and roads completed to the border were pointed out.

[109] This was the crux of Plan "N," drawn up by the French military mission and Czechoslovak General Staff in 1921 in the later stages of the German-Polish conflict in Upper Silesia. See Wandycz, *France and Her Eastern Allies*, pp. 235, 280-81. In talks with Soviet representatives in December of the same year, Seeckt had indicated

oslovakia to join France against German attempts to revise the Polish borders by force. It was less likely that Czechoslovakia would support unprovoked attacks against Germany by France or Poland, although the Foreign Office reminded the Army that Prague might not be able to withstand French pressure to enter the conflict.[110]

The two departments traded intelligence of Czechoslovak politico-military activity, notably the extent of military ties with France and Poland.[111] Shortly after the signing of the Franco-Czechoslovak political alliance on 25 January 1924, the Foreign Office sent the Defense Ministry details of joint planning between the French and Czechoslovak General Staffs.[112] The Army apparently accepted without skepticism, however, the opinion of the Foreign Office that Beneš had declined to bind his country militarily.

In the summer of 1925, when Poland sought closer ties in eastern Europe on the eve of Locarno, members of the Polish and Czechoslovak General Staffs held talks. As Rauscher observed from Warsaw, however, Czechoslovakia was against a military pact with Poland.[113] A few years later Dirksen received credible evidence from Lieutenant Colonel Schwante (T3) that the French were urging the Czechoslovaks to increase the size of their Army, and that changes and improvements were being made in Czechoslovak plans for mobilization and combined operations in the event of war against Germany.[114] But neither ministry inferred from this activity a definite military commitment from Czechoslovakia.

---

his certainty that France and Czechoslovakia would intervene if Germany supported the Soviet Union in the event of another Soviet attack on Poland. Carsten, *Reichswehr and Politics*, p. 137.

[110] See below, chap. 6.   [111] *AA*, K94/K009940ff.

[112] *AA*, Bülow to Defense Ministry, 7 February, *ibid.*, K010054-6.

[113] *AA*, Rauscher to Foreign Office, 11 September 1925 (transcript to Defense Ministry on 22 September), 6190/E465097-8.

[114] *AA*, Dirksen minute of 19 April 1928, K16/K002661-2. On 31 August 1929 the Prague mission reported to Berlin that Czechoslovak tactics in a war with Germany would include an air offensive against

Rumania might also provide help for France and Poland in a conflict with Germany, but its military planning, as Berlin came to realize, was guided by the desire for defense against Soviet aggression. In 1926 the Foreign Office kept the Defense Ministry informed of reports from Bucharest concerning Polish-Rumanian military talks. The Defense Ministry studied the text of the Polish-Rumanian military convention of May 1926, agreed with the Wilhelmstrasse that it improved Poland's strategic position in the event of a war with Germany, but soon realized that the revised convention bound Rumania to no military commitments against Germany.[115]

In 1928 persistent rumors spread—most of them first peddled in Moscow—that Rumania had joined an eastern European bloc, led by Pilsudski and supported by Britain and France, which was plotting an offensive against the Soviet Union. But Colonel von Blomberg, Chief of the *Truppenamt*, agreed with Rauscher that there was no colorable evidence for such reports and that Polish-Rumanian military arrangements dealt only with a common defensive strategy against the Soviet Union.[116]

The Defense Ministry—T3 of the *Truppenamt*—in the late 1920s held a high regard for the Hungarian Army, and a low opinion of the Italians.[117] But the German Army did not count on Hungary to neutralize Czechoslovakia in a European conflict, for Hungary was itself held in check by the other two members of the Little Entente, Yugoslavia and Rumania.[118] The German Navy hypothesized active Italian

---

bridges on the Elbe, Oder, and Main rivers, railroad yards, and electricity plants; K94/K010114.

[115] See above, chap. 1.

[116] *AA*, Rauscher to Foreign Office, 6 December 1928, K178/K030939-42; and 26 February 1929, 4569/E169196-7; Blomberg to Foreign Office, 28 March, K178/K030972.

[117] Castellan, *Réarmement*, pp. 492, 463.

[118] The French General Staff studied the possibility of Hungary's coming to the aid of Germany; *ibid.*, p. 492. On military contingency

support against France, but the Army was not inclined to rate Italy as an ally in a continental war.[119] Finally, although aware of the pressure that an *Anschluss* with Austria would have put on Czechoslovakia, most officers still thought of *Anschluss* in terms of *Deutschtum*, not part of a grand strategic design against the French alliance system nor—like the Corridor—an absolute strategic necessity for the Reich.[120]

By and large, the Army's strategic appraisal of eastern and southeastern European affairs corresponded to that of the Foreign Office: Poland was Germany's only avowed enemy in that part of Europe; the Soviet Union, Germany's single likely military ally; and the individual members of the Little Entente, although antirevisionist, had not promised Poland military support against Germany. During the first half of the decade, the Army was more eager for a German-Soviet military pact than the Foreign Office was, and acted independently in the early stages of secret military collaboration with the Red Army. But after 1925, the Army was more disposed to accept the Wilhelmstrasse's authority over Germany's eastern policy and military enterprises in the Soviet Union.

---

plans of the Little Entente in 1929, when the three staffs held the first of their annual meetings, see Rudolf Kiszling, *Die militärischen Vereinbarungen der Kleinen Entente 1929-1937* (Munich, 1959), pp. 10-11, 14ff.

[119] See below, chaps. 6, 7.

[120] Interviews with General Flörke and others. Austria, completely omitted from the Army's operational studies of the late 1920s, appeared for the first time in the General Staff tour of 1931; below, chap. 9.

CHAPTER IV

The West

TO GERMANY'S west lay the perpetrators of the Versailles *Diktat*. Their occupation of part of Germany deprived it of sovereignty; their military restrictions and surveillance impaired Germany's means of self-defense; and their territorial changes mutilated the organic Bismarckian Reich. This record was hardly one to engender a mood of reconciliation in the German Army, which viewed its mission as the preservation of a fully sovereign and militarily powerful state. On the other hand, persuasive arguments favored a general rapprochement with the West: there Germany might discover its best chance of gaining political support for revision of the economic, military, and territorial clauses of the treaty; there Germany might work out an intelligent method for avoiding a future war on two fronts. Two closely related facets of the Army's politico-military thinking therefore need to be considered: its attitude toward Germany's western policy; and its assessment of Germany's military security against France and the French alliance with Poland.

POLICY

In the Seeckt era, the Army Command neither regarded the West as a solid anti-German bloc nor upheld Stresemann's policy of understanding. In 1920 Seeckt and the *Truppenamt* had blamed the Entente for conspiring to create Poland and destroy Germany.[1] But when Anglo-French differences (in the Near East and North Africa, and over reparations and the resumption of trade with the Soviet Union) began to

[1] See above, chap. 3, p. 98.

erode the Entente, Seeckt thought that Germany might eventually answer Britain's quest for a continental ally in a war against France.[2] By 1922 Anglo-German relations had improved enough to raise the question of consistency between secret collaboration with the Soviet Union and cooperation with Britain, whose Foreign Secretary, Conservative Lord Curzon, was vehemently anti-Soviet. Seeckt answered that to side with Britain against France did not stand in the way of Germany's military relations with the Soviet Union, and that German-Soviet relations " 'would not have a decisive influence on Britain's attitude in searching for an ally.' "[3]

In 1925, Seeckt's interest in an Anglo-German understanding cooled as Stresemann stepped up his policy of rapprochement with the West. In January, he reassured the Soviet Ambassador that it was " 'impossible [for Germany] to lean either on France or Britain,' " and that Germany would not

[2] Seeckt memorandum of 11 September 1922, in Freund, *Unholy Alliance*, p. 136. Major Oskar Ritter von Niedermayer must have found it particularly difficult to adjust to Germany's transformation from Britain's world-political rival to its potential continental ally. In February 1920 Niedermayer, the "German Lawrence" of the World War, read a paper in the Defense Ministry describing his expedition to the Middle East and outlining the means of invading India so as to precipitate the total collapse of the British Empire. He granted, however, that political conditions would have to change before such an attack would be possible. "Beurteilung der Militärgeographischen Verhältnisse eines Angriffs auf Indien," in Nachlass Gessler, no. 55, Bundesarchiv (Koblenz). Early in the war Seeckt too had found attractive the "Alexander idea" of an offensive toward India, as a means of "remedying [Germany's] restricted insular position." Letter to Joachim von Winterfeldt-Menkin, 25 January 1915, Seeckt Papers (microfilm), roll 20, Stück 90.

[3] Seeckt memorandum of 11 September 1922, in Freund, *Unholy Alliance*, p. 136. Seeckt had taken the same position in a conversation with Karl Radek in January 1922; Carsten, *Reichswehr and Politics*, p. 138. Four years earlier, on the other hand, he had suggested that Britain would do well to align with Germany after the war for assistance against Britain's two real commercial and colonial rivals, the Soviet Union and the United States; letter to Arnold Rechberg, 3 October 1918, Seeckt Papers (microfilm), roll 19, Stück 89.

ally with Britain to oppose the Soviet Union. Still, Seeckt believed that Germany would eventually be able to take advantage of an Anglo-French conflict.[4] This view was shared by Lieutenant Colonel Joachim von Stülpnagel:

> Germany must exploit the conflicts between Britain and France, which in the long run cannot abate; she must not mitigate them by sacrificing her own interests, but must on the contrary sharpen them, so that the impression is created abroad that not Germany, but France, is responsible, if the British proposals for a League of Nations, disarmament, and economic pacification cannot be realized. If we succeed in this, Britain will in the long run only be able to obtain her aims vis-à-vis France by force of arms at the side of Germany. To work towards this should be the duty of German diplomacy, and is the task of the soldier.[5]

Fundamental to the Army Command's western demeanor was its strong anti-French prejudice and its conviction that nothing short of force would induce France to " 'right the wrong' " of Versailles and save Germany from its " 'final destruction . . . as a power.' "[6] Germany should endeavor to build an international constellation that would force France and Poland to make concessions to Germany. To Seeckt, Stresemann's western policy seemed to do just the opposite. At a cabinet meeting on 24 June 1925, which lasted almost six hours, the general voiced his strong opposition to Germany's reaching an understanding with the western powers. The security pact would be advantageous to France, not Germany, for it would alleviate France's real (not pretended) fear of Germany. It would mean a recognition of the current Franco-German border, thus a renunciation of Alsace-Lor-

[4] In Carsten, *Reichswehr and Politics*, pp. 235-36.

[5] Memorandum of 20 February 1924, *ibid.*, p. 199.

[6] *Ibid.* During the war Seeckt had contrasted British objectivity with the French psychological illness that made them aspire to an "orgy of conquest." Letter to von Winterfeldt, 4 August 1916, Seeckt Papers (microfilm), roll 20, Stück 90.

raine. To Stresemann's assertion that the security pact would not stand in the way of future agreements concerning borders between two states, Seeckt replied that borders were changed not by treaties but by force, a viewpoint that the military believed had been repeatedly validated in the recent past. After Stresemann's rejoinder that Germany could not think of recovering Alsace-Lorraine, Seeckt chided, "That is the only thing Germany *should* think of." Furthermore, Seeckt feared that rapprochement with the West would knock Germany's good relations with the Soviet Union into a cocked hat, and on this point he was supported by Brockdorff-Rantzau.[7]

Much the same reasoning prompted Seeckt's opposition to Germany's entry into the League of Nations. Seeckt suspected that German membership would give France even greater control over Germany's military affairs, and would alienate the Soviet Union.[8] At that same heated cabinet meeting, he averred that in the interests of good German-Soviet relations German entry was "impossible."[9] In March 1925 in a long conference with Secretary of State Schubert, General Hasse, the Chief of the *Truppenamt*, also warned that Germany's entry would contradict its Soviet policy, so that Germany "would then have to choose between the League and Russia." He listened skeptically to Schubert's opinion that Germany, as a member, would in fact be in a position to help the Soviets, and argued that joining the League would put Germany "in tow of the Allies."[10]

Neither Seeckt nor the other military leaders were totally

[7] *RK*, cabinet protocol, 24 June, 3543/D765055-7; a complete account of the meeting in Meier-Welcker, *Seeckt*, pp. 470-77. Seeckt was not always so talkative in cabinet meetings. According to Chamberlain, Stresemann could not decide whether Seeckt's usual taciturnity "concealed real ability or merely an empty mind." Chamberlain (Geneva) to Foreign Office (Tyrrell), 6 December 1926, *DBFP*, Ser. IA, II, 580.

[8] Rabenau, *Seeckt*, p. 407; Carsten, *Reichswehr and Politics*, pp. 200, 206f. See below, n. 11, for evidence to the contrary.

[9] *RK*, cabinet protocol, 24 June 1925, 3543/D765055-7.

[10] *AA*, Schubert notes, 19 March, 4562/E155091-2.

oblivious to the advantages of cooperating with the West. General Hasse, no supporter of Stresemann's League policy, resisted the other extreme of aligning with the Soviet Union and sacrificing "all the advantages that we can and must get from joining the League," in particular, the evacuation of the Rhineland.[11] In 1924 Seeckt worked with Schleicher to win acceptance of the Dawes Plan, which regulated Germany's payment of reparations and brought about an end to the Ruhr occupation, and was annoyed at those inveterate Nationalists who voted against it. Furthermore, Seeckt was too sensible of Germany's politico-military weakness to deny Gessler's judgment that a pact with the Allies to safeguard the Franco-German border would bring Germany a certain degree of security in the west.[12]

Nevertheless, Seeckt's antagonism toward Stresemann's policy was bitter, and his wife helped to advertise it in Berlin's social circles.[13] Differences between the two men were exacerbated during the presidential election campaign of 1925, when Stresemann opposed the general's candidacy. Personal animosity aside, Seeckt's political contrariness stemmed in large part from his limited view of Germany's foreign policy objectives. Seeckt believed that only after Germany had regained its political and military power could it adopt an "active" foreign policy, appear attractive to Britain as a continental ally, and be able "to regain everything we have lost."[14] The mid-1920s, he emphasized in his criticism of Stresemann, was not the opportune time for such a policy:

[11] *AA, ibid.*, E155092. According to Gessler, this had also been Seeckt's advice to the cabinet in the autumn of 1924; *Reichswehrpolitik*, pp. 317-18.

[12] Gessler's opinion in *RK*, cabinet protocol, 24 June 1925, 3543/D765061-2.

[13] Frau von Seeckt's activity did not escape Stresemann's attention; *AA*, Stresemann note of 26 July 1925, 7129/H147935.

[14] *AA*, Stresemann note of 26 June, *ibid.*, H147890. Meier-Welcker emphasizes that the phrase about regaining everything, attributed to Seeckt, is not in the protocol; *Seeckt*, p. 473n.

In foreign affairs I view the Locarno-Geneva policy as a mistake because it ties us down and is of no advantage to us. We are still too weak to share in taking the lead, and are thus to others an object, not a subject, at most a compliant ally who can be dropped when differences have been reconciled or a better ally can be found. We could have waited and strengthened ourselves internally first, and above all we could have kept a completely free hand toward the east. That we no longer have. We have succumbed to British influence and are subservient to British interests.[15]

The attitude of both Seeckt and Hasse toward Britain is a measure of the muddle in the Army's attitude toward the West. Seeckt foresaw an eventual Anglo-German tie directed against France, and Hasse "could envision a settlement of the general situation only with the aid of Russia *and* England."[16] Yet to cooperate too much with Britain in 1925—that is, to sign the security pact and join the League—was to be Britain's bondsman. Similarly, to reach an understanding with France before Germany possessed sufficient means for effective political authority was to sink deeper into international serfdom.

Stresemann agreed that Germany could resume its position as a Great Power only after recovering its economic and military power, but he did not believe that Germany would soon be in a position to " 'pound the table with her fist.' "[17] Nor

[15] Seeckt letter to his sister, 4 April 1926; Rabenau, *Seeckt*, p. 430. See also *ibid.*, p. 422. Concerning Germany's eastern policy, however, Seeckt's interpretation of what constituted an "active" policy was different: Germany could strengthen itself politically and militarily by cooperating with the Soviet Union, a "policy of action" the goal of which was to increase Germany's means of pursuing a still " 'more active policy' " in the future. See Seeckt memorandum of 11 September 1922, in Freund, *Unholy Alliance*, pp. 136-37.

[16] *AA*, Schubert notes of conversation with Hasse, 19 March 1925, 4562/E155092.

[17] *RK*, cabinet protocol, 24 June 1925, 3543/D765060; Gasiorowski, "Stresemann and Poland before Locarno," p. 41.

138

would he accept that the only alternative in the west to what Seeckt described as a "policy of action" was immobility. Indeed his western policy met the prerequisite set forth by Seeckt in his memorandum of 11 September 1922: " 'An active policy must have a goal and a driving force. To carry it out it is essential to assess one's own strength correctly and at the same time to understand the methods and aims of the other Powers.' "[18] Stresemann correctly judged that his policy did not mean servitude. Quite the contrary, it was a move toward regaining international status and national sovereignty, and a shrewd gambit in the game of peaceful treaty revision by a second-rate military power.

Seeckt viewed Locarno as the project of " 'officious upstarts who must have a hand in everything, like Stresemann, the man of general distrust. . . .' "[19] But Stresemann was supported by men in the Foreign Office and cabinet who valued understanding for its design. Hans Luther, Chancellor during the Locarno negotiations, defended Stresemann's policy in contrast with "the policy of those who simply wait for the day when we once again have a great army, and until then twiddle their thumbs and trust that Providence will one day provide us some miraculous means of defending ourselves against our enemies. . . ."[20]

Although Gessler supported Seeckt on matters of special interest to the Army, on the main lines of foreign policy he "stood behind Stresemann against the opposing views of Seeckt."[21] In cabinet discussions on the security pact, for example, he upheld Stresemann, a surprise to the Foreign Minister. Moreover, in contrast to Seeckt, who questioned the competence of the Wilhelmstrasse to shape and conduct Germany's foreign policy, Gessler affirmed that it was up to the Foreign Office to decide "whether the security pact was politi-

[18] In Freund, *Unholy Alliance*, p. 135.
[19] Seeckt letter to his sister, 4 April 1926; Rabenau, *Seeckt*, p. 430.
[20] *AA*, Stresemann note of 26 June 1925, 7129/H147890 (also in *Vermächtnis*, II, 110).
[21] Gessler, *Reichswehrpolitik*, p. 314. But see below, n. 26.

cally a necessity."[22] Personal relations between Stresemann and Gessler were never very cordial, and Stresemann made no secret of his opposition to the Defense Minister's presidential candidacy in 1925.[23] Moreover, Gessler was less optimistic than Stresemann that rapprochement with France would have quick and favorable results. But Gessler himself rejects as "a myth" the opinion that the Bendlerstrasse campaigned behind the scenes against Stresemann's western policy. He concludes that the forces of attraction between the two departments were stronger than their differences over minor points.[24]

After Seeckt's dismissal these forces combined more sympathetically to improve Germany's international situation. The Army's attitude toward the West after 1926 was not so boldly proclaimed as when Seeckt had been Chief of the Army Command, for General Heye was politically less aggressive, and the energies of the Defense Minister and his most influential assistant, Kurt von Schleicher, were bent largely toward internal civil-military matters. Still, they were more willing than Seeckt to collaborate with the Foreign Office and less adamant in naming rapprochement with the West a political blunder. Colonel Erich von Bonin, chief of T2, the Organization Section (*Organisationsabteilung*) in the *Truppenamt*, shared this cooperative spirit. Late in 1926 he ob-

[22] *AA*, Stresemann note of 19 July 1925, 7129/H147917 (also in *Vermächtnis*, II, 152); Gessler, *Reichswehrpolitik*, pp. 167ff.

[23] See Turner, *Stresemann and Politics*, pp. 193-94. Prof. Turner points out that Stresemann's reasons were not chiefly personal but political: ". . . according to reports from the Paris Embassy, the election of [Gessler] would have much the same effect as the election of Seeckt, since the French were convinced that the Minister was simply a tool of the Army. Even though Stresemann agreed that this was an inaccurate assumption on the part of the French, he felt that it would definitely be a foreign policy handicap. . . ."

[24] Gessler, *Reichswehrpolitik*, pp. 314-15, 317, 320. We may wonder, however, whether the Skoblevsky affair was not a major exception to interdepartmental attraction. See above, chap. 3. Gessler does not mention the Skoblevsky incident in his book.

140

served that the Treaty of Locarno, by which Germany had recognized its western borders, had contributed to the current atmosphere of peace and arbitration and reduced the threat of war. Bonin asked that the Army concede these positive effects of Germany's western policy.[25]

Objectivity and patience in the sphere of foreign policy were essential qualities for the civilians and officers in the Defense Ministry if they were to develop a closer relationship with the Foreign Office. Wilhelm Groener possessed both. On better personal terms with Stresemann than Gessler was, and more conscientious about maintaining friendly cooperation between his ministry and the Wilhelmstrasse,[26] the new Defense Minister since the end of the war had advocated cautious waiting and cultivating good relations with the West. In 1919 he had written: "In our situation we cannot exercise enough reserve in the area of foreign policy. We must learn to wait for things to develop in order to recognize for certain where our advantage lies. But we must pursue one assignment energetically, tenaciously, and with all means: the revision of the Treaty of Versailles." Thus, he had urged that, although it remained to be seen whether the League would provide a stage for pacifists or an arena for new alignments of power, Germany must use the League "as a political means toward revision" of the intolerable terms of the peace treaty. And in 1926 he warned against the consequences of combining with the Soviet Union to oppose France, falling out with

[25] Müller, *Vaterland*, p. 297. For a T2 memorandum (probably by Bonin) of 6 November 1926, see Rabenau, *Seeckt*, pp. 482-83.

[26] Groener-Geyer, *General Groener*, pp. 251-52; Theodor Eschenburg, *Die improvisierte Demokratie: Gesammelte Aufsätze zur Weimarer Republik* (Munich, 1963), p. 244. Stresemann told Eschenburg more than once that "Groener showed very much more understanding for his foreign policy than Gessler," who had been afraid of Army officers. While Gessler was still Defense Minister, Stresemann remarked " 'that in all countries the relations between Defense Ministry and Foreign Ministry can, at best, be called correct. . . .' " Speech before leaders of the DVP, 22 November 1925, in Turner, "Rede Stresemanns," pp. 427-28.

141

Britain over the Soviet Union (which would be to France's advantage), and becoming involved in a conflict between the West and the Soviet Union.[27]

Schleicher, too, was a cautious realist. In dividing Germany's objectives into three main categories, he drew an indissoluble connection between domestic and foreign policy, between internal strength and external gains. First in importance was full state sovereignty, which required internal political unity, the freedom of German soil from Allied occupation, and an end to Allied military surveillance in Germany. Second, Germany had to achieve economic stability, which demanded an expeditious settlement of the reparations question. These two objectives, he believed, could be reached only by cooperating with the West, not by continually affronting the Allies by demanding the abrogation of the "war guilt clause" (Article 231) of the Treaty of Versailles, a tiresome and ineffectual habit of the parties of the Right. Finally, after accomplishing these first priorities, Germany could essay a foreign policy strong enough to insure territorial revision in the east.[28]

Schleicher supported Stresemann's policy of understanding, the essentials of which were similar to his own program for German recovery.[29] Neither he nor Stresemann, however,

[27] Groener memorandum of late July 1919, in Wilhelm Groener, *Lebenserinnerungen*, ed. Friedrich Freiherr Hiller von Gaertringen (Göttingen, 1957), pp. 517-18; also above, chap. 3, n. 103.

[28] Müller, *Vaterland*, pp. 199, 224-25, 293; Eugen Ott, "Ein Bild des Generals Kurt von Schleicher; aus den Erfahrungen seiner Mitarbeiter dargestellt," *Politische Studien*, x (1959), 365-66; interview with Ambassador Ott. Both Müller and Ott (who became military attaché to Japan, 1934-38, and German Ambassador to Tokyo, 1938-43) were members of Schleicher's staff for most of the 1920s. On differences between Schleicher and Seeckt over priorities, see Rabenau, *Seeckt*, pp. 117-18; Carsten, *Reichswehr and Politics*, p. 17; Gordon, *Reichswehr and Republic*, p. 312.

[29] Ambassador Ott recalls that Schleicher was disappointed at Stresemann's slowness in building up closer relations with Briand; interview. On the frequent evening chats between the two—Schleicher

accepted Arnold Rechberg's reasons for Franco-German rapprochement. Rechberg, an industrialist and political gadfly, had sounded out Stresemann in 1923 concerning Franco-German relations.[30] He had proposed industrial settlements between the two countries to ease the pressure France was exerting on German heavy industry in Rhineland-Westphalia in response to the Treaty of Rapallo and agreements between the Soviet Union and German industrial interests headed by the Krupp firm.

But the anti-Soviet bias in Rechberg's plan for a military alliance between Germany, France, and Britain proved too fervid for the Foreign Office and Defense Ministry, both of which wanted to preserve ties with Moscow in spite of rapprochement with the West. In 1925 Stresemann cautioned against paying any attention to Rechberg's ideas.[31] Two years later, when Rechberg talked with Schleicher about a Franco-German industrial and military alliance, Schleicher referred him to Gessler. The Defense Minister in turn told Rechberg to go to the Foreign Office, since he himself was in no official position to deal with such a question of foreign policy. This Rechberg declined to do, because he believed that Stresemann was too engrossed in his Locarno policy to give him a fair hearing. Instead he went to London, where anti-Soviet feeling had been high since the "Zinoviev letter" episode of

---

preferred Mosel wine, Stresemann Pilsener beer—see H. R. Berndorff, *General zwischen Ost und West* (Hamburg, 1951), pp. 141f.

[30] *AA*, Rechberg to Stresemann, 6 April 1923, 7114/H145292-7; also letters of 20 and 26 April, 7115/H145370-2, 408. During the war Rechberg had campaigned for an early peace by means of a separate understanding with France. See Eberhard von Vietsch, *Arnold Rechberg und das Problem der politischen West-Orientierung Deutschlands nach dem 1. Weltkrieg* (Koblenz, 1958), pp. 23ff. Stresemann's brother-in-law, Kurt von Kleefeld, had been a strong supporter of Rechberg's ideas both during and after the war. The first contact between Stresemann and Rechberg had occurred about 1917; *ibid.*, p. 41 and n.

[31] *AA*, Stresemann note, 24 July, 7129/H147925.

October 1924. There, according to a report in the Wilhelm-strasse, his ideas met with some support among those who thought that the Soviet threat to British colonial interests must one day be ended by force.[32]

Rechberg was deprived of a useful ally by the death of General (Ret.) Max Hoffmann in July 1927, who since the war had prescribed a western European alliance for the "liberation of Russia."[33] But Rechberg and a fellow industrialist, Moritz Klönne, continued their campaign. In February 1929 Rechberg and General (Ret.) Georg von der Lippe met in Paris with Poincaré and former French War Minister and Premier Paul Painlevé, and showed them Rechberg's memorandum on an alliance between Germany and the West. In it he enthusiastically outlined Franco-German cooperation against the double menace of Bolshevism and American financial and industrial hegemony. Poland would cede Danzig and the Corridor to Germany, and in return the three allies would guarantee Poland its borders with the Soviet Union, free use of the Vistula, a free harbor in Danzig, and a harbor in Memel. If in addition Poland joined the military alliance, it would become "the advance post of France and Germany against Bolshevism." Ambassador Hoesch reproved Rechberg and Lippe for not consulting the Foreign Office before coming to Paris, and reminded them of Germany's relations with the Soviet Union, but he did not dissuade them from holding further talks with French political leaders, for he found most interesting the solicitous reception given Rechberg by Poincaré and Painlevé.[34]

[32] *AA*, memorandum by Karl Ritter, 10 June 1927, 4506/ E124003-8.

[33] See Hoffmann's essay, "Moscow, the Root of All Evil; the Problem of Bolshevism," in his *War Diaries and Other Papers*, trans. Eric Sutton (2 vols.; London, 1929), II, 363ff. See also Walter Schellenberg, *The Labyrinth: Memoirs of Walter Schellenberg*, trans. Louis Hagen (New York, 1956), pp. 24-25. Some of Rechberg's letters to Hoffmann are printed in Vietsch, *Rechberg*, pp. 167-72.

[34] *AA*, Hoesch to Foreign Office, 28 February, 1 and 4 March 1929, 4506/E124014-31.

In Geneva in March, Briand told Stresemann of Rechberg's activities in Paris, including his statement that the proposition of a joint military invasion of the Soviet Union had advocates in the German Army. Stresemann replied that this was nonsense, that Rechberg spoke in no official capacity, and that "no one else in Germany would have anything to do with a military attack against Russia."[35] At the urging of Schleicher, however, Stresemann permitted Schubert to grant General von der Lippe an interview in the Foreign Office. Schubert tried to weigh down Lippe's inflated impression that Paris and London were all agog over Rechberg's plan; he questioned whether the French government would really take it seriously and reminded Lippe that Germany's geopolitical situation required "a very farsighted and also often very complicated foreign policy."[36] Schleicher's recommendation that the Foreign Office receive Lippe stemmed not from any indulgent interest in the Rechberg plan, but from a desire to see that Lippe was swayed by responsible authorities before eagerly disseminating Rechberg's ideas even more widely around Berlin. Schleicher himself viewed these ideas as "absolute fantasies" and "complete nonsense," and refused to discuss them further with General Lippe.[37]

Stresemann, Groener, and Schleicher had already tacitly agreed that the Polish question could not be resolved by forming a western bloc against the Soviet Union.[38] In spite

[35] *AA*, Foreign Office minute, 5 March 1929, 2945/D573885-6.

[36] *AA*, Schubert notes, 11 April 1929, 4506/E124042-8. Later in the month, Schubert gave similar advice to Klönne, who had been present at a recent meeting in Berlin between Rechberg and Paul Reynaud, son-in-law of M. Schneider-Creuzot (the French industrialist), and a rising political figure on the French Right; *ibid.*, E124066-70.

[37] *AA*, Schubert notes of 4, 5, and 9 April, 21 May, *ibid.*, E124037-41, 078. On relations between Schleicher and Rechberg, see Vietsch, *Rechberg*, pp. 102-105, 207-10.

[38] This—as well as their objection to General Heye's unusual step of acting on his own in foreign policy matters—explains their annoyance upon learning that the Chief of the Army Command had sanctioned Rechberg's trip to Paris in February. Heye himself re-

of its anti-Bolshevism, the Army had no intention of forfeiting its ties with the Soviet Union by forming a military alliance with France, whose government was itself working for closer relations with Moscow. For Groener and Schleicher, as for Stresemann, the most favorable international circumstances for Germany included both western and Soviet support for territorial revision in the east.

SECURITY

The military threat from France took two forms; either a unilateral move against Germany from the west or a combined attack by France and its eastern allies, Poland and Czechoslovakia. The French were unlikely to attempt the first following the adverse domestic and international reaction against the Ruhr occupation in 1923; moreover, agreements with the West established concrete preventive measures. The Dawes Plan afforded Germany legal and procedural protection against arbitrary and unilateral sanctions in the event of a German default in reparations payments.[39] And the guarantors of Locarno, Britain and Italy, were obliged to come to Germany's aid 1) if, before the evacuation of the Rhineland, France committed an act of unprovoked aggression, such as an invasion across the Rhine; and 2) if, after the evacuation, France flagrantly violated the Franco-German border or reoccupied the demilitarized Rhineland.[40]

---

assured Stresemann that he had said nothing to Rechberg and Lippe about the political question of a Franco-German understanding, but had merely warned them of the "spirit of revenge" still strong in Germany. On Rechberg and the anti-French *Stahlhelm*, see Vietsch, *Rechberg*, pp. 112, 118, 124.

[39] Northedge, *Troubled Giant*, pp. 191-92; Eyck, *Weimar Republic*, I, 308.

[40] See above, chap. 2. Although Chamberlain told the Committee of Imperial Defence that Locarno obligated Britain to come to Germany's aid if France repeated the Ruhr invasion, it is unlikely that Britain would have intervened against France in a Franco-

Against a two-front attack, the deterrent power of Locarno and the policy of understanding was less precise. In 1924, when T3 of the *Truppenamt* requested information on Franco-Polish agreements, the Foreign Office replied that these included a secret military pact. The French had not promised Poland unconditional support in a war with the Soviet Union: "the Franco-Polish alliance system should be viewed as directed primarily against Germany."[41] The Wilhelmstrasse continued to view that alliance as the foundation of French efforts to surround Germany, and did not rush to the reassuring conclusion that Locarno would effectively block French intervention even if Poland were the aggressor.[42] Still, the diplomats were quicker than the generals to see in Locarno a sign of Germany's international resurgence, temper their anti-French prejudice, minimize the actual current threat to Germany, and concede that defects existed in the French system of security.[43]

Ulrich Rauscher seconded suspicions in the Wilhelmstrasse concerning the validity of what T3 regarded as a renewal of the Franco-Polish military convention of 1921, allegedly signed on 18 January 1926.[44] In May 1928 he told of the skepticism among military observers in Warsaw over whether Pilsudski would allow large numbers of French troops to en-

---

German conflict; Jacobson, *Locarno Diplomacy*, p. 24; Wolfers, *Britain and France between Two Wars*, pp. 230-31, 260-61.

[41] *AA*, Foreign Office to T3, 2 December 1924, K177/K030294-5.

[42] See below, chap. 6.

[43] This troubled General Wetzell, who, while still Chief of the *Truppenamt* early in 1927, thought that the Foreign Office did not realize the full extent to which the youth of France and Poland were being trained militarily; *AA*, minute (by Dirksen?) of talk with Major Fischer about a recent conference between Wetzell and Schubert, 27 January, 6698/H111747.

[44] *AA*, T3 (Colonel Wichmann) to Foreign Office, 28 January 1928; Zechlin to Colonel Wichmann, 6 March; K177/K030318-20, 360. The version of the convention enclosed in T3's message was identical to the first of two texts sent by T3 to the Foreign Office in 1931; see below, chap. 9, n. 47.

ter Poland in a Polish-Soviet war, whether the French would risk landing troops and munitions in Danzig, and whether France's domestic situation would permit it to send an expeditionary force to Poland. Rauscher recommended that Franco-Polish military agreements be considered as part of the entire complex of such accords between France and each member of the Little Entente, and between Poland and Rumania, and he doubted that their sum "rigidly controlled" the strategic situation in the east.[45]

Nor did the Foreign Office trust the reports received by T3 of talks in Copenhagen among French, Danish, and Polish officials concerning a common military strategy in the Baltic. Ulrich von Hassell, the Minister to Copenhagen, agreed that the French wanted an arrangement with Denmark to secure its sea communications with Poland, but argued that the Danish government and Navy were opposed to allying with France and Poland against the Soviet Union and Germany.[46]

Franco-Polish strategic accord was confounded by Pilsudski's proud recalcitrance in discussions with the French General Staff, and embarrassed by the realization in both capitals that French foreign policy and military planning implicitly weakened the Franco-Polish alliance. The Treaty of Locarno restricted France's freedom of movement in the event of a

[45] *AA*, Rauscher to Foreign Office, 16 May (transcript to T3 on 18 July), *ibid.*, K030362-7. On these various military arrangements and the difficulty of coordinating military planning among allies with different political objectives, see Maurice Gamelin, *Servir* (3 vols.; Paris, 1946-47), II, 24-27, 465-74. The question of whether and how France was obligated to intervene in the event of German paramilitary offensives—supported by Berlin—into Danzig and the Corridor troubled the Quai d'Orsay and French General Staff, both of which believed that the secret convention of February 1921 committed France too much and was a victory for the Polish negotiators, Pilsudski and General Kazimierz Sosnkowski. Wandycz, *France and Her Eastern Allies*, pp. 217-19.

[46] *AA*, T3 to Foreign Office, 29 February 1928; Hassell to Foreign Office, 19 March, 13 April, 23 May; K154/K017469-71, 473-6, 527, 529.

German-Polish conflict.[47] And once French troops evacuated
the Rhineland, France would lose not simply a defensive buffer but a staging area on German soil for an attack into the
very heart of the Reich. In anticipation of this strategic
change, and facing troop reductions, the French Army urged
the construction of a heavily fortified barrier near the Franco-
German border. Construction began early in 1930. Named
after the Minister of War at that time, the Maginot Line was
expected to provide cover or protection (*couverture*) against
a sudden German attack while French reserves mobilized for
a counteroffensive. Yet French military planning in the 1920s
already contained a strategic bias that viewed the projected
fortress system almost exclusively as a defensive device, not
as a base for offensive operations. France, in short, was about
to relinquish its forward positions in the Rhineland, and
seemed also to be abdicating its responsibility to support Poland effectively from French soil.[48]

[47] See above, chap. 2; below, chap. 6.

[48] On the Maginot Line, evacuation, military reorganization, and
French defensive doctrine in the late 1920s and early 1930s, see
Tony Albord, *La défense nationale* (Paris, 1958), pp. 287-89; Philip
C. F. Bankwitz, *Maxime Weygand and Civil-Military Relations in
Modern France* (Cambridge, Mass., 1967), pp. 40-47, 83-92, 116-24;
Édouard Bonnefous, *Histoire politique de la Troisième République*
(7 vols.; Paris, 1956ff.), IV, 210-12, 240-41, 244-45; Richard D.
Challener, *The French Theory of the Nation in Arms, 1866-1939*
(New York, 1955), chaps. 4, 5, pp. 215-24; Jacques Chastenet,
Histoire de la Troisième République (7 vols.; Paris, 1952-63), V,
192-94; Gamelin, *Servir*, II, 7-10, 21-24, 41-45, 66-72; Irving M.
Gibson, "The Maginot Line," *Journal of Modern History*, XVII
(1945), 130-46; Jacobson, *Locarno Diplomacy*, pp. 104-13, 322-28;
Enno Kraehe, "The Motives behind the Maginot Line," *Military
Affairs*, VIII (1944), 109-22; Paul-Marie de La Gorce, *The French
Army: A Military-Political History*, trans. Kenneth Douglas (New
York, 1963), pp. 270ff.; Jacques Nobécourt, *Une Histoire politique
de l'armée* (2 vols.; Paris, 1967), I, chap. 13; Paul-Émile Tournoux,
*Haut commandement, gouvernement et défense des frontières du nord
et de l'est, 1919-1939* (Paris, 1960), especially chap. 10, and pp.
335ff.

The vision of a "war of liberation" against France, inspired both by obvious strategic vulnerability in the west, where the Rhineland was occupied and demilitarized, and by hatred of servitude to the Versailles *Diktat*, did not encourage the Army to entertain the idea that Locarno and French strategy might have opened a fissure in the encirclement of Germany. The French preponderance in the west had been a check against German intervention in the Polish-Soviet war of 1920, and had dissuaded Seeckt from using regular troops against the Polish rising in Silesia in the spring of 1921, for fear that France would retaliate by occupying further German territory.[49] In 1923, after the French marched into the Ruhr, Seeckt ordered various measures begun for mobilization and supply in the event that the German policy of passive resistance changed to active military prevention of deeper French penetration. In spite of emergency preparations, however, Seeckt had to advise Chancellor Cuno that the Army was not capable of an offensive in case of war.[50]

In the annual "generals' tours" he conducted, Seeckt repeatedly stressed defense, usually against France in the west but also in the east against Czechoslovakia and Poland.[51] Seeckt's long-range strategic plan for Germany, however, contained an ultimate departure from the defensive: although Germany must avoid conflict while it remained militarily weak, it should strive for an international alignment—Anglo-French discord and German-Soviet understanding—that would enable it to carry out an "active" policy of revision (or "liberation") against both France and Poland.

The logical consequence of Seeckt's strategy was a war on two fronts, for Seeckt seems to have concluded fatalistically that because Germany was surrounded by enemies its destiny

[49] Gordon, *Reichswehr and Republic*, p. 343.

[50] *Ibid.*, p. 255. "Some officers, like the normally moderate Lieutenant Colonel Joachim von Stülpnagel, wished to sponsor a popular rising against the French, but Seeckt emphatically forbade such a course."

[51] Interview with General Friedrich Wilhelm Hauck; Rabenau, *Seeckt*, pp. 520, 522.

was to fight them all. The general, who during the World War had demonstrated an unusually flexible and broad view of international relations, rejected the notion that rapprochement with France might break Germany's encirclement and peacefully lay the specter of a two-front war.[52]

Again the year 1926—Seeckt's dismissal—marks a temporal divide. Avoiding a war on two fronts, though not a novel post-Seecktian conception, became the outstanding feature of German politico-military activity after 1926. Having studied Germany's wartime economic problems, the Army Ordnance Office (*Heereswaffenamt*) drew up recommendations for economic mobilization in a future conflict, emphasizing that, because of Germany's lack of raw materials, it must "never again get into a two-front war."[53] The Defense Ministry clearly accepted this admonition by agreeing with Stresemann that Germany should try to neutralize the western front through a policy of rapprochement with France. Gessler, Groener, and Schleicher, all of whom upheld the primacy of the Foreign Office in the sphere of foreign policy, backed Stresemann's policy of understanding, and thus its corollary, to take no steps in the west in transgression of the Treaty of Versailles. Strategically, Groener and Schleicher were particularly vehement against fighting a war in the west, which Germany could not possibly win. They believed it wiser to look after the eastern defenses, for Poland was the most immediate threat.[54]

[52] See Seeckt's memorandum of 11 September 1922. " 'The whole policy of reconciliation and appeasement towards France . . . is hopeless in as far as it aims at political success.' " France's objective, in Seeckt's view, was " 'the complete destruction of Germany, not yet fully brought about. . . .' " Wheeler-Bennett, *Nemesis of Power*, p. 135. (Freund omits part of this in *Unholy Alliance*, p. 136.)

[53] Müller, *Vaterland*, p. 297.

[54] Meinck, *Deutsche Aufrüstung*, pp. 12-13; interviews with Ambassador Ott and General Hans Speidel, who in 1930 joined the French section of T3 and gave Groener quarterly briefings on the French Army. In the autumn of 1926, Colonel von Bonin explained that Germany had recognized its western borders in the Treaty of Locarno and was "not militarily strong enough to take any steps in

This reorientation of defense policy did not elicit the wholehearted approval of that office in the *Truppenamt* which planned mobilization and operations, the *Heeresabteilung* (Army Section), or T1. In March 1929 General von Blomberg, Chief of the *Truppenamt*, had T1 prepare a long memorandum on the conclusions drawn from its "winter studies" of 1927-28 and 1928-29. The former study assumed a Polish attack against Germany; the latter, a French invasion of Germany in order to come to Poland's assistance in a Polish-Soviet war. "Both winter studies," the report affirmed, "as well as other considerations, show that a *one-sided* politico-military entanglement is unlikely. Thus, national defense should not be focused exclusively on defense against a Polish attack. Rather, in addition to defense in the east, we must also prepare for defense in the west and on the remaining borders of the Reich, insofar as this is at all possible considering our many obligations."[55]

Blomberg sent copies of the memorandum to the chiefs of the other bureaus in the ministry—*Wehramt, Waffenamt, Personalamt,* and *Ministeramt*—and asked for their differences, if any, with the *Truppenamt* on lesser points or "fundamental questions," so that he might mention them when he presented the T1 report to General Heye. On one "fundamental question," Schleicher informed the *Truppenamt* of the following objections of the *Ministeramt*:

> In opposition to T[ruppen] A[mt], which . . . designates a *one-sided* military-political imbroglio as unlikely and hence concludes that we must also in effect make defensive preparations in the west, M[inister] A[mt] is of the

---

the west, which would in any case be possible only outside the demilitarized zone. It was all the more worthwhile to strengthen the border defense in the east." Müller, *Vaterland*, p. 297 (his paraphrasing of Bonin's memorandum).

[55] *RWM, Truppenamt* (T1), "Folgerungen aus den Studien des T.A. im Winter 27/28 und 28/29," 26 March 1929, II H 597, p. 3; hereafter abbreviated to "Folgerungen."

opinion that such a situation [i.e., war on two fronts] is completely hopeless if general political conditions do not fundamentally change.

For the present, therefore, M.A. considers only the one-sided defense in the east as correct. The practical provision of our defense in the west, repeatedly demanded in the report of the T.A., is, moreover, unfeasible in view of the decisions of the government which are currently in effect.[56]

Schleicher's criticism of the *Truppenamt* stemmed in large measure from his interest in mending domestic civil-military fences, one of the major responsibilities of the *Ministeramt*. In the second paragraph above, Schleicher alluded to the policy of cooperation among the military, cabinet, and Prussian government in the field of border defense. Since Seeckt's departure, civil-military relations over this question had improved, but were subject to constant strain because of the contacts between the Army and right-wing paramilitary organizations. In 1928 the Prussian police learned that the *Feldjäger*—an irregular formation founded in 1923 to conduct sabotage behind the French lines in case of open conflict—still existed. In response to pressure from the Prussian government, the Defense Minister's office promptly prohibited " 'any practical frontier defence measures in the west and any military activity in the demilitarized zone' of the Rhineland."[57]

Both before and after this ban, the *Truppenamt* acknowledged that cooperation with local civil authorities was necessary, and confessed that Locarno made defensive measures in the west unnecessary.[58] And in its memorandum of March 1929 T1 referred only to the *"theoretical* studies" used for western defense discussions in the absence of "practical meas-

[56] *RWM*, Schleicher to *Truppenamt*, 22 April 1929, II H 597.
[57] In Carsten, *Reichswehr and Politics*, pp. 300-301. On the *Feldjäger*, see also Meinck, *Deutsche Aufrüstung*, p. 9; Generaloberst Gotthard Heinrici, Zeugenschrifttum no. 66 II, Institut für Zeitgeschichte (Munich). Heinrici recalls that Schleicher knew about the *Feldjäger* but did not approve.
[58] See n. 54 above; below, chap. 5.

ures."[59] Nevertheless, the *Truppenamt* continued to advocate the organization of a western border defense. It was reluctant to accept for long the official prohibitive policy of the Defense Minister and Foreign Office,[60] and it did not completely discontinue unofficial collaboration with irregular organizations for illicit "practical measures" in the west.

In the spring of 1929, while this intradepartmental conflict between the *Truppenamt* and *Ministeramt* was still unresolved, Schleicher notified Blomberg of the furor caused by the latter's indiscretion of attending a maneuver by illegal western defense formations. Blomberg believed that he was subsequently removed from Berlin and the *Truppenamt* because of Schleicher's political machinations.[61] But ascribing Schleicher's motives to personal preference and political ambition failed to account for the likelihood that major differences over defense policy were decisive in drawing the fire of the *Ministeramt*, which brought about Blomberg's transfer to command of *Wehrkreis* (Military District) I in East Prussia.

The Blomberg incident offended Schleicher for two major reasons. In the first place, because it violated the official prohibition of the Defense Minister, it threatened to destroy the delicate web of civil-military relations that Groener, Schleicher, the Foreign Office, the cabinet, and local governments were spinning in the interests of national defense.[62] Second, since Blomberg's act amounted to an endorsement of illegal defensive measures in the demilitarized west, it contravened

[59] *RWM, Truppenamt* (T1), "Folgerungen," 26 March, II H 597, pp. 6, 11.

[60] *RWM, ibid.*, pp. 5-6, 11.

[61] On Blomberg's bitterness, recorded in his "Erinnerungen bis 1933," see Carsten, *Reichswehr and Politics*, p. 301. Blomberg accused Groener and Schleicher of setting him up as a sacrificial lamb. Prof. Carsten views the episode chiefly in the context of Schleicher's rise to power, citing the "Lebenserinnerungen" of Colonel (later General) von Mittelberger to show that the Schleicher " 'clique' " often made things difficult for Blomberg; *ibid.*, p. 300.

[62] See below, chap. 5; also Carsten, *ibid.*, pp. 301, 305.

154

Stresemann's policy of rapprochement with France. In short, Blomberg's imprudence jeopardized current progress toward Germany's internal political unity and economic stability, national goals that, according to Schleicher and the Foreign Office, required civil-military cooperation and, with French concurrence, an end to military occupation and reparations.

There was also a more distinctly strategic side to this confrontation between Schleicher and Blomberg. In Schleicher's opinion, "one must summon up the courage to admit that there might be politico-military involvements in which a struggle can be termed hopeless from the outset. . . ."[63] But Blomberg—that is, T1, whose conclusions Blomberg supported—urged the Army to prepare for the worst, a two-front war that France might force upon Germany in disregard to treaties and compromises.[64]

The difference between these two viewpoints did not signify a division into two opposing schools of strategic thought. Both the *Ministeramt* and the *Truppenamt* firmly believed that revision in the east was necessary; that a war to regain the lost territories must be limited if Germany, even with an expanded armed force, was to have any hope of success; and that restricting the war to one front required a previous political understanding with France.[65] The two outlooks were separated because they rested on different priorities. Schleicher, like the Foreign Office, stressed political conditions: Germany's weak international position and dependence on French cooperation or acquiescence for treaty revision, and the certainty that the government would not order military resistance if both Poland and France attacked Germany. Under Blomberg's guidance, the *Truppenamt*, although conscious of political realities, attached greater importance to the military necessity of defensive preparedness on all fronts, which it placed ahead of the political dictate of reaching an

---

[63] *RWM*, Schleicher to *Truppenamt*, 22 April 1929, II H 597.

[64] *RWM*, *Truppenamt* (T1), "Folgerungen," 26 March 1929, *ibid.*, pp. 2-3.

[65] These considerations are discussed in chap. 6.

understanding with France.[66] Although the *Truppenamt* concurred with the Foreign Office and *Ministeramt* that rapprochement with France afforded the most promising egress from encirclement, it favored a western defense policy which, since it violated the Versailles and Locarno treaties, might have alienated France sufficiently to insure French intervention in a German-Polish war.

In their defense planning in the late 1920s, the Army Command was preoccupied with questions of organization, training, and operations; the office of the Defense Minister, with relations between military and civilian authorities. Neither the Chief of the Army Command and *Truppenamt* nor the Defense Minister and *Ministeramt* tried to usurp the power over foreign policy. Nevertheless, the intradepartmental collision between the *Truppenamt* and the *Ministeramt* over western defense had foreign policy implications, for the whole question of national defense could not be aired in isolation from Germany's international situation. Although Schleicher, as head of the *Ministeramt*, properly dealt with internal political matters such as parties, paramilitary groups, and civilian support for defensive measures, he invaded the organizational sphere of military planning when he rejected a western border defense, and the operational sphere when he declared that some possible conflict situations must be viewed as "hopeless." No doubt this latter strategic argument was of less importance to Schleicher than the necessity of preserving civil-military cooperation when he reproved Blomberg and

[66] In his discussion of American strategic doctrine after the Second World War, Janowitz considers the formative effects not simply of particular wartime experiences, but also of "a system of personal alliances, centering around loyalties to strong leaders," and of "organizational self-interest" (in which cases "doctrine is irrelevant, or at best a rationale for the pursuit of personal glory or organizational success"); *Professional Soldier*, pp. 284-85. Although not immune to "personal alliances" and "organizational self-interest," the *Truppenamt*'s strategic doctrine seems to have been determined chiefly by the experience of the First World War and by the politico-military exigencies of Germany's postwar situation.

helped engineer his replacement in the *Truppenamt* by General Kurt Freiherr von Hammerstein-Equord, an old friend of both Schleicher and Groener. Still, Schleicher encroached upon the responsibility of the *Truppenamt* for military planning, and this interference probably added to the animosity felt toward him and the *Ministeramt* by many of his fellow officers, who were suspicious of his political motives and less attuned to the political precedence of winning the diplomatic understanding of France and the domestic support of the civilian authorities and the Social Democratic Party.

The particulars of the Schleicher-Blomberg clash assume wider proportions when viewed in connection with Schleicher's personal ascendancy in the Defense Ministry and, as a result, his potential influence on military planning. Schleicher was Groener's most trusted political adviser, and by 1929 his power had undermined the authority of the mild and pliable General Heye, Chief of the Army Command.[67] Because of Schleicher's influential position in the ministry, his advice to the *Truppenamt* on questions of national defense was less easily overruled by the Chief of the *Truppenamt* and more readily followed by General Heye.[68] Furthermore, replacing Blomberg with Hammerstein, who favored closer relations between the Army and republican groups, and between Germany and France, assured Schleicher of greater influence on planning in the *Truppenamt*.

After 1926 the military officials in the Bendlerstrasse, although not of one mind on the question of western defense,

[67] Heye was not, however, oblivious to Schleicher's increasing power, and complained to Groener about it; see Carsten, *Reichswehr and Politics*, pp. 296ff.

[68] In 1929, as an example, Heye accepted Schleicher's criticisms of the *Truppenamt* report of 26 March. The steps by which Schleicher won this argument over defense planning can be traced in a series of documents in *RWM*, II H 597, including the following: Schleicher to *Truppenamt*, 22 April; Heye's handwritten comment (19 June) in the margin of Blomberg's cover note to the *Truppenamt* report of 26 March; Blomberg to department chiefs in the *Truppenamt*, 24 June; Schleicher to *Truppenamt*, 8 July; Blomberg to chiefs, 12 July.

assented to the judgment of the Foreign Office that rapprochement with France offered the possibility of rupturing the Franco-Polish alliance, among other advantages. French military planning at the time was increasingly defensive. In addition, the French were willing to settle the issue of evacuation of the Rhineland without answering Polish demands for a compensatory security pact in the east. The signs augured ill for Poland. But no amount of wishful thinking could erase the fact that France and Poland were still allied. Germany was militarily too weak to fight an offensive war on one front, and internationally too exposed to be confident that a conflict with Poland would not bring French intervention.

CHAPTER V

Force and Foreign Policy: Rearmament

THE GERMAN officer, like Stresemann, thought of national power in terms of armed forces, internal unity of purpose, and economic resources. To the officer, however, *Macht* had a more immediate professional relevance. Charged with maintaining the nation's standing military force, he was on call either to defend the fatherland or to provide the necessary means for an aggressive policy by the political leadership. Whether he could execute either mission depended not simply upon the international situation, but also upon military planning: the size and organization of the armed force; and the operational employment of that force. Moreover, he performed this twofold task with a set of assumptions about the use of force in foreign policy, and the relationship between military planning and foreign policy.

FORCE AND FOREIGN POLICY

Part V of the Treaty of Versailles, in disarming Germany as the first step toward "a general limitation of the armaments of all nations," was designed to reduce the likelihood of wars of aggression. The treaty did not, however, expunge a nation's right to defend itself against attack. Seeking to protect this right, and believing that the treaty had not insured everlasting peace, the German Army continually urged an increase in Germany's military power, by publicly demanding a revision of the disarmament terms or secretly circumventing them. General von Seeckt summed up the Army's view in a letter to Chancellor Cuno in April 1923. The French, he wrote, could not "deny us the right of defense," a deprivation for which there was no justification in international law. Germany's vulnerability to external threats was the greater because its borders were not—nor should they be—guaranteed. To guard its borders and rights, every German government had "not only the right but the duty" to take any defensive measures so long as they were "not *explicitly* prohibited by the Treaty of Versailles."[1]

Until such time as Germany was allowed a larger armed force, Seeckt refused to permit the 100,000-man Army to be converted to merely a border police force, a transformation that, Seeckt affirmed, would have been " 'entirely contrary to the principles according to which I have trained and educated it. . . .' "[2] Seeckt wanted to prepare the tiny force prescribed by the Treaty of Versailles to be the nucleus of an expanded regular force in the future, one really capable of shielding Germany against its enemies.

Seeckt's plan was firmly advocated by the civilian heads of the Defense Ministry. In cabinet meetings Gessler upheld measures that exceeded the provisions of the Treaty of Versailles but were "indispensable for Germany's security." He also promoted Seeckt's design of the current Army as the kernel of a larger one.[3] Groener appealed to the German public to back national defense programs, in the interest of German security.[4]

[1] *RK*, Seeckt to Reich Chancellor, 16 April 1923, K953/K249558-61. See also Gordon, *Reichswehr and Republic*, pp. 270-75; Manstein, *Soldatenleben*, pp. 116ff. This argument for self-defense was repeated by the *Truppenamt* in 1929, when there was no doubt in either the Army or the Foreign Office that many measures were "explicitly prohibited" by the terms of the Versailles Treaty; *RWM*, "Folgerungen," 26 March, II H 597, p. 4.

[2] Seeckt to Chancellor Joseph Wirth, 10 June 1922; in Carsten, *Reichswehr and Politics*, p. 119.

[3] *AA*, notes of session of 6 June 1925, 7133/H148798; *RK*, cabinet protocol, 29 November 1925, 3543/D770971. See also Gessler, *Reichswehrpolitik*, p. 430; Gordon, *Reichswehr and Republic*, p. 332.

[4] Groener drew examples from some of the speeches of Bismarck, who, like Groener, had had to defend the military budget in debates in the Reichstag; letter from the Reichsarchiv to Groener, 15 June

The Foreign Office supported the imperatives of Seeckt's military policy more strongly than he realized or chose to admit. For Stresemann, while negotiating for a foreign policy that Seeckt bitterly attacked, resolutely defended Germany's right to national security. A sore point in talks between the Allies and Germany about a western security pact in 1925, the German Army's infringements of the Treaty of Versailles irritated the French in particular. They would not be disposed to reach a political understanding with Germany so long as they had evidence that the Army was violating the treaty by retaining the General Staff in all but name, caching weapons illegally, and training the *Schutzpolizei*—a police force commanded by former regular Army officers—as a reserve. An Allied note to this effect was the subject of discussion at a cabinet meeting in Berlin early in June 1925. Stresemann rallied to the Army's defense. "The Allied point of view regarding our Reichswehr," he said, "is wrong; the Treaty of Versailles does not state that we may not further develop our Reichswehr in case of an attack, and that we may not defend ourselves if we are attacked. . . ."[5]

Seeckt's successor as Chief of the Army Command, General Heye, was more appreciative of Stresemann's efforts in behalf of the Army. Stresemann acknowledged Heye's grati-

---

1928, enclosing material for the latter's study on Bismarck's national defense and armament policy, Nachlass Groener, no. 39, Bundesarchiv-Militärarchiv. The Defense Ministry did not always easily persuade a majority of Reichstag delegates that marked increases in the official defense budget—from 490 million marks in 1924 to 827 million in 1928—were necessary for armed forces whose size the Treaty of Versailles had fixed. See Eyck, *Weimar Republic*, II, 143-44; Wheeler-Bennett, *Nemesis of Power*, p. 187 and n.

[5] *RK*, cabinet protocol, 5 June, 3543/D764856f. On the Allies' knowledge of the military character of the *Schutzpolizei*, see W. M. Jordan, *Great Britain, France and the German Problem 1918-1939* (London, 1943), pp. 143-44; on the organization, training, and activities of the Berlin *Schutzpolizei*, Hsi-Huey Liang, *The Berlin Police Force in the Weimar Republic* (Berkeley, Calif., 1970), chap. 3.

tude. He assured the general that, as Foreign Minister, his "gravest concern" was Germany's military weakness. Whereas other states could protect "hearth and home," Germany was so powerless that it could not defend itself against a minor power "without having to fear sacrificing the lives of our soldiers in a useless struggle."[6]

German political representatives emphasized their country's military inferiority in the many discussions about disarmament that took place during the 1920s. The Wilhelmstrasse hoped that the Treaty of Locarno had satisfied the French demand for security as a precondition to revision of Part V of the peace treaty, and that as a member of the League Germany could press continually and forcefully for either general disarmament or German rearmament. In the spring of 1927, after a year of debate, the Preparatory Commission appointed by the League had made little progress toward eliminating the main differences between the two major parties, Britain and France, an important step toward a final Disarmament Conference. Count Johann von Bernstorff, head of the German delegation to the Preparatory Commission, became increasingly disillusioned, persuaded that the French never intended to disarm.[7] In November 1927 this sober pessimism shaded a Foreign Office minute to Stresemann on the question of national defense. The Great Powers at Geneva showed every sign of wanting to preserve their military superiority against Germany. Therefore Germany must not give them any cause to accuse it of paralyzing disarmament talks, but must cautiously conduct its policy so that only they would be blamed in the event of a breakdown of negotiations.[8]

---

[6] *AA*, Stresemann to Heye, 13 August 1927, 7346/H164800-1.

[7] Zimmermann, *Deutsche Aussenpolitik*, pp. 446-49.

[8] *AA*, "Aufzeichnung über die Pläne des Reichswehrministeriums betreffend den 'Landesschutz,'" 21 November, K6/K000310-11. Although signed by Gerhard Köpke, the memorandum (to Stresemann) was probably prepared by Dirk Forster, a military expert in the Wilhelmstrasse. The section on disarmament, except for the last few sentences, is identical to Forster's note of 21 June, 3177/D683185-6.

Some of the other representatives to the Preparatory Commission—notably the French, who were not confident that Locarno provided a sufficient degree of European security to permit general disarmament—suspected the Germans of undermining the idea of general disarmament "so as to clear the ground for the rearmament of Germany."[9] Their suspicion had some foundation in fact. The Germans were less interested in French ideas of security than in equality of armaments, by which they meant a level that would require France to reduce and allow Germany to increase the size of their standing Armies. General von Seeckt, who in retirement had become friendly toward Stresemann, advised the Foreign Minister that the size of a nation's peacetime army should be relative to its population: excluding the United States and the Soviet Union, first-class powers (Germany, France, Great Britain, and Italy), with over 30 million population, should have armies of 250,000 men. Germany required a force of at least that size to protect its "natural right of self-defense" and to enable it to fulfill possible future military obligations to the League of Nations.[10] To what extent this advice influenced Germany's position in talks at Geneva is uncertain, but it agreed with the broad outlines of official German policy in the late 1920s: since general disarmament was impracticable, Germany must be allowed to rearm after an international agreement was reached on military levels corresponding to the size and requirements of individual nations.

The Army, then, justified its rearmament policy—just as the Foreign Office did Locarno—in terms of German security and European peace, both of which remained imperiled as long as a disarmed Germany created a "military-political

[9] Gathorne-Hardy, *History of International Affairs*, p. 187. See also Jacques Benoist-Méchin, *Histoire de l'armée allemande* (6 vols.; Michel ed.; Paris, 1964-66), II, 353ff.

[10] *AA*, Seeckt memorandum to Stresemann on the subject of peacetime armaments, 29 November 1927, 7371/H166716-25; Seeckt study on the disarmament question, which he sent to Stresemann on 18 August 1928, shortly before Germany joined in the signing of the Kellogg Pact, 7150/H151344-62.

163

vacuum" in Central Europe.[11] In this emphasis on security against aggression the Army conformed to the Kellogg Pact, signed on 27 August 1928 by representatives of Germany and fourteen other nations, which renounced war as an instrument of national policy while reserving to each nation the right of self-defense.[12]

But at the same time the Army, again like the Foreign Office, contradicted the Kellogg Pact by retaining the fundamental assumption that war—or the application or threat of force short of war—is a means of foreign policy. The Army Command believed that it must be ready to carry out an order of the political arm to attack as well as defend, for the government, having weighed such factors as international alignments and the absence of international agreement on the definition of aggression, might decide to resort to war in order to further national interests.[13] The Army did not subscribe to the idea of military preparedness simply out of deference to possible political commands, but had strong convictions about the meaning of power in international affairs. The German military's notion of *Machtpolitik* did not differ fundamentally from the diplomats' synthesis of force and foreign policy. It

[11] In an interview, General Flörke emphasized this term as a component of European power politics. Compare Lord D'Abernon's opinion of the drastic reduction of German strength "far beyond the point where any danger need be feared by England." The ambassador thought it "probable, should the 'balance of power' theory again become a dominant English conception of policy, that future critics will consider that a mistake has been made in 1922 in disarming Germany so far without disarming other Powers of Europe." *Diary*, II, 167-68. See also Seeckt's *Gedanken eines Soldaten* (Berlin, 1929), pp. 76-77.

[12] On self-defense as defined in the Kellogg Pact, see Ferrell, *Peace in their Time*, chaps. 12, 13. The editors of a leading German military journal were skeptical about the ideal and the effectiveness of the pact, for "defensive war" was subject to many interpretations, and German security had still not been guaranteed. "Militärpolitischer Abriss 1928," *Wissen und Wehr*, x (1929), 59-63.

[13] Seeckt pointed this out to Stresemann in August 1928, above, n. 10 (*AA*, 7150/H151358); see also chap. 6.

164

comprehended the following, which were both goals and means of national policy and which implied a broader and more elastic definition of national security than defense against attack: the restoration of Germany's status as a European Great Power and the commensurate military strength to protect its vital interests, attract allies, and regain the Corridor and Danzig by force if necessary.

With some differences in emphasis, these dimensions of *Machtpolitik* as understood in the Bendlerstrasse continued throughout the Weimar period. Seeckt spoke of Germany's need to regain its power, for only with power was an active foreign policy of revision possible. Meanwhile Germany should make itself attractive as an ally by developing its small armed force into an efficient fighting unit.[14] The accession of Groener and the parallel rise of Schleicher after 1926 marked a change from Seeckt's policy in a number of senses. These men were determined to cooperate with the government and Foreign Office. They were also more sensitive to questions of domestic policy, recognizing that internal consolidation was a long process requiring patience and joint civil-military effort. Further, they rejected the fantasy of a war against France that beguiled Seeckt and other Francophobes. Finally, in public addresses and debates in the Reichstag on the military budget, Groener stressed the advantages of an armed force that, though large enough to deter an army from attacking German territory, was not so formidable as to threaten the Great Powers.[15] Yet Groener and Schleicher, no matter

[14] Rabenau, *Seeckt*, pp. 118, 463. *RK*, Seeckt to Prussian Minister of the Interior (Carl Severing), 29 December 1923, K951/K248468. See also above, chap. 4.

[15] Groener speech before the "Deutsche Gesellschaft 1914," 27 November 1928, Nachlass Groener, no. 149, Bundesarchiv-Militärarchiv (the copy in *RWM*, II M 57/60, establishes the exact date). For excerpts from some of Groener's speeches in the Reichstag, see Groener-Geyer, *General Groener*, pp. 250ff. On Groener's rejection of an aggressive foreign policy in the manner of Seeckt, see also Herzfeld, *Problem des Heeres*, p. 13; Schüddekopf, *Heer und Republik*,

how much more temperate than Seeckt, were still advocates of *Machtpolitik*. Their program was to strengthen Germany internally as a necessary step toward the eventual re-establishment of Germany's "external power."[16]

Never divorced from its reflections on power was the Army's feeling of subjugation to the *Diktat* of Versailles. Germany lacked the freedom to build up its armed forces for self-defense, to enter into a favorable alliance system, and to defend its "rights" by force of arms if necessary. "Liberation" (*Befreiung*) was a common and highly emotive ideal in the officer corps, particularly in the years before Locarno; and Prussia's war of liberation against Napoleon was the precedent immediately recalled. Whether the two situations were very similar was the subject of Lieutenant Hans Speidel's doctoral dissertation at the University of Tübingen. Speidel concluded that Germany in 1924 lacked the three major elements that had contributed to Prussia's recovery and liberation: the restoration of political and military power; a favorable international situation; and an idealistic and patriotic national spirit. The key to freedom, in Speidel's view, was power: political power is built upon military strength, and "it is always

---

pp. 235ff.; Helmut Haeussler, *General William Groener and the Imperial German Army* (Madison, Wisc., 1962), pp. xiiff.

16 On Schleicher, see above, chap. 4. In public, Groener recommended "a sound and sensible pacifism," meaning that Germany should be proud and strong enough to defend itself. But in a memorandum Groener used during cabinet discussions in the autumn of 1928 concerning the construction of the first "pocket-battleship," the argument went beyond mere self-defense. The stronger Germany became, the better its chances of improving its position in the event of a European war, which Germany should enter only if it had "real prospects of success." For the text of this confidential memorandum, which was leaked to the British press, see Nauticus, "New Germany's New Navy," *The Review of Reviews*, LXXVIII (1929), 16-21; Schüddekopf, *Heer und Republik*, pp. 251-54. See also Wheeler-Bennett, *Nemesis of Power*, pp. 192-93; Wolfgang Wacker, *Der Bau des Panzerschiffes 'A' und der Reichstag* (Tübingen, 1959), pp. 35-38; below, chap. 7.

on power that right among nations depends."[17] This consciousness of the significance of power—and the relationship between power and freedom—was widespread in the German Army. To the German officer, powerlessness was the root of Germany's ills, and France the nation most responsible for Germany's military impotence, lessons bitterly reinforced during the French occupation of the Ruhr.[18]

The spirit for a "war of liberation" against France waned in the late 1920s as the Army Command admitted the advantages of a rapprochement with France and grew generally more circumspect in its strategic thinking. But there was no similar change in the Army's attitude toward Poland. Most officers, believing that Poland would never surrender the Corridor without an armed struggle, continued to doubt that Germany could peacefully regain its lost territorial "right," and to favor force as a means of territorial revision. This particular application of force to an objective beyond mere self-defense was always implicit in the rubric *Machtpolitik* as conceived by the German Army and its civilian head in the Defense Ministry.

CLAUSEWITZ

In its view of force as an instrument of foreign policy, the Army retained the dictum of Karl von Clausewitz that "war is a mere continuation of policy by other means," not an entirely separate form of activity "subject to no laws but its own."[19] Moreover, recognizing the political character of war, the Army also revived that vital principle of civil-military

[17] Hans Speidel, "1813/1924: Eine militärpolitische Untersuchung" (unpublished Ph.D. dissertation, University of Tübingen, 1925), notably pp. 36, 80-81. For Stresemann's similar views on right and power, see above, chap. 2.

[18] Interviews with Generals Brennecke, Flörke, Hauck, Heusinger, Lanz, and Speidel.

[19] Carl von Clausewitz, *On War*, trans. Colonel J. J. Graham (3 vols.; rev. ed.; London, 1940), I (Bk. I), 23; III (Bk. VIII), 121.

relations which Clausewitz had laid down: the military point of view must be subordinate to the political. According to Clausewitz, policy

> is the intelligent faculty, War only the instrument, and not the reverse. . . . Experience in general also teaches us that notwithstanding the multifarious branches and scientific character of military art in the present day, still the leading outlines of a War are always determined by the Cabinet, that is . . . by a political not a military organ. . . . When people speak, as they often do, of the prejudicial influence of policy on the conduct of War, they say in reality something very different to what they intend. It is not this influence but the policy itself which should be found fault with.[20]

The President of the Weimar Republic exercised supreme command over the armed forces, but even under President Hindenburg the Army, when it referred to the "political arm," "political leadership," and "political control" in correspondence pertaining to organizational and operational matters, consistently meant the Chancellor and cabinet (i.e., the government). Moreover, the Army considered the Foreign Office a departmental segment of the political leadership, the most important department not only for the integration of military planning with the foreign policy adopted by the government, but also for the subordination of military planning to that policy. The primacy of the political regime of the Second Empire had been paralyzed during the First World War, when the Army High Command under Hindenburg and Ludendorff established a supremacy over the civilian authorities which was " 'the very essence of militarism,' " in the retrospective judgment of a retired German general.[21] This

[20] *Ibid.*, III (Bk. VIII), 125-26; also I (Bk. I), 22-23.
[21] General Freiherr von Schoenaich, quoted in Telford Taylor, *Sword and Swastika: Generals and Nazis in the Third Reich* (New York, 1952), p. 16. See also Jehuda L. Wallach, *Das Dogma der Vernichtungsschlacht: Die Lehren von Clausewitz und Schlieffen*

was not the only lesson of the war. In 1920 the *Truppenamt* condemned the lack of cooperation between the military and the political leadership, the failure to coordinate operations with policy prior to the outbreak of war in 1914. As a result Germany had become entangled in a prolonged two-front war for which it lacked sufficient military strength. To preclude such a blunder, the *Truppenamt* warned, the diplomats and generals had to work with instead of against each other: "A solution *must* be found which insures cooperation between the Foreign Office and the Army Command."[22]

At the Foreign Office Gustav Stresemann was a staunch upholder of political primacy. Predominance in civil-military relations, he declared, depends on "who has the stronger will." Bismarck, he recalled, had carried out his "political will" notwithstanding the increasing political influence of a victorious and prestigious military command after the Franco-Prussian War.[23]

---

und ihre Wirkungen in zwei Weltkriegen (Frankfurt am Main, 1967), chap. 8; Ritter, *Staatskunst und Kriegshandwerk*, IV. On the waning influence of the Foreign Office under William II, see Craig, *Prussian Army*, chap. 7; Holborn, "Diplomats and Diplomacy," in Craig and Gilbert, *Diplomats*, pp. 125ff. Among the reasons for this decline of political control was William's own preference for the advice of the military over that of professional diplomats. On policy and strategy in wartime, the Kaiser's dictum was the antithesis of that of Clausewitz. " 'Politics,' " William said, " 'must keep its mouth shut during the war until strategy allows it to talk again.' " *Ibid.*, p. 129.

[22] *RWM*, T4 (Training Section) memorandum, March 1920, II H 221. The memorandum began with a quotation from Clausewitz on war as a continuation of policy. See Seeckt's criticism of both arms for failing to cooperate in 1914, and his argument for collaboration between the Foreign Office and military, in *Gedanken*, pp. 60-63.

[23] *AA*, Stresemann speech before the "Arbeitsgemeinschaft Ostpreussischer Regimentsvereine," 1 April 1928, 7375/H167552, 555-6. As a member of the Reichstag in 1918, however, Stresemann had not demonstrated this conviction. In reply to another member's criticism of the Treaty of Brest-Litovsk, he had said, " 'We do not wish to annex parts of Poland; but if our High Command tells us that we must improve our frontier by removing it farther east to prevent future in-

The hope shared by the Army and Foreign Office for harmonious interdepartmental relations and the principle of political primacy were never more seriously in jeopardy than during the intense feud between Seeckt and Stresemann in 1925. Seeckt's hostile position was inconsistent with his own views about civil-military relations, for his letters, publications, and training policy reveal an allegiance to Clausewitz. Early in 1917 he had written to a friend, "The military chief should always recede behind his Commander in Chief and, after the old Prussian custom, have no name."[24] And a few years after resigning as Chief of the Army Command he observed: "Armaments races and armaments restrictions, despite their military appearance, are both political questions. A soldier cannot be blamed if he makes high demands in regard to matters that are his responsibility. To keep these matters within the framework of general policy, however, is the task of the statesman."[25]

Like Clausewitz, Seeckt believed that policy determines military planning, not the reverse. " 'The current objection that a strong army induces a policy of conquest is untenable. National policy determines the employment of the army. If it is a bad policy, it will use the army incorrectly; a good policy effects a proper use.' "[26] Again in the manner of Clausewitz, Seeckt held that the statesman, although responsible for the decision whether to make war, must weigh the advice of the military chief concerning military preparedness and strength relative to the enemy.[27]

---

vasions, no one will take on himself the responsibility of opposing such a need.' " In Ralph H. Lutz (ed.), *Fall of the German Empire 1914-1918* (2 vols.; Stanford, Calif., 1932), I, 786.

[24] Seeckt to von Winterfeldt, 1 January, Seeckt Papers (microfilm), roll 20, Stück 90.

[25] Seeckt, *Gedanken*, pp. 56-57.

[26] Seeckt memorandum, 17 February 1919; in Rabenau, *Seeckt*, p. 463.

[27] Clausewitz, *On War*, III (Bk. VIII), 125-26; Seeckt, *Gedanken*, pp. 58, 115.

Clausewitz accommodated no exceptions to his general prescription that the political arm sets the policy to which the military must adapt its activities. Nor, at first academic glance, did Seeckt, who defined "statesman" as "the political leadership of the state," that man or body—absolute or constitutional monarch, dictator, president, or cabinet—responsible for the conduct of "state life" (*Staatsleben*) through such departments as finance, foreign service, and the armed forces.[28] In practice, however, Seeckt sometimes failed to heed his own warning against merely reciting Clausewitzean principles "instead of studying him."[29] For his independent military policy toward the Soviet Union and his keen opposition to Brockdorff-Rantzau and Stresemann exceeded the bounds that both he—at least in theory—and Clausewitz put on the military's advisory role in political affairs.

Seeckt's deviation from the principle of political control was the consequence of facing new political facts that Clausewitz could not have foretold: a republican form of government in which party politics affected the composition of cabinets and the making of defense and foreign policies; and a bureaucracy whose heads of department were likely to be party politicians.[30] Seeckt, a monarchist and professional sol-

[28] Seeckt, *ibid.*, p. 55.

[29] *Ibid.*, p. 17. As an example, Seeckt observed, "The principle that war is a continuation of policy with other means has become a catchword and thus dangerous. One can just as well say war is the bankruptcy of policy." *Ibid.*, p. 74. For a similar warning, and a criticism of Seeckt's inconsistency, see Wallach, *Vernichtungsschlacht*, pp. 19-26, 347-48.

[30] On the little attention (but attention nonetheless) that Clausewitz paid "the internal politics of foreign-policy making," see Mayer, *Political Origins*, p. 2n., and "Internal Causes and Purposes of War in Europe, 1870-1956: A Research Assignment," *Journal of Modern History*, XLI (1969), 292-93; also Peter Paret, "Clausewitz and the Nineteenth Century," in Michael Howard (ed.), *The Theory and Practice of War: Essays Presented to Captain B. H. Liddell Hart on His Seventieth Birthday* (London, 1965), p. 34; Hans Rothfels, "Clausewitz," in Edward Meade Earle (ed.), *Makers of Modern Strategy: Military Thought from Machiavelli to Hitler* (Princeton,

dier, had to protect the Army's interests in the politically un-
familiar and (among the parties of the Left) anti-military
surroundings of the Weimar Republic. Seeckt's intense distrust of parliamentary politics prompted him to order the
Army to stay above party. This ban condemned activity in
party politics; it did not prohibit advising "the political leadership of the state." But his arrogant disdain for politicians
led him to define that leadership in a manner harmful to cooperation in the executive-departmental sphere delineated by
the constitution. Seeckt refused to observe that Stresemann
was a foreign policy expert, a head of department who himself resented the intrusion of party politics into vital politico-
military issues. Instead, Seeckt described Stresemann pejora-
tively as a "politician," deficient in the understanding of
politico-military affairs and the qualities of leadership he admired in Bismarck, his ideal of a *Staatsmann* (an ideal Stresemann shared).[31]

Seeckt reserved to himself the right to ignore or combat the
Foreign Office when its policies clashed with what he considered to be the Army's interests, even though these policies
had been officially adopted by the cabinet. He would, when
he preferred, be selectively obedient to the President, or to
the state as an organic whole, but not to the Chancellor, cabinet, or a bureaucratic adjunct to the government such as the
Foreign Office.[32] His prerogative based on contempt was at

N.J., 1943), pp. 105-107; for contrasts between Clausewitz's "classic
theory of intergovernmental war" and recent forms of "intrastate
war," Samuel P. Huntington, "Patterns of Violence in World Politics,"
in Huntington (ed.), *Changing Patterns of Military Politics* (New
York, 1962), pp. 19-20.

[31] For Seeckt's characterizations of *Staatsmann* and *Feldherr*, see
his *Gedanken*, pp. 55ff.; Rabenau, *Seeckt*, p. 588.

[32] The Army, Seeckt wrote, "is subordinate to the state as a whole,
which is embodied in its leadership, not . . . to particular parts of
the state organism." *Gedanken*, p. 115. See also Claus Guske, *Das
politische Denken des Generals von Seeckt: Ein Beitrag zur Diskussion des Verhältnisses Seeckt-Reichswehr-Republik* (Lübeck, 1971),
pp. 131-38.

once limited in its definition of "political leadership" and in its understanding of subordination, injurious to the healthy growth of civil-military relations at the departmental level where politico-military planning took place, and detrimental to a reconciliation between Clausewitzean theory and Weimar institutional practice.

Beneath the surface of this high-level discord, however, a Clausewitzean renaissance had already begun, building a doctrinal foundation for cooperation and subordination after Seeckt's dismissal. The Training Section (T4) of the *Truppenamt* assigned the writings of Clausewitz for the instruction of officers in military history and theory. Officers applied to the Bismarck era and the World War Clausewitz's theory of the proper relationship between policy and military planning. In the latter instance the two had not been coordinated, and the political arm not forceful enough to remain in control of the conduct of the war. On the other hand Bismarck had preserved the Clausewitzean conception: the armed force is the instrument of and subordinate to the political arm; the political leadership must clarify the international situation and explain the state's political objectives to the military; the military leadership then advises whether, and in what manner, it can carry out the military mission in pursuit of these objectives.[33]

This code of civil-military conduct, emphasized in contemporary writings as well,[34] was also explicitly stated in the cor-

[33] Interviews with Generals Brennecke (who was an instructor of military history in the Army's training program for General Staff officers), Flörke, Maximilian Fretter-Pico, Heusinger, and Max von Viebahn (a member of T4 from about 1925 to 1930). On Ludwig Beck's advocacy of the "primacy of policy," see the introduction by Hans Speidel to Beck's *Studien* (Stuttgart, 1955), pp. 14-15.

[34] Otto von Moser, *Das militärisch und politisch Wichtigste vom Weltkriege* (Stuttgart, 1926), and *Die obersten Gewalten im Weltkrieg* (Stuttgart, 1931); Max von Szczepanski, *Politik als Kriegführung* (Berlin, 1926); (Colonel) Curt Liebmann, "Die Entwicklung der Frage eines einheitlichen Oberbefehls im Weltkriege," *Wissen und Wehr*, VIII (1927), especially pp. 95-100. For a study of the rebirth

respondence of the Foreign Office and Defense Ministry. A memorandum in the Wilhelmstrasse called attention to Germany's military weakness, which justified illegal rearmament and necessitated careful diplomacy to keep Germany out of war. In order to subordinate the Defense Ministry's preparations to political considerations, it was the duty of the Foreign Office "more than ever to preserve the primacy of foreign policy."[35] Similarly, in a discussion with representatives of the Foreign Office in November 1927, Colonel Werner von Fritsch (head of T1, the Army Section in the *Truppenamt*) correlated defensive measures with Germany's foreign policy. No preparations could be made in western Germany, since the government had decided to base German security there on the Locarno understanding with France. Steps taken in the eastern provinces to guard against a Polish attack "should not be an end in themselves, but should serve foreign policy."[36] The military arm was to remain subordinate to the political in the event of war. The *Heereswaffenamt* (Army Ordnance Office) observed "that today even a purely defensive struggle cannot be conducted without persuasive and alert political leadership by the government."[37]

The role of the political arm was considered in the Army's war games and other operational studies. Foreign Office participants in these exercises noted among officers of the *Truppenamt* a reassuringly balanced appraisal of Germany's international situation, and a sincere willingness to increase co-

---

of Clausewitz in the 1920s, see Wilhelm Ritter von Schramm, "Wege und Umwege der deutschen Kriegstheorie," *Revue militaire générale* (1960), nos. 8 and 10. Wallach has assembled an exhaustive bibliography of works on Clausewitz, in *Vernichtungsschlacht*.

[35] *AA*, Köpke memorandum (see above, n. 8), 21 November 1927, K6/K000309, 311-12; also Forster minute of 12 May 1928, *ibid.*, K000388-9.

[36] *AA*, Foreign Office notes of conference, 21 (?) November, *ibid.*, K000305.

[37] *RWM*, *Waffenamt* memorandum, 26 October 1927, II M 2.

operation with civilian agencies.[38] A military expert from the Wilhelmstrasse met with no demur when he told officers that they must accustom themselves to the fact that "the armed forces, even on strictly military grounds, are much more dependent on foreign policy than before." Until 1927, this official recalled, the Defense Ministry had worked independently in matters that affected foreign policy, particularly in interpreting disarmament regulations, with the unhappy result that the Foreign Office had sometimes been hard-pressed to explain illegal or questionable military practices to the Allies. In 1927, however, the Defense Ministry and Foreign Office had begun to work together in these sensitive areas. He concluded that further participation in operational exercises would give the Foreign Office the opportunity to strengthen in the Army "the feeling for foreign policy and for the dependence of the armed forces on the Foreign Office."[39]

The Bendlerstrasse's interest in foreign policy was also manifested in the directives of the Defense Minister, Wilhelm Groener. Groener encouraged cooperation in war games, for he believed that such studies must be built on "a foundation that corresponds to [Germany's] actual situation."[40] In an instruction to the two service chiefs, Groener stated that measures for expanding and employing the armed forces depended on the assignments designated "by the responsible political leadership."[41]

Thus the theory and spirit of the dependence of military

[38] *AA*, Forster notes, 2 May and 2 October 1928, K6/K000380-3, 399-403.

[39] *AA*, Forster notes, 2 October 1928, *ibid.* From late 1925 through January 1927, Forster, as a member of the Paris embassy, had been active in negotiations to end Allied military control in Germany. For an exploration of German civil-military friction over this question—demilitarization, the Inter-Allied Military Control Commission, and Stresemann's policy of understanding—see Michael Salewski, *Entwaffnung und Militärkontrolle in Deutschland 1919-1927* (Munich, 1966).

[40] *AA*, Groener to Foreign Office, 14 June 1928, K6/K000393-4.

[41] See below, chap. 6, p. 232.

planning on foreign policy was very much in evidence in the late 1920s. But was this principle yet deeply enough ingrained in practice to give the Foreign Office unreserved confidence in its own ascendance? And if, in attempting to adapt Clausewitzean theory to the Weimar constitution, the Army corrected Seeckt's conditional interpretation of subordination to the political leadership, did it do so without conceding to the Reichstag a degree of control over politico-military activity commensurate with the post-Clausewitzean development of parliamentary government? To answer these questions requires a more detailed examination of civil-military relations in the two areas of military planning: the organization and expansion of defensive preparations; and operations.

GRENZSCHUTZ AND LANDESSCHUTZ

After the war ended late in 1918, one of the major tasks of the German Army was to defend Germany's borders against Poland. For this purpose the Army created the Border Defense East (*Grenzschutz-Ost*), which was made up largely of volunteers who belonged to politically conservative veterans' associations. The existence of these paramilitary units posed a dilemma that neither the civilian authorities nor the Army could resolve during the Weimar Republic. The central government, the Prussian government, and the Foreign Office all admitted Germany's need for defensive forces in excess of the 100,000-man Army. But they were nervously aware of the veterans' hostility toward the republic, and knew that such illegal military measures would irritate the Allies. The Army justified the *Grenzschutz* as a necessary expression of Germany's "right of self-defense," yet struggled to gain control over the training and tactical use of irregulars, and realized that their effectiveness would be impaired unless the active cooperation of civilian officials were obtained. As the *Grenzschutz* became incorporated in a larger scheme of national defense (*Landesschutz*), civil-military cooperation gradually increased in the executive-departmental sphere, in spite of

176

persistent differences of opinion with the Prussian government over the question of the composition and control of irregular units.

Before 1924 a series of crises had cast shadows of distrust on civil-military relations. The regime of President Ebert had turned to the Army for defense of the republic against internal rebellion from the Left and Right, and had witnessed General von Seeckt's hesitation to act decisively in response to that call during the Kapp *Putsch* of March 1920 and again at the most inflammatory stage of the Bavarian separatist movement in the autumn of 1923. Externally, Upper Silesia had been under constant pressure from bands of Polish insurgents, East Prussia and Pomerania had anticipated Polish aggression, and western Germany would have become a battleground if German resistance to the French occupation of the Ruhr early in 1923 had compelled the French to seize more German territory. These external threats had swelled the ranks of *Verbände* (patriotic organizations) such as the *Stahlhelm, Heimatverbände, Jungdeutscher Orden*, and *Arbeitskommandos*, which provided emergency defensive troops who were politically right-wing and unwilling to follow the orders of the regular cadre.

After 1923 internal order was restored, Stresemann's Locarno policy relieved Franco-German tension, and the problem of national defense was concentrated in the east. But the issue of irregular forces remained. Prussia's Socialist government, headed by Prime Minister Otto Braun and Minister of the Interior Carl Severing, both of whom had sanctioned the use of irregulars in time of emergency, must either be courted or deceived if the Army were to continue the *Grenzschutz* and other secret defensive preparations. By mid-1923 the Defense Ministry had already, apparently, elected courtship. In June, after months of bickering between the Defense Ministry and the Prussian government, Gessler and Severing reached an agreement on national and border defense.

The subsequent "regulations" (*Richtlinien*) issued by Gessler defined *Landesschutz* as defense of the borders against enemy attack, and internal protection against rebellion and other violent disruptions of public order. The *Grenzschutz* was a part of *Landesschutz* on Germany's eastern boundaries, including East Prussia. The "regulations" called for close cooperation between civilian and military authorities, and control over stores of arms by politically reliable personnel, forbidding participation of paramilitary *Verbände* in the implementation of these measures.[42] Early in 1926 the Army Command gave evidence that it was asserting control over border defense. Seeckt issued a directive centralizing all matters pertaining to frontier defense in a new department within the *Truppenamt*, T2III. And General Wetzell, Chief of the *Truppenamt*, reiterated the Army's policy of refusing to collaborate with the *Verbände*.[43]

The Prussian government, however, viewed as insufficient and insincere the Army's efforts to abide by the defense "regulations" of 1923. In a meeting with Gessler and Stresemann on 29 October 1926, Otto Braun complained about the illegal military training of civilians, and the participation of *Stahlhelm* members in the construction of concrete bunkers near Küstrin on the Oder.[44] A few days later, Braun received a long report from the new Prussian Minister of the Interior, Albert Grzesinski, declaring that the Army had violated the "regulations" of 1923 by acting on its own to undertake

[42] The "regulations" of 30 June 1923, in *RK*, K951/K248617-19; Müller, *Vaterland*, pp. 324-25; Severing, *Lebensweg*, II, 129-30.

[43] Chief of the *Truppenamt* to chiefs of staff of Group Commands, *Wehrkreis* Commands, and cavalry divisions, 1 April 1926; in Carsten, *Reichswehr and Politics*, p. 231. " 'The importance of the army in the state rests in particular on the fact that we have succeeded, in six years of hard work, in detaching the soldiers from the struggle of political opinions and the conflict of interests; the same rule applies with equal force to our efforts in the realm of frontier defence.' "

[44] *AA*, Stresemann notes, 29 October, 7155/H151923-5; Eyck, *Weimar Republic*, II, 91-92. In this conference Braun also stated that Severing doubted whether Gessler took Prussian complaints seriously, and that Schleicher had replied with rancor to Prussian disapproval of the military training of civilians.

measures not envisaged in that document. The frontier defense organization, he continued, " 'is *politically completely one-sided*. It leans mainly on circles which are hostile to the republic. The nucleus of the organization is the *Kreis* officers, who are officers of the old army and stand, almost without exception, politically on the right.' "[45]

Civil-military relations concerning border and national defense were still rancorous at the end of Seeckt's tenure as Chief of the Army Command. Shortly after Seeckt's dismissal, one high-ranking officer wrote a friend that " 'in questions of defence we have made no progress for years, only because S[eeckt] could not be persuaded to discuss all these matters openly with the government.' "[46] For the same reason Gessler was glad to be rid of Seeckt, and promised the cabinet that he and the new Chief of the Army Command, General Heye, would work closely with the Prussian civilian authorities. Gessler and Heye would submit to the cabinet those steps that they thought were required for border defense. The measures the cabinet approved, thereby assuming political responsibility for them, would then be discussed with the Prussian government and its consent obtained.[47]

[45] Grzesinski to Braun, 6 November 1926; in Carsten, *Reichswehr and Politics*, p. 229; the complete report in *RK*, K951/K248620-44. Grzesinski had served for a very short time as Undersecretary (or State Secretary) to the Defense Minister, resigning on 1 September 1920. On the *Kreis* (district) officers and their recruiting of irregular troops, see Carsten, *ibid.*, pp. 147ff., 225ff., 269ff.

[46] Colonel Joachim von Stülpnagel to Colonel Alexander Freiherr von Falkenhausen, 20 November 1926; in Carsten, *ibid.*, p. 212.

[47] Gessler's attitude toward Seeckt in *AA*, Stresemann notes of meeting with Gessler and Braun, 29 October 1926, 7155/H151924. The new cooperative course of Gessler and Heye is discussed by Carsten, *Reichswehr and Politics*, pp. 265ff. Stresemann told Chamberlain he was glad that Seeckt had retired, and that relations between Army Command and government had already improved. Heye "had come frankly to Stresemann saying that he should regard himself merely as an organ of the government, that he perfectly recognized that there could not be two governments or two policies in the Reich, and that he was merely a part of the administration. He should make

Heye, Schleicher, and Gessler's successor, Wilhelm Groener, shared this more conciliatory attitude. Indeed Schleicher's memorandum of December 1926 sketched the outlines of civil-military cooperation for the next few years. The Army, he wrote, must improve its relations with the political arm by clearly and truthfully presenting Germany's minimum defensive needs, rather than parading as many wants as possible and then awaiting the inevitable decimation of the list by the politicians. The minimum program was " 'a well-prepared border defense in the east and all preparations for a rapid and complete mobilization of the military forces on hand in peacetime.' "[48]

In February 1927 General Heye reported to the cabinet the current status and future needs of the Army's frontier defense program. Chancellor Wilhelm Marx (Center Party) and the cabinet (a new, Rightist coalition that included four Nationalists) endorsed this program, which called for civil-military collaboration in the maintenance of secret arms stores and units of civilian volunteers as the first line of defense against Polish invasion.[49] But Otto Braun was unwilling to accommodate the cabinet and Defense Ministry. The Prussian Prime Minister did not reject border defense in principle. Nor was his opposition grounded simply in his distrust of the political leanings of the civilian volunteers. Braun and other Socialist leaders in Prussia realized that the Army's program for border defense was but a part of its larger plan

his proposals to the government, take his instructions from them and carry out their policy." Chamberlain (Geneva) to Foreign Office (Tyrrell), 6 December 1926, *DBFP*, Ser. IA, II, 580.

[48] In Vogelsang, *Reichswehr und NSDAP*, p. 412. See also Müller, *Vaterland*, pp. 221-22. On Groener's professional military background and political acceptability as reasons for his suitability as Defense Minister, and on the opponents and supporters of his appointment, see Craig, *Prussian Army*, pp. 429-31; Eyck, *Weimar Republic*, II, 146ff.; Wheeler-Bennett, *Nemesis of Power*, pp. 194ff.

[49] Protocol of cabinet meeting of 26 February 1927; in Carsten, *Reichswehr and Politics*, p. 267. See also Rosenbaum, *Community of Fate*, pp. 238-39.

for national defense that would enable the Army to mobilize during peacetime,[50] an eventuality that the anti-military Social Democratic Party did not contemplate with equanimity.

In the Army's proposal of early 1928 for new "regulations," *Landesschutz* encompassed the following general requirements: the storage and safekeeping of armaments and other military supplies; the organization and training of the *Grenzschutz*; personal and material preparations for the mobilization of the peacetime fighting force into a battle-ready and expanded field army (*Feldheer*); and records of statistics related to these measures kept by civil authorities. In implementing the above, civil-military cooperation was imperative; the responsibility for it being delegated to the Military District (*Wehrkreis*) commanders and provincial *Oberpräsidenten*.[51]

The Foreign Office declared its readiness to back this plan in further discussions in the cabinet and with Prussian officials.[52] The Wilhelmstrasse agreed in principle with a system of national defense not confined to Germany's border provinces. In addition, the provisions outlined by the Army did not exceed what the Foreign Office regarded as the limits of the politically permissible. But perhaps most important, the diplomats were conscious of a growing spirit of cooperation in the military and were eager to foster interdepartmental accord by extending their support. The Wilhelmstrasse, it is true, harbored misgivings over the degree of autonomy the Army had previously enjoyed in this sphere, and over the military's past disregard for questions of foreign policy. But these doubts were considerably allayed when the Defense Ministry,

[50] On this, see Carsten, *Reichswehr and Politics*, p. 268; also *AA*, Foreign Office minute, 21 November 1927, K6/K000311-12. In November 1926, Grzesinski had called attention to the " '*secret system of mobilization*' " of the Army, which went " 'far beyond the framework of the preparations permitted for the eastern frontier areas.' " Carsten, p. 229.

[51] *AA*, Army memorandum entitled "Landesschutz," undated, K6/K000384-7. See also Gerhard Thomée, *Der Wiederaufsteig des deutschen Heeres 1918-38* (Berlin, 1939), pp. 75-76.

[52] *AA*, Forster minute, 12 May 1928, K6/K000388-9.

appreciative of the Wilhelmstrasse's industrious and successful efforts to procure the withdrawal of the Inter-Allied Military Control Commission on 31 January 1927, evinced and
acted upon a genuine concern for subordinating military planning to foreign policy, in conferences concerning defense policy as well as in joint planning for war games.[53]

A number of meetings and memoranda between representatives of the Foreign Office and Defense Ministry in the last
quarter of 1927 familiarized the diplomats with the details
of the Army's plan.[54] Stresemann, though sensitive to the effects that public knowledge of illegal defense measures might
have on Germany's foreign policy, subscribed to "the fundamental need for certain measures in the sense" recommended
by the Defense Ministry.[55] Another Foreign Office official ob-

[53] In January 1927 the two ministries cooperated during discussions
in Paris with the Inter-Allied Control Commission on the subject of
fortifications; Germany was allowed to keep some, but was ordered
to dismantle others and to refrain from constructing new positions
in certain border areas. *AA*, 4530/E142539ff. See also Salewski,
Entwaffnung und Militärkontrolle, pp. 369f.; the text (in French) of
the Allied-German agreement of 31 January in *DBFP*, Ser. IA, II,
797-98.

[54] In October, Schleicher presented to Stresemann the Defense Ministry's study, "Vortrag vor dem Herrn Reichsaussenminister über
'Landesschutz' "; *AA*, Gessler to Stresemann, 28 October, K6/
K000300; the text of the study, *ibid.*, K000301-4. Also Foreign Office
minute of conference with Colonel von Fritsch, 21 (?) November,
ibid., K000305-8; Köpke to Stresemann, 21 November, *ibid.*, K000309-
15; Stresemann to Gessler, 25 November, *ibid.*, K000316; Gessler to
Foreign Office, 6 December (with handwritten note at bottom by
Forster indicating that the Foreign Office gave its views to Fritsch
and Blomberg on 20 December), *ibid.*, K000327. There were further
talks on 6 February 1928 (Stresemann, Schubert, Groener, and Blomberg), and on 12 May (Bülow, Köpke, Forster, and Blomberg); these
as well as other correspondence on this question in *ibid.*, K000367-89.

[55] *AA*, Stresemann to Gessler, 25 November 1927, *ibid.*, K000316.
This and further evidence of Stresemann's support of secret rearmament for affirmative reasons (to increase Germany's defensive capability) should be contrasted against the view of Wolfgang Sauer.
Stresemann, Sauer says, tolerated illegal measures not because he
thought them necessary alongside his official foreign policy, but

served that, as long as the cabinet and the Prussian government had acknowledged the necessity of establishing a system of national defense, it was impracticable to restrict preparations to the border areas as the Prussian government insisted. To accept this restriction, and to limit defensive measures elsewhere in the Reich to the safeguarding of arms depots, was to invite instant defeat in the event of a Polish attack. Germany's best hope of delaying such an invasion lay in a defense program which, like the Defense Ministry's, demanded close coordination between the border districts and the interior in the mobilization of men and matériel, and evacuation of civilians from the forward zone.[56]

In spite of support from the Foreign Office and cabinet, the Defense Ministry continued to meet resistance in the halls of the Prussian government. One Prussian condition required that a clear distinction be drawn between *Grenzschutz* and *Landesschutz*, which neither the "regulations" of 1923 nor the Army's proposal of 1928 did satisfactorily. In reply, the new "regulations," which the cabinet of Hermann Müller (led by Social Democrats, but including ministers from the Center, Bavarian People's, German People's, and Democratic parties) finally passed on 26 April 1929, defined frontier defense as pertaining exclusively to the eastern borderlands: East Prussia, Pomerania, *Grenzmark* Posen-West Prussia, Frankfurt/ Oder, and Upper and Lower Silesia. National defense re-

---

because he found them already in progress when he assumed office, and he and other civil authorities were "unable to prevail against the military." Stresemann "appears fundamentally to have rejected illegal secret rearmament because it threatened his policy of revision based on understanding." "Die Mobilmachung der Gewalt," in Karl Dietrich Bracher, Sauer, and Gerhard Schulz, *Die nationalsozialistische Machtergreifung* (2d ed., Cologne & Opladen, 1962), p. 773. At least one official in the Wilhelmstrasse, however, did advise Stresemann that unless the civilian arm cooperated in defense preparations the Army would doubtless revert to the hazardous practice of collaboration with the *Verbände* of the Right; see Carsten, *Reichswehr and Politics*, p. 272.

[56] *AA*, Forster memorandum, 13 April 1928, K6/K000370-2.

ferred to all Germany, although no *Landesschutz* preparations (and no *Grenzschutz*) were permitted in the western border areas.[57] Apparently Braun's objection to planning for mobilization was either overruled or weakened by separating the two categories of defense measures.[58] But before Prussia would agree to the new "regulations" it wanted to discuss the Army's continued reliance on volunteers from nationalistic organizations hostile to the republic. Thus almost two years elapsed before Severing, once again Prussian Minister of the Interior, notified Groener that the new "regulations" would be in effect on Prussian territory beginning 1 January 1931.[59]

By its very nature, this area of civil-military relations contained questions bearing upon both foreign and domestic politics. The Foreign Office endangered its western policy by permitting and, more seriously, by collaborating in secret rearmament. The diplomats admitted this, but judged the risk worth taking for a modicum of defensive capability: Germany must violate the Treaty of Versailles in order to be in a position to attempt the self-defense sanctioned by the same treaty. Any violations must be cautious, limited, and approved by the Foreign Office, even after the withdrawal of the Inter-Allied Military Control Commission, when it would be increasingly difficult for a foreign power to petition the League of Nations to investigate German military preparations without alienating world opinion, which was becoming more and more friendly to Germany. The Allies would eventually learn of illegal measures, but would have less cause to intervene if

[57] Memorandum in the Reich Chancery, 20 February 1930; in Vogelsang, *Reichswehr und NSDAP*, pp. 413-14.

[58] See the discussion of the *Aufstellungsplan* below.

[59] Severing, *Lebensweg*, II, 188ff.; Otto Braun, *Von Weimar zu Hitler* (2d ed., New York, 1940), pp. 265-68; Carsten, *Reichswehr and Politics*, pp. 305-306, 355-56; *RK*, Schleicher to State Secretary in the Reich Chancery, 22 January and 3 February 1930, K953/ K249717, 719; Groener to Chancellor Müller, 17 February, *ibid.*, K249721-5; Severing to Groener, 23 December, *ibid.*, K249733-4; Groener to Chancellor (Brüning), 9 January 1931, *ibid.*, K249732.

those projects were "apparently harmless in intent" and strictly subordinated to the overall political interests of Germany.[60] This policy of calculated risk paid off. The French, although apprehensive about German paramilitary organizations and German rearmament in general, were to some extent reassured by Stresemann's firm grip on the conduct of a foreign policy of understanding. And in London, the Chief of the Imperial General Staff reported that Germany's military preparations "are in many cases in contravention both of the spirit and the letter of the Treaty of Versailles, but the nature of the information is such as to make it impossible for a charge to be made against Germany of breach of faith."[61]

The relaxation of international tensions and the improvement of relations between the Army and the Foreign Office did not completely eliminate potential interdepartmental ruptures over foreign policy, for the Army retained attitudes and practices not designed to humor either France or the Foreign Office. The Foreign Office correlated rearmament with international circumstances favorable either for *de jure* agreements with Germany's former enemies, or for open *de facto* rearmament with little chance of foreign intervention. Yet the Army, assuming that civil-military cooperation over *Landesschutz* had cleared the way to Germany's rearmament, might injure Germany's foreign policy by a premature *de facto* ex-

---

[60] *AA*, Köpke to Stresemann, 21 November 1927, K6/K000309-15; Forster minute, 12 May 1928, *ibid.*, K000388-9.

[61] Memorandum by the Chief of the Imperial General Staff, Field Marshal Lord Milne, 11 February 1930, "The Military Situation in Germany, January 1930," reinforcing and expanding upon a similar report of December 1928, *DBFP*, Ser. 2, I, 598. See also notes of a British Foreign Office official (referring to a letter from the War Office), 25 August 1927, *ibid.*, Ser. IA, III, 531-36; Carsten, *Reichswehr and Politics*, pp. 359-60; Manstein, *Soldatenleben*, p. 116. For the moral indignation of the chief British member of the Control Commission toward German breaches of the Treaty of Versailles, see J. H. Morgan, *Assize of Arms: The Disarmament of Germany and Her Rearmament, 1919-1939* (New York, 1946).

pansion large enough to fill even friendly powers with alarm.[62] The Foreign Office proscribed secret defensive measures in the westernmost provinces, realizing that the western powers would consider this a violation of the demilitarization clauses of the Versailles and Locarno treaties; yet the *Truppenamt* advised the formation of a *Grenzschutz* in the west.[63] Finally, although the Defense Ministry prohibited the incorporation of the *Verbände* in national defense, it unofficially maintained its close liaison with the openly anti-French *Stahlhelm* and other *Verbände* for purposes of recruiting regular and eastern *Grenzschutz* personnel.[64]

In domestic affairs, the most divisive issue remained border defense in the east. By 1930, civilian and military leaders had agreed that defense was their common concern and, accordingly, established channels of responsibility for secret measures that involved the cabinet, the budget committee of the Reichstag, the Defense Ministry, and local magistrates and commanders.[65] This and other gestures in the late 1920s indicated that the Army was trying to win the cooperation and respect of civilian authorities and political parties. Nevertheless, the traditional antipathy between officers and Social Democrats persisted with the result that conciliatory efforts by military spokesmen like Heye, Schleicher, Bonin, and Otto Hasse, and civilians like Severing and Chancellor Müller, did

[62] The Foreign Office sounded this warning in memoranda of 21 November 1927 and 12 May 1928 (see above, n. 60).

[63] On the question of a western *Grenzschutz*, see above, chap. 4.

[64] Müller, *Vaterland*, pp. 222, 324ff.; Carsten, *Reichswehr and Politics*, pp. 256-57, 264-66. At Thoiry in September 1926, Briand remarked to Stresemann that the French were worried about the *Stahlhelm*. Stresemann replied that Gessler and Seeckt had taken steps to exclude the *Stahlhelm* from military activities; Stresemann, *Vermächtnis*, III, 18-19 (an unabridged version of this part of their talk in *AA*, Stresemann notes, 20 September 1926, 7332/H162521).

[65] Carsten, *Reichswehr and Politics*, pp. 274-75; Vogelsang, *Reichswehr und NSDAP*, p. 157; Müller, *Vaterland*, pp. 317-18; recommendations of the *Truppenamt* concerning civil-military collaboration in *RWM, Truppenamt* (T1), "Folgerungen," 26 March 1929, II H 597, pp. 7-8.

not convince either side of the good will and understanding of the other.[66] The officer, who was ordered to stay "above politics," valued the patriotism and military usefulness of political groups like the paramilitary *Verbände*. The Social Democrat, for whom national defense was indeed and properly a party-political issue, believed that recruiting antirepublicans to defend the republic was not unlike asking a bear to guard the honey. The Socialist Prussian government could point on the one hand to defense "regulations" and orders from the office of the Defense Minister prohibiting inclusion of the *Verbände* in border and national defense; on the other to the fact that, although units of the *Stahlhelm* and Hitler's *Sturmabteilungen* did not belong to the *Grenzschutz*, many individual *Stahlhelm* and S.A. members did.[67]

Differences of opinion between the Army and the Foreign Office over defense policy could be surmounted, provided that the prevailing winds of cooperation continued to blow and the leadership in the Defense Ministry and Wilhelmstrasse concurred in subordinating military planning to foreign policy. Soldiers and diplomats shared a belief conducive to cooperation: military planning and foreign policy, whether secret or overt, should be nonpartisan. In their view, Social-

[66] Carsten, *Reichswehr and Politics*, chap. 6, *passim*; Heinrici, Zeugenschrifttum no. 66 II, and General Hermann Foertsch, Zeugenschrifttum no. 37, Institut für Zeitgeschichte (Munich); interviews (all). On the Army and the Social Democratic Party, see Gustav Adolf Caspar, *Die sozialdemokratische Partei und das deutsche Wehrproblem in den Jahren der Weimarer Republik* (Frankfurt am Main, 1959); also the excellent analysis in Gordon, *Reichswehr and Republic*, pp. 372-95. Gordon (p. 380) finds that Severing "wavered between half-hearted cooperation with the Heeresleitung and open hostility to everything military." In a speech before the Reichstag on 20 January 1928, Severing warned that the Army seemed determined to restore its wartime control over foreign and domestic policy; Craig, *Prussian Army*, p. 425.

[67] On the *Stahlhelm* and defense, see Volker R. Berghahn, *Der Stahlhelm: Bund der Frontsoldaten 1918-1935* (Düsseldorf, 1966), pp. 55-63, 131-42; the *Stahlhelm* and other *Verbände*, Carsten, *Reichswehr and Politics*, chaps. 5, 6, *passim*.

ists had on more than one occasion jeopardized Germany's politico-military position by making illegal activities a partisan issue, and the strong suspicion that Socialists could not be trusted to keep national secrets lingered on.[68]

Believing that their areas of responsibility should be above party scrutiny, and mistrusting Germany's largest political party, the Army and Foreign Office confronted the truth that national defense was a volatile political issue exposed to discussion by parties, general public, and state (*Land*) governments. The Weimar constitution empowered the Reichstag to enact all Reich legislation including the budget (Arts. 68 & 85), to express its confidence in the Chancellor and individual Reich ministers or withhold it from them (Arts. 54 & 56), and to impeach the President, Chancellor, and ministers for criminal violations of the constitution or Reich laws (Art. 59). Each state, which must be a republic with a representative assembly (Art. 17), retained the right of jurisdiction "so long and in so far as the Reich does not exercise its jurisdiction," except "in cases where the Reich possesses exclusive jurisdiction" (Art. 12).[69]

Because of these republican and federal emphases in the constitution, civil-military relations in the Weimar Republic posed a more complicated problem than they had in Bismarck's day. At both parliamentary and federal levels, the defense policy of the government and departments was subject to criticism, amendment, and delay. The Reichstag (which voted the military budget annually rather than every seven years, the interval established by Bismarck in 1874) had in effect entered the lists to struggle over policy-making. In Prussia, the largest *Land* and the one most vital for *Grenzschutz* and *Landesschutz*, the Social Democrats controlled the state government. And, since the Weimar Chancellor was not

[68] See Hilger, *Incompatible Allies*, p. 203.

[69] Gerhard Anschütz, *Die Verfassung des Deutschen Reichs vom 11. August 1919* (rev. ed., Berlin, 1926); translated passages (here and below) from E. A. Goerner (ed.), *The Constitutions of Europe* (Chicago, 1967), pp. 102-33.

—like Bismarck—Prime Minister of Prussia, and the President not—like the Kaiser—also titular head of Prussia, there was greater chance that the central and Prussian governments might disagree over an issue of national policy.[70]

Vulnerability to parliamentary and Prussian interference was a thorn in the side of those involved in joint planning, and how to pluck it out became an increasingly imperative assignment: the Reichstag showed no symptoms of maturing into a law-making body capable of united and sustained effort for national defense; the parties frequently refused to co-operate in providing Chancellors with stable majorities, and their parliamentary delegations exercised often crippling control over their respective leaders who occupied cabinet posts; Prussia, in the judgment of the Foreign Office and Defense Ministry, cooperated only reluctantly and partially. In their search for an Androcles, both departments looked back wistfully to Bismarck as the man who had successfully subordinated military to political considerations, pushed military budgets through the Reichstag, and made Prussia the central pillar of a powerful Reich. This sort of nostalgia was undemocratic, but not reactionary, for the two ministries—and the executive—began to shape a novel system of civil-military relations within the flexible constitutional framework of the republic.

The Weimar system, that is, the paradigm of institutional civil-military relations that emerged during the years of stability, concentrated power in the executive-departmental sphere and stressed interdepartmental planning. At the federal level, the cabinet, Foreign Office, and Defense Ministry together exerted pressure on Prussia to accept the new defense "regulations." Since these "regulations" violated the Treaty of Versailles, they could not be made Reich law, and,

[70] In a letter to Groener of 3 September 1928, Schleicher pointed out that the Prussian government was as dissatisfied with the handling of military questions by a cabinet led by Social Democrats as it had been earlier with a conservative cabinet; in Carsten, *Reichswehr and Politics*, pp. 304-305.

therefore, the constitution did not clearly spell out the respective powers of the Reich and Prussian governments over *Landesschutz*.[71] In the opinion of those Germans who advocated the complete subordination of the separate states to the central control of the Reich, this executive-departmental constraint was a temporary and unsatisfactory solution to the problem of Reich-Prussian dualism.[72] Barring constitutional reform, however, it would probably have become normal procedure.

Even before the crisis of the early 1930s, the executive and departments increased their power at the expense of the Reichstag, for Hindenburg, Chancellor Müller, Stresemann, Groener, Schleicher, and the bureaucracy all believed that the political parties were too factional and not national enough in their interests. The reformers in the Bendlerstrasse were more averse to parliamentary sovereignty than either Müller or Stresemann, but they could not completely eliminate the legislative assembly from the region of policy-making—notably, with regard to the budget and votes of no confidence. Groener and Schleicher therefore solicited the participation of the Social Democrats in the hopes of composing a parliamentary majority that would support legal and overt national defense policies, such as naval construction. But simultaneously they began to erect institutional obstacles to parliamen-

---

[71] Although national defense came under the exclusive jurisdiction of the Reich, the constitution (Art. 79) required that in "the organization of the German people for defense . . . due consideration [be given] the peculiarities of the people of the separate states." The constitution also anticipated that regional "peculiarities" might lead a state government to pass a law not in harmony with Reich law, or to be lax in its execution of Reich law (Arts. 13-15). Thus, the constitution eliminated neither the federal level nor federal disputes from civil-military relations concerning defense policies that—unlike *Grenzschutz* and *Landesschutz*—were established by Reich law.

[72] See Earl R. Beck, *The Death of the Prussian Republic: A Study of Reich-Prussian Relations, 1932-1934* (Tallahassee, Fla., 1959), chap. 1; Bracher, *Auflösung*, pp. 559-65; Carsten, *Reichswehr and Politics*, pp. 167-68, 190-91; Eyck, *Weimar Republic*, ii, 139-42; Schultz, *Demokratie und Diktatur*, chap. 12.

tary control. Groener and Schleicher viewed the Defense Minister as a champion for the military rather than a watchdog for the electorate, responsible to the President rather than the Reichstag. They created the *Ministeramt* as a bureaucratic state secretaryship to assist the minister and represent him before the Reichstag and cabinet, instead of the parliamentary secretaryship demanded by the SPD, responsible to the Reichstag, and therefore providing an opportunity to increase parliamentary control over military affairs. Finally, they sanctioned presidential intervention to build stable majority governments or, failing that, governments enjoying the President's confidence above party.[73]

The Weimar system left unresolved a number of constitutional problems belonging to the executive-departmental sphere of the republic. At the executive level, the President and Chancellor remained potential rivals, for the constitution not only drew a distinction between the presidency and the government, but also gave executive and appointive powers to each. Ministers might consider themselves responsible either to the Reichstag or the President; they might be party men, who tried with little success to free themselves from the control of their parliamentary delegations, or bureaucratic "experts" bound to no party. The Chancellor or a head of department might assume more than one cabinet portfolio, a latent threat to the autonomy of individual ministries and to

[73] See Caspar, *Sozialdemokratische Partei und deutsche Wehrproblem*, pp. 29ff.; Schmädeke, *Militärische Kommandogewalt*, pp. 160ff., 176-81, 182ff.; Wohlfeil, *Heer und Republik*, pp. 121-24; Schleicher's proposal to President Hindenburg in the aftermath of the political crisis of December 1926–January 1927, in Dorpalen, *Hindenburg*, p. 127; documentary article by Becker, "Politik der Wehrmachtabteilung." Haungs rejects Schmädeke's view that the Groener-Schleicher formula for ministerial responsibility represented "nothing but a juristic construction derived from a reactionary ideology." Schmädeke, p. 117; Haungs, *Reichspräsident*, p. 191 and n. Although Haungs correctly points to the ambivalence of the constitution in his criticism of Schmädeke, neither author examines interdepartmental relations; both concentrate on the parliamentary and presidential dimensions of civil-military relations.

the distribution of political influence among many departments. Finally, departments might battle among themselves over particular issues. But in spite of all this, the Weimar system had begun to work. The President and Chancellor left the formulation of foreign policy and military planning to the departments. Neither the Chancellor nor any of his ministers took over additional portfolios. Müller's government, viewed by the Defense Ministry as the political arm, pushed the controversial naval budget through the Reichstag, voted to finance the *A-Plan* without an explicit legislative act, and passed the new "regulations" without the aid of a presidential decree.[74] Party leaders (Stresemann and Severing) and a nonparty expert (Groener) concurred that their departments must cooperate in the implementation of illegal measures. Stresemann and Groener shared the belief that their own interdepartmental relations must be based on the primacy of foreign policy.

The secrecy and illegality of the *Landesschutz* program contributed persuasively to the argument for executive-departmental control and interdepartmental solidarity. But the Weimar system—or something like it—would have developed even if the Treaty of Versailles had not restricted Germany's military power; because of their mistrust of parties and parliamentary sovereignty, the departments would have acted in very much the same way no matter what the terms of Versailles. The departments encountered impotent resistance at the parliamentary level when they declared that politico-military activity was the responsibility of the executive and bureaucracy. The moderate parties (People's, Center, Democrats) and SPD could not agree on a clear definition of civil-military relations or on concrete reform to insure parliamentary control.[75]

[74] On the *A-Plan*, see this chapter; on the battle cruiser issue, chap. 7.

[75] On the parties' failure to develop a stable parliamentary majority and the consequent increase in the political initiative and power of the President after 1925, see Bracher, *Auflösung*, pp. 29-37, 47-51;

Moreover, the Weimar system owed its growth to its apparent legitimacy (or, perhaps better, its lack of a constitutional bar sinister) and to the initiative and adroitness with which the departments and the executive reached out for control in a constitutional penumbra. The advocates of executive-departmental control could argue that their interpretation of political primacy was not unconstitutional, since the founding documents did not clearly establish parliamentary control over foreign policy and military planning. The Weimar system was *sui generis*, a peculiar adaptation of the principles of Clausewitz to a new set of political circumstances.[76] In politico-military activity, the Foreign Office and Defense Ministry concurred that it was easier theoretically and more efficient practically to preserve the idea of political primacy in an authoritarian policy-making network that operated chiefly at the departmental level and severely limited parliamentary participation.

AUFSTELLUNGSPLAN

The Army's defensive preparations included a plan for its expansion and mobilization in an emergency. The *Truppenamt* justified this *Aufstellungsplan*, or *A-Plan* as it was abbreviated, on the grounds that the government, confronted with an imminent invasion of German soil, might decide to declare a state of war, and that it was the Army's responsibility to be prepared to carry out the President's order to form a wartime force.[77]

Dorpalen, *Hindenburg*, chaps. 4, 5; Eyck, *Weimar Republic*, II, 50-52, 102-103, 145-46, 149, 164-65, 196-98; Haungs, *Reichspräsident*, pp. 192, 274, 280, 287-93; Schmädeke, *Militärische Kommandogewalt, passim.*

[76] There are similarities between the Weimar system and what Janowitz describes as "the pattern of decision-making" in the United States since World War II: the emphasis on administrative or managerial techniques and the limited power of Congress over politico-military decisions. *Professional Soldier*, especially part 7.

[77] *RWM*, preliminary outline of *A-Plan* drawn up by T2 and sent

As early as January 1921, during a period of tension on the Silesian frontier, Seeckt had recommended trebling the Army to 21 infantry divisions in the event of conflict.[78] This remained the kernel of subsequent planning in the Defense Ministry. In 1925, the *Waffenamt* envisaged increasing the number of cavalry divisions from 3 to 5, and adding 39 border defense units and an air force to the trebled infantry divisions.[79] By 1929, the number of projected border defense units had been reduced to 23 because of the prohibition against a western border defense. In addition, the *Truppenamt* designated the following as components of the "first organizational goal": preparations for fortifications, demolitions, and civilian evacuation in the east; war economy; supply; studies of possible operations in case of conflict (*A-Fall*, short for *Aufstellungsfall*); transportation; air force; training of civilians to fill border defense units and new regular divisions; cooperation of civilian authorities; and preparations for a *Grenzschutz* in the west as well as the east.[80]

---

to other sections in the *Truppenamt*, as well as the *Waffenamt*, Naval Command, and other offices, 30 June 1927, II H 135/2; also *Truppenamt* (T1), "Folgerungen," 26 March 1929, II H 597, pp. 2-4.

[78] Rabenau, *Seeckt*, pp. 480-81.

[79] Carsten, *Reichswehr and Politics*, p. 220; Burkhart Mueller-Hillebrand, *Das Heer 1933-1945*, I: *Das Heer bis zum Kriegsbeginn* (Darmstadt, 1954), pp. 17ff. Testifying at the Nürnberg trials, Manstein and other high-ranking officers gave the impression that mobilization planning did not begin until 1929-30, although perhaps they meant to imply that before 1929 only preliminary studies existed. See their statement in *Trials of War Criminals before the Nuernberg Military Tribunals under Control Council Law No. 10* (15 vols.; Washington, D.C., 1949ff.), x, 525.

[80] *RWM, Truppenamt* (T1), "Folgerungen," 26 March 1929, II H 597. According to General Heinrici, the *A-Plan* really began to move forward when Colonel von Mittelberger replaced Colonel Bonin as chief of T2 early in 1927. Bonin, Heinrici recalls, had misgivings about the *A-Plan* because it violated the Treaty of Versailles; interview. See Bonin's memorandum on mobilization measures, 18 January 1927, in *Trials of War Criminals*, x, 428-31.

194

The Army cherished no illusion that it would soon be able to muster a *Kriegswehrmacht* of 21 infantry divisions, for it lacked the necessary trained reserves, ammunition, and strategic raw materials. Nor could it be confident of a "mobilization period" (*Rüstungszeit*, or *Anlaufzeit*) before the outbreak of hostilities. To provide such a prelude was "the task of diplomacy," but the probability that Germany's borders would be suddenly overrun required immediate defensive countermoves by whatever force Germany had ready for battle. And faced with these two realities—inadequate numbers and matériel, and the time factor—as of mid-1927 the Army and Navy could assemble no more than an "emergency armed force" (*Not-Wehrmacht*), the Army itself no more than an "emergency army" (*Notstandsheer*).[81]

Admitting its military limitations, however, the Army laid the foundations for the restoration of Germany's defensive capability during what it hoped would be a prolonged period of European peace. This gradual process was to be based on an annual reevaluation of preliminary studies by appropriate units and authorities, emphasizing simplicity and, "unfortunately, the *lower* limits of the necessary."[82] At the end of the first stage of rearmament, 31 March 1933, the *Truppenamt* hoped to have the resources to field 16 fully equipped infantry divisions, with enough men (but not weapons) for the remaining 5 divisions, plus 3½ cavalry divisions, 23 *Grenzschutz* units, and related support troops.[83]

[81] *RWM*, preliminary outline of *A-Plan* by T2, 30 June 1927; memorandum (by T2?) marked "Isar . . . Weser," code names by which the Defense Ministry designated *A-Plan* records, 23 November 1927; II H 135/2.

[82] *RWM*, preliminary outline of *A-Plan* by T2, 30 June 1927, *ibid.*; *Truppenamt* (T1), "Folgerungen," 26 March 1929, II H 597, p. 5.

[83] *RWM*, *ibid.*, p. 4; also Manstein, *Soldatenleben*, pp. 111f.; Georg Thomas, *Geschichte der deutschen Wehr- und Rüstungswirtschaft (1918-1943/45)*, ed. Wolfgang Birkenfeld (Boppard, 1966), pp. 53-61, 488-97; Wohlfeil, *Heer und Republik*, pp. 228-33; coordination of the national railroad system with the Army's strategic needs, in *RWM*, II H 570, 572.

Germany's weak politico-military situation dictated the tactical organization of this expanded force. An inspection of Germany's border defenses late in 1923 yielded a sobering conclusion:

> Even without regard to East Prussia, the border situation in the east is not favorable to strategic defense. Considering the current ratio of military power, any attempt to hold the entire border defensively must fail. Even with a considerable inferiority in forces, we will be able to seek a decision only on the offensive. Still, a well thought out system of defense in the east is necessary, for we can attack decisively only at one point, while for the rest we must strive to surrender as little as possible of German territory with its irretrievable resources, and, in so doing, expend as few forces as possible.[84]

The Army Section (T1) in the *Truppenamt*, responsible for operations, agreed with this assessment and with the distinction made in the report between "border positions" (*Grenzstellungen*) and "fallback positions" (*Rückhaltsstellungen*). The mission of the units in the "border positions" was to delay the enemy's advance, giving the main force behind them time to mobilize.

This conception of two lines of defense was continued in the *A-Plan* of the late 1920s. The front line, or *Grenzschutz-Zone* as it came to be called, would be guarded by border defense units under their local commanders. The area east of the Oder river was such a zone; since it was within 50 kilometers of the border, fortifications were prohibited by the Treaty of Versailles (Article 180), but there the Army hoped to construct permanent works as soon as the political situation allowed.[85] The main line of defense to the rear, or *Rück-*

[84] *RWM*, report by the Inspector of Engineers and Fortifications, "Die Landesverteidigung im Osten," to *Truppenamt* (T1), 24 October, II H 518.

[85] The Foreign Office, having been consulted by the Defense Ministry, said that there were no political objections if the Army built

196

halt-Zone (also referred to as the *operative Rückhalt-Zone*), to which any regular troops in the forward zone would withdraw in case of attack, would be manned chiefly by regular units. Examples were the *Oder-Rückhalt-Zone* (the left bank of the Oder), and the "Heilsberg triangle" in East Prussia, both of which were more than 50 kilometers from Germany's borders and therefore areas in which (with the exception of Küstrin and Glogau on the Oder, too close to Poland in the opinion of the Allies) heavy fortifications were not outlawed by the Treaty of Versailles or subsequent multilateral agreements. These rearward zones would receive reinforcements as mobilization progressed and as *Grenzschutz* units withdrew, and could provide both defensive lines and points of concentration for offensive counterattacks.[86]

The *A-Plan* went into effect on 1 April 1930. In a related directive to the Chiefs of the Army and Naval Commands, Groener made it clear that Germany was still many years away from possessing a force of 21 divisions. What Germany did have immediately available was an "army ready for action" (*marschbereites Reichsheer*)—presumably a gradually expanding equivalent to the "emergency army" mentioned above[87]—which could be employed partly, entirely, or with reinforcements. The *Reichsheer* could be prepared for action, without "extraordinary legal measures and without risking

---

positions in peacetime along the left bank of the Oder so long as it did not include Küstrin and Glogau (the Army plan did not). *RWM, Truppenamt* (Blomberg) to *Wehrkreis* III, 14 June 1928, and Schubert to Defense Minister, 28 March 1929, II H 525; *AA*, Köpke memoranda, 28 August 1928, 9481/H276241-2, and 23 March 1929, 3170/D681189-93.

[86] Various documents in *RWM*, II H 518, 524/2; preliminary outline of *A-Plan* by T2, 30 June 1927, II H 135/2. For more on tactics and fortifications, see Mueller-Hillebrand, *Das Heer*, pp. 38-41 (includes maps); also Manstein, *Soldatenleben*, pp. 120ff.; Müller, *Vaterland*, pp. 322-23; Vogelsang, *Reichswehr und NSDAP*, pp. 31ff. In interviews, Generals Brennecke, Hauck, Hausser, Heinrici, Fritz Kühne, and Walther Nehring provided useful information.

[87] See p. 195.

foreign policy complications," within one or two days after the order to mobilize. According to projections, however, Germany would have a field army (*Feldheer*) of 21 regular divisions in addition to the *Grenzschutz* units, or conceivably even a "further reinforced field army" (*weiter verstärktes Feldheer*). The *Feldheer* would be expected to complete its mobilization within five to eight days. Because of its size and material needs, it required a "mobilization period" (*Anlaufzeit*) before the outbreak of hostilities. The Army's objectives, therefore, were to train and equip the *Reichsheer* with the most modern weapons, and to progress steadily with plans for the men, matériel, and training necessary for the *Feldheer*.[88]

The *A-Plan* provided for mobilization of Germany's available military resources, a form of planning that the Treaty of Versailles outlawed, but that the German Army deemed necessary for any army, even one on the defensive.[89] This illegality of mobilization plans was a major stumbling-block in civil-

[88] *RWM*, Groener to Chiefs of Army and Naval Commands, "Die Aufgaben der Wehrmacht," 16 April 1930, PG 34072.

[89] By "mobilization" is meant "the transition of the 'immobile' to the 'mobile' army, that is, all necessary forces and means are provided to the army, quartered during peacetime in its garrisons, so that it can move freely 'in the field,' 'operate,' and supply itself"; as in Mueller-Hillebrand, *Das Heer*, p. 47. General Heusinger's brief description is the "assembling and arming of an expanded army"; interview. By these definitions, and by design of military planners in the 1920s, the *A-Plan* was clearly a mobilization plan. Although it did not provide for a mass mobilization of the kind employed in 1914, it still had political implications for both foreign and domestic policy, for it was in violation of international law (the Treaty of Versailles) and thus the law of the Reich. Therefore, the milder word "Aufstellung" was preferred to "Mobilmachung," which seldom appears in the documents. On this, see Müller, *Vaterland*, pp. 317-18; also the memorandum by Herr Semler, General Counsel in the Defense Ministry, 7 January 1927, in *Trials of War Criminals*, IX, 254-55. Semler distinguished between the probable legality of mobilizing only those forces allowed Germany by the Treaty of Versailles and the distinct illegality of the more extensive mobilization envisaged in current planning.

military collaboration. In 1926 Schleicher, optimistic that the part of a minimum defense program that called for an eastern *Grenzschutz* would be endorsed by most politicians, cautioned that plans for mobilization would " 'meet with little support.' " Schleicher's warning proved correct when Otto Braun and the Prussian government demanded that a clear distinction be made between national and border defense, and that measures for the former be confined to safeguarding stores of arms.[90]

Schleicher opposed Braun on this issue, and the most that he would concede to the Social Democrat's aversion to mobilization was that the *A-Plan* must be regulated by cabinet decisions concerning *Landesschutz*.[91] In these decisions the predominantly Socialist cabinet—and, eventually, the Prussian government—yielded to the Army's persuasive argument that plans for mobilization were vital to Germany's "right of self-defense," and that frontier defense was but a part of national defense. In early October 1928 the cabinet of Chancellor Müller approved the Defense Ministry's recommendations for financing the *A-Plan*.[92] And the new defense "regulations" passed by the cabinet in 1929, though distinguishing between *Grenzschutz* and *Landesschutz*, did not prohibit measures the civilian authorities knew to be included in the *A-Plan*.

The expanded army would be formed in three "waves," the first two containing the great bulk of the regular troops; the third, with a very small percentage of regulars, was not expected to be ready for immediate use at the start of hostilities. But even those divisions in the first two "waves" would include untrained men, whose numbers would increase proportionately as the percentage of veterans (still trained secretly)

[90] Schleicher memorandum, December 1926; in Vogelsang, *Reichswehr und NSDAP*, p. 412. See the discussion of *Grenzschutz* and *Landesschutz* above.

[91] *RWM*, Schleicher to *Truppenamt*, 22 April 1929, II H 597.

[92] Müller, *Vaterland*, pp. 317-18. Apart from the regular defense budget, the Defense Ministry drew from secret funds and the budgets of other ministries to pay for rearmament.

declined due to old age.[93] Where, then, would these untrained reserves come from? In 1929 the *Truppenamt* assumed that enough able-bodied civilians would volunteer, and concentrated on the problem of giving them some military training in peacetime. The *Waffenamt*, however, rejected this supposition. "The influence of family and neighbors," its chief observed, was "too great for men to undertake military service without compulsion." The only way to insure sufficient personnel for both the *Grenzschutz* and regular divisions, he asserted, was to follow the example of East Prussia and obtain special legislation obligating all able-bodied men to perform labor service. From this large number, some could be selected for military training.[94]

As the chief of the *Waffenamt* realized, the question of manpower had far-reaching political implications because it was national and, ultimately, legislative in its dimensions. To finance, recruit, and equip an army of trebled size required cooperation between military and civilian officials, and reconciliation with the Social Democratic Party. Groener and Schleicher shared the burden of these requirements, and this largely accounted for Schleicher's increasing political activity as head of the *Wehrmachtsabteilung* and, beginning in 1929, the *Ministeramt*. Both offices were charged with superintend-

[93] In 1929 it was suggested that each division in the first two "waves" consist of approximately equal numbers of active troops, former soldiers, and untrained personnel; *RWM, Truppenamt* (T1), "Folgerungen," 26 March 1929, II H 597, pp. 10, 17. For a plan of March 1928, with different percentages, see Carsten, *Reichswehr and Politics*, pp. 272-73. In some Army District Commands resentment arose because the *A-Plan* required existing divisions to give up so many of their regulars to new divisions in an emergency; interview with General Heinrici. But to General Flörke, who as Captain was Adjutant of the 12th Infantry Regiment in Halberstadt, supply was a greater problem than the trebling of units in the event of conflict; interview.

[94] *RWM, Truppenamt* (T1), "Folgerungen," 26 March 1929, II H 597, pp. 9-11, 16-17; General Ludwig (head of the *Waffenamt*) to Chief of *Truppenamt*, 6 April, *ibid.*

ing relations between the Army on the one side, and civilian leaders and political parties on the other.

The rise of Schleicher and the *Ministeramt*, though contributing to cooperation with the Foreign Office, cabinet, and parties of the center and Left, at the same time sowed dissension in the Army. The Chief of the Army Command, through his subordinates in the *Truppenamt* and other offices, was responsible for *Landesschutz* and *A-Plan* preparations. In practice, however, Schleicher interloped into this organizational area of planning. For example, in reply to its long report of 26 March 1929, he curtly reminded the *Truppenamt* that *A-Plan* activities must remain within the political framework of current decisions regarding *Landesschutz*, and that the *Ministeramt* would have an important share in evaluating the details of the report.[95] Schleicher considered this a legitimate intrusion in view of the designated role of the *Ministeramt* and the interrelationship between domestic politics and military planning. But the domineering manner in which he interposed—then and on other occasions—offended many officers, who were already irritated by the meddling of the *Ministeramt* in military affairs they considered none of its business, and by the attempts of Groener and Schleicher to make peace with the Social Democrats in behalf of national defense.[96]

This intradepartmental friction, caused not simply by personality conflicts but also by pressures inherent in the process of institutional adjustments—the price of trying to establish the Weimar system on solid institutional footing—seems not to have destroyed the belief of most officers in the interdependence of foreign policy and military planning. The Army had taken the initiative in drawing up studies to show what

[95] *RWM*, Schleicher to *Truppenamt*, 22 April 1929, *ibid.* See also above, chap. 4.

[96] On antagonism in the officer corps toward Schleicher and the *Ministeramt*, see Carsten, *Reichswehr and Politics*, pp. 262-63, 297ff.; also Sauer, "Die Reichswehr," in Bracher, *Auflösung*, pp. 273, 276.

preparations were necessary, a proper exercise of its advisory function. The Foreign Office endorsed these recommendations and assisted the Defense Ministry in overcoming political opposition to the *A-Plan*, not because it had been browbeaten by the military leadership, but because the diplomats fundamentally agreed with the need for a plan for mobilization. Leaving the Defense Ministry to determine what specific measures should be adopted in proceeding with the *A-Plan*, the Foreign Office reserved the right to prohibit any such projects endangering Germany's foreign policy.[97] And the Defense Ministry realized that it must coordinate its planning with the Foreign Office in order to expedite mobilization of either 1) the *marschbereites Reichsheer* in an emergency, without discrediting Germany internationally, or 2) the *Feldheer* in a situation in which Germany had the benefit of a "mobilization period" before a conflict and could risk diplomatic repercussions by readying an expanded force during what was technically still a time of peace.

The officials in the Foreign Office, including Stresemann, concurred with the Defense Ministry that an intricate politico-military issue like the *A-Plan* should be decided upon and administered by professional experts. Within that province of expertise, as in the case of *Grenzschutz* and *Landesschutz*, the foundations of joint interdepartmental planning and executive-departmental authority had been laid, the Clausewitzean principle of the subordination of military planning to foreign policy preserved, and parliamentary control averted.

[97] *AA*, Forster minute, 12 May 1928, K6/K000388-9.

CHAPTER VI

Force and Foreign Policy:
Operations

IN ADDITION to questions of organization, German military planning included the "dynamic issue" of operations, or the method by and circumstances under which armed force might be employed.[1] In this operational sphere, the German Army relied on war games and other devices to study both methods and contingencies. Of particular influence on the Army's operational principles were the lessons of the First World War and the conditions of Germany's current strategic situation.[2] German operations on the western front in August 1914 had religiously adhered to a preestablished and highly detailed plan of concentration, deployment, and attack, for the General Staff had concluded that unless it followed this design to the letter the grand enterprise of enveloping and annihilating the enemy was unlikely to succeed. But the German offensive in the west had miscarried. Memories of that failure, of executing a plan that assumed Germany's engagement in a two-front war and therefore required Germany to attack France and violate Belgian neutrality even if Russia were the major enemy, and of the ensuing years of trench warfare in the west, caused a reaction among German officers against rigidly defined operation plans.

This reaction had boiled up during the war, and would surely have spilled over to influence postwar German military thinking whatever the size of the Army. Still, the severely

[1] This distinction between two major areas of military planning is a modified version of the threefold division made by Huntington in *Soldier and State*, p. 1.

[2] Manstein, *Soldatenleben*, pp. 125-26; Meinck, *Deutsche Aufrüstung*, p. 12; interviews (all).

reduced numbers and striking power of the German military force after the Treaty of Versailles in themselves also determined the Army's view of operations. Offensive operations were out of the question unless the international situation changed markedly. Defensively, Germany faced superior forces on both fronts. In the event of war, the French, Polish, and Czechoslovak Armies could choose from a number of avenues of attack. The location of the theater of operations depended, therefore, on the enemy's plan of operations. The German Army could only study various contingencies, making tentative plans for defensive measures—and, in some cases, counterattack—at each likely point of enemy invasion.[3] Aware of this interrelationship between operations and international politics, the Army solicited the collaboration of the Foreign Office in this second major area of military planning.

OPERATIONAL STUDIES

The German Army's strategic thinking during the Weimar period manifests itself most clearly in operational studies.[4] By about 1927 at the very latest, the Army was performing these at various levels. At the highest echelon, General von Seeckt had established annual generals' tours (*Führerreise*), in which the Chief of the Army Command conducted a large-scale tactical exercise on paper, with headquarters near the

---

[3] Correspondence from General Franz Halder and Field Marshal Erich von Manstein; interviews with Generals Hans von Ahlfen, Brennecke, Hauck, Hausser, and Heusinger.

[4] In interviews and correspondence with former officers, the words "operations" and "strategic planning" required definition. Some—e.g., Ahlfen, Halder, and Manstein—understood "operations" to connote the offensive, and emphasized that Germany had no such plans until after 1935. The broader definition used throughout this chapter encompasses, however, both theoretical studies and actual plans for defensive as well as offensive use of the armed forces. For an East German view of the operational doctrine of Heusinger, Manstein, and "other militarists" in the *Truppenamt*, see Wolfgang Wünsche, *Strategie der Niederlage* ([East] Berlin, 1961), pp. 66-67.

front under consideration. All or most of the commanding officers of the two Group Commands, 7 infantry divisions, and 3 cavalry divisions, participated in these tours.[5] Their field problem often explored further the questions previously deliberated in the General Staff tour. At the staff level, the Chief of the *Truppenamt* led annual General Staff tours (*Truppenamtsreise*) of group and division chiefs of staff and other General Staff officers of the rank of major and above. They, in turn, usually based their problem on the war game (*Kriegsspiel*) conducted annually by the *Truppenamt*. The *Truppenamt* held its war game in the winter, sending out theoretical assignments to other departments in the Army Command and to unit headquarters. It directed the game from the Defense Ministry, where it assembled and evaluated incoming reports in preparation for the General Staff tour that followed in the spring.

In conjunction with its war game, the *Truppenamt* required all General Staff officers to submit their solutions to operational problems (*operative Aufgaben*) assigned once or twice yearly. The Chief of the *Truppenamt* then sorted the answers (which had to be written in a mere few hours) into groups based on particular solutions, criticized each group, and presented his own solution. This practice had a twofold purpose. It provided the *Truppenamt* with useful material for planning the General Staff tour, and it continued the training of General Staff officers in operations. These officers, called *Führergehilfen*, or leader's assistants, a label that did not technically violate the prohibition in the Treaty of Versailles against a General Staff, were really General Staff officers in all but name. A remarkably select group, only about 15 (or less than 5 percent) of some 350 junior officers who took the qualifying examination each year were accepted as officers of the General Staff. To reach that plateau they had to score high marks in three years of training: two at Military District

[5] Group Command 1, its headquarters located in Berlin, controlled Military Districts I-IV; Group Command 2, at Kassel, Military Districts V-VII. Each Military District contained an infantry division.

205

Headquarters (*Wehrkreiskommando*), where their instruction by officers of their district (i.e., division) was under the general supervision of the *Truppenamt*; and (after 1923) a third year in Berlin at the Defense Ministry.[6]

Both during and after their formal training, General Staff officers worked under the watchful eye of the central office for military strategy and tactics, the *Truppenamt*.[7] By means of annual problems and General Staff tours, the *Truppenamt* continually sharpened the operational thinking of those officers picked for the highest command and staff positions. Moreover, General Staff officers joined the troops in the field in summer and fall maneuvers of units from company to division size. During the seasonal sequence of this integrated training program—from winter studies and war games, to spring General Staff tours, late spring or summer generals' tours, and unit maneuvers in the fall—the guidance of the *Truppenamt* came largely from two of its four sections. T4, the Training Section (*Ausbildungsabteilung*), issued tactical manuals and supervised the three-year training program for General Staff candidates. T1, the Army Section (*Heeresabteilung*), assembled in its Group I what was essentially the operations staff of the Chief of the Army Command.[8] Some of Germany's greatest operations specialists of the Second World War served in Group I during the Weimar period, planning the annual war games and the General Staff and generals' tours.

[6] On the *Führergehilfen*, see Carsten, *Reichswehr and Politics*, pp. 209-10; Waldemar Erfurth, *Die Geschichte des deutschen Generalstabes von 1918 bis 1945* (Göttingen, 1957), pp. 125-26; Walter Görlitz, *History of the German General Staff, 1657-1945* (New York, 1953), pp. 225-27; Gordon, *Reichswehr and Republic*, pp. 300-301; Manstein, *Soldatenleben*, p. 90.

[7] Gordon discusses the organization and political influence of the *Truppenamt* in *Reichswehr and Republic*, pp. 178-80, 314-15.

[8] See Manstein, *Soldatenleben*, pp. 105ff. Manstein headed Group I from 1929 to 1932, serving under Colonel Geyer (chief of T1), who, as a captain in the Operations Section of the High Command in the First World War, had written a study of "The Defensive Battle."

206

With this degree of centralized control from the *Truppenamt*, it is not surprising that a common operational spirit permeated the officer corps. Strategically, Germany stood clearly on the defensive, but nevertheless the Army did not adopt static and passive defensive tactics. The cardinal tactical rule called for flexible delaying action (*hinhaltender Widerstand*), allowing time to concentrate forces for offensive counterattacks at weak points in the enemy's advance. Flexibility required close cooperation between the combat arms and between the field commanders, more initiative on the part of unit leaders in planning the tactical execution of missions than they had been allowed in the war, and mobility before and during the battle.[9]

The operational spirit generated by these tactical doctrines reinforced the professional *esprit de corps* that Seeckt had instilled in the Army during its formative years.[10] The 100,000-man Army, he had emphasized, established the nucleus for a larger force of at least 21 divisions. Every officer and enlisted man, rather than thinking of himself as a member of a small police force, should ready himself technically and psychologically for greater responsibilities once the expansion occurred. The *Truppenamt* usually built its exercises around

[9] Annual "transportation exercises" (*Transport-übungsreise*) examined the use of railroads to move troops to areas of concentration, in contingencies similar to those of the operational studies mentioned above; interviews with Generals Ahlfen, Donat, Kühne, Nehring; *RWM*, II H 560.

[10] Some younger officers, however, criticized Seeckt for being unreceptive to innovations in tactics; Carsten, *Reichswehr and Politics*, pp. 213-14. On General Staff training and tactics, see also Craig, *Prussian Army*, pp. 393ff.; Demeter, *Offizierkorps*, pp. 103-106; Gordon, *Reichswehr and Republic*, pp. 297ff.; Robert J. O'Neill, "Doctrine and Training in the German Army, 1919-1939," in Howard, *Theory and Practice of War*; Rabenau, *Seeckt*, pp. 498ff.; Rosinski, *German Army*, pp. 211ff., 291ff.; Thomée, *Wiederaufsteig*, pp. 85-92; Wallach, *Vernichtungsschlacht*, pp. 335-44; Wheeler-Bennett, *Nemesis of Power*, pp. 100-102. For secret training in air tactics, see Völker, *Entwicklung der militärischen Luftfahrt*, pp. 136-39, 148-51, 170-71; also his *Dokumente und Dokumentarfotos*, pp. 93-102.

the theoretical existence of an enlarged armed force, an assumption that encouraged more confidence and imagination in the solution of operational problems. On a larger scale than maneuvers, which trained all field officers and troops in small unit battle tactics,[11] operational studies were designed to test the skill of select officers in commanding large units in theoretical situations.[12] In General Staff tours, for example, a regimental chief of staff often commanded a division.

One task in the tours of generals and General Staff officers required the actual control of large units—communications between units and with headquarters in the rear, movement of troops, and so on. Another assignment, central to the written operational problems prescribed by the *Truppenamt* for all General Staff officers, was the unraveling of theoretical predicaments. A frequent tactical question asked, "How would you defend against a Polish attack on East Prussia?" Or, on a strategic scale, "How would you distribute Germany's defenses in a two-front war with France and Poland?" Neither question, the *Truppenamt* realized, could be isolated from foreign policy, for German operations—whether on one front or in a larger war—depended on Germany's international situation.

[11] Hans von Seeckt, *Bemerkungen . . . bei Besichtigungen und Manövern aus den Jahren 1920 bis 1926* (Berlin, 1927), p. 8; Erich von Tschischwitz, *Manöver und grössere Truppenübungen* (Berlin, 1930), p. 4. The primary manual for small unit infantry tactics after the war was "Führung und Gefecht der verbundenen Waffen" ("F.u.G."), revised from 1930 to 1932 by Ludwig Beck and retitled "Truppenführung" ("T.F."); Erfurth, *Geschichte des Generalstabes*, p. 129; Wolfgang Foerster, *Generaloberst Ludwig Beck: Sein Kampf gegen den Krieg* (Munich, 1953), p. 24; Wallach, *Vernichtungsschlacht*, pp. 332-34.

[12] See Seeckt's view in Rabenau, *Seeckt*, pp. 519-21; also Manstein, *Soldatenleben*, p. 126; Friedrich von Cochenhausen, *Kriegsspiel-Fibel* (Berlin, 1930?), p. 5. In the third year of their training program, General Staff officers studied the deployment of units of up to division size. Courses were expanded in 1930 to include units of corps and army size; Erfurth, *Geschichte des Generalstabes*, p. 126.

General von Seeckt had shown no interest in inviting Foreign Office officials along on the generals' tours he conducted, an exclusiveness entirely consistent with his hostility toward Stresemann's foreign policy, but at variance with the Clausewitzean principle to which Seeckt himself subscribed in his training doctrine pertaining to such tours: the dependence of military operations on foreign policy and the political situation.[13] Following Seeckt's dismissal and the departure of the Inter-Allied Military Control Commission, the improvement in interdepartmental relations extended into operational studies, in which joint planning became accepted procedure.

Cooperation between the Army and Foreign Office began in 1927 on the initiative of the military. In November Colonel von Blomberg, Chief of the *Truppenamt*, invited the Foreign Office to send a representative to the winter war game in the Defense Ministry. He believed the game would afford valuable insights into Germany's defensive capability, demonstrating to the cabinet the absolute necessity of *Landesschutz* in the east.[14] The *Truppenamt* hypothesized a war between Germany and Poland at the current military strength of each. Relations between the two countries, it was assumed for the game, had deteriorated beyond any chance of bilateral reconciliation; anti-German feeling in Poland was unusually high and, at the same time that the League of Nations began to consider the matter at Germany's request, Poland prepared to invade Germany. Intelligence reported the Polish plan of

[13] See Seeckt's concluding remarks at the *Führerreise* of 1923 in Schleswig-Holstein, in Rabenau, *Seeckt*, p. 521; also Seeckt, *Gedanken*, p. 59: the military commander is responsible for preparing contingency plans, but to do this he needs basic instructions from the statesman concerning the political situation and national objectives.

[14] *AA*, Blomberg to Foreign Office (Schubert), 12 November, K6/K000318; Forster notes of Blomberg's briefing of officers in the Defense Ministry, 22 December, *ibid.*, K000329-31. It is quite likely that the findings of this game and joint discussions related to it increased the Wilhelmstrasse's support for the Army's national defense proposals; see above, chap. 5.

operation: a main thrust against East Prussia to seize that province, with supporting attacks from the Corridor against Pomerania and from southwestern Posen against Silesia.

The German government, weighing whether to sacrifice East Prussia and withdraw behind the Oder river, decided instead to defend the beleaguered province. Its decision was facilitated by Germany's favorable international situation: Germany's relations with France were strong enough to rule out French intervention on the side of Poland. Poland, meanwhile, could concentrate its forces against Germany, for the Soviet Union was preoccupied with internal political disorder.[15]

Following border violations by Polish insurgents, and advised by the Chief of the Army Command that the Polish Army was poised for an invasion of East Prussia, the cabinet appointed a Chief of the Armed Forces (*Chef der Wehrmacht*) to take charge of defensive preparations: positioning *Grenzschutz* units along the border; empowering the military commander in East Prussia to take all measures necessary to hold the province; readying the regular armed forces for march and deployment; and mobilizing further divisions. The Chief of the Armed Forces ordered the Chief of the Army Command to repel any enemy incursions, ascertaining which were made by Polish regulars, but not—for the time being—allowing German troops themselves to cross the border into Poland. The latter part of this order was rescinded when Polish regulars invaded, and the German military therefore no longer had to restrict its operations to German soil. The outbreak of hostilities caused no significant changes in the international constellation, although the United States government protested against the sinking of an American vessel near Kiel by a Polish warship, the League stepped up its efforts to end the conflict, and Lithuania declared its neutrality.[16]

---

[15] *AA*, Forster notes, *ibid.*

[16] *AA*, situation report sent to Schubert by Blomberg on 14 January 1928, *ibid.*, K000336-41. Schubert, Dirksen, and Forster had

The diplomatic alignment initially presupposed by the *Truppenamt* drew caustic criticism from Stresemann: "Further," he elaborated, "it is apparently assumed that England was the victim of a seaquake and that America—as a result partly of tornadoes and partly of unsound speculations—fell into ruin, while Czechoslovakia was totally preoccupied with the conclusion of concordat negotiations."[17] A less biting critique, prepared by legal and military experts in the Wilhelmstrasse, was presented orally at a conference in the Defense Ministry on 25 January 1928. Representing the Foreign Office were Herbert von Dirksen, then director of the Eastern Department, and Dirk Forster, whose area of responsibility included disarmament and other military questions. Dirksen and Forster advised the *Truppenamt* that, under current international circumstances, "a German-Polish war without the intervention of France or other powers" was improbable. Still, France might hesitate to intervene in the first phase of the conflict. Since Poland was the aggressor, French action against Germany would violate the Treaty of Locarno. As a guarantor of that treaty, Britain was legally bound to intervene on Germany's side. It appeared "most highly unlikely" that Britain would do so, but Anglo-French differences over treaty obligations in such a conflict might be intense enough to weaken resolve in Paris and delay the French decision to attack Germany.

Answering the *Truppenamt*'s query about the reaction of the United States to the loss of a ship, the Foreign Office counselled that harsh American countermeasures—such as breaking off diplomatic relations with Poland—might occur only if Poland failed to pay reparations for the act. Regarding the Soviet Union, the Foreign Office concurred with the

---

attended the first session of the war game on 11 January; *ibid.*, K000332-3.

[17] *AA*, Stresemann's handwritten marginal comment on his copy of Forster's notes of 22 December 1927 (see above, n. 14), 7414/ H175358.

Truppenamt, finding active Soviet participation doubtful. Perhaps the German government, however, could prevail upon Moscow to create anti-Polish demonstrations, through diplomatic channels and by troop movements along the border with Poland, forcing Poland to keep more than a token force in its eastern provinces and out of the campaign against Germany.

Germany's best chance of delaying or weakening the Polish attack, the diplomats observed, rested with the League of Nations. The League's General Secretary would have to call an emergency meeting of the League Council at the request of Germany or another League member. As parties to the dispute, Germany and Poland were obligated—by Article 12 of the League Covenant—not to resort to war until three months after the Council had made its final report. Poland's aggression was clearly a violation of Article 12, and economic sanctions should be imposed on Poland by the other members of the League, as stipulated by Article 16. But the Foreign Office did not expect economic sanctions to be very effective nor to be supported by Czechoslovakia or Hungary.

The weapon the League afforded Germany was not economic but political: although German protests to the League would not effect an immediate halt of the Polish advance, they should inflame opinion against Poland, thereby weakening the aggressor's international position. In this and subsequent critiques, the Foreign Office made one thing about the League absolutely clear: there must be no doubt among the member states that Poland was the aggressor; otherwise the hope of League intervention on behalf of Germany would be illusory.[18] For this reason, Friedrich Gaus objected to that

18 *AA*, notes (no date) used by Dirksen and Forster at the conference of 25 January 1928, K6/K000342-4; their observations on the League and the United States were taken from a memorandum by Friedrich Gaus (prepared perhaps by Georg Mutius, his assistant in the Legal Department), 20 January, *ibid.*, K000345-6; Foreign Office minute (no date) concerning the *Truppenamt*'s proposed situation for the war game of the following year (Bülow represented the

part of the *Truppenamt* war game that permitted field commanders to cross the Polish border once Polish regulars had invaded German soil. This would have constituted a counterattack, whereas Gaus held that the Polish attack justified only purely defensive measures. Any deviation from the defensive would prejudice Germany's case before the League Council.[19]

Before either the *Truppenamt* or the Foreign Office could sort out their disparate views of the situation assumed in the war game, a new operational exercise was in the planning stage in the Defense Ministry. The General Staff tour, for which Blomberg again requested the participation of representatives from the Wilhelmstrasse, was scheduled for 17-27 April in Silesia. Based on the same political situation as the war game, the tour would consider a continuation of military operations from the cessation of combat at the end of the game.[20] After nearly a month of fighting (in October 1927), the Polish Army held East Pomerania, Silesia, and all of East Prussia except Königsberg. Both sides had observed the neutrality of Danzig. The League, galvanized finally by repeated German entreaties and the energetic efforts of Britain, had compelled Poland to cease fire and had established demarcation lines in East Prussia and along the Oder and Neisse rivers. While awaiting the outcome of peace talks, Germany and Poland were each limited to one division for every 30 kilometers of front within a zone extending 50 kilometers to either side of the demarcation lines.

During the ensuing winter months, however, the international situation changed in Germany's favor. The Soviet political leadership strengthened its position by channeling popular discontent into anti-Polish war fervor. At the beginning of April (1928) the Red Army invaded Poland, and Rumania (pursuant to the Polish-Rumanian alliance of 1926)

Foreign Office at a conference with Blomberg on 8 November 1928), *ibid.,* K000409.

[19] *AA*, Gaus memorandum (see preceding note).

[20] *AA*, Blomberg to Schubert, 27 January 1928, K6/K000354.

entered on Poland's side. On 8 April the League prorogued discussion of the German-Polish conflict until May. Britain and France, having been sharply at odds in the debate in Geneva over the German-Polish question, found their differences somewhat blunted after the Soviet attack on Poland. The French press demanded active French intervention for Poland. Save France and Belgium, the states bordering on Germany declared their neutrality. On 10 April, the day after the Red Army roundly defeated the Polish First Army near Baranowitz (Baranowicze), the Soviet Union asked Germany to attack Poland. If Germany did not, the Soviet note declared, then the Soviet Union alone would decide "the fate of Poland."

The German government, meanwhile, received an optimistic report from the Chief of the Armed Forces. Germany had increased its military strength enough during the armistice to expect victory should it reenter the conflict. This assessment presupposed "that *all* energies could be directed against Poland, and that the political leadership is able to keep other states—especially England and France—from actively intervening against Germany."

Having described its assumptions, the *Truppenamt* concluded its situation report by requesting the opinion of the Foreign Office. "Under what circumstances," the *Truppenamt* wanted to know, "does Germany's participation in the fight against Poland—without the immediate active intervention of England and France—appear possible?"[21] In reply, the Foreign Office informed the Defense Ministry "that a situation in which Germany and Russia conduct a war against Poland without the appearance of France and England is politically unthinkable."[22] The *Truppenamt* went ahead with its tour fixed on this theoretical situation, however, for it wanted to test General Staff officers' operational ingenuity against an enemy of approximately equal strength, at a moment when

21 *AA*, situation report sent to Schubert by Blomberg on 27 January 1928, *ibid.*, K000347-50.
22 *AA*, *ibid.* (handwritten note by Forster on K000350).

the Soviet Union pressed Poland from the east and France prepared to intervene from the west.[23]

The war game of the following winter (1928-29) was designed to point out the need for *Landesschutz* in the west. Germany's military strength for the game was not based on current figures, but on resources projected for 1 April 1933.[24] Would that expanded force be able to withstand a French attack? Germany faced enemies on two fronts: Poland, at war with the Soviet Union, and France, determined to come to Poland's aid. The Council of the League failed to agree that the Soviet Union was the aggressor, but this did not deter the French from planning to intervene according to the terms of the Franco-Polish alliance. France demanded passage for its troops through Germany, and, following Germany's justifiable refusal, invaded Germany. Fortunately, Germany could concentrate most of its strength against the French attack, since Poland's armed forces were battling the Red Army and posed no offensive threat to Germany's eastern provinces. The theoretical conflict was between France and Poland on the one side, and Germany and the Soviet Union on the other, with major operations along the Franco-German and Polish-Soviet borders. The other European states and America watched from off-stage.[25]

The Foreign Office accepted this general situation as not improbable. But Herr von Bülow voiced the Wilhelmstrasse's telling reservations about those states that the *Truppenamt* had relegated to the wings, in a conference with Colonel von Blomberg at the *Truppenamt* on 8 November 1928. It was unlikely, Bülow said, that Britain would remain neutral for long, for British interests were bound up with events in Eu-

[23] Forster, who represented the Foreign Office at the tour in Silesia, reported that, "from a military standpoint, the operations turned out to be interesting and instructive." *AA*, Forster notes, 2 May 1928, *ibid.*, K000380-1.

[24] See above, chap. 5, p. 195.

[25] *RWM, Truppenamt* (T1), "Folgerungen," 26 March 1929, II H 597, p. 1; *AA*, minute (no date) on the *Truppenamt's* proposed situation, K6/K000407-9.

215

rope. Moreover, at least currently, Britain was "politically too closely connected with France," and was remarkably solicitous toward Poland (an allusion by the Foreign Office to Britain's break with the Soviet Union and consequent increase in concern for Poland). France would surely try to win British approval before resorting to military action. Even if Britain balked, it would probably soon intervene "on the side of our enemies."

Nor could one assume the neutrality of Czechoslovakia, Bülow continued. Considering its precarious strategic position in relation to Germany, the Soviet Union, and Hungary, and its anti-Polish sentiments, Czechoslovakia would prefer to promise no more than benevolent neutrality to France and Poland. But it was very doubtful that Czechoslovakia would be able for very long to resist pressure from France to enter the conflict, for to France Czechoslovakia was "militarily important as an ally." Rumania would probably not remain neutral, although internal unrest might dictate such a policy. Lithuania, which was barely mentioned in the war-game situation report, could not be ignored; in the situation assumed by the *Truppenamt*, Poland would probably attack Lithuania. The United States would be sure to protect its freedom of trade, at least at the beginning of the conflict. As for the *Truppenamt*'s inclusion of a communication from Washington to Paris protesting French war preparations (a reference by the *Truppenamt* to the Kellogg Pact), the Foreign Office considered such a note improbable.[26]

JOINT OPERATIONAL PLANNING: AN ANALYSIS

Mutual understanding and the reconciliation of differences in the interdepartmental dialogue over operational studies was impeded by the Army's failure to explain carefully and consistently the purpose of war games. On the one hand, the *Truppenamt* stated their theoretical nature, during training and in correspondence with the Foreign Office. By inventing

[26] *AA, ibid.*

situations in which Germany could conceivably have some chance of holding off an enemy attack, the *Truppenamt* was able to accomplish two objectives: the training of General Staff officers in large-unit operations, and the demonstration of Germany's military deficiencies even in hypothetically favorable circumstances. On the other hand, in an effort to approach political reality, Colonel von Blomberg posited "a politically possible conflict situation" for the winter game of 1927-28.[27] And the *Truppenamt* asked the diplomats under what conditions such a conflict was indeed possible (Germany against Poland without the intervention of France and Britain), a query that conveyed the Army's interest in the actual international situation and how it might be expected to change.

As a result of statements like Blomberg's, the Foreign Office was not convinced that the Army's games were purely theoretical, but suspected that the military, in juggling European political alignments allegedly only to create an approximate parity of forces on one of Germany's fronts, was in fact seriously misjudging the "politically possible." In December 1927 Stresemann took at face value the situation outlined by the *Truppenamt* for its war game, concluding that only a fortuitous conjunction of disasters could have made that constellation at least plausible. Stresemann's attitude is not surprising, for he could recall Seeckt's narrow view of what Germany's policy toward the Soviet Union and the West should be, and he had no explicit evidence in the situation report of this first cooperative war game that the Army Command had grown strategically much the wiser since Seeckt's dismissal.

But Stresemann was too hasty in diagnosing severe military myopia in the *Truppenamt's* studies, for some apparent symptoms of that malady were in fact signs of a cautious reappraisal of Germany's strategic situation, delayed but analogous to that reassessment in the Wilhelmstrasse that had led

[27] *AA*, Blomberg to Foreign Office, 12 November 1927, K6/K000318.

217

to the Treaty of Locarno. Herr Forster became aware of the Army's increasing prudence during his participation in the General Staff tour of April 1928. In his report to the Foreign Office he praised the military's "sober evaluation of our political and military-political situation, and, resulting from this, the limitation . . . of the military-political problems with which the *Truppenamt* busies itself. This conscious 'renunciation of romanticism' was a note sounded in numerous conversations."[28]

As a "very interesting" example of the new realism, Forster called attention to the Army's view of France. Officers had remarked to him that there might well come a time when "the emotional antipathy of the Army toward France would have to recede in the face of political developments."[29] The Army was not suddenly oblivious to the Franco-Polish alliance and the French system of security against Germany: the war game of 1928-29 visualized a French invasion of Germany to aid its Polish ally. But neither was the Army blind to the enormous strategic benefit to Germany should France somehow refrain from joining the conflict. Seeckt had hoped that France would be held in check by a Britain allied with Germany or at least hostile to France's continental policy; but in the late 1920s the Army's operational studies did not include any suggestion of an Anglo-German coalition. The Army Command now saw Franco-German rapprochement as a means to the same end, a possibility that the *Truppenamt* considered in the war game and staff tour of 1927-28.

It might be argued that this allusion to Franco-German understanding in the operational studies of 1927-28 was merely lip service to appease the Wilhelmstrasse, disguising the Army's unchanged conviction that Germany must one day fight a "war of liberation" against France. But Forster's report and corroborating evidence indicate that, although anti-French feeling was still alive, it had begun to yield to a more

[28] *AA*, Forster notes, 2 May 1928 *ibid.*, K000381-2.
[29] *AA*, *ibid.*, K000382.

218

realistic estimate of the advantages of an understanding with France.[30] The question of the degree of hostility toward France did not perturb the Foreign Office in this instance; rather, the Foreign Office did not share the Army's apparently sanguine expectation that Franco-German understanding would be substantial enough to enable the political arm to dissuade France from intervening against Germany.

It might also be maintained that the *Truppenamt's* insistence on *Landesschutz* in the demilitarized west, which was bound to antagonize France, betrayed the military's true opinion of that country—as a hostile power whose system of security would continue to surround Germany, and which, in defiance of international agreements, might attack Germany, either to impose arbitrary military sanctions or to intervene in a war in eastern Europe.[31] More than a measure of residual Francophobia, however, this *Landesschutz* policy was the mark of a military mind concerned about national defense in any conceivable conflict, including one that the Army hoped the political leadership could prevent.

Yet the *Landesschutz* question did present a dilemma in strategic planning with regard to France. The *Truppenamt* recommended a comprehensive *Landesschutz* system. The Foreign Office—and Schleicher—thought that *Landesschutz* preparations in the west would jeopardize the policy of rapprochement with France. Even as the *Truppenamt* was beginning to appreciate the utility of an understanding with France, it advised defensive steps which might foil that accord. And while the diplomats warned that any conflict be-

[30] On Groener and Schleicher, see above, chap. 4. Interviews with various officers indicate that many were influenced more by considerations of national security than by hatred of France.

[31] The *Führerreise* of 1928, in which the Army and Navy collaborated (apparently they did not invite Foreign Office participation), hypothesized *Fall West*: German defense against a Franco-Belgian invasion of the Ruhr, with Poland and Czechoslovakia remaining neutral. The Army based its portion of the exercise on a major enemy advance from the Ruhr toward the Thuringian Forest. Documents in *RWM*, II M 100/17, 100/18.

tween Germany and Poland without the intervention of France was unlikely, they restricted the military's defensive capability against a French attack.

Landesschutz was one problem piece in the politico-military puzzle of Franco-German relations. Others were the Anglo-French tie, Locarno, and the Franco-Polish alliance. The Foreign Office reminded the *Truppenamt* that Britain's political disposition would have some influence on France's willingness to intervene in either a German-Polish war or a Polish-Soviet war. The Foreign Office questioned how Britain would interpret the Treaty of Locarno in either of these situations. In a German-Polish war, the Foreign Office observed, it was doubtful that as a guarantor of Locarno Britain would join Germany if France violated Germany's western border. In this situation Germany could at most expect British pressure on France to refrain from military action. In a larger war involving the Soviet Union, Poland, Germany, and France, Britain was still less likely to invoke Locarno and more apt to intervene on the side of Germany's enemies.

In spite of Locarno, then, Germany could not yet be confident that its western front would be secure in even a purely defensive war against Poland. The dangers inherent in the Franco-Polish alliance weighed more than the strategic advantages Stresemann and others had discerned in the Treaty of Locarno.[32] That alliance was defensive, and thus France had no legal grounds for attacking Germany unless Germany had actually attacked or provoked Poland; but neither the Foreign Office nor the Army viewed this as an absolute deterrent against French invasion.

Notwithstanding Forster's testimony to the Army's increasing strategic realism, the Foreign Office had good reason to doubt that the military surveyed the international scene broadly enough to include prominently the two greatest maritime powers, Britain and the United States. Stresemann, it will be recalled, was irritated that the *Truppenamt* had ig-

[32] See above, chap. 2.

220

nored Britain and America in its first situation outline for the game of 1927-28. In subsequent reports the *Truppenamt* did introduce those two powers, but in a very perfunctory manner. The Army had not forgotten that British and American sea power had strangled Germany's commerce during the World War, doing incalculable damage to war industry and civilian morale. That experience had alerted the military to the unequivocal necessity that Germany enjoy at least the neutrality of Britain and America in any future continental war.[33] But the Army seems to have been too eager to translate necessity into reality, succumbing to the illusion that because Britain and America must remain friendly and neutral, they would. When Britain, for example, did play a part in these war games and staff tours, it was as a champion of Germany (and an opponent of France) in debates in the League, or as a neutral. This presumptive benevolence—and the rather facile expectation that the political arm would be able to arrange it—was rejected by the Foreign Office. The diplomats calculated that Britain was still too closely linked to France and too interested in continental politics to be counted out of a future anti-German coalition, and that America would bring less pressure to bear on France or Poland than the Army imagined.

Neither the generals nor the diplomats overestimated the strength of the League of Nations as an international policeman. The League, they agreed, would not be able to prevent Poland's occupation of German territory. At best—that is, if it decided unanimously that Poland was the aggressor—the League might intervene to effect a cease-fire and draw demarcation lines between the two antagonists. Failing League unanimity, France would be less hesitant to invoke its alliance with Poland and attack Germany. In spite of its weaknesses, however, the League was still a political force with which Germany had to reckon in its defense policy. The Defense

[33] Interviews, notably with Generals Brennecke, Flörke, and Nehring.

Ministry recognized that the League served as a tribunal of international opinion that Germany was not strong enough to risk alienating. The Foreign Office, even more sensitive to possible reactions in the League, opposed the counterattack in the war game of 1927-28 on the grounds that it would weaken the political remonstrances of German leaders before the League Council. Because the Army's tactical doctrine stressed the counterattack and every tactical move might cause widespread political repercussions, this politico-military problem would require careful joint deliberation.[34]

Of minor or no significance in these operational studies were Czechoslovakia, Rumania, and Lithuania. Stresemann's sarcastic rebuke of the war-game situation proposed by the *Truppenamt* late in 1927 attested to the Wilhelmstrasse's vigilance toward Czechoslovakia even in a situation in which Germany was the victim of Polish aggression. In the opinion of the Foreign Office, French pressure on Czechoslovakia to tighten the strategic noose around Germany would probably overcome Prague's desire to remain neutral in the larger conflict hypothesized in the following year's war game. In the staff tour of 1928 the *Truppenamt* supposed that Rumania would enter after its Polish ally had been attacked by the Soviet Union, yet in the war game of 1928-29 Rumania stayed neutral, a proposition the Foreign Office doubted. According to the *Truppenamt*, Lithuania declared its neutrality in the German-Polish conflict of the game of 1927-28; in the following game, the Foreign Office considered Lithuania a probable victim of Polish aggression.

In their treatment of the Soviet Union in these studies, the two ministries introduced the current military and diplomatic information that Moscow was beset by internal difficulties

[34] We may wonder whether the *Truppenamt*, in spite of its political awareness, was not impatient with the legalism of Friedrich Gaus in his interpretation of Germany's military situation opposite Poland; on the other hand, regard for international opinion induced the *Truppenamt*'s opposition to a surprise attack on Gdingen (Gdynia) before the actual outbreak of a German-Polish war; below, chap. 7.

222

that demanded attention. In the game of 1927-28, the *Truppenamt* dismissed Soviet intervention in the event of a Polish invasion of Germany, and the most that the Foreign Office expected was a sympathetic movement of Soviet troops along the border with Poland. The staff tour that followed assumed a Soviet attack against Poland as the Soviet regime sought to convert internal unrest into external aggression, and the game of 1928-29 again projected the Soviet Union at war with Poland.

Germany's affirmative answer to the Soviet request in the staff tour of 1928—that Germany attack Poland or forfeit any share in determining the subsequent "fate of Poland"—was assumed by the *Truppenamt* to issue from the political leadership. The Foreign Office did not reject the idea of forceful German-Soviet resolution of Poland's future, but criticized the notion that the political arm (the cabinet and Foreign Office) would be able to keep Britain and France out of the conflict and would therefore be free to enter on the side of the Soviet Union. Similarly, in the war game of 1928-29, the Foreign Office did not dismiss a Polish-Soviet war as improbable (although intelligence in both ministries disclosed that Moscow lacked both the resources and the intent to conduct an offensive)[35] but questioned the *Truppenamt*'s predilection for assigning neutral postures to other capitals.

The staff tour of 1928 offered the opportunity for theoretical joint German-Soviet operations against Poland, and Forster reported that the commanders' decisions took into account the Soviet advance from the east.[36] But Forster also noticed in the officers present a political awareness of Soviet

[35] See above, chap. 3.

[36] *AA*, Forster notes, 2 May 1928, K6/K000381. Whether Soviet officers were present and joint planning actually occurred during the tour has not been established, but such planning as there might have been was probably an improvisation for the immediate purpose of the exercise rather than an implementation of plans on which the two staffs might have already agreed. We still have no evidence that German-Soviet military collaboration in the late 1920s included operation plans.

policy that did not suggest a reckless search for joint operational obligations in fact. In spite of their plans to send officers to the Soviet Union, Forster observed, Army leaders advised caution in military relations, for they recognized "the fundamental unreliability of the Soviet leadership in the case of its drawing closer militarily to capitalistic Germany."[37]

The Army's intention of meeting with reserve "any enticement coming from outside for a military understanding" was, according to Forster, an outgrowth of its increasing political realism. Not only was the military leadership cautious about ties with the Soviet Union, but it also viewed warily "the inclination of many Italian personages to speak of future military cooperation between Germany and Italy."[38] In the operational planning of the German Navy, Italy was a natural ally against France, for Italian naval presence in the Mediterranean could be expected to draw French warships away from Germany's shores and lanes of communication in the North Sea. But, even though Italy was a guarantor of Locarno, not until the early 1930s did the Army begin to include Italy—as Germany's ally—in its broad operational studies.[39]

Both the *Truppenamt* and the Foreign Office dwelt on the wider repercussions of any German-Polish conflict, fearing that it would escalate into a two-front war. In its critiques of the operational studies of 1927-29, the Foreign Office insisted that France—and eventually Britain—would surely intervene at some stage against Germany. To the *Truppenamt*, these studies demonstrated that a war limited to one front was unlikely, and therefore that *Landesschutz* should be organized on Germany's western borders. Limiting a war with Poland to one front was a common goal of the Foreign Office and the *Truppenamt*. The latter's operational hypotheses and queries

[37] *AA, ibid.*, K000382. This stands in contrast to the opinion of Prof. Hans Gatzke that "Germany's political leaders realized, as their military colleagues did not, that it was impossible to have . . . trust in a government whose aims threatened the very existence of friend and foe alike." "Russo-German Military Collaboration," p. 597.
[38] *AA*, Forster notes, *ibid.* [39] See below, chaps. 7, 9.

to the Wilhelmstrasse evidenced a search for some means of escaping Germany's "strategic fate," a war on two fronts.

The two offices disagreed, however, over whether to extend defensive preparations to the demilitarized west, a question which had strategic implications. The Foreign Office—and Schleicher—took the stand that, in current international circumstances, to confine a German-Polish conflict to one front would be almost impossible; therefore, Germany should not jeopardize relations with France by organizing *Landesschutz* in the west, but should seek to deepen the understanding founded at Locarno so that territorial revision would be possible. The *Truppenamt* also looked forward to the day when Germany, thanks to understandings with France and Britain, need no longer fear the intervention of the Entente powers; but meanwhile the *Truppenamt* advocated a western defense policy that risked inciting French indignation. The Foreign Office, Defense Minister, and *Ministeramt* were attuned to political expediency, the *Truppenamt* to overall military preparedness.[40]

It was going to be difficult to harmonize military and political viewpoints on subjects such as western border defense, British continental commitments, League intercession, Czechoslovakian dependence on France, and avoidance of war on two fronts. Interdepartmental accord would probably have been facilitated had the Army and Foreign Office agreed upon an official canon defining the purpose of operational exercises and clarifying the relationship between theoretical situations and political reality. In the absence of such a standard, the Foreign Office remarked on the flaws in the assumed situations of the studies and remained apprehensive that the *Truppenamt*'s simplification of international relations betrayed a real lack of political astuteness.

On the other hand, the Foreign Office received reassurances that the Army wanted to continue and strengthen joint operational planning. Herr Forster, after conversations with

---

[40] See also chap. 4.

Army leaders during the staff tour of April 1928, was pleased to report that they were sincerely in favor of closer cooperation between the two departments. The officers whom General Heye had appointed to the *Truppenamt* thought of themselves "with a certain pride as a 'young generation,' " willing to bridge the troubled waters of civil-military relations, to adapt to changing international alignments, and to derive some good from the disarmament requirements of the Treaty of Versailles by doing away with "obsolete institutions and ideas."[41]

Although the "renunciation of romanticism" had begun in the Army Command before Groener became Defense Minister in January 1928, he did much to reinforce it by cultivating interdepartmental understanding with the Foreign Office. The recent war game, he acknowledged in a note of 14 June 1928 to Minister Director Gerhard Köpke, revealed "that it is often difficult to base games on a foundation that corresponds to the actual situation." For this reason, and also to acquaint the Foreign Office with military needs, Groener proposed expanding joint participation in future war games.[42]

[41] *AA*, Forster notes, 2 May 1928, K6/K000381-3. Forster also commented on the officer corps' high regard for Blomberg's personal qualities and professional competence. Other leaders in the Army Command with whom Forster conversed informally were Colonel von Fritsch (chief of the Army Section, T1), General Joachim von Stülpnagel (head of the Personnel Office, *Heerespersonalamt*), and Colonel Kühlenthal (head of the Statistical Section, T3).

[42] *AA*, Groener to Köpke, 14 June, *ibid.*, K000393-4. Groener's *Panzerschiff* memorandum (see above, chap. 5, n. 16), however, seemed to contradict his principle of basing operational studies on Germany's "actual situation," since it envisaged exploiting a future European conflict. When published in *The Review of Reviews*, it drew angry protests from the Left because of its militant tone. The Foreign Office notified its embassies in Washington and Paris that the memorandum gave the opinion of the Defense Ministry, not the cabinet, and that it was based "on military considerations, without regard for foreign policy matters." *AA*, message of January 1929, 5551/E391383. But the discussion of interdepartmental collaboration in this chapter shows that this message was an understandable attempt to silence possible public outcries abroad against German "militarism" rather than

Further, the Defense Ministry invited the Foreign Office (and the Finance and Transportation Ministries) to send representatives to the autumn maneuver in Silesia, not to compare strategic notes—for maneuvers dealt only cursorily with the international situation—but to help restore a spirit of cooperation and mutual respect to interdepartmental relations.[43]

By 1930 collaboration in war games and staff tours had become an institutional custom. Foreign Office participants in the war game of 1927-28 had merely advised. For the larger game of the following winter, however, Blomberg invited more active participation by the Foreign Office, one of whose representatives was to act as Foreign Minister during the game.[44] This high degree of cooperation would have been impossible had not the Army and Foreign Office learned through increasing contact that they shared two central convictions: Germany's defense required greater military power; and foreign policy and military planning are interdependent, a relationship that demands the regular airing of differences and the practice of joint planning. The Clausewitzean principles of interdependence and political primacy were applied conscientiously by diplomats and generals to relations between the two departments regarding operational planning. They viewed the operational portion of politico-military activity as of no direct concern to the Reichstag; it belonged exclusively to the Foreign Office and Defense Ministry, and to the cabinet if orders to mobilize and fight were required. The

---

evidence of a fundamental aversion in the Wilhelmstrasse to using the Army as a means of policy in the future. Nor should this Foreign Office reaction be construed as an attack against the Defense Minister for not subordinating "military considerations" to "foreign policy matters" in his defense planning. In the cabinet meeting of 14 November 1928 Stresemann did not criticize the substance of the memorandum, but simply warned Groener to keep it confidential for fear of diplomatic repercussions; *RK*, notes of meeting, K955/ K251009-10.

[43] *AA*, Forster notes, 2 October 1928, K6/K000400.

[44] *AA*, Blomberg to Foreign Office, 16 October 1928, *ibid.*, K000404-6.

Foreign Office (and cabinet) had, therefore, growing cause to be confident of its own authority in the operational sphere and to trust the Army's declaration of dependence.

DEFENSIVE AND OFFENSIVE WAR

The *Truppenamt's* studies recognized international relations and military readiness as the conditions that would determine Germany's fate in a defensive war. Both war games highlighted the persuasion that Poland was the major threat to Germany's national security. Neither the Foreign Office nor the Defense Ministry expected Pilsudski to invade German territory in these years of improvement in German-Polish relations. Nevertheless it was the military's duty to weigh Germany's defensive capability in the event that political change brought about the unexpected. From the war game of 1927-28 the *Truppenamt* concluded that, with the resources available on 1 October 1927, in a fight against a Poland that could commit almost all of its forces, Germany "could offer *somewhat promising resistance only for a short time and with the loss of further German territories*."[45] One of the purposes of that game had been to show the political arm that security in the east required a comprehensive *Landesschutz* organization and an increase in the number of troops and amount of matériel ready for combat. The *Truppenamt* was cautiously optimistic that by 1 April 1933 (when the first stage of the rearmament program was to have been completed) Germany would be in a much better position to defend itself against Poland, although still not strong enough

[45] *RWM, Truppenamt* (T1), "Folgerungen," 26 March 1929, II H 597, p. 1. Upon assuming command of the Army, General Heye promised Stresemann "that if East Prussia were attacked by Poland he should do his best to defend it. Whether he could succeed he did not know. . . ." Chamberlain (Geneva) to Foreign Office (Tyrrell), 6 December 1926, *DBFP*, Ser. IA, II, 580. Compare the more optimistic appraisal noted above, chap. 3, p. 107. Perhaps the Army Command was inclined to pessimism when trying to persuade the government of Germany's minimum defensive needs.

228

to execute large-scale offensive operations. By the same date it would be able to muster a stronger defense against French attack. The operational study of 1928-29, the *Truppenamt* noted,

> showed that, after reaching the desired state of preparedness of 1 April 1933, our military prospects for defense in the west, under certain political and military conditions and in spite of the disproportion in military power, are not so hopeless as may first appear. Of course, a military victory in the west cannot be contemplated. The objective of military action can be, to begin with, *not decisive battles but only slowing down the enemy's advance and weakening him.*[46]

But Germany's international position and military preparedness also affected when and how to wage an offensive war, which the German Army accepted in theory as a legitimate means of attaining national objectives. Whether the Army in fact contemplated an offensive war, notwithstanding its increasingly realistic assessment of Germany's power and international position in the late 1920s, is a question that calls for a reexamination of its operational planning and expansion program.

Operational studies may illuminate the strategic thinking of the period, but they do not chart a narrow course of preparations for war that the military intends to follow to its conclusion. In reviewing every contingency that was even remotely possible, the *Truppenamt* gave those situations that were most likely to occur more attention in war games and other studies and more space in its files. It would be ill-advised, however, to expect these studies to prefigure closely the German Army's campaigns under Hitler, not simply because the studies (except the staff tour of 1928) placed Germany on the defensive, but also because the Army itself was averse to binding plans and viewed its operational exercises as reflec-

[46] *RWM, Truppenamt* (T1), "Folgerungen," 26 March 1929, II H 597, p. 2.

229

tions of the strategically possible, not as declarations of the inevitable.[47]

Still, two themes recurred in the *Truppenamt*'s operational deliberations about Poland. At the tactical level, the very areas of Germany that were most exposed—East Prussia and the salients of Silesia and Pomerania—provided excellent bases for attacks against the enemy's flanks. Although on the defensive, the German Army preserved the spirit and methods of the tactical counteroffensive. The fortifications existing or planned in East Prussia, Pomerania, and east of Küstrin and Frankfurt on the Oder, would not merely delay the Polish advance, but would afford protection for the concentration of troops in the rear and "pivots" or "hinges" for the ensuing counterattack.[48]

The flank attack and envelopment of the enemy's forces, a common answer of General Staff officers to tactical problems set by the *Truppenamt*, prevailed in military planning for a number of reasons: the idea of envelopment, basic to the Schlieffen Plan, had not been discredited in 1914;[49] a war

[47] The late B. H. Liddell Hart refers to Colonel Fritsch as the man "largely responsible for devising the plan, in case of war, for a swift offensive against Poland combined with a defensive in the West to hold France in check." Furthermore, he continues, this "was the embryo of the plan that was actually executed in 1939, although then amplified in scale and resources." *The German Generals Talk* (New York, 1948), p. 26. In all likelihood, Fritsch's plan was a part of the operational studies of the late 1920s, when he was head of T1, and thus a contingency plan for possible adoption in a particular defensive situation.

[48] Interviews with Generals Ahlfen, Busse, Donat, Fretter-Pico, and Lanz. See also above, chap. 5; Roos, *Polen und Europa*, pp. 6-7; British staff (G-2) report of 24 December 1927, cited in Jacobson, *Locarno Diplomacy*, p. 95n.

[49] Interviews with Generals Flörke and Nehring, in addition to those officers mentioned in the preceding note. Groener eulogized Schlieffen in two books (*Das Testament des Grafen Schlieffen* [Berlin, 1927]; and *Der Feldherr wider Willen* [Berlin, 1931]), in which he wanted to hand down to the younger military generation "the strategic thinking of his master." Groener-Geyer, *General Groener*, p. 227. On the members and ideas of the Schlieffen school during the

of mobility was preferable by far to a static war of attrition, particularly in view of Germany's limited resources; and by means of Germany's excellent railroad system, fresh units of an expanded army could be rapidly moved and concentrated where necessary to exploit any weakness in the Polish offensive. To mount a successful counteroffensive would require a more favorable balance of forces than existed in the late 1920s, a presupposition that underlay both the Army's war games and its plans for expansion. Nevertheless, it was hoped that, in a future war with Poland, a flexible plan of operation against the enemy's flanks would prove decisive.

A second theme, at the strategic level, was the Army's persistent avowal that Germany must regain its lost territories from Poland. The introduction of hypothetical Polish-Soviet wars conveniently enabled Germany to group its forces on the eastern front in the staff tour of 1928, and on the western front in the war game of 1928-29. But the political motivation assumed by the *Truppenamt* in the former study was that Germany must exploit a conflict between Poland and the Soviet Union, and be one of the active agents in deciding "the fate of Poland." Again, in the second study, Germany's inclination to fight France was probably determined by more complex motives than defense of German neutrality against the illegal transit of French forces. Also at stake were its pledges to the Soviet Union that Locarno and membership in the League would not oblige Germany to assist an anti-Soviet coalition, its desire that Poland emerge the loser in any confrontation with the Soviet Union, and its hope of winning territorial concessions in the peace settlement afterwards.

These currents in the Army's operational planning flowed into its expansion program: as one part of *A-Plan* preparations for conflict (*A-Fall*), the *Truppenamt* prescribed operational studies like those mentioned above.[50] Shortly after the

Weimar period, see Wallach, *Vernichtungsschlacht*, pp. 305-19, 349-51.

[50] *RWM, Truppenamt* (T1), "Folgerungen," 26 March 1929, II H 597, p. 7.

THE MILITARY AND JOINT PLANNING

A-Plan became effective on 1 April 1930, Defense Minister Groener sent copies of a highly secret directive to the two service chiefs. Entitled "The Assignments of the Armed Forces," it prescribed general guidelines for continuing the national defense programs. The development and employment of the armed forces would be based on the assignments "set by the responsible political leadership." Apart from quelling internal outbreaks of violence, the armed forces might be employed for two tasks. The first was self-defense:

1) to repulse illegal border violations (by guerrillas), where it is expected that the violation can be quickly suppressed without leading to a conflict with the legal armed forces of the state concerned;

2) [to resist] an enemy attack, only if the invading state is militarily heavily engaged elsewhere, or if resisting will prevent a *fait accompli* or cause the intervention of other powers or international courts;

3) to ward off imminent—or to settle actual—border violations by retreating troops (cf. Russo-Polish war 1920) as well as the danger of inadmissible pursuit by the victorious party.

In these defensive circumstances, the directive added, the military force employed might be the "army ready for action" (*marschbereites Reichsheer*) or the 21-division field army (*Feldheer*), the latter only under the conditions described in the second situation and only if Germany had the necessary extra time to mobilize.

The second assignment was the "exploitation of a favorable political situation," without Germany's being "directly attacked," in the following circumstances:

1) in response to the pressure of a group of combatant states, insofar as we can improve our political or military position through such a connection with a power or power bloc. It will be particularly advantageous for us if our commitment is discharged simultaneously by defending our neutrality against a common enemy;

2) by our own independent decision, provided that a favorable international constellation allows us to take the risk of such a resolution.

Here the field army or "further reinforced field army" (*weiter verstärktes Feldheer*) would be engaged, and Germany would enjoy, "more or less, the initiative to complete . . . preparations to a certain extent (mobilization period), and to determine the moment of entry."[51]

Neither the Army's operational studies nor its expansion program demonstrates the actual planning of an offensive war. They do indicate explicitly the Army's determination to ready itself for any future decision by the political arm to defend Germany or resort to war for national objectives. They also evince the Army's utmost concern for a "favorable international constellation." International conditions, as the military realized, determined whether Germany would have the benefit of a "mobilization period," and limited the extent to which Germany's "political or military position" might be improved even with a fully prepared field army.

In 1929, General Joachim von Stülpnagel, pleased that the Army had finally abandoned "utopian schemes" and started to concentrate on the "immediate future," believed that in the next ten to twenty years a " 'Great War' " was unfeasible. On the other hand, he pointed out, the limited conflicts theorized in the two studies of 1927-28 and 1928-29 were possible.[52]

[51] *RWM*, Groener to Chiefs of Army and Naval Commands, "Die Aufgaben der Wehrmacht," 16 April 1930, PG 34072. Major Ott may have drawn up this text, which is similar in some of its phraseology to the *Panzerschiff* memorandum that he prepared for Groener in 1928; see above, chap. 5, n. 16; below, chap. 7. On the *Reichsheer* and *Feldheer*, see above, chap. 5.

[52] *RWM*, Stülpnagel to *Truppenamt*, 3 April 1929, II H 597. Stülpnagel, head of the Personnel Office, believed that practical and theoretical training should be adapted to Germany's needs in the "immediate future," and wondered whether operational exercises in fact took this realistic view sufficiently into account. Contrast his own emotional and "utopian" ideas in 1924 of a "war of liberation" against France; above, chap. 4, p. 135 and n. 50; Carsten, *Reichswehr and Politics*, p. 200.

There is, in point of fact, an unmistakable analogy between the war game of 1928-29 and the first of the two situations Germany might "exploit," according to the Groener directive. Germany could expect territorial rewards if, in defending its neutrality in a Polish-Soviet war, it denied French aid to Poland. The correspondence is admittedly implicit, but it is entirely consistent with the exigencies of Germany's international situation and the strategic thinking in the Defense Ministry.

Again, it is not too audacious to infer a particular case from Groener's second general proposition of exploitation, Germany's "independent decision" to resort to war for national objectives. Regaining the lost territories in the east, a limited objective, was probably the most likely cause for which Germany might decide to apply force offensively and unilaterally once it possessed a field army and the necessary freedom of diplomatic movement. An irreducible politico-military aim, it offered sufficient grounds for war in the opinion of the officer corps.

The Army contemplated a limited war over the Polish question: Germany as the victim of a Polish attack, or as a participant in and beneficiary of a Polish-Soviet war, or—most distantly—as the aggressor to recapture Danzig and the Corridor. If aspirations for a great continental war for hegemony over eastern and southeastern Europe or visions of a "war of liberation" against France lurked in the minds of some officers, they were branded as "utopian" by responsible Army leaders who planned operations and expansion, and whose increasing objectivity concerning Germany's limited politico-military capabilities and aims was appreciated by the Foreign Office.

CONCLUSION

During these stable years of the republic, Stresemann's foreign policy was an amalgam, in which he and his supporters "saw no contradiction between the policy of Locarno, German membership in the League of Nations, . . . and German revisionism."[53] He viewed rapprochement with the West as a necessary precondition to territorial revision in the east, hoping that, just as western representatives had assembled in London and Locarno in the interests of European economic stability and peace, so they would one day come together to revise the German-Polish border. But even in that event, which German diplomats expected too confidently, the Wilhelmstrasse received no indication that Poland would peacefully surrender former German territories. Perhaps after his conversation with Pilsudski in December 1927 Stresemann was optimistic on this point. If so, he seriously misjudged the marshal's intentions and the prohibitive force of Polish nationalism. In spite of the improvement in German-Polish relations in the late 1920s, Germany's policy of border revision could not succeed in regaining the Corridor and Danzig unless it abandoned peaceful for forcible means.[54]

German diplomats were less inclined than the Army to resort to force, and more patient in the peaceful pursuit of political objectives. Therefore they reacted with greater political sensitivity to any public revelations of German politico-military activity—such as secret collaboration with the Red Army—that might set back Germany's program of treaty revision by a policy of understanding. Yet officials in the Wilhelmstrasse did not enter the 1920s with blank slates poised for peaceful Wilsonian inscriptions; they made their way forward with the memory of defeat in a two-front war and the knowledge that military power was an invaluable national asset.[55] This power-political persuasion remained strong in

[53] Kordt, *Nicht aus den Akten*, p. 37.

[54] Territorial revision was but one part of what Prof. Thimme calls Stresemann's "dynamic" policy, which she contrasts with the "stagnant" French policy of security. The simultaneous pursuit of two contradictory policies, she concludes, made unlikely a "peaceful solution of the question of Germany and Europe." *Gustav Stresemann*, p. 128.

[55] Wolfgang Sauer asserts that Weimar statesmen should have adopted a "political security system" based on Wilsonian principles,

the Foreign Office during a period of international conciliation and German military weakness. It formed the basis for
the diplomats' concurrence with the generals that military
force was at once a defensive and exploitative instrument of
German foreign policy, whose application depended on politico-military circumstances: international alignments; Germany's military capability; and civil-military relations.

The Foreign Office and Army did not view Germany's international situation with equal immediacy or breadth, but
they agreed that Germany must avoid a war on two fronts in
any future continental conflict over the Polish question. Just
as the Army Command valued the advantages of its clandestine ties with the Red Army above the political damage
their discovery might cause, so it found military preparedness on both fronts more important than the political consideration of adverse reactions in France. And the *Truppenamt*,
in the opinion of the Foreign Office, neglected extra-continen-
tal maritime powers in its operational studies. In the same
studies, however, Foreign Office officials observed among the
officers in the *Truppenamt* promising signs of strategic circumspection, such as caution about establishing too close a
bond with the Soviet Union, and the acknowledgment that
Germany might one day neutralize the western front by an
understanding with France. Whereas the diplomats criticized
some of the military's political hypotheses in war games and
staff tours, they accepted without flinching the persistent
theme expressed in all these exercises: whether and how Germany might take advantage of future conflict situations—

rather than the "military security system" advocated by the Reichswehr, for the necessary rearmament would jeopardize Germany's
international position; "Die Reichswehr," in Bracher, *Auflösung*, pp.
233-37. See also *ibid.*, p. 269; the same author's "Mobilmachung der
Gewalt," in Bracher, *Machtergreifung*, pp. 768, 770-72, 775, 784; the
similar view of the Socialist writer, Carl Mertens, in *Reichswehr oder
Landesverteidigung?* (Wiesbaden, 1927), *passim*. For a telling criticism of Sauer, see Herzfeld, "Zur neueren Literatur über das Heeresproblem," pp. 375-76.

notably a Polish-Soviet war—to regain the Corridor and Danzig. For both the Foreign Office and Defense Ministry, "favorable" implied something beyond what was politically necessary for Germany to reestablish its sovereignty or strategically necessary to defend its remaining territory against attack. An alignment of European powers that promised western cooperation or inaction was indispensable to either a peaceful or a forcible resolution of the Polish question in Germany's favor. As the Foreign Office pointed out in joint operational planning, Germany had not yet achieved that much western support or security.

Before attempting either a defensive or exploitative assignment, Groener's directive of 1930 emphasized, Germany had to be certain of success.[56] The prerequisites for success were a favorable international situation, as well as a strong military establishment. By 1930 the Army's secret preparations were not extensive enough for even a defensive war without risking a "catastrophe" for Germany.[57] "In the current political situation," the Groener directive declared, "we have to take into account that a responsible government might have to decide upon a *renunciation* of military resistance or military attack, as the case may be."[58]

With the common aim of improving Germany's politico-military position, the Foreign Office and Defense Ministry established guidelines for civil-military collaboration on rearmament and operations. The Army, quoting the theory of Clausewitz, acknowledged also in practice the subordination of both branches of military planning to the policies of the Foreign Office and cabinet. The Foreign Office, encouraged by this departure from Seeckt's uncooperative and refractory conduct of military policy, supported the Army's eastern border defense and *A-Plan* programs, and increased its participation in operational exercises. Civil-military relations had

[56] *RWM*, Groener to Chiefs of Army and Naval Commands, "Die Aufgaben der Wehrmacht," 16 April 1930, PG 34072.

[57] *RWM*, *Truppenamt* (T1), "Folgerungen," II H 597, p. 2.

[58] *RWM*, Groener to Chiefs (see n. 56 above).

improved by 1930, and there was a reasonable chance that, barring a recurrence of the acute domestic and international instability of the early 1920s, differences over issues like a western border defense could be settled above the party factionalism in the Reichstag and within existing interdepartmental and executive-departmental procedures for joint planning.

CHAPTER VII

The Navy

THE NAVAL component of the armed forces, the *Reichsmarine*, was the junior partner in German military planning throughout the Weimar period.[1] In the era of Admiral Alfred von Tirpitz, the Imperial Navy had expanded rapidly as an agent of William II's *Weltpolitik* and as a sponsor of his belated attempt to establish a *Pax Germanica*. But the Weimar Republic promised little excitement to those naval officers and civilians who preferred world maps to continental ones. The diplomatic and military consequences of having lost a struggle for world power reduced Germany's capacity to regain even its continental stature. Diplomats and generals rediscovered in both the war and the peace the dictate that Germany, by nature of its geopolitical situation, had always been and would remain a land power first and foremost. The Navy also reevaluated its performance in the war, and began to adjust to the postwar politico-military realities that placed the Navy on the periphery of civil-military relations and operational planning as well. The Navy shared the view of the Foreign Office and Army that the Polish question must be resolved

[1] The major secondary works used for the Navy are the following: Kurt Assmann, *Deutsche Seestrategie in zwei Weltkriegen* (Heidelberg, 1957); Carsten, *Reichswehr and Politics*; Carl-Axel Gemzell, *Raeder, Hitler und Skandinavien: Der Kampf für einen Maritimen Operationsplan* (Lund, 1965); Fritz E. Giese, *Die Deutsche Marine 1920 bis 1945* (Frankfurt am Main, 1956); Walther Hubatsch, *Der Admiralstab und die obersten Marinebehörden in Deutschland 1848-1945* (Frankfurt am Main, 1958); Erich Raeder, *My Life*, trans. Henry Drexel (Annapolis, Md., 1960); Wacker, *Bau des Panzerschiffes*. In the late 1930s the German Navy summarized planning after Versailles: *RWM*, PG 26648 (also in *Trials of War Criminals*, x, 433ff.); PG 31039; PG 31871; PG 33965b.

by force if necessary. Although the Naval Command admitted the Army's relatively greater importance, it nevertheless sought for itself a major role that neither the Navy's size nor Germany's international situation seemed to permit.

The Treaty of Versailles reduced the Navy to an active strength of 6 battleships (of the "Deutschland" class, older and smaller than the "Dreadnought" class), 6 small cruisers, 12 destroyers, and a like number of torpedo boats. In addition, the treaty prohibited submarines and airplanes, required Germany to disarm its Baltic coastal fortifications, and limited the officer corps to 1,500 members (with a 25-year term of service), and lower ranks to 15,000 (12-year term).[2] The Weimar constitution threw overboard the imperial system of command, which had allowed direct contact between the service chiefs and the Kaiser without civilian intervention.[3] The Weimar command system subordinated the Chief of the Naval Command to the civilian Minister of Defense, whom the President entrusted with the power of issuing orders to both services.[4] The Naval Command, formally established in 1920, resided in the Defense Ministry; the *Marineleitung* combined both administration and command, an internal improvement over the separation and rivalry between these two offices in the Imperial Navy. The Naval Command included the staff of the Chief of the Naval Command (the *Zentralabteilung*, or Central Department), Naval Command Office (*Marine-Kommando-Amt*), General Naval Office (*All-*

[2] Rolf Bensel, *Die deutsche Flottenpolitik von 1933 bis 1939: Eine Studie über die Rolle des Flottenbaus in Hitlers Aussenpolitik* (Frankfurt am Main, 1958), pp. 6-7; Wacker, *Bau des Panzerschiffes*, pp. 1-3. For a contemporary view, that the Treaty of Versailles was meant to crush Germany's naval power and remove Germany from world maritime competition, see Admiral (Ret.) Hollweg, "Das Versailles Diktat und die deutschen Seeinteressen," *Nauticus*, XVII (1923), xvii-xxviii.

[3] On command, within both the constitutional framework and the Navy's own organization, see Hubatsch, *Admiralstab*, pp. 184-87, 193, 255; Wacker, *Bau des Panzerschiffes*, pp. 3-8.

[4] See above, chap. 3, p. 90.

gemeines Marine-Amt), and Naval Administration Office (*Marine-Verwaltungs-Amt*). The Fleet Department (*Flottenabteilung*), located in the Naval Command Office, handled all operational questions.[5]

Naval planning accented a number of persistent themes: Germany required a stronger Navy to be *bündnisfähig*, and to defend Germany in a two-front war against France and Poland; the North Sea was of central importance to Germany's maritime security; an offensive strike against the Polish base at Gdingen (Gdynia) would be a major action in a German-Polish war. The 1920s witnessed a shift in operational emphasis from the Baltic to the North Sea; the early 1930s, the elaboration of *Studie Gdingen* (or *Studie Ost*) as part of the Navy's *A-Plan*. In both periods, the Navy's assumptions concerning Germany's strategic situation, rearmament, and operations obliged it to communicate with the Foreign Office, the Defense Minister, and the Army Command, but not always harmoniously.

STRATEGY, REARMAMENT, AND OPERATIONS

After the First World War, France replaced Britain as Germany's naval arch-enemy; the Franco-Polish alliance encircled Germany by land and sea. In a conflict with Poland, German naval forces could easily overpower the infant Polish Navy, but other exigencies of war would require the German Navy to close the Baltic Sea to French ships and keep open Germany's own sea lanes to isolated East Prussia. In 1926, Admiral Hans Zenker (Chief of the Naval Command, 1924-28) advised the cabinet that command (*Seeherrschaft*) of the North Sea was out of the question; on that front, the Navy

---

[5] The operations staff was not subordinated to the Chief of the Naval Command, but remained under the direction of the Naval Command Office (just as in the Army T1 was under the Chief of the Truppenamt, not the Chief of the Army Command); Hubatsch, *Admiralstab*, p. 187.

could only protect the German coast. Command of the Baltic, on the other hand, was attainable.[6]

In 1924 the Fleet Department referred to Germany's current international isolation.[7] To remedy this, in anticipation of the struggle against France and Poland, naval leaders examined alignments that might be of value to Germany. Contacts with Soviet naval representatives, resumed in 1926 (earlier relations had been of little consequence), encouraged the Naval Command to weigh the strategic advantages of a naval tie with the Soviet Union. If Germany and the Soviet Union together fought Poland, or France and Poland, the Soviet Navy might secure the Baltic and enter the Mediterranean, simultaneously freeing the German Navy for operations against the French in the North Sea and diverting some French forces from the Atlantic. But the naval leadership rejected any idea of close collaboration with the Soviets because of their pernicious ideology, their unstable politics, and their position as Germany's potential rival for naval supremacy in the Baltic. For these reasons, and because the German Navy (in contrast to the Army) did not depend heavily on the Soviets for its illegal activities, the *Reichsmarine* maintained a very cautious attitude in its relations with the Soviet Navy.[8] Looking to the west, the Naval Command favored rapprochement with Britain; Germany needed British support for revision of the peace treaty, and British neutrality was an absolute necessity in a future continental war. Italy posed a threat

[6] *RK*, excerpt from cabinet protocol, 29 November 1926, Akten betr. Reichswehr, Volkswehr, und Wehrpflicht, Band 5 (not filmed); correspondence between the Navy and Foreign Office concerning the Baltic, *AA*, file K154. See also Assmann, *Deutsche Seestrategie*, p. 104; Hubatsch, *Admiralstab*, p. 185. In July 1926, Zenker remarked to Naval leaders that " '*Poland* will disintegrate.' " Carsten, *Reichswehr and Politics*, p. 240.

[7] *RWM*, *Flottenabteilung* memorandum, 25 July, II M 62/1.

[8] *RWM*, Naval Command memorandum (no date) and *Flottenabteilung* notes, 29 July 1926, PG 33617; Carsten, *Reichswehr and Politics*, pp. 146-47, 238-42, 245; Erickson, *Soviet High Command*, pp. 251-55, 274.

to French naval superiority in the Mediterranean and might one day provide a counterweight against France in a European conflict, although Admiral Zenker himself discounted the possibility of German-Italian cooperation, since Germany might " 'have to pull Italian chestnuts out of the fire without receiving anything in return . . .' " and could not expect much Italian military support in any case.[9]

By 1929, in the opinion of the Fleet Department, Germany had not yet broken out of strategic isolation. Would Germany remain neutral in future conflicts among the world's Great Powers? Or would Germany have to fight "in the interests of its existence and in order to gain its freedom"? The answers remained uncertain. For the moment, Germany must strengthen its armed forces for self-defense against the immediate threat posed by France and the French vassal, Poland—confederates who would like to see Germany destroyed. Germany could not, in its current military situation, defeat France and Poland alone. To form an alliance with the Soviet Union, the only current possibility, would be strategically suicidal because it would alienate the British and align them with Germany's enemies. Thus, Germany must develop *Bündnisfähigkeit*, flexible enough to adjust to changes in the "power constellation" but in the hope that Italy would hold France in check and so reduce the French naval strength which might be launched against Germany.[10]

After 1925, the development of a new class of ship to re-

---

[9] Carsten, *Reichswehr and Politics*, p. 240; *RWM, Flottenabteilung* notes, 29 July 1926, PG 33617. Zenker also considered rapprochement with the other "Anglo-Saxon power," the United States, a major objective of naval policy in the interests of treaty revision; *RWM, ibid.* On the other hand, Captain Wilfried von Loewenfeld, chief of the Fleet Department, believed that " 'the *U.S.A.* is too far away and too little interested in the details of Europe.' " Carsten, *ibid.* The Navy's concern for Britain and Italy derived from naval strategic conditions that would have obtained even without the British and Italian guarantee of the Franco-German border in the Treaty of Locarno.

[10] *RWM, Flottenabteilung* paper (Captain Hermann Boehm), January 1929, II M 57/58.

place the obsolete "Deutschland" battleships stimulated planning in the Naval Command, whose strategic ambition ranged far beyond coastal defense and the Baltic Sea. Some officers had recommended the construction of the "Monitor" type of ship—heavily armed and armored, but slow and limited in its operating range—for coastal and Baltic use, but the Naval Command adopted plans for *Panzerschiff A*, the first of a series of "pocket-battleships," or battle cruisers.[11] Although naval leaders publicly extolled the advantages of such a ship for major engagements in the Baltic, they used the terms *Kreuzerkrieg* (or *Handelskrieg*) and *Seegeltung* when discussing among themselves the operational capability of the battle cruisers. They envisioned a ship that could operate independently in the North Sea and more distant sea lanes, defending German shipping and carrying out long-range offensive assignments against enemy communications (the new craft would have a range of 20,000 nautical miles); they anticipated a naval force that would begin to restore Germany's maritime prestige and power, an impossible prospect if the *Reichsmarine* restricted itself to the Baltic and coastal defense.[12]

[11] Assmann, *Deutsche Seestrategie*, pp. 105-110; Bensel, *Deutsche Flottenpolitik*, p. 14; Wacker, *Bau des Panzerschiffes*, pp. 45-50.

[12] Interviews with Admiral of the Fleet Karl Dönitz, Admiral Gerhard Wagner; *RWM, Flottenabteilung* paper (Captain Kurt Assmann), 2 November 1928, II M 57/57; PG 31039; PG 31871; PG 33965b; also Gemzell, *Raeder, Hitler und Skandinavien*, pp. 32-33, 151. *Kreuzerkrieg* meant cruiser warfare; *Handelskrieg*, economic or commercial warfare. *Seegeltung*, more difficult to translate, did not necessarily signify command or mastery of the seas; rather, it suggested the awareness of—and the power to defend—the nation's maritime prestige and interests. Interviews with Admirals Dönitz and Wagner; *RWM*, PG 33965b. See also Gerhard Bidlingmaier, *Seegeltung in der deutschen Geschichte* (Darmstadt, 1967), pp. 3-8; Walther Hubatsch, "Zur Frage der deutschen Seegeltung," in Wilhelm Schüssler (ed.), *Weltmachtstreben und Flottenbau* (Witten, 1956), pp. 196-97. *Weltgeltung*, used less frequently than *Seegeltung* in the naval documents of the 1920s, contained political coloring derived from the *Weltpolitik* of William II and Tirpitz. According to Captain

Aroused by the image of battle cruisers dashing about the Atlantic, the Navy also prepared for the less fanciful but more immediate tasks of mobilization and operations in the event of conflict. Preliminary mobilization measures had been initiated during the Polish-Soviet war in the winter of 1920-21; more comprehensive provisions for expansion and rearmament were included in the new naval *Aufstellungsplan* for 1926 and beyond.[13] In the autumn of 1929, Admiral Erich Raeder (who succeeded Zenker as Chief of the Naval Command in October 1928) directed officers to forgo war games for the coming winter and turn their attention instead to "measures that are necessary and possible in the event of a sudden outbreak of war, *without a mobilization period and with the means at hand.*"[14] Included in these *A-Plan* preparations, *Studie Gdingen* was a plan of attack against Poland's Baltic port if Poland should invade Germany.[15]

In *Studie Gdingen*, in war games and other theoretical exercises, the Navy's immediate task remained defense of the

---

Boehm, world prestige required public consciousness of the need for great national power, will, and maritime strength. He quoted Tirpitz, that Germany had never been a "servile people" (*Sklavenvolk*); *RWM*, Boehm paper, January 1929, II M 57/58.

[13] *RWM*, *Flottenabteilung* memorandum, 1 September 1926, PG 34061; also summarized in Hubatsch, *Admiralstab*, p. 191. The Navy made the same distinction as the Army between *A-Fall*, a conflict before which the armed forces would enjoy a "mobilization period," and an emergency situation (*Not-A-Fall* in naval documents), in which the forces would have to grant priority to the most pressing requirements for defense against sudden attack; *RWM*, *Flottenabteilung* memorandum, 16 May 1927, PG 34168/1.

[14] *RWM*, Raeder critique of an operational exercise, late autumn, PG 34048/3.

[15] *Studie Gdingen* (referred to after 1929 as *Studie Ost*) was one part of the larger "Study Baltic Sea Defense," which assumed the likelihood of French entry into the Baltic and included mining and other measures to hinder French operations in the narrow entrances to the Baltic; Raeder, *My Life*, pp. 151-52; *RWM*, *Flottenabteilung* paper (Commander Marwitz), 1929, II M 57/46; documents in files PG 34066, 34101.

Baltic in a two-front war, for the Navy assumed that France would intervene in a German-Polish conflict. At the same time, however, the Navy placed increasing importance, in its operational planning, on world maritime communications and, consequently, on operations in the North Sea, and on the attitudes of Britain and Italy in the Atlantic and Mediterranean, respectively.[16]

In war games in the early 1920s, the Naval Command accorded the Baltic strategic priority, even for the relatively favorable contingencies that allowed Germany to concentrate its forces against France.[17] In this period, the Naval Command either rejected North Sea operations or limited them to the defense of German communications and the German coast.[18] Subsequent exercises beginning in 1925, however, reveal the Navy's growing inclination toward operations outside the Baltic in a two-front war; Germany might even conduct offensive strikes against French maritime commerce, channel ports, and troop transports en route from North Africa to France.[19] At the end of 1929 Admiral Raeder announced to

[16] Operational exercises took place at different levels: the Station Commands of the North Sea and Baltic Sea forces (located in Wilhelmshaven and Kiel, respectively); the Fleet Command (in Wilhelmshaven until 1930, when it moved to Kiel); and the Fleet Department. The Naval Archives (*Marinearchiv*) assumed responsibility for training the Navy's *Führergehilfen*, a select number of junior officers who, like their counterparts in the Army, would become staff officers in all but name. On training and tactics, see Assmann, *Deutsche Seestrategie*, pp. 113-15; Bidlingmaier, *Seegeltung*, p. 214; Karl Dönitz, *Mein wechselvolles Leben* (Göttingen, 1968), pp. 144-66, *passim*; Hubatsch, *Admiralstab*, pp. 186-87; Raeder, *My Life*, pp. 187-96, 235-36.

[17] *RWM, Flottenabteilung* situation reports, 1922-24, PG 34073, 34073/1, II M 100/1; also directive of Admiral Paul Behncke (Chief of the Naval Command, 1920-24) for wartime deployment, May 1922, extended in February 1923, PG 31039; Hubatsch, *Admiralstab*, pp. 186-87.

[18] Sources in preceding note; also *RWM, Flottenabteilung* situation report and critique of war game 1924-25, PG 31039.

[19] *RWM, Flottenabteilung* memorandum, 8 June 1925, PG 34061; war game 1925-26, PG 31039; also Hubatsch, *Admiralstab*, pp. 188-89.

246

senior command and staff officers that careful study of the North Sea during recent months had convinced him of its vital importance to Germany, even if the French intended to enter the Baltic in a Franco-Polish combination against Germany. The Baltic, he concluded, demanded attention only insofar as Germany must free itself there "to turn to the main tasks in the west."[20]

This shift to the North Sea and maritime communications signalled the Navy's renunciation of the role of a mere "coastal navy." In the opinion of most naval officers, a coastal force could not secure Germany's maritime communications or effectively interdict those of the enemy; maritime communications were both a criterion and an objective of a nation's sea power.[21] For the remainder of the decade, naval planning and literature demonstrated this maritime emphasis in which the naval battle (*Seeschlacht*) constituted not the end of operations, but a means to a broader strategic objective—control of sea communications, chiefly through flexible operations by single ships or small groups of ships.[22] At the

[20] *RWM*, Raeder critique of an operational exercise, PG 34048/3.

[21] In 1924, while Inspector of Naval Education, Raeder had criticized a junior officer's recommendation that Germany refrain from commercial warfare because of the possible adverse diplomatic repercussions. Raeder admitted that Germany must take care not to violate international law and alienate neutrals, but he pointed out that *Handelskrieg* was an effective means of injuring the enemy. *RWM*, Raeder critique of an operational problem, 20 August, II M 57/32. Raeder compiled that part of the official naval history of the First World War that dealt with cruiser warfare (*Der Krieg zur See 1914-1918: Der Kreuzerkrieg*, 2 vols., Berlin, 1922-23); see Raeder, *My Life*, p. 114.

[22] The most outspoken representative of the strategy of maritime communications was Admiral Wolfgang Wegener. Wegener, then Inspector of Naval Artillery, sent Zenker an essay condemning the Navy's traditional emphasis on the strategic defensive, in which the battle had become the focal point of naval planning. Instead, Wegener urged an offensive strategy, by which he meant gaining that "strategic-geographic position from which the fleet can operate, i.e., can control avenues of communication and thus exercise command of the sea [*Seeherrschaft*]." *RWM*, Wegener to Zenker, 28 September 1925,

same time, however, the Navy preserved the inheritance of Tirpitz, who had concentrated the Imperial Navy in home waters, ready for a decisive battle with the British Home Fleet.[23]

Operational exercises from 1927 through 1929 assumed the following conditions: two-front wars (and *Fall West*) in which Britain remained neutral and Italy supported Germany either as an ally or as a benevolent neutral; cruiser warfare in the North Sea; and battles against the Polish fleet in the Baltic and French forces in either the Baltic or the North Sea.[24] In these studies, the *Reichsmarine* never entirely resolved the dichotomy between the maritime and Tirpitzean schools. The latter owed its persistence to the thorough indoctrination of naval officers during the era of Tirpitz, and to Germany's unfavorable politico-military situation: the Navy could not disperse its forces without increasing the vulnerability of Germany's coasts and Baltic communications; to maintain their security might require a *Seeschlacht*. The maritime school drew encouragement from the optimistic long-range hypothesis that Germany would eventually enjoy the necessary sea power and international position to wage economic warfare against France on the high seas. Naval planners of both schools were not blind to the transition in time from the reality of current limitations to the theory of future capabil-

---

"Gedanken zu den Grundlagen unserer Kriegsspiele und Kriegsuntersuchungen," PG 34177. On the anti-British bias in Wegener's subsequent book, *Seestrategie des Weltkrieges* (privately published in 1926, publicly—minus the parts relating to a future maritime war against Britain—in 1929), see Gemzell, *Raeder, Hitler und Skandinavien*, pp. 15-25; also Hubatsch, *Admiralstab*, p. 190 and n.

[23] Interview with Dr. Jürgen Rohwer; Gemzell, *Raeder, Hitler und Skandinavien*, pp. 25-26, 38-39.

[24] *RWM*, Zenker critique of war game, December 1927, II M 100/14; documents pertaining to joint *Führerreise* with the Army (*Fall West*), 1928, II M 100/17, 100/18; Fleet Command to Naval Command concerning war games to be conducted by the two Station Commands, 7 November 1928, II M 100/1; Raeder critiques of operational exercises, 8 January and late autumn 1929, PG 34048/3.

ities, nor did they believe that hypothetical exercises necessarily represented actual operation plans.[25] Still, the Navy habitually projected naval strengths and international alignments which transcended the temporal world of expectations that appeared reasonable to the Foreign Office and Army.[26]

THE NAVY AND THE FOREIGN OFFICE

The Navy's relationship to the civilian departments of the government sought an even keel after the failure of the Kapp *Putsch* in March 1920. Naval units had participated in this Rightist attempt to overthrow the republican regime, and the Chief of the Naval Command had given ready and open support to the illegitimate Kapp-Lüttwitz government. But subsequently the Naval Command tried earnestly to keep naval personnel out of party politics, avoid contacts with the National Socialists, and sever connections with the *Verbände* of the Right. The Navy endeavored to adjust to the new constitution as the Army did: defend the state; obey the constitutional authorities, the President and the "political leadership" (by which the Navy meant the Chancellor and his cabinet); and confine politico-military activity to the executive-departmental sphere, especially the departmental level of civil-military relations.[27]

Although correspondence between the Foreign Office and the Defense Ministry concerning Germany's strategic situation usually pertained to the Army, certain strategic dimensions of the Polish question (in northern and eastern European affairs) required the attention of the Navy as well: Franco-Polish naval activity in the Baltic, and Germany's

[25] Admiral Oldekop, the Fleet Commander, cautioned against overestimating Germany's available resources for *Studie Gdingen* and allowing fantasy so much latitude in Baltic war games; *RWM*, Oldekop to Chief of the Naval Command, 29 September 1929, PG 34066.

[26] In at least one war game, the Navy pitted its battle cruisers against obsolete French ships; Hubatsch, *Admiralstab*, p. 192.

[27] On the Navy, the republic, and the constitution in the 1920s, see Carsten, *Reichswehr and Politics*, pp. 83-84, 133-35, 288-90.

relations with the Soviet Union. German diplomats at Baltic posts and in Berlin recognized the threat of Polish naval expansion and French entry into the Baltic in a German-Polish conflict, but they also admitted the diplomatic usefulness of this anti-German maritime expansion, which might increase British sympathy for Germany in discussions about border revision.[28] The diplomats questioned the actual strength of a Franco-Polish combination in the Baltic,[29] controverted reports of an imminent Polish seizure of Danzig in 1926,[30] and, apparently unable to convince a stubborn Naval Command, persuaded Groener to cancel a naval maneuver scheduled for September 1928 in the Bay of Danzig which might have damaged foreign policy.[31]

Control over the *Reichsmarine*'s contacts with the Soviet

[28] *AA*, Dirksen (Danzig) to Foreign Office, 25 October 1924, K170/K025442-5; Zechlin to missions, 31 October, K191/K037101-4; Rosenberg (Stockholm) to Foreign Office, 19 November, with memorandum enclosed, K154/K017379-97. Dirksen advised the Wilhelmstrasse not to oppose Polish plans for ordering the construction of submarines in the Danzig dockyard; the Naval Command rejected his economic reasons for allowing such an expansion of Polish naval strength through German firms in the Free City. Dirksen to Foreign Office, 30 August and early September 1924; Naval Command to Foreign Office, 9 October; K191/K037091, 095, 098.

[29] France, Rauscher reported from Warsaw, had not promised Poland a major naval intervention in the Baltic, and the French considered the dispatch of a small force to the Baltic an extraordinary risk; *AA*, Rauscher to Foreign Office, 7 March 1929, K190/K036279-80; see also above, chap. 2, n. 20. Von Hassell, Minister to Copenhagen, reassured Berlin that Denmark had no intention of joining the Franco-Polish bloc; above, chap. 4; Hassell to Foreign Office, early November 1928 (to Defense Ministry on 14 November), K154/K017573-5. See also Wacker, *Bau des Panzerschiffes*, pp. 40-45.

[30] See above, chap. 3; also *AA*, Dirksen to Köpke, 26 May 1926, 5462/E371068.

[31] *AA*, memorandum (Köpke?), 11 July 1928; Foreign Office (Schubert?) to Groener, 13 July; 4569/E169137-40, 141-3. *RK*, Schubert to Chancellor (with marginal note by the Chancellor's Secretary of State), 12 July, Akten betr. Reichsmarine, Band 2 (not filmed); *RWM*, Naval Command minute, 20 July, II M 66/1. On a projected maneuver in the same area in 1929, see below, n. 59.

Navy never became an issue, for naval collaboration was neither mutually beneficial nor regular.[32] The Foreign Office did worry that German-Soviet relations might suffer from the ostensibly anti-Soviet implications of some statements concerning naval planning. In 1926, Brockdorff-Rantzau asked Berlin whether Chicherin's information was correct: in a Reichstag debate over enlarging the naval budget, the Navy's representative had mentioned the necessity for a defensive capability against the Soviet Baltic fleet. If this report were true, the ambassador fumed, the German government must disavow such "irresponsible utterances . . . of military armchair politicians," which would make the conduct of a sensible policy toward the Soviet Union impossible.[33] Two years later, the *Panzerschiff* debate evoked a Soviet request for clarification of Germany's naval policy in the Baltic. Schubert instructed the Moscow embassy to reassure Litvinov that Groener, in his *Denkschrift* supporting the Navy's proposed battle cruiser, meant no unfriendliness toward the Soviet Union when he argued that, among its other advantages, the new ship would improve Germany's ability to defend its neutrality against the Soviet Union.[34]

[32] Judging from the Wilhelmstrasse's anxious reaction to rumors of a joint German-Soviet naval maneuver in the eastern Baltic in 1924, the diplomats would probably have demanded control over any serious program of collaboration the Navy might have developed; *AA*, Dufour (London) to Foreign Office, 30 September 1924; Foreign Office to Defense Ministry, 20 (?) October; Naval Command to Foreign Office, 23 October; Foreign Office to London and Paris missions, 24 October; K170/K025378-81, 404, 412-14, 416-17. The Naval Command clung to its denial of such a joint exercise; Schubert to Defense Ministry, 27 December, and Naval Command to Foreign Office, 15 May 1925, K299/K105011-12, 028-9.

[33] *AA*, Brockdorff-Rantzau to Foreign Office, 9 and 10 March; Wallroth to Brockdorff-Rantzau, 11 March; 9524/E671570, 572-3, 574-5. Wallroth reassured Brockdorff-Rantzau that the report was sheer fabrication, that the naval spokesman had merely alluded to the progress being made by the Soviet Navy.

[34] *AA*, Schubert to Moscow, 24 January 1929, 2860/D560135; see also Carsten, *Reichswehr and Politics*, p. 238.

Admiral Raeder, referring to the Baltic and Germany's dependence on the postures of the Scandinavian states, called for cooperation in peacetime with the Foreign Office. If at all possible, the Navy should, with the help of the diplomats, "influence the political situation" in order to benefit Germany's naval interests.[35] In the *Flottenabteilung*, Captain Hermann Boehm also emphasized the close connection between foreign policy and naval strategy.[36] The training of the naval *Führergehilfen* included two Clausewitzean principles: war is a means of national policy, not an end in itself; military planning belongs in a position subordinate to political considerations and the political arm.[37] These tenets, the interdependence of foreign policy and military planning and the primacy of the political leadership, should be examined in the context of the Navy's rearmament and operations.

Both the clandestine and the legal rearmament of the Navy came under civilian attack, with the result that the Naval Command acknowledged its subordination to the cabinet and Foreign Office. By 1926 the Navy had established secret contacts in various countries for the study and construction of forbidden weapons: airplanes, small torpedo boats, and submarines. In 1927, the public revelation of the Navy's investment of secret funds earmarked for rearmament caused a scandal that forced Gessler to resign his post as Defense Minister. His successor, Groener, demanded a detailed account of naval activities in violation of the Treaty of Versailles; henceforth, the Chief of the Naval Command would have to

[35] *RWM*, Raeder critique of operational exercise of autumn 1928, 8 January 1929, PG 34048/3. In time of war, Raeder added, the Navy must not risk damaging Germany's relations with another country unless the proposed action were decisively in Germany's favor.

[36] The Navy, Boehm asserted, must maintain a close relationship with the Foreign Office "in order to inform those who conduct our foreign policy what is advantageous for the Navy and its strategy, and . . . to help expedite the attainment of these objectives inasmuch as such a peacetime strategy is currently possible." *RWM*, Boehm paper, January 1929, II M 57/58.

[37] Interviews with Admirals Dönitz and Wagner.

apprise the Defense Minister and cabinet of any such activities.[38]

Shortly after this episode the Defense Minister submitted the construction proposal for *Panzerschiff A* to public debate, since the project would require an explicit allocation from the Reichstag. After months of prolonged political battle, the Navy could congratulate itself on having gained support, even from the liberal Democratic Party, in a crucial vote in November which defeated a resolution of the SPD against the cruiser.[39] But the cruiser debate confirmed the power of the Reichstag over the national budget, and because future Reichstag majorities might not protect the Navy's legal construction program from the fiscal shears of the Social Democrats, the Naval Command and the office of the Defense Minister concurred in the desire to restrict defense policy to the cabinet and departments as much as possible.

Stresemann told the Reichstag that he supported the construction of *Panzerschiff A*, since it did not conflict with his foreign policy.[40] Still, the Wilhelmstrasse's regard for British

[38] Carsten, *Reichswehr and Politics*, pp. 242-45, 284-90; also Assmann, *Deutsche Seestrategie*, p. 115.

[39] *RK*, documents in file K955; Braun, *Weimar zu Hitler*, pp. 250-53; Eyck, *Weimar Republic*, II, 153-65; Raeder, *My Life*, pp. 147f.; Wacker, *Bau des Panzerschiffes*, pp. 62-167; also Arnold Brecht, *Mit der Kraft des Geistes: Lebenserinnerungen, 1927-1967* (Stuttgart, 1967), pp. 49-55; Gordon A. Craig, "Quellen zur neuesten Geschichte: ii. Briefe Schleichers an Groener," *Die Welt als Geschichte*, XI (1951), 124-26. On internal divisions in the Social Democratic Party over questions of naval rearmament, see Caspar, *Sozialdemokratische Partei und deutsche Wehrproblem*, chap. 7; Wacker, *Bau des Panzerschiffes*, pp. 11-24, 128-45.

[40] Wacker, *ibid.*, p. 54. Prof. Eschenburg told Wacker that Stresemann "in his heart" opposed the battle cruiser, but decided he could not resist its construction because of pressure from his own party, the Right, and the armed forces; *ibid.*, n. Be that as it may, Stresemann's support of the *Panzerschiff* was consistent with his practice of sanctioning rearmament activities as long as they did not jeopardize his foreign policy; see Stresemann's warning to Groener above, chap. 6, n. 42. Stresemann almost certainly believed that the Navy intended

opinion overrode the Naval Command's proposal to increase the caliber of the cruiser's main guns beyond the original figure.[41] The scandal and the cruiser issue chastened the Naval Command and alerted the Foreign Office. In the future, the Navy told a representative from the Wilhelmstrasse, the Navy would make no decisions concerning rearmament without first consulting the Foreign Office, a pledge welcomed by the diplomats because it promised closer cooperation and the prevention of "foreign policy difficulties."[42]

Differences of opinion over the Baltic front, German-Soviet relations, and naval reconstruction were minor in comparison to the Navy's fundamental divergence from the western policy of Stresemann. The Foreign Office realized this when it began to collaborate with the Navy in operational planning. Late in 1927, to increase cooperation between the Navy and Foreign Office, Admiral Zenker invited officials from the Wilhelmstrasse to participate in the Navy's operational exercises.[43] Although Dirk Forster and the other Foreign Office representative attending the winter war game of 1927 did not have the opportunity to speak during the conduct and critique of the game, they discovered in the course of many informal conversations that the Naval Command was sincerely endeavoring "to take into account foreign policy and the leading role of the Foreign Office in that province, and, therefore, to seek closer liaison with the Foreign Office."

to use the new cruisers primarily in the Baltic, not as raiders of French commerce in the North Sea.

[41] Assmann, *Deutsche Seestrategie*, p. 110; Hubatsch, *Admiralstab*, pp. 192-93; Wacker, *Bau des Panzerschiffes*, p. 48n.; British Foreign Office memorandum, 19 May 1927, and Berlin embassy to London, 2 June, *DBFP*, Ser. IA, III, 314-17, 317n. The original caliber was itself in excess of the maximum stipulated for cruisers in either the Treaty of Versailles or the Five-Power Naval Treaty, signed at the Washington Conference on 6 February 1922 by the United States, Britain, France, Italy, and Japan.

[42] *AA*, Forster notes of conversation with the head of the Naval Command's Special Section for League of Nations Affairs, 23 April 1928, K6/K000379.

[43] *AA*, Zenker to Schubert, 1 December, *ibid.*, K000320-1.

Naval leaders had shown keen interest in the diplomats' judgment that "in view of the complicated European situation and the effects of Geneva and Locarno, the sudden outbreak of armed international conflict was unlikely . . ." and that therefore, the central politico-military problem was to determine what military measures Germany should take "during a political crisis in Europe in order to protect itself and avoid, for as long as possible, being dragged into a war."[44]

But Forster observed something else. Even though the Naval Command admitted that the conflict situation did not correspond to reality, Forster believed that the Navy was inclined "to overrate the importance of Italy as a comrade in arms for us, and to consider France as the given enemy." Moreover, in the Navy's explicit effort to free its thinking "from the narrow limits imposed by postwar circumstances and turn it once again toward a great European conflict," Forster detected "a certain optimism about the importance of Germany as a maritime factor."[45] A few months later, having compared the Navy's assumptions and aspirations with those of the Army, Forster concluded that the Navy had not made as much progress in abandoning "romantic" notions in its operational planning.[46]

Naval planning in the 1920s looked forward to a "war of liberation" against France. If a German-Polish conflict should erupt, the Navy would of course engage in Baltic operations against Poland; but at the same time the Navy would hope to set in motion its anti-French western maritime strategy, depending upon *Handelskrieg* in the Atlantic, British and American neutrality, and Italian support. In view of this strategy, the Navy could probably not have defined the purpose of war games, nor explained the connection between operational hypotheses and politico-military circumstances to the

[44] *AA*, Forster memorandum on the game in Kiel, 7 January 1928, *ibid.*, K000324-6. Forster's colleague was Georg Mutius, a member of the Wilhelmstrasse's Legal Department.

[45] *Ibid.*

[46] *AA*, Forster report on the Army's General Staff tour of April 1928, 2 May, *ibid.*, K000382.

satisfaction of the Foreign Office. In the Wilhelmstrasse, Stresemann and the career diplomats regarded the policy of understanding as a means of preventing a war with France. In the event of a conflict with Poland, the diplomats were determined to confine hostilities to the eastern front. When they pointed out the weaknesses of the Franco-Polish naval combination in the Baltic and supported construction of the battle cruiser, they did not imply that Germany must attain *Seegeltung*, or assume that the "Anglo-Saxon" naval powers would remain neutral in a continental war, or expect that Italy might solve Germany's strategic problems.[47]

Had the diplomats demanded access to the Navy's operational exercises in the early 1920s, they might have been able to restrain some of the Navy's assumptions. In any case, by the time joint operational planning had been established, Francophobia and *Seegeltung* permeated naval strategy. The Navy granted the primacy of the Foreign Office in foreign policy and the interdependence of policy and strategy; but the Navy apparently expected foreign policy to serve naval planning and not the reverse. The Foreign Office had evidence of the "romantic" tendencies in naval planning, but made no concerted attempt to conform naval strategy more closely to continental realities. The Navy's presumptuousness and the Wilhelmstrasse's negligence shared this root: the Navy was clearly of secondary importance in national defense.

INTER-SERVICE COOPERATION

The two service chiefs confessed that joint planning between the Navy and Army had been conspicuously deficient before and during the war, vowed that the services would no longer follow independent paths, and agreed in the autumn of 1920 that they must encourage inter-service cooperation in de-

[47] The Navy's planning for North Sea operations included measures which might have forced the British to abandon their neutrality and aid France. Britain was unlikely to stand by idly if German naval forces attacked French channel ports; Hubatsch, *Admiralstab*, p. 190.

fense planning.[48] Moreover, both services affirmed their determination to study operational contingencies jointly:[49] an officer from the Naval Command was attached to the Army Command; an Army officer, to the Fleet Department; the Army and Navy conducted joint operational exercises, some at the regional or unit level, others involving senior command and staff members; and each service sent officers to observe the field maneuvers of the other. But the resultant camaraderie did not eliminate essential differences over Germany's politico-military situation and requirements. Although the Navy acknowledged its secondary role, it refused to strike its flag meekly in inter-service quarrels; these quarrels were both symptomatic of the difficult but necessary process of grafting the armed services to each other, and a constant hindrance to closer collaboration.

In view of Groener's vigorous defense of the battle cruiser in Reichstag budget debates, the charge that he was unsympathetic to naval needs (or much less sympathetic than Gessler had been) should be moderated.[50] Still, Groener and Schleicher rejected the Naval Command's draft on the value of the cruiser. The Navy's terms *Seegeltung* and *Kreuzerkrieg* would have been unpalatable to the majority in the Reichstag; this language reminded Schleicher of German maritime

[48] *RWM*, Seeckt to Chief of the Naval Command, 4 September, Behncke to Seeckt, 11 November, Fach 7896; also Hubatsch, *Admiralstab*, p. 184. The Navy rejected the Army's subsequent proposals for centralizing the administration of military and naval ordnance in a *Kriegsamt* and promoting the Chief of the Army Command to the position of supreme commander of the armed forces in the event of war; the Naval Command did, however, agree in principle to a joint command system for the sake of expediency. *RWM*, documents in file II M 2; Assmann, *Deutsche Seestrategie*, p. 126; Hubatsch, *Admiralstab*, p. 188; below, chap. 9, n. 108.

[49] *RWM*, Fleet Department *Denkschrift* (Capt. Gladisch), May 1921; *Truppenamt* to Naval Command Office, December 1925; PG 31039; also memorandum in Naval Command, "Die Aufgaben der Marine im Kriege. Zusammenarbeit mit dem Heere," PG 34065.

[50] Assmann, *Deutsche Seestrategie*, pp. 111-12; Raeder, *My Life*, pp. 136-37, 140.

aspirations to a world strategy in the Tirpitz era, which he dismissed as " 'far removed from all reality' " in the 1920s. Thus, Groener and Schleicher assigned Major Ott—an Army officer—the task of composing a politically more acceptable and strategically more realistic memorandum to guide the Defense Minister in cabinet discussions and in the Reichstag debate in November 1928.[51]

This confidential Groener *Denkschrift* gave three major reasons for strengthening the armed forces by measures such as providing the Navy with battle cruisers: defense against Polish attack; protection of Germany's neutrality during a conflict among other states; and assurance of Germany's *Bündnisfähigkeit* in the event that joining in a coalition might benefit Germany in a future war. Groener emphasized that the Navy's primary responsibility was Germany's security in the Baltic, where it should safeguard sea communications with East Prussia, support land battles in coastal regions, protect land forces against enemy assault from the sea, and blockade Poland. He would restrict naval operations in the North Sea to coastal defense.[52]

The Navy did not share the Army's continental formula, implicit in the Groener *Denkschrift*, that Germany should confine its naval operations to the Baltic and the coasts because it was a land power.[53] In the opinion of naval planners,

[51] Müller, *Vaterland*, p. 315; interview with Ambassador Ott; *RWM, Flottenabteilung* paper, "Der militärische Wert der Panzerschiffneubauten," 2 October 1928, II M 69/1, perhaps the draft that Groener could not accept. Although formulated by Ott, the memorandum was ascribed to Groener, and the ideas in it can legitimately be viewed as Groener's own.

[52] For the text of the *Denkschrift*, see sources in chap. 5, n. 16; discussion of its contents in Wacker, *Bau des Panzerschiffes*, pp. 35-40, 47, 50-53; also *RK*, excerpts from cabinet protocols of 14 and 15 November 1928, and Groener speech to party leaders, 16 November, K955/K251009-11, 013, 018-39; Groener address before "Deutsche Gesellschaft 1914," 27 November, Nachlass Groener, no. 149, Bundesarchiv-Militärarchiv.

[53] Groener's defense of the cruiser for employment in the Baltic did not receive the support of T3 in the *Truppenamt*, which feared

the Army's continental point of view served as a strong lever to dissuade the government and Reichstag from reducing the Army's budget to free funds for naval construction. The Army's strategy also demonstrated to the Navy an inability to grasp the importance of sea power and *Handelskrieg* to Germany's survival in a prolonged continental war.[54] This clash between the continentalism of the Army and the maritime strategy of the Navy had sharp repercussions, producing inter-service discord over more pressing questions which the Army and Navy had to settle jointly in the interests of national defense: protection of the North Sea ports and coast; and Baltic operations against Poland.

In 1924, Admiral Zenker read Oswald Spengler's fatalistic theory of French expansionism, the outcome of which would be " *'the triumph of the Romance world over the Germanic.'* " The Chief of the Naval Command doubted Spengler's gloomy assertion that Germany lacked the power to prevent the French from seizing Germany's North Sea ports and turning them into air and submarine bases for the struggle against the "Anglo-Saxon" and Germanic world.[55] But perhaps Spengler estimated German power more accurately than the Navy did. In correspondence and joint exercises, the Navy too readily assumed that, if the French invaded on land, the Army would be able to defend Wilhelmshaven, Bremen, and Hamburg, and at the same time contribute units to a joint force to oppose French amphibious landings behind the German lines. The Army's western con-

---

possible damage to military collaboration with the Soviet Union; Carsten, *Reichswehr and Politics*, p. 282.

[54] Assmann, *Deutsche Seestrategie*, p. 104; Raeder, *My Life*, pp. 139-40; interviews with Admirals Dönitz and Wagner. Cooperation between the representatives of both services in the *Wehrmachtsabteilung* (and *Ministeramt*) was close (interview with Ambassador Ott), but it was limited to questions of internal politics and did not resolve inter-service differences over strategy; Hubatsch, *Admiralstab*, p. 193.

[55] *RWM*, Zenker marginal question mark on copy of short article by Spengler, "Frankreichs Weltmacht; die Wiederaufbau der napoleonische Pläne," October (?), PG 34463.

tingency planning envisaged a strong defensive line north of what it considered the most likely and most dangerous axis of French advance, along the Main valley toward the Thuringian Forest and Czechoslovakia. Although the Army would try to hold positions near and along the Ems and Weser rivers, it could not maintain them indefinitely if the French prepared to advance from the Main valley into the heart of the Reich; in that event, Germany might have to sacrifice most if not all of its North Sea coastline.[56]

Joint planning for Baltic operations embraced transportation, amphibious landings, and an attack against Gdingen. Army and Navy units together studied possibilities for the transportation of troops and matériel to and from East Prussia; the Army Command did not rely upon supplying that province by land through the Corridor in a German-Polish war, and contemplated shipping reinforcements from East Prussia to the western front in a one-front conflict with France.[57] Naval officers collaborated with units of Army District II on defense against an enemy amphibious landing on the Baltic coast, and with the Second Engineer Battalion (Stettin), the Army's first amphibious unit, on loading and disembarking troops on beaches.[58] Cooperation at these unit-levels was friendly and regular, although the landlubber *Truppenamt* did not display much enthusiasm for amphibious operations.[59]

[56] *RWM*, Behncke directive, May 1922, PG 31039; Naval Command note on joint *Führerreise*, June 1923, PG 34073/1; *Flottenabteilung* memorandum, 8 June 1925, PG 34061; documents pertaining to joint *Führerreise (Fall West)*, 1928, II M 100/17, 100/18; Boehm paper, January 1929, II M 57/58; interview with Admiral Dönitz; Hubatsch, *Admiralstab*, pp. 188-90.

[57] Interviews with Generals Hauck and Kühne; *RWM*, Army transportation exercises of 1922, 1925, 1927-28, II H 249, 561, 562; Army Command memorandum to Chief of the Naval Command, "Seetransporte des Reichsheeres," 28 September 1922, II M 62/1.

[58] Interviews with Generals von Ahlfen (a junior officer in the Second Battalion, 1926-28), Hauck, and Hausser (Chief of Staff of the Second Division, Stettin, 1925-28).

[59] The initiative in amphibious planning came from interested

In 1924, four years before his promotion to Chief of the Naval Command, Raeder skeptically dismissed the supposition of some naval officers that the Army would participate in a combined land and sea assault on Polish coastal installations.[60] Raeder's judgment proved correct. In subsequent war games and staff talks, the Navy reluctantly acceded to the *Truppenamt*, which declared that the Army's part in *Studie Gdingen* must be severely restricted if not eliminated. Whether the operations of the *Feldheer* (in an *A-Fall*) might include a minor attack against Gdingen would depend on circumstances. Preparations for a surprise raid by a force of irregulars might take place in peacetime; such a mission, if feasible at all without detriment to the mobilization of the *Feldheer*, would have to be executed after the outbreak of hostilities because of foreign policy considerations. Should Poland occupy Danzig and use it as a naval base, a land assault on Gdingen simply to destroy its air fields and coastal artillery would not be worth the cost.[61] By mid-1928, *Studie*

---

tacticians and technicians in the lower echelons of the services, not from their Berlin command offices or operations sections. As Chief of the *Truppenamt*, Blomberg concurred with the Foreign Office that the Navy's joint amphibious maneuver scheduled for September 1929 in the Bay of Danzig should be cancelled because of possible diplomatic repercussions. He also stated that the Army, which had virtually no interest in the maneuver, had reluctantly placed units at the Navy's disposal solely to accommodate the Navy. *AA, Flottenabteilung* to Foreign Office, 5 January 1929; Köpke notes of conversation with Blomberg, 6 April; 4569/E169190, 202-4.

[60] *RWM, Flottenabteilung* papers (Lieutenant Schenk), 1922, II M 57/5; (Captain von Ditten), 1924, with critique by Raeder, 20 August, II M 57/32. Schenk's proposal for an offensive into Poland, with numerous primary and secondary land attacks, assumed a politico-military superiority which not even the most "romantic" Army officers could have imagined.

[61] The *Truppenamt* also declared that "the possibility of conducting a land operation against Danzig if [Poland] should violate its neutrality does not exist and cannot be taken into consideration." *RWM, Truppenamt* (T1—Fritsch) to Military District II (Stettin) and Group Command 1 (Berlin), 20 June 1928, PG 34101. Zenker

Gdingen had become the Navy's sole responsibility, and the Naval Command continued this operational segment of its *A-Plan* without any guarantee of assistance from the Army.[62]

On both fronts, the Navy overestimated the Army's willingness to commit forces to coastal regions and did not fully appreciate the Army's strategic preoccupation with the security of Germany's heartland.[63] In the west, the Army had begun to favor a political understanding with France in order to neutralize that front in a German-Polish war. In the east, the Army viewed the Polish question with great urgency, the German-Soviet tie with high strategic hopes, and Gdingen with little tactical interest. The Navy shared the Foreign Office's concern for the neutrality of Britain and the United States in a future war. But the Army comprehended the relationship between foreign policy and military planning on the continent, and this no doubt enabled the soldiers and diplomats to develop a more harmonious relationship in joint planning, and to extend their general strategic agreement—on Germany as a continental rather than maritime power—into the particulars of rearmament and operations.

---

critique of war game, December 1927, II M 100/14; this and other exercises, Zenker concluded, showed "that there can be no successful land operation against [Polish] bases so long as the Army Command is not in the position to include an attack against Danzig/Gdingen in the general plan of operations." See also Hubatsch, *Admiralstab*, pp. 188, 190.

[62] *RWM*, Naval Command paper, PG 31039; Fleet Command (Oldekop) to Chief of the Naval Command, 29 September 1929, PG 34066.

[63] In its *A-Plan*, the Army took into consideration the economic potential of "Innerdeutschland," for Germany could not count on the heavy industry of the vulnerable border regions in the east and west; Thomas, *Wehr- und Rüstungswirtschaft*, pp. 55, 59-60. In the Naval Command, however, this conception of "Innerdeutschland" (which disappeared after 1933) must have reinforced the determination to protect Germany's maritime links with industrial nations and sources of raw materials.

THE YEARS OF CRISIS, 1930-33

Official departments should maintain an attitude of reserve toward the question of the Corridor problem until an international constellation favorable to us permits its being opened.

Hans Adolf von Moltke, August 1930

In the struggle for the recovery of its complete freedom, Germany concluded a secret treaty with Russia [according to which] Germany's old eastern borders should be restored.

Army *Führerreise*, 1933

Part III

The Naval Command is currently working on a study concerning measures at sea should a conflict with Poland suddenly break out.

Naval Command memorandum, January 1930

CHAPTER VIII

Policy in the Foreign Office

STRESEMANN'S long tenure had created an atmosphere of foreign policy stability and expertise above party and had reduced the contrast between a party minister and his staff of career diplomats. After 1929, however, party ministers in the Foreign Office and other departments gradually succumbed to attacks from two sides: opposition in the Reichstag curtailed their ministerial longevity; the Chancellor, President, and bureaucracy questioned their political usefulness.

The political turmoil of the early 1930s heightened the antipathy with which the Wilhelmstrasse contemplated parliamentary control over foreign policy.[1] The Foreign Office could not escape public criticism, most vocal during a period of instability and harmful to the domestic base of national policy. Midway through his brief term of office as Stresemann's successor, shortly after the astounding success of the National Socialist Party in the election of September 1930, Julius Curtius observed that the government's survival depended on its ability to impress the German people with concrete results in foreign policy.[2] Curtius himself became a casualty of Nationalist pressure; he was forced to resign in October 1931 after the government abandoned the Austro-

---

[1] Kordt, *Nicht aus den Akten*, p. 46; Weizsäcker, *Memoirs*, pp. 85-86.

[2] Sir Horace Rumbold (British Ambassador to Berlin, 1928-33) to Arthur Henderson (Foreign Secretary, 1929-31), 27 October, *DBFP*, Ser. 2, I, 525. The day after the election, Secretary of State Bülow had advised Curtius (then in Geneva) that, in view of the election results, he should phrase his speech to the League Assembly " 'in a way acceptable to the Right.' " Edward W. Bennett, *Germany and the Diplomacy of the Financial Crisis, 1931* (Cambridge, Mass., 1962), pp. 11-12.

German customs union project. Even Stresemann, an adept mediator between his department and the public, probably could not have endured the intense politics that suffused foreign policy issues from the election campaign of 1930 to the end of the republic, nor would he have survived the elimination of party ministers from the cabinets of Papen and Schleicher.

The Chancellor, President, and career diplomats concurred that the Wilhelmstrasse should no longer be headed by a party minister; they preferred instead a bureaucratic expert dependent upon their support.[3] Heinrich Brüning (March 1930-May 1932), whose interest in and influence over foreign policy far exceeded that of any Chancellor under whom Stresemann had served, assumed Curtius' portfolio in October 1931, a move that "increased the importance of the state secretary for foreign affairs."[4] But Brüning's experiment—extending the foreign policy domain of the Chancellor while encouraging departmental expertise—did not last. Constantin Freiherr von Neurath joined Franz von Papen's "cabinet of barons" (May-November 1932) as Foreign Minister on the conditions that, as a head of department in a "presidential system," he would have the full sanction of the President, and that the cabinet itself would be a true presidential cabinet above party, that is, with presidential support against the Reichstag. A professional diplomat, not a party man, Neurath viewed foreign policy as the province of the Foreign Minister and Foreign Office; he enjoyed the approbation and close co-

[3] On the tendency toward expertise and bureaucratic "efficiency," see Bracher, *Auflösung*, Pt. I, chap. 7; Heineman, "Neurath as Foreign Minister," pp. 23-32; Kehr, "Die Diktatur der Bürokratie," in *Primat der Innenpolitik*, pp. 251-53; Kordt, *Nicht aus den Akten*, pp. 51-52; Seabury, *The Wilhelmstrasse*, p. 21.

[4] Eyck, *Weimar Republic*, II, 331-32. See also Groener to Gleich, 20-21 September: Brüning would like to get rid of Curtius and be his own Foreign Minister, relying on a skillful Secretary of State; in fact Brüning " 'already works with state secretaries in other departments similar to Mussolini.' " Phelps, "Aus den Groener Dokumenten," p. 1016.

operation of his career subordinates, as well as the favor of President Hindenburg, to whom alone he considered himself responsible. Under Chancellors Papen and Schleicher (December 1932-January 1933), Neurath struggled to define and defend this institutional basis for German foreign policy in the *Präsidialstaat* of the "Old Gentleman."[5]

The domestic instability that altered the executive-departmental setting also influenced the diplomatic methods of German policy. The "tendency to complain of the cabinet's foreign policy as insufficiently aggressive"[6] was displayed not only by the political extremes, for even the parties that had formed the last pro-republican Great Coalition under Müller (People's Party, Center, Democratic Party, and Social Democrats) thought that they could perceive an intimate connection between domestic socio-economic misfortunes and Germany's international situation. Partly in response to this public pressure, accepting the equation between domestic survival and foreign policy success, German diplomats and Chancellors accelerated the pace for attaining revisionist goals, announced some policies peremptorily, and adopted a more "forward" or aggressive manner in negotiations, abandoning Stresemann's patient and conciliatory method of pursuing national interests.

The foreign policy goals themselves, however (and, to some extent, the quickened tempo of diplomacy), were inherent in Germany's revisionist policy of the 1920s: should Germany not move on to the next stage of revisionist demands after the first had been reached? In June 1929, when the Foreign Office anticipated the evacuation of the Rhineland and a new reparations settlement in 1930, Bülow thought that the accomplishment of these objectives might signal the moment

[5] On Neurath's civil-servant authoritarian ideology, his refusal to serve as minister in the quasi-parliamentary regime of Brüning because it was not "presidential" enough, his candidacy in May 1932, and his popularity in the Wilhelmstrasse, see Heineman, "Neurath as Foreign Minister," chap. 2, pp. 81-91, 132-33.

[6] Hilger, *Incompatible Allies*, p. 225.

for Germany " 'to embark on a greater activity.' "[7] During the following winter, the financial crisis in the United States began to complicate European diplomacy and exacerbate Germany's formidable problems of taxation and unemployment. But rather than allow these changing circumstances to postpone a new stage of revisionism or reduce Germany's revisionist claims, as Stresemann might have done, the Foreign Office and Chancellor went ahead with "a greater activity," often pleading that domestic pressure required this activity, seldom admitting that it possessed an internal momentum of its own.[8]

The extent of Germany's eastern territorial aims remained virtually the same as in the Stresemann era. In a long directive to German missions in March 1931, Curtius adduced both ethnographic and strategic arguments for the return of Danzig, the Corridor, western Posen, and Upper Silesia. Curtius enjoined German envoys to keep these claims alive in diplomatic circles and to avoid any fractional measures such as reconstituting the Corridor as an independent territory with Danzig as the capital.[9] In June 1930 Bernhard W. von Bülow replaced Schubert as Secretary of State; in the autumn

[7] Bülow to Rome mission, 5 June, in F. G. Stambrook, "The German-Austrian Customs Union Project of 1931: A Study of German Methods and Motives," *Journal of Central European Affairs*, XXI (1961), 20.

[8] For a persuasive criticism of the opinion that Brüning's foreign policy was all blunder simply for the sake of "activity," see Wolfgang J. Helbich, "Between Stresemann and Hitler: The Foreign Policy of the Brüning Government," *World Politics*, XII (1959), 24-44. Helbich argues that Brüning was concerned more with foreign than with domestic policy, and that we must view his policy of "activity" in relation to German revisionism between Stresemann's policy of understanding and Hitler's campaign for *Lebensraum*.

[9] *AA*, Curtius memorandum, 7 March (to missions on 17 March), L575/L185481-98. Like Stresemann, Curtius extended the Corridor south of the limits of the area that had been ethnographically German even before the Polish policy of de-Germanization had begun. He also emphasized the importance of railroad lines in the Corridor and western Posen.

268

of 1931 Richard Meyer succeeded Oskar Trautmann, Chief of the Eastern Department since 1928; and Hans Adolf von Moltke, director (or deputy chief) under Trautmann, became Minister to Warsaw after Rauscher's death in December 1930.[10] In spite of this changing of the guard, the official correspondence of these diplomats in the early 1930s echoed Curtius' prohibition against a partial settlement of the Polish question, an eventuality that Rauscher had believed Germany "must fear like poison."[11]

EASTERN EUROPE

Germany's Polish policy after Stresemann continued to reflect the deadlock between the two countries over the territorial status quo, but German diplomats became more and more entangled in a web that they themselves helped to spin.[12] Realizing that a final solution to the Polish question must await a more favorable international situation, they nevertheless kept that question in full view of the German public and foreign officials. The Foreign Office had to show the German voter that the government was adamantly revisionist, and it wanted no misunderstanding abroad that Germany might compromise its territorial demands in conversations about reparations, the customs union project, and disarmament. As a result, in dealing with the question of border revision, reacting to the alleged threat of Polish aggression, and maintaining relations with Poland, the Foreign Office steered erratically between procrastination and public display.

The diplomats postponed the border settlement but were

[10] See Curtius, *Sechs Jahre Minister der Deutschen Republik* (Heidelberg, 1948), pp. 146-47. The Poles had feared that Zechlin would become the new Chief of the Eastern Department; a high official in the Polish Foreign Office regarded him as "one of the most rabid opponents of any sort of understanding with Poland." Lipski, *Diplomat in Berlin*, p. 29.

[11] *AA*, Rauscher (from his residence on Lake Constance) to Bülow, 13 August 1930, 2945/D575226.

[12] See the analysis by Kimmich, *Free City*, pp. vii, 102ff., 165.

269

careful not to imply any recognition of the existing borders. Late in 1929 Curtius reassured a Social Democrat (Rudolf Breitscheid) and a retired Army officer that the recent German-Polish agreement governing the rights of Germans in former German territories contained no secret attachments, such as a recognition of the eastern borders.[13] In the election campaign of 1930, the Foreign Office and Brüning were vexed when a member of the cabinet took up the Polish question in strident nationalistic tones.[14] Bülow "was clearly embarrassed by [this incursion] into the domain of foreign policy," and Moltke reaffirmed that German officials should maintain a reserved attitude toward the Corridor question "until an international constellation favorable to us permits its being opened."[15]

In March 1931 Curtius reiterated that the time for formally broaching the border question had not yet arrived.[16] Although this official stance still found some public support, Curtius' position was neither as zealous nor as simplistic as demonstrations and propaganda by the Nazis and the *Stahlhelm*, who demanded an immediate revision of the borders.[17]

[13] *AA*, Curtius to Moltke, 30 November, and Curtius to Lt. Col. (Ret.) Kurt Graebe, 7 December, 2945/D574391, 408-9.

[14] *RK*, cabinet protocol, 20 August, 3575/D784627ff. Gottfried Treviranus, Minister for Occupied Territories and recent co-founder (with Count Kuno von Westarp) of the Conservative People's Party, committed that indiscretion before a congregation of "Patriotic Eastern Leagues" in Berlin. Although the cabinet did not disavow this speech by one of its members, Brüning subsequently cautioned his ministers not to overexpose the Polish question and asked that they check with him before making public statements on foreign policy.

[15] Rumbold (Berlin) to Henderson, 18 August, *DBFP*, Ser. 2, I, 500; *AA*, Moltke to Rintelen (Warsaw), 28 August, L558/L161931-2.

[16] *AA*, Curtius memorandum, 7 March (to missions on 17 March), L575/L185481-2.

[17] For an essay supporting the government's policy, see Werner Freiherr von Rheinbaben, "Deutschland und Polen; zwölf Thesen zur Revisionspolitik," *Europäische Gespräche*, IX (1931), 83-99. Although the Foreign Office would not allow chauvinists to force its hand, it

270

The Foreign Office also had to guard against a premature opening of the Polish question by conciliatory groups like the Pan-European Union, which urged a compromise solution because a restoration of the entire Corridor to Germany without war was virtually impossible. Bülow observed that, although the Foreign Office was fully aware of the difficulties that blocked revision "in the German sense," it must insist that notions of compromise would mislead other states concerning Germany's official policy and would be domestically unpalatable.[18] Postponement continued through the final year of the republic. In a conversation with Zaleski in Geneva, Brüning ignored the Polish Foreign Minister's remark that perhaps a *modus vivendi* could be found. And, a few days before Hitler became Chancellor, Neurath noted that any partial solution must be avoided, for it would only prejudice the desired outcome of the Polish question.[19]

During the years of crisis, the Foreign Office and the Reich Chancery were flooded with reports from the borderlands of Polish incursions onto German soil, and Polish concentrations for military invasion. The Wilhelmstrasse brought border incidents to the attention of foreign diplomats to help prove that the German-Polish borders were untenable.[20]

---

parried Polish protests with a stern reminder that the *Stahlhelm* was a private organization and that foreign governments had no business telling German authorities how to treat such groups; *AA*, documents concerning a mass *Stahlhelm* demonstration in Breslau on 30-31 May 1931, L558/L162650-3, 661-4. On the *Stahlhelm's* Polish policy, see Siegfrid Wagner (*Bundeskanzler* of the *Stahlhelm*), *Die Polnische Gefahr* (Berlin, 1930); also Berghahn, *Stahlhelm*, pp. 163-64, 169-71. Nazi foreign policy prior to 1933 is summarized in Hans-Adolf Jacobsen, *Nationalsozialistische Aussenpolitik 1933-1938* (Frankfurt am Main, 1968), pp. 1-15.

[18] *RK*, correspondence with and about the Pan-European Union, 1931, Akten betr. Polen, Band 9 (not filmed).

[19] *AA*, Bülow (Geneva) to Foreign Office, 25 April 1932, 2945/D575710-12; Neurath notes for speech before Reichstag Foreign Affairs Committee, 26 January 1933, 6601H/E495035-6.

[20] *AA*, K190, *passim*; *RK*, Akten betr. Polen, Bände 9 and 10, *passim* (not filmed); *DBFP*, Ser. 2, I, 490-91.

Moreover, Brüning's government and the Army feared Polish seizure of German territory while they might be preoccupied with, at worst, a full-scale civil war. According to Brüning, this anxiety increased in 1931, after the Germans learned of Polish mobilization plans and the League failed to take action against Japanese aggression in Manchuria.[21] German diplomats in Poland and Danzig, however, discounted rumors of an impending invasion.[22] Similar alarmist reports reached Berlin in the first half of 1932, when many Germans—not merely the nervous borderland residents—suspected that Pilsudski intended to launch a preventive war to seize Danzig, parts of East Prussia, and perhaps even Silesia. But again German diplomats (and the Prussian Interior Ministry) tried to temper public excitement (stirred up by the oratory during the presidential and Prussian election campaigns and by the government's own revisionist propaganda) with evidence that Poland was not massing troops for an attack.[23]

The thaw in German-Polish relations in the late 1920s did not last. Curtius, like Stresemann, declared his determination to normalize relations with Poland so long as the border question remained on a back burner.[24] But his decent efforts to aid

[21] Heinrich Brüning, "Ein Brief," *Deutsche Rundschau*, LXX, no. 7 (July 1947), 2; also Roos, *Polen und Europa*, pp. 37-39.

[22] *AA*, reports from missions in Poland and Danzig, 1931, K190/K036654-772, *passim*.

[23] *AA*, reports from German diplomats in Poland and from the Prussian Interior Ministry, K190/K036810-900 and ff. In June, Pilsudski ordered the Polish destroyer "Wicher" to enter the Danzig harbor as a protest against a recent international ruling prejudicial to Poland's naval interests in Danzig, and as a demonstration of Polish firmness at a time when Germany had stepped up its campaign for Franco-German reconciliation and equality of armaments. For conflicting interpretations of Pilsudski's plans and the "Wicher" incident, see Beck, *Final Report*, pp. 14-15; Breyer, *Deutsche Reich und Polen*, pp. 31-32, 37; Zygmunt Gasiorowski, "Did Pilsudski Attempt to Initiate a Preventive War in 1933?," *Journal of Modern History*, XXVII (1955), 139-40; Kimmich, *Free City*, pp. 118-20; Roos, *Polen und Europa*, pp. 39ff., 47f.; Von Riekhoff, *German-Polish Relations*, pp. 367-74.

[24] Curtius, *Sechs Jahre*, pp. 98-101. Rauscher, in one of his last

272

the German minority in Poland and to improve economic relations between the two countries were denounced by those who believed that the government should give more sustenance to *Deutschtum* abroad; by agrarian groups on the Right demanding higher protective tariffs in a period of deepening agricultural depression; by subscribers to the view that great political leverage could be gained by economically isolating Poland; by skeptics who saw lurking behind any agreement with Poland an eastern Locarno or some other form of recognition of the borders; and by irreconcilables who simply despised not only the Poles but the Berlin government as well.[25] Under this hostile domestic fire, the Reichstag refused to ratify the commercial agreement, signed in Warsaw in March 1930 after years of stuttering negotiations, and the tariff war intensified.[26] Exacerbating German-Polish relations further were border incidents, nationalistic pride, the increasing Polish economic and political pressure on Danzig, and Polish suspicions of collusion between German officials and Ukrainian nationalists inside Poland.[27]

Germany's Polish policy had become anachronistic and faltering. Postponement rested in part on the assumptions that the German minority would remain at least large enough to justify argument from the Wilsonian principle of self-determination and that Danzig would be able to survive with German help until the Polish question could be resolved. As a result of postponement, neither of these suppositions was valid in 1932, except by the farthest stretch of the imagina-

---

memoranda, remained a staunch advocate of normalizing German-Polish relations; *AA*, Rauscher to Bülow, 13 August 1930, 2945/D575226-9.

[25] *RK*, Akten betr. Polen, Bände 8-10, *passim* (not filmed); Korbel, *Poland between East and West*, pp. 261ff.

[26] Kruszewski, "German-Polish Tariff War," pp. 309-11; Von Riekhoff, *German-Polish Relations*, pp. 190-93.

[27] Kimmich, *Free City*, pp. 109-26; Von Riekhoff, *German-Polish Relations*, pp. 330-38; *Papers Relating to the Foreign Relations of the United States*, 1931 (3 vols.; Washington, 1946), I, 595-604, and 1932 (5 vols.; Washington, 1948), I, 861-64.

tion. Ethnic Germans constituted only about 14 percent of the population in the Corridor, contrasted with 70 percent in 1910; Danzig's economy, dependent on international trade, was suffering heavily as a result of the world depression.[28] Yet Weimar diplomats and politicians seemed frozen into the official position of insisting upon but deferring revision; hoping for an international situation advantageous to territorial revision, they were distracted by one that could scarcely have been less favorable.

Germany's Lithuanian policy remained essentially the same after Stresemann's death: economic and political support short of binding agreements. The Wilhelmstrasse still considered Lithuania part of a useful land bridge to the Soviet Union, and a possible ally against Poland, since Lithuania had not forgiven Poland's seizure of Vilna. But Lithuania's possession of Memel during a period of rising agitation for the return of borderland *Deutschtum* restrained Germany from drawing still closer;[29] indeed, Lithuania's military occupation of and imposition of martial law on Memel in February 1932 severely strained German-Lithuanian relations.

Berlin had compelling reasons for maintaining ties with Moscow: Germany needed a staunch revisionist supporter and anti-Polish partner; and the economic benefits promised in the treaties of Rapallo and Berlin, so far disappointingly meager, might help to compensate for Germany's share in the overall decline in western European trade, and for the com-

[28] Kimmich, *Free City*, pp. 104-105, 124, 162-63.

[29] Curtius seems to have believed that Pilsudski was willing to surrender the Corridor in return for Memel and a free hand against Lithuania; Curtius rejected this compensation idea, since it would only antagonize Lithuania, and advised that the Memel and Polish questions be kept separated. Curtius, *Sechs Jahre*, pp. 98-99; *AA*, Curtius to Groener, 30 January 1931, 2945/D575540-1; Curtius memorandum, 7 March (to missions on 17 March), L575/L185498; Curtius minute of conversation with André François-Poncet (then Under-Secretary to the French Premier's Office) in London, 22 July, 2945/D575657.

mercial losses sustained in the fierce tariff war with Poland. The Rapallo relationship deteriorated, however, because of circumstances that German actions alone did not create and could not control.

First, the revolutionary activities of the German Communist Party and the Comintern revived the ideological animosities of the early 1920s. The German public grew more agitated than the Foreign Office about the threat of *Bolschewismus*, and found in its fears yet another foreign policy issue with which to harangue the government. Second, a Franco-Soviet rapprochement developed after the Franco-German Locarno understanding broke down and a brief French diplomatic offensive against the Soviet Union failed. Finally, Polish-Soviet relations improved. Before 1930 Pilsudski had already determined the direction of Polish foreign policy: rather than rely on the West to maintain the Treaty of Versailles, Poland must follow an independent path between Germany and the Soviet Union, negotiating with each of them separately. Under the direction of Colonel Jozef Beck, appointed deputy to Zaleski in 1930 and to replace him —Zaleski was neither a Pilsudski man nor an admirer of his policy—as Foreign Minister in November 1932, Warsaw pursued this policy energetically as German-Polish tension mounted.[30] Moscow was receptive to Polish and French diplomatic probes and proffered some of its own because it wanted to avoid a war in Europe: Japanese expansion into Manchuria threatened the Soviet Union in the Far East; Germany was internally unstable and could not be counted on as an ally; and the Soviet regime faced serious domestic problems associated with Stalin's program of rapid industrialization and collectivization.

By the winter of 1929-30 Germany and the Soviet Union

[30] Beck, *Final Report*, pp. 6-10; Korbel, *Poland between East and West*, pp. 272ff.; H. L. Roberts, "The Diplomacy of Colonel Beck," in Craig and Gilbert, *Diplomats*, chap. 19. The Wilhelmstrasse characterized Beck as "crafty and ruthless" ("schlau und rücksichtslos"); *AA*, Trautmann to Bülow, 11 February 1931, 2945/D575565.

had almost annulled the "marriage of convenience" they had maintained during the last years of Stresemann's Soviet policy. The Soviets believed that Germany had gone too far with the West in negotiations over reparations and the Rhineland. In Germany, public opinion bore witness against the government's Soviet policy, blaming Moscow for social unrest in Germany and repressive domestic policies injurious to Russian peasants of German stock. Before revitalizing the "spirit of Rapallo," Curtius concluded, the Wilhelmstrasse would have to persuade the German public that the Soviet Union did not menace Germany's internal security, a threat the diplomats thought had been distorted by the press. Gradually, but not completely, Curtius succeeded, helped by Moscow, which began "a series of accommodating gestures" in an effort to preserve Rapallo. Relations improved markedly during the summer of 1930, and, the next autumn, the Soviet Union changed its trade policy in favor of Germany.[31]

Although the economic advantages of Rapallo increased, its strategic value waned. Curtius, Trautmann, and Dirksen stressed the importance of the Soviet Union as a future ally against Poland.[32] In March 1931 Curtius urged a renewal of the Berlin Treaty because of the utility of Soviet power as a counterweight against Poland, even though the Red Army was a purely defensive force. Germany, militarily weak, could afford to give up Soviet support only when it became strong

[31] Dyck, *Weimar Germany and Soviet Russia*, pp. 152-208, 216-21; also Carr, *German-Soviet Relations*, p. 101; Curtius, *Sechs Jahre*, p. 157; Dirksen, *Moscow, Tokyo, London*, pp. 97ff.; Hilger, *Incompatible Allies*, p. 227.

[32] Dyck, *Weimar Germany and Soviet Russia*, pp. 187-88, 204; *AA*, Trautmann to Foreign Minister, 20 June 1930, 2945/D575150-6. Dyck observes that Dirksen put more emphasis than the others on Russia "as a counterweight to the west," a view that had become "outdated." According to a Soviet interpretation, the ruling imperialistic circles in Germany, who wanted to end Rapallo, could not ignore mass opinion favoring an improvement in economic relations with the Soviet Union; Ushakov, *Deutschlands Aussenpolitik*, pp. 153ff.

enough to conduct its eastern policy without Moscow or able to substitute the backing of other powers for that of the Soviet Union. Besides, Curtius added, keeping Moscow on a string would prevent the Soviet Union from conducting a pro-Polish policy.[33]

But Franco-Soviet and Polish-Soviet rapprochement virtually broke the strategic promise implicit in the Protocol for the Renewal of the Berlin Treaty (signed in June 1931). In the spring of 1931 France admitted the failure of its campaign against Soviet dumping, and wanted additional security in response to the Austro-German customs union project. And Soviet foreign policy under Litvinov, who in July 1930 succeeded Chicherin as Commissar for Foreign Affairs, began to move toward antirevisionism and better relations with France, Poland, and the Baltic States as the best guarantee against the possibility of Germany's upsetting the European status quo in a manner unfavorable to the Soviet Union.[34]

Germany lacked the international prestige to block the negotiations that led to the Franco-Soviet Nonaggression Pact (initialed August 1931, signed November 1932, ratified May 1933) and Polish-Soviet Nonaggression Pact (initialed January 1932, signed July, ratified December). But the Wilhelmstrasse did try to prevent the Soviet Union from construing the Polish agreement as an eastern Locarno. Bülow stated Berlin's position in a message to the Moscow embassy in November 1931: Germany could not risk international disfavor by opposing a normalization of Polish-Soviet relations in a pact that renounced an offensive war by one party on another, even though such an arrangement would alleviate pressure on Poland's eastern flank; but the inclusion of any guarantees of Polish territory would seriously harm German-Soviet relations, since it would be incompatible with Germany's major

[33]*AA*, Curtius to missions, 16 March, K290/K101432-43; Dyck discusses the directive in *Weimar Germany and Soviet Russia*, pp. 231-33.

[34]*Ibid.*, pp. 156, 209-15, 236ff.; H. L. Roberts, "Maxim Litvinov," in Craig and Gilbert, *Diplomats*, pp. 349-50.

goal of "revision of the borders—even if by peaceful means."[35]

The Soviet Union gave Germany some reassurances, and, in spite of antigovernmental violence by the German Communist Party, German-Soviet relations survived the year 1932 in a "generally muddled" state. With some skepticism, but with no alternative, the Foreign Office accepted Moscow's interpretation that recognizing Poland's territorial integrity was neither a " 'recognition of the Versailles system' " nor of Poland's frontiers.[36] Moscow, though now in the stronger bargaining position, did not wish to sever the Rapallo tie, for it did not entirely trust France or Poland. Reports that Papen sought reconciliation with France as the first step toward an anti-Soviet bloc, which would include Poland, cast a shadow over relations between the Soviet Union and the three capitalist states. But Schleicher, who as Defense Minister under Papen had energetically promoted the secret military collaboration, promised Moscow in a December (1932) statement that his position as Chancellor " 'was a guarantee of friendly relations toward the Soviet Union, and so it would remain as long as he occupied this office.' "[37]

With German-Polish tension at a high point in March 1932, Brüning had told the Reichstag that the Soviet Union was not bound to its nonaggression pact with Poland "if Po-

[35] *AA*, Bülow to Moscow embassy, 4 November, K290/K101535-9. This file (K290) contains many documents dealing with technicalities related to the Polish-Soviet pact, such as the obligations of one signatory if the other waged war on a third party (see below, chap. 9, n. 29). Dirksen recalls that Bülow and Meyer were very upset over Soviet diplomacy toward France and Poland; he himself remained calm, although aware that German-Soviet relations were indeed deteriorating. *Moscow, Tokyo, London*, pp. 114-17.

[36] Dyck, *Weimar Germany and Soviet Russia*, pp. 247, 249; Brüning speech before Reichstag Foreign Affairs Committee, 24 May 1932, in Brüning, *Reden und Aufsätze eines deutschen Staatsmanns* (ed. W. Vernekohl, Münster, 1968), p. 168.

[37] Dyck, *Weimar Germany and Soviet Russia*, p. 254; also Korbel, *Poland between East and West*, p. 277.

land attacked another power."[38] In view of Moscow's reluctance to become engaged in a European war, however, Brüning's reading of Rapallo—that one partner would defend the other—was moot. The likelihood of "pushing Poland back to her ethnographic frontiers" in collaboration with the Soviet Union receded still further from political reality. Moscow had made accords with the intended victim of the Rapallo combination and with Germany's major western antagonist, both of which were antirevisionist powers.

Prague, still apprehensive about German revisionism, protested against the Austro-German customs union project, which Beneš considered a breach of the Treaty of Versailles and a threat to the Czechoslovak economy.[39] In 1932 German diplomats received reports from "reliable sources" that Czechoslovakia was holding military talks with France, Poland, and its partners in the Little Entente, anticipating that their governments might agree to joint military sanctions should Germany shatter the peace settlement by withdrawing from the reparations and disarmament conferences.[40] Czechoslovakia did not sign a military alliance with France, nor enter into a military arrangement with Poland. But the German ministers to Warsaw and Prague noted closer contacts between the two military staffs and referred to the "logic" of Polish-Czechoslovak military cooperation: both countries feared Germany; Poland had secured its rear by the nonaggression treaty with the Soviet Union; and Poland could expect no more than meager assistance from Rumania in a German-Polish conflict.[41] To sum up, Poland's antirevisionist

[38] Roos, *Polen und Europa*, p. 42.

[39] Bennett, *Financial Crisis*, pp. 58, 79-81.

[40] *AA*, K177/K030489-548, *passim*; von Hassell (Belgrade) to Foreign Office, 25 May, M342/M015591-2.

[41] *AA*, Koch (Prague) to Foreign Office, 21 November 1932, 6190/E465124-9; Moltke to Foreign Office, 7 December, K177/K030552-6; Forster (Paris) to Foreign Office, 18 January 1933, 5964/E438401. When the Polish-Rumanian mutual defense treaty came up for renewal in March 1931, so did its ancillary military

position among the states of eastern Europe was stronger than in the late 1920s, and Germany's revisionist leverage correspondingly weaker. The Polish-Soviet Nonaggression Pact lessened the chance of a war with the Soviet Union. And, although Czechoslovakia retained "liberty of action" in its relations with Poland and France, common fear of German revisionism during a period of heightened international tension had brought Czechoslovakia closer to the other two countries.

Perhaps not so aware of the current drift of eastern affairs as some of the diplomats in the field, Bülow speculated on a connection between the project of a customs union with Austria and the weakening of Poland's international position. Czechoslovakia, he surmised in 1931, would soon find it economically necessary to join the proposed customs union, even as an inferior partner; if this bloc were strengthened by closer economic ties between Germany and the Baltic States, Germany would gain enormous economic and political advantages over Poland. Germany would " 'have [Poland] in a kind of vise which might sooner or later put her in a state of mind to consider further the idea of exchanging political concessions for tangible benefits.' "[42] The Secretary of State had

---

convention. Moltke reported from Warsaw that the renewed agreement contained no provisions for Rumania to guard Poland's Soviet border in a German-Polish war. Although the recent treaty, like the old one, pledged mutual assistance "against all external aggression," Polish-Rumanian military negotiations centered upon questions of command and tactics in joint anti-Soviet operations. *AA*, Moltke to Foreign Office, 2 September 1931, 6188/E464977-8; text of the new treaty (signed 15 January, ratified 26 March), in Horak, *Poland's International Affairs*, pp. 160-62.

[42] Bülow to Koch (Prague), 19 April, in Bennett, *Financial Crisis*, pp. 79-80. Implicit in Bülow's analysis is the view of the increasingly popular school of geopolitics that German hegemony over "Middle Europe" was an "organic" economic and political necessity. On *grossdeutsch*, *gesamtdeutsch*, and geopolitical sentiments during the Weimar Republic, see Henry Cord Meyer, *"Mitteleuropa" in German Thought and Action 1815-1945* (The Hague, 1955), pp. 292-310.

designated Austria a link between Germany's western and eastern policies, without the assurance that Germany could successfully manage the western diplomacy requisite to the formation of any kind of union with Austria.

THE WEST

Although Curtius did not subscribe to the most extravagant interpretation of Germany's western policy, that it served merely to free Germany's hands in the east, he, like Stresemann, viewed revision in the west—reparations, disarmament, the status of the Rhineland, and the Saar—as both an end in itself and as an intermediate step toward revision of the eastern borders. Germany could neither align itself with the West nor compromise its goals in the east, but must, for the time being, remain "balanced" between the West and the Soviet Union.[43] But how should Germany conduct its western policy? By conciliation, which Stresemann had believed indispensable to an understanding with the West? Or by bluntness and "greater activity," on the assumption that this diplomatic method would compel the West to accede to a more grudging kind of understanding with Germany? Stresemann's successors chose the latter, impelled by the surge of critical and impatient public opinion during a period of crisis in Germany, and encouraged by the apparent logic of proceeding in orderly sequence to the next stage of revisionist demands, regardless of the vicissitudes that altered the international and domestic climate.

In August 1930 Rauscher accurately affirmed that the West would be reluctant to grant new treaty revisions soon after the early evacuation of the Rhineland, which many Europeans regarded as a major concession in itself.[44] Since Curtius was advised after the election of September 1930 to avoid the term " 'policy of understanding' " and to stress Ger-

[43] *RK*, cabinet protocol, 20 August 1930, 3575/D784627ff.; *AA*, Curtius to missions, 16 March 1931, K290/K101432-43.
[44] *AA*, Rauscher to Bülow, 13 August, 2945/D575226-9.

many's " 'long-standing poverty in diplomatic successes,' "[45]
the chances of gaining western sympathy were even slimmer.
Yet Curtius and Brüning hoped to convince the West and the
League of Nations that revisionist victories were necessary
for the reestablishment of public confidence in the government, that Germany should not be expected to make any sacrifices in return for revision, and that the Polish question must
be resolved in Germany's favor after temporary postponement—all this in a domestic atmosphere charged with
antagonism toward both France and Poland.

The abortive customs union project with Austria was the
most daring and least successful venture of German foreign
policy during the years of crisis. Stresemann had deferred the
question of *Anschluss*, a major revisionist objective, which
he believed Germany could effectively pursue only after his
policy of understanding had freed the Rhineland of foreign
troops and nudged France into a more cooperative attitude
toward Germany's further demands. When those conditions
seemed nearly satisfied in 1929, Bülow wrote that, although
the Polish question would deserve priority in 1930, " 'it could
be that the time for raising the Eastern problems may not be
ripe, and that we must tackle the Anschluss question in some
form or other.' "[46] Evidently, Curtius and Bülow concurred
late in 1930—without the knowledge of the Brüning cabinet
and lesser officials in the Wilhelmstrasse—that Germany
must seize the opportunity of Austria's economic plight to
form a customs union as the first step toward a political
Anschluss. By early February 1931 they had persuaded
Brüning that the project should be expedited before disen-
tangling the reparations question with the West.[47]

[45] Bülow to Curtius (Geneva), 15 September, in Bennett, *Financial Crisis*, pp. 11-12. In his speech to the League Assembly that month, Curtius in fact "followed closely the line laid down in Bülow's tele-gram." *Ibid.*, p. 13.

[46] Stambrook, "Customs Union Project," pp. 18-20.

[47] *Ibid.*, pp. 19, 41-42; Bennett, *Financial Crisis*, pp. 44-51, 78-79; Heinrich Brüning, *Memoiren 1918-1934* (Stuttgart, 1970), pp. 263-

Germany's sudden announcement of the project in March 1931, without that prior consultation with the West that had accompanied Stresemann's diplomatic moves, strained Germany's relations with the West and jeopardized the accomplishment of *Anschluss* and eastern revision in the near future. Although irritated by Germany's behavior, the British government continued to respect Brüning's argument that timely revision would bolster the Chancellor against extremist attacks from the Nationalists and Nazis. In negotiations surrounding the implementation of the Young Plan, the Hoover Moratorium, and the subsequent diminution of reparations payments, Britain urged an alleviation of the financial difficulties of Germany as one of the nations most severely affected by the European economic depression. And British mediation proved invaluable to Germany in the meetings of the Disarmament Conference at Geneva, where, in December 1932, Germany finally won recognition of the principle of equality of status. But the British were annoyed at Germany's repeated refusal to make concessions commensurate with western compromises over reparations: Germany would not jettison the customs union project (Austria dropped it in September 1931, forcing Germany to do the same), trim military expenditures, nor completely shelve the Polish question for a designated number of years. Berlin did not applaud Ramsay MacDonald and Arthur Henderson for their roles as mediators, but expected a more pro-German scenario in London.[48] So long as Britain participated in continental affairs as an intermediary rather than a champion of Germany, the British could recommend a peaceful compromise solution to the Polish question—one repellent to Germany. The Wilhelmstrasse had neither secured Britain's unqualified support

---

70; Curtius, *Sechs Jahre*, chap. 12; Eyck, *Weimar Republic*, ii, 304-307; Helbich, "Between Stresemann and Hitler," pp. 40-42.

[48] Henderson's careful handling of the legal questions involved in the customs union project seemed unfair to the Germans; Bennett, *Financial Crisis*, pp. 64-70, 108-11.

for border revision nor witnessed a collapse of the wartime and Versailles Entente, despite Anglo-French dissonance over reparations, *Anschluss*, and disarmament.

Franco-German hostility had already begun to mount before Berlin and Vienna publicly and ungraciously revealed their plan for economic union. The Germans blamed their economic ills on the Versailles *Diktat*, and the idea of a "war of liberation" regained the popularity it had enjoyed in the early 1920s. The French, alarmed by the Nazi election successes of September 1930, suspected that western foreign policy concessions would not buttress Brüning's government. The customs union project intensified French fears of a resurgence of German power in Central Europe, threatened Briand's plan for European security through a larger European federation, contributed to his defeat in the presidential election of May 1931, and forced the French government into a more dogged position during reparations talks. In return for financial assistance, the French wanted Germany to declare a moratorium on political questions (e.g., the Corridor), abandon the customs union project, and reduce the military budget.[49]

In spite of Franco-German differences over Austria, and Germany's refusal to trade political concessions for economic aid, Paris and Berlin avoided a serious diplomatic rupture in 1931 and remained hopeful about reaching a general agreement in which "the French longing for security and the German need for capital would somehow be balanced."[50] At the Lausanne Reparations Conference in June 1932, Chancellor Franz von Papen (who had criticized Brüning for antagonizing the French rather than winning their good will) offered a compromise to the new French Premier, Edouard Herriot: Germany would form a customs union and military entente

[49] *Ibid.*, chap. 8.

[50] *Ibid.*, pp. 85, 111-12, 178ff. See also Jacques Bariéty and Charles Bloch, "Une tentative de réconciliation franco-allemande et son échec (1932-1933)," *Revue d'histoire moderne et contemporaine*, xv (1968), 433-65.

with France, to prove Germany's sincere interest in security, in return for a cancellation of reparations.[51] Although this startling proposal came to nothing, it did signal a brief change in Germany's disarmament policy. In an attempt to isolate the French and compel them to accept the principle of equality of status, Brüning had sought the support of Britain and the United States, but Papen, Schleicher, and Neurath tried to initiate bilateral negotiations with the French. Their bold tactics, however, did not impress the French as conciliatory. Ultimately, French recognition of the German claim to equality of status (which the French read as German rearmament) was not the result of bilateral rapprochement. After months of increasing Franco-German enmity and Germany's boycott of the deliberations that resumed in Geneva in September, Herriot feared that France had indeed become isolated at the Disarmament Conference, and he assented to the British formula for bringing Germany back to the conference table. In a declaration signed on 11 December, the West recognized Germany's "equality of rights in a system which would provide security for all nations," and Germany joined Britain, France, and Italy in a pledge to settle grievances without resorting to force.[52]

In the 1920s the Poles had believed that French gestures of conciliation to Germany, without an eastern Locarno in compensation, weakened the Versailles system and the strategic foundations of the Franco-Polish alliance. After the last French units were evacuated from the Rhineland (Mainz zone) in June 1930, five years earlier than stipulated in the Treaty of Versailles, the prospect of more French concessions continued to trouble Warsaw. The French began to show signs of yielding to British pressure to accommodate the Ger-

[51] On Papen's surprise move and opposition to it in the Wilhelmstrasse, see Dyck, *Weimar Germany and Soviet Russia*, pp. 252-54; Eyck, *Weimar Republic*, II, 402ff.; Heineman, "Neurath as Foreign Minister," pp. 103-104, 144-50; Papen, *Vom Scheitern einer Demokratie 1930-1933* (Mainz, 1968), pp. 93-122.

[52] The disarmament issue is discussed in more detail below, chap. 9.

285

man position on the disarmament question. Hoesch reported from Paris, shortly after the return of a Left majority to the French Chamber of Deputies in the elections of May 1932, that most Frenchmen were recoiling from a chauvinistic foreign policy, preferred to see France part company with Poland, and opposed renewal of the Franco-Polish military pact.[53] The formation of the Papen cabinet in June increased Pilsudski's anxiety, for he was aware that Papen sought Franco-German rapprochement, and that Schleicher leaned toward a German-Soviet combination against Poland.[54] These developments encouraged Pilsudski and Beck to pursue an independent policy toward Germany and the Soviet Union, but not to break the alliance with France.

German diplomats knew that French leaders endorsed the idea of German-Polish discussions of the border question;[55] they could see that Locarno had damaged the Franco-Polish alliance; they realized that Germany's politico-military situation was improved by the early evacuation of the Rhineland, with neither an eastern Locarno nor a "commission of verification" to discover and report German violations of the demilitarized zone; and they observed that discord between Pilsudski and the French continued unabated. But, although Ambassador Hoesch believed that a "most significant revolution in French foreign policy" was occurring in 1932,[56] and although Pilsudski harbored very deep misgivings about French political loyalty and military planning, the Franco-Polish alliance remained intact. France had neither promised Germany support in regaining its eastern territorial objectives peacefully, nor abrogated its treaty obligation to come to Poland's aid against a German revision by force.

[53] *AA*, Hoesch to Foreign Office, 31 May, K177/K030484-7.

[54] Breyer, *Deutsche Reich und Polen*, p. 35; Roos, *Polen und Europa*, pp. 51-52.

[55] *AA*, Curtius minute of conversation with François-Poncet in London, 22 July 1931, 2945/D575656-8; also Sir R. Lindsay (Washington) to Lord Reading, 26 October 1931, *DBFP*, Ser. 2, II, 307.

[56] *AA*, Hoesch to Foreign Office, 31 May, K177/K030484-7.

In the early 1930s more and more German voters viewed German membership in the League of Nations as a liability to treaty revision rather than an asset. They ignored or considered insufficient that the League Council upheld German complaints against Polish mistreatment of the German minority, and that the Disarmament Conference recognized Germany's right to equality of status. The collapse of the Austro-German venture proved to many Germans, including not a few diplomats, that the victors "controlled" the League and would continue to use it to keep Germany from revising the peace settlement.[57]

Italy had joined Britain as a guarantor of the Locarno Pact in 1925 but had not immediately plunged into vigorous activity in the diplomacy between the West and Germany. In 1930, however, Mussolini began to show more interest in affairs of common concern to the three major Locarno parties. Berlin watched Italy's early moves during the years of crisis without much pleasure: in March 1931 a Franco-Italian naval agreement appeared likely; a few months later, disturbed about an eventual *Anschluss*, Italy joined the opposition to the customs union project.[58] But Franco-Italian mistrust helped scuttle the planned naval compromise, and, in talks with Brüning and Curtius in Rome in August, Mussolini evinced greater concern about French aspirations to European hegemony than about Austro-German relations.[59] Italy's usefulness and sympathy for Germany did not go unnoticed in the Wilhelmstrasse, but neither did the baffling inconsistency of Italian revisionism. Mussolini called for a broad revision of the peace settlement, agreed to a reduction of German

[57] On German resentment of League intervention in the customs union affair, see Bennett, *Financial Crisis*, pp. 64-71, 107-11; Eyck, *Weimar Republic*, II, 307-10.

[58] Dirksen viewed the impending naval agreement as further evidence " 'that the great political decisions in Europe are being decided against us, or at any rate, without Germany. . . .' " Dyck, *Weimar Germany and Soviet Russia*, p. 224. On Italian opposition to the customs union, see Bennett, *Financial Crisis*, pp. 74-78, 168-69.

[59] Bennett, *ibid.*, p. 298n.

287

reparations at the Lausanne Conference in the summer of 1932, and backed Germany in the disarmament negotiations of the fall and winter; yet he remained opposed to *Anschluss* and gave Germany no more than token support for a peaceful revision of the Polish borders.

After the evacuation of the Rhineland, Germany's "active" policy toward the West achieved revision of the reparations and disarmament portions of the peace settlement, in spite of running aground on the customs union project. But those revisionist successes had not improved Germany's situation for revising the eastern borders. Germany had introduced the Polish question into negotiations with the West as a constant reminder of Germany's eastern claims; but the West had responded by treating the matter as a political issue that Germany might agree to suspend in return for western concessions. Britain, France, and the United States agreed with Germany that the current borders were intolerable, but afforded Germany no assurance that their cooperation in an eventual revision would go beyond a compromise solution that fell short of Germany's minimal demands.

FORCE AND FOREIGN POLICY

The more divisive international and domestic winds of the early 1930s disseminated in Germany the belief that the application or threat of force is a legitimate means of foreign policy. Even those German diplomats and voters who had supported peaceful (although aggressive) methods to attain intermediate goals were now restive; they pointed out that Germany was still denied the interwoven long-range objectives: sovereignty, national security, and border revision. The Rapallo tie still implied an encirclement of Poland; but it was of dubious strategic value after the Soviet Union made non-aggression agreements with France and Poland. The evacuation of the Rhineland eliminated a major obstacle to the reestablishment of full sovereignty, and removed a French foothold on German soil for intervention in a German-Polish war;

288

but Germans considered the demilitarization of the Rhineland an affront to the right of any sovereign nation to exercise military as well as political control over all its territory. Locarno afforded Germany security against unprovoked French aggression, and weakened the Franco-Polish alliance; but France might still impose military sanctions (e.g., by reoccupying the Rhineland) in spite of Locarno and the Young Plan if Germany withdrew from the reparations and disarmament conferences,[60] and the Franco-Polish alliance continued to encircle Germany. The West conceded that the German-Polish borders were unworkable, but had not completely forsaken the Polish side of the territorial argument. The West recognized the principle of equality of status in disarmament talks, but did not grant Germany the freedom to rearm to the level Germany deemed adequate to defend itself against a two-front attack, or to initiate a war for the lost territories.

Germany appeared to be half-sovereign, isolated between the West and Poland, vulnerable to invasion, and unable to accomplish all its policy objectives by peaceful means. As a panacea for these politico-military ills, Germans from the right wing of the SPD to the extreme Right and the Nazi Party demanded an increase in Germany's military power.[61] In disarmament negotiations, German representatives rested their case on the inadequacy of their current armed forces to provide security against external threats, so long as general European disarmament did not follow Germany's disarmament. But the use of force for purposes other than defense against attack was an accepted politico-military doctrine in the Wilhelmstrasse, notwithstanding Germany's signing of the joint declaration of 11 December 1932, which acknowledged Germany's equality of rights and rejected forcible means for

[60] On the Young Plan and sanctions, see below, chap. 9.

[61] Weizsäcker recalls the intense public pressure on German negotiators at the Disarmament Conference; *Memoirs*, p. 66. Some SPD delegates in the Reichstag believed that Germany must arm itself " 'according to its needs' " if the conference failed to arrive at a fair compromise; Caspar, *Sozialdemokratische Partei und deutsche Wehrproblem*, pp. 20f., 69.

settling international disputes. About two weeks before that declaration, Bülow rejected any notion of an international resolution of the border question while Germany remained in a militarily inferior position.[62] Military power, Bülow implied, would improve Germany's politico-military situation for either negotiations or war.[63] In view of the uncertain international situation and the need to rearm for security and greater freedom of action to revise the borders, the Foreign Office knew that joint planning with the Defense Ministry was imperative.

[62] *AA*, Bülow to London embassy, 29 November, 6176/E476373-4. Hoesch had named Winston Churchill as one who favored a resolution of the border question while Germany was still weak; Hoesch (Neurath's successor as Ambassador to London) to Foreign Office, 24 November, *ibid.*, E463369-72. The British Ambassador to Warsaw, Sir William Erskine, considered a German-Polish war inevitable in view of the refusal of either side to compromise; *AA*, Moltke to Foreign Office, 25 May 1932, K1949/K507122-5. See also Rumbold to Henderson, 26 February 1931, *DBFP*, Ser. 2, I, 569, 572; Lipski, *Diplomat in Berlin*, pp. 29, 45.

[63] In a lecture to naval officers, Weizsäcker declared that Germany did not want war, but simply the military power to pursue a successful "Friedenspolitik"; *AA*, 8 January 1931, K6/K000558, 560-1. Neurath nurtured a "great respect for power [and] distrust of international organizations. . . ." Heineman, "Neurath as Foreign Minister," pp. 67-68.

CHAPTER IX

The Military and Joint Planning

THE ECONOMIC depression and political crisis of the early 1930s increased authoritarian politics in Germany and transformed the Weimar system of civil-military relations into a crisis system, in which the institutional elements of its predecessor were exaggerated, strained, and disrupted. Chancellors Brüning, Papen, and Schleicher all subscribed to the theory of a presidential regime (*Präsidialstaat*), and based their governments on the power of the presidential decree (Art. 48), a procedural means of governing in the absence of a parliamentary majority.[1] They concentrated more power in the chancellorship, Defense Ministry, and central government than had been the case during the years of stability. In October 1931 Brüning assumed the post of Foreign Minister, Groener that of Interior Minister; the following year Papen became Reich Commissioner for Prussia, and, after Papen's fall, Schleicher simultaneously held the offices of Chancellor, Defense Minister, and Reich Commissioner for Prussia. The dormant rivalry between the Chancellor and President quickened as President Hindenburg chose to intervene in politics and stretch the limits the constitution had placed on his authority.[2]

[1] Bracher, *Auflösung*, pp. 51-63, Pt. II, *passim*; Haungs, *Reichspräsident*, pp. 278-79; also three works by Werner Conze: "Brünings Politik unter dem Druck der Grossen Krise," *Historische Zeitschrift*, CXCIX (1964), 529-50; "Die deutschen Parteien in der Staatsverfassung vor 1933," in Erich Matthias and Rudolf Morsey (eds.), *Das Ende der Parteien 1933* (Düsseldorf, 1960), pp. 3-28; "Die politischen Entscheidungen in Deutschland 1929-1933," in Conze and Hans Raupach (eds.), *Die Staats- und Wirtschaftskrise des Deutschen Reichs 1929/33* (Stuttgart, 1967), pp. 176-252.

[2] Dorpalen, *Hindenburg*, chaps. 6-12, *passim*; Eyck, *Weimar Republic*, II, 254, 316-17, 328ff., 369f., 389f.

Groener, Schleicher, and Hammerstein (who succeeded Heye as Chief of the Army Command in October 1930) redoubled their political activities as the intensity of the domestic crisis increased. The military leadership believed that the maintenance of internal order and defense against foreign attack, the Army's responsibility, was jeopardized by the revolutionary extremism of the Nazis and Communists and by the political influence of the Social Democrats, the Reichstag, and the Prussian government. The Bendlerstrasse wanted to see the *Präsidialstaat* solidly established. The government, backed by the expanded authority of the President and the power of the armed forces, should try to win the allegiance of a people tired of party squabbling and build a parliamentary majority if possible; but it should rule by decree if necessary. In either case, ministers would be answerable to the President, not the Reichstag.[3]

The intervention of the military leadership increased civil-military tensions in the executive-departmental sphere. At the executive level, Groener and Schleicher helped to make and unmake cabinets. In the Bendlerstrasse, within their own department, they exacerbated differences. In September 1930, three lieutenants were tried before the Supreme Court at Leipzig on charges of treason; Groener (and Schleicher, apparently reluctantly) had decided to bring the matter before the civil authorities rather than confine it to the normal channels of military discipline, a decision that offended the officer corps' sense of military privacy and propriety. The trial in-

[3] See above, chap. 5; Carsten, *Reichswehr and Politics*, pp. 306ff.; Werner Conze, "Zum Sturz Brünings," *Vierteljahrshefte für Zeitgeschichte*, I (1953), 268; Craig, *Prussian Army*, pp. 436ff.; Dorpalen, *Hindenburg*, pp. 169-71; Otto Meissner, *Staatssekretär unter Ebert-Hindenburg-Hitler* (Hamburg, 1950), pp. 256-57; Müller, *Vaterland*, p. 199; Sauer, "Die Reichswehr," in Bracher, *Auflösung*, pp. 276-78; Vogelsang, *Reichswehr und NSDAP*, pp. 68ff.; Wheeler-Bennett, *Nemesis of Power*, pp. 198ff.; interview with Ambassador Ott. Groener's political ideas hardly warrant the "democratic" evaluation of the Defense Minister found in Eschenburg, *Improvisierte Demokratie*, p. 243, and Krosigk, *Es Geschah in Deutschland*, pp. 97-106.

sinuated that the officer corps was being swept by the rising tide of national revolutionary sentiment on the Right. Not since the Bavarian separatist crisis of 1923 had the question of the Army's loyalty to the republic been raised so urgently.[4] Groener, Schleicher, and Hammerstein viewed this event as evidence of a "crisis of confidence," the Army's loss of confidence in the leadership of the government and Defense Ministry. But their exhortations to shun extremism and party politics neither restored confidence nor healed divisions in the officer corps, which watched the political machinations of the military leaders with mistrust and alarm.[5]

At the departmental level, both the Defense Ministry and Foreign Office still preferred to keep the details of foreign policy and military planning to themselves, and to maintain joint planning. At the General Staff tour in May 1930, Heye, Hammerstein, Joachim von Stülpnagel, and other senior officers frequently emphasized the need for "the best possible relations between the Defense Ministry and Foreign Office in the interests of overall policy."[6] Groener commended "the

[4] Carsten, *Reichswehr and Politics*, pp. 313-19; Sauer, "Die Reichswehr," in Bracher, *Auflösung*, pp. 282-83. Peter Bucher rejects three common interpretations of the Leipzig trial: that it revealed the spread of Nazi doctrine among junior officers; that it represented a conflict between young "front" officers and older "office" generals in the Bendlerstrasse; that it was an example of Hitler's tactical skill in using the Army in his rise to power. See his *Der Reichswehrprozess: Der Hochverrat der Ulmer Reichswehroffiziere 1929/30* (Boppard, 1967), especially pp. 130-43; and, for the role of Groener and Schleicher in the prosecution of the lieutenants, pp. 42-48.

[5] On this campaign by the military leadership, see Bucher, *Reichswehrprozess*, pp. 143-52; Carsten, *Reichswehr and Politics*, pp. 319-29; Müller, *Heer und Hitler*, pp. 28-34; Hammerstein briefing of officers in Kassel, 24 April 1931, in Thilo Vogelsang, "Neue Dokumente zur Geschichte der Reichswehr 1930-1933," *Vierteljahrshefte für Zeitgeschichte*, II (1954), 410-11. Bucher maintains that, in spite of the Army's crisis of confidence, its "structure" remained intact; although the Army had never been politically homogeneous, its professional homogeneity survived.

[6] *AA*, Schlimpert notes, 3 June 1930, K6/K000479-80. The Foreign Office conducted periodic lectures before Army and Navy officers

excellent cooperation of the Foreign Office with the Defense Ministry."[7] Young men from both ministries gathered regularly for informal evening meetings to develop personal contacts and mutual understanding.[8]

After some differences, both departments cooperated in reintroducing military attachés. Because of the possibility of unfavorable diplomatic repercussions during Germany's campaign for equality of status in disarmament negotiations, Neurath and Bülow urged caution in 1932. But they agreed with Defense Minister Schleicher that Germany's right to attachés, taken away by the Treaty of Versailles, must be restored; military attachés would enable the Army to increase its intelligence about foreign armies and present its armaments plight to them. Schleicher's representatives reassured the Wilhelmstrasse that the attachés would not be allowed to dabble in politics or illegal activity, that they would be subordinate to the chiefs of mission, and that all their correspondence would go through these chiefs and the Foreign Office. In January 1933, after Germany had improved its status at the Disarmament Conference, the Defense Ministry publicly announced that beginning on 1 April Germany would resume sending military and naval attachés to its principal missions abroad. Without question this represented a revisionist triumph for both ministries, and illustrated the principle of the subordination of military to diplomatic representatives.[9]

But the political crisis also dislocated interdepartmental relations. It is surely an exaggeration to say that in the early 1930s the Army "designated the enemies, made the alliances,

on politico-military questions; Weizsäcker to Forster, 12 January 1931, *ibid.*, K000577.

[7] Schleicher to senior officers in Berlin, 11-12 January 1932, in Vogelsang, "Dokumente," p. 414.

[8] Ott, "Ein Bild," p. 364; interviews with Ambassador Ott, Generals Heusinger and Speidel.

[9] Kehrig, *Wiedereinrichtung*, pp. 126-32, 144-54, 158-63; also Leo Freiherr Geyr von Schweppenburg, *Erinnerungen eines Militärattachés* (Stuttgart, 1949), pp. 9-10, 15.

and dictated the attitudes" in German foreign policy,[10] for the Army's view of Germany's territorial interests and strategic situation corresponded in general to that of the Foreign Office. With its rearmament program, however, and in contributing to the disorder in the executive-departmental sphere, the Army threatened both interdepartmental harmony and the subordination of military to political considerations.

EASTERN EUROPE

Poland, as the British military attaché reported from Berlin late in 1931, remained "the *bête noire* of the German military mind."[11] The racial prejudice and vengeful sentiments of some Germans clouded their perception of clear boundaries.[12] But the military leadership continued to designate border revision a national interest and to justify it primarily in terms of strategic necessity, by which standard Germany must regain at least the Corridor and Danzig. The recovery of these territories, by force if necessary, would depend on Germany's politico-military situation.

Because of Germany's military weakness and internal instability, the Army increasingly feared a Polish attack, and anxiously gathered intelligence from various sources in an attempt to trace Polish troop movements and verify rumors of imminent invasion. Reports from German diplomats or the Prussian Ministry of the Interior were usually calm; from

[10] This is Castellan's contention, *Réarmement*, p. 447.

[11] Colonel Marshall-Cornwall memorandum, 9 December, *DBFP*, Ser. 2, II, 521. He attributed this animosity to "the claim to moral and cultural superiority coupled with a sense of the military and political disadvantages imposed by the treaty." Seeckt considered Poland the major enemy "in all questions of German foreign policy," and believed a German-Polish compromise to be impossible; General Hammerstein called the Corridor situation unbearable and saw in it the seeds of a future conflict. Seeckt, *Wege deutscher Aussenpolitik* (Leipzig, 1931), pp. 16-17; Castellan, *Réarmement*, p. 472.

[12] On Seeckt's idea of a "racial struggle" against Poland, see his *Wege, passim*; Korbel, *Poland between East and West*, pp. 258-59.

T3 and the *Abwehr* Department, moderate but apprehensive; and from civilians and some officers in the borderlands, hysterical. In answer to queries from the *Abwehr* Department in October 1930, Rauscher said that the recent Nazi success in the election, and the Corridor propaganda that had preceded it, had heightened Polish fears of isolation. But he could not predict whether events in Germany would alter the Polish Army's attitude toward war. Meanwhile, not Germany, but the Soviet Union, Pilsudski's ideological enemy, remained the major opponent in Polish military planning.[13] A few months later, the German mission in Warsaw observed that the Polish officer corps considered a German-Polish conflict a "theoretical possibility" but very unlikely at the present time, and many Polish officers shared the "fatalistic conviction that alone Poland was not in the position to fight a war with Germany."[14]

In the spring of 1932, the officers stationed in the border areas resented the decree of 12 April banning the *S.A.* and *S.S.* because they thought it would weaken the *Grenzschutz*. East Prussian civilians protested against the removal of their *Wehrkreis* commander, General von Blomberg, for temporary duty at the Disarmament Conference at a time of extraordinary danger to the province. And a lieutenant, writing under the auspices of the District Command, aggravated local alarm with a news-like account of a Polish invasion of East Prussia.[15] The Foreign Office noted an increase in Polish mil-

[13] *AA*, Bredow (*Abwehr*) to Foreign Office, 10 October; Rauscher to Trautmann, 31 October; M342/M015365, 434, 437-40. Contrast the unfounded opinion of a German lieutenant that Poland would soon attack Germany as a means of escaping internal political troubles; in Hans Rothfels, "Ausgewählte Briefe von Generalmajor Helmuth Stieff," *Vierteljahrshefte für Zeitgeschichte*, II (1954), 296.

[14] *AA*, Rintelen to Foreign Office, 20 February 1931 (transcript to Defense Ministry in early March), K190/K036596-8.

[15] Von Weiss-Plauen to Schleicher, 5 February 1932, Nachlass Schleicher, no. 44, Bundesarchiv-Militärarchiv. H. Nitram (pseudonym for Hans Martin) wrote the booklet, published in January and February, entitled *Achtung! Ostmarkenrundfunk! Polnische Truppen*

itary activity but discounted wild rumors of Polish concentrations for attack.[16] In the Bendlerstrasse, Hammerstein told senior officers that the Polish threat to Danzig and East Prussia was real, but not acute while Pilsudski remained at the helm.[17] T3 and the *Abwehr* Department distinguished the irresponsible allegations of borderland informants from the reliable intelligence that anti-German feeling in the Polish government was rising sharply. Even though some Polish officers apparently favored an offensive against Germany to seize Danzig in the spring and summer, most of the officer corps, as well as the government, opposed any such use of force. For the rest of the year, military intelligence had nothing startling to report.[18]

Responsible officials in both Berlin and Warsaw did not want war, but feared that a border incident—militant nation-

---

haben heute Nacht die ostpreussische Grenze überschritten! When red placards appeared on kiosks advertising the book, many East Prussians thought its title was true, and some sought cover in the woods. With proceeds from its sale, Martin bought a small car and a fur for his wife; officers in his unit called the fur "der Nitram Pelz." Interviews with Generals Heinrici (Martin's battalion commander at the time), Hauck, and Heusinger. The Foreign Office was not amused by Herr "Nitram's" literary endeavors; *AA*, Windecker to Meyer, 19 March, Abteilung IVPo, Akten betr. Politische Beziehungen Polens zu Deutschland, Band 36 (not filmed).

[16] See above, chap. 8; also *AA*, Moltke to Foreign Office, 23 March, K190/K036873.

[17] Hammerstein briefings, 27 February, 21 May, in Vogelsang, "Dokumente," pp. 420, 425. Groener apparently shared Brüning's opinion that "so long as Pilsudski is in control, the Polish government would hardly take a step against Danzig, since Pilsudski contemplates restoring the Corridor to Germany in return for compensation through Lithuanian territory." *RWM*, Naval Command minute, 6 May 1932, PG 34089.

[18] Interview with General Lanz; *RK*, *Abwehr* to Reich Chancery, 22 February, Akten betr. Polen, Band 10 (not filmed); *RWM*, *Abwehr* reports of May-December, PG 49031. Groener believed that one of the functions of the *Abwehr* Department was to "prevent wild rumors"; *AA*, Groener to Curtius, 18 December 1930, 3177/D683338-9.

alists belonged to border defense groups on both sides of the border—might bring open conflict. Berlin's nightmares also included a Polish preventive move to seize Danzig and widen the Corridor before the Nazis gained control of the Free City (not to mention the Reich government), and Polish participation in military sanctions in retaliation for German obstinacy over reparations and disarmament. In spite of intelligence denying an impending Polish attack, these contingencies along with the menace of internal civil war moved Hammerstein to state in February 1932 that the Army must consider the worst possible eventuality.[19]

Should Germany and Poland come to blows, Lithuania remained a possible ally and a part of the Baltic territorial bridge to the Soviet Union. Polish-Lithuanian relations had improved, but the unresolved Vilna question and the anti-Polish sentiment in the Lithuanian Army inhibited a rapprochement.[20] The maintenance of good relations between the German and Lithuanian Armies, "a corollary to the Polish enmity" in the German Army according to a British observer, was cited by Curtius as grounds for not antagonizing Lithuania by discussing the compensation plan.[21] Similarly,

[19] Hammerstein briefing of senior officers, 27 February 1932, in Vogelsang, "Dokumente," p. 420. The Foreign Office, Hammerstein said, had told him that German policy would be conducted in such a way as to preclude that eventuality; Aufzeichnungen Generals Curt Liebmann (Befehlshaberbesprechungen), Institut für Zeitgeschichte (Munich). Some of Liebmann's notes of this conference are not included in Vogelsang, "Dokumente."

[20] *AA*, Bredow (*Abwehr*) to Foreign Office, 10 October 1930; Rauscher to Trautmann, 31 October (to Defense Ministry, 19 January 1931); M342/M015365, 441-2. Also *RWM, Abwehr* reports, 1932, PG 49029.

[21] British military attaché report, 9 December 1931, *DBFP*, Ser. 2, II, 521; *AA*, Curtius to Groener, 30 January 1931, 2945/D575540-1. We do not know exactly when Lithuanian officers began to participate in German General Staff courses, nor what was the nature of the " 'active military policy' " that the *Truppenamt* declared it was conducting with Lithuania; the latter almost certainly did not imply binding military agreements unknown to the Foreign Office. See T3 report, December 1930, in Carsten, *Reichswehr and Politics*, p. 284.

Hammerstein counselled even temper after the Lithuanian government, in an act which Germany viewed as hostile, sent troops into the Memelland in February 1932 and forcibly ousted the local administration.[22]

Not only the Foreign Office, but the Defense Ministry as well, found itself in an awkward position concerning German-Soviet relations; both tried to preserve a balance between the Soviet Union and the West, and to maintain Rapallo in spite of the resurgence of Bolshevik revolutionary agitation. Just as in the late 1920s, the Foreign Office evinced a greater concern for overall policy (very close military ties might jeopardize Germany's western policy and make it difficult to withdraw from Rapallo if that became necessary); the Defense Ministry was more intent on securing military advantages.

In January 1930, when German-Soviet relations had sharply declined, the Wilhelmstrasse objected to the German armament industry's expansion of programs of assistance to the Soviets. But the Defense Ministry replied that Germany could not halt this recent amplification of secret collaboration without imperilling its military interests in the Soviet Union, so the Foreign Office withdrew its opposition.[23] In pressing for the continuation of collaboration, the Defense Ministry rejected the entreaties of German conservatives to abandon all ties with the atheistic and revolutionary Bolsheviks.[24] Groener, Schleicher, and Hammerstein refused to renounce

[22] Hammerstein briefing, 27 February, in Vogelsang, "Dokumente," p. 419. On the probability that Lithuania cooperated with Poland in applying pressure on Germany in 1932, see Roos, *Polen und Europa*, pp. 40-41.

[23] Dyck, *Weimar Germany and Soviet Russia*, pp. 189-90; Gatzke, "Russo-German Military Collaboration," pp. 589-94.

[24] Werner von Alvensleben (secretary of a special committee appointed by the *Herrenklub* to lobby for an anti-Soviet policy) to Schleicher, 21 May 1930, Nachlass Schleicher, no. 35, Bundesarchiv-Militärarchiv. The continuation of collaboration with the Red Army provoked Arnold Rechberg's savage criticism of Schleicher in 1930, but Schleicher still rejected Rechberg's plan for a Franco-German (and Polish) combination against the Soviet Union; correspondence to and about Schleicher, *ibid.*

Rapallo simply because of domestic political considerations, although Hammerstein conceded that it was a "pact with Beelzebub," and Schleicher anticipated that "the Russian sphinx" would continue to play an important role in German internal politics.[25]

The Army still valued collaboration because of its actual usefulness in the development and testing of military aircraft, tanks, and poison gas, and its potential strategic benefit in case of a German-Polish conflict.[26] In 1932 German-Polish tension and international fluctuations caused the Army to re-examine its strategic assumptions, but not to reject them. The Bendlerstrasse knew that the Red Army concentrated on the defensive in its operational planning;[27] that the Polish-Soviet Nonaggression Pact signed on 25 July 1932, though not a cure for Polish-Soviet enmity, would give Poland some protection against a Soviet surprise attack from the east; and that the Soviet Union would not position the bulk of its forces along the Polish-Soviet border as long as the Sino-Japanese dispute in the Far East threatened Soviet security.[28] In spite

[25] Hammerstein briefing in Kassel, 24 April 1931, in Vogelsang, "Dokumente," pp. 409-10; Schleicher to Niedermayer (in Moscow), 24 April 1930, Nachlass Schleicher, no. 35, Bundesarchiv-Militärarchiv.

[26] Carsten, *Reichswehr and Politics*, pp. 357-58; Erickson, *Soviet High Command*, pp. 272ff.; George H. Stein, "Russo-German Military Collaboration: The Last Phase, 1933," *Political Science Quarterly*, LXXVII (1962), 54-71. Before Colonel Köstring departed for Moscow to assume his duties (see following note), President Hindenburg enjoined him to " 'keep good relations with the Red Army for me!' "; Hindenburg added that, although the time had not yet arrived, he would like to teach the Poles a lesson. Köstring, *General Köstring*, p. 55.

[27] *AA*, report of General Hans Halm following his return from the Soviet Union, 22 June 1930, 9480/H276083-8; its text (German) in Carsten, "Reports by Two German Officers," pp. 241-44; also, for General Adam's observations in 1931, Manstein, *Soldatenleben*, pp. 138ff. On the duties and special positions of Halm and Köstring (who was a military attaché in all but name), see Kehrig, *Wiedereinrichtung*, pp. 63-65; Köstring, *General Köstring*, pp. 54-63.

[28] Hammerstein briefing of senior officers on *Führerreise*, 21 May

of the fact that these conditions weakened the strategic utility of Soviet cooperation, the Army preserved its contingencies of the 1920s: Soviet intervention (or at least major demonstrations at the border) in a German-Polish war; and German intervention in a Polish-Soviet war.[29]

The desire to clarify military interests and intentions was perhaps Schleicher's main motivation for inviting Marshal Mikhail Tukhachevsky and other Soviet officers to Germany in September 1932.[30] And because of his pro-Soviet politico-military attitude, Schleicher's elevation to the chancellorship in December 1932 might be interpreted as the high-water mark of German-Soviet military collaboration.[31] In any case, under Schleicher the predicament inherent in Weimar foreign policy and military planning persisted. Although the West had begun to accommodate Germany on the disarmament question, the Foreign Office and Defense Ministry believed that Germany still lacked both the political advantage of western sympathy (or acquiescence) and the military power necessary to adopt an eastern policy that did not rely on Soviet support.

In 1932, the Army Command concurred with the Foreign Office that Czechoslovakia might participate in military sanc-

---

1932, in Vogelsang, "Dokumente," p. 425; *RWM, Abwehr* report, 4 August, PG 49031; also Castellan, *Réarmement*, pp. 483-84.

[29] The first of these contingencies was compatible with Art. 2 of the Polish-Soviet Nonaggression Pact: the Soviet Union would be released from the treaty if Poland committed "an act of aggression against a third state." On the other hand, the treaty bound the Soviet Union "not to give aid or assistance, either directly or indirectly," to any state that attacked Poland. Text of the pact in Horak, *Poland's International Affairs*, pp. 162-65.

[30] On this visit, see Castellan, *Réarmement*, pp. 484-86; Erickson, *Soviet High Command*, pp. 341-42.

[31] The French General Staff could not say for sure whether a definite German-Soviet commitment for a joint offensive against Poland existed; Castellan, *Réarmement*, pp. 486-87. General Heusinger believes not, but General Lanz recalls that late in 1932 the *Truppenamt* weighed the possibility of a German-Soviet offensive (interviews); see also Roos, *Polen und Europa*, p. 57.

tions against Germany.[32] The Army apparently also agreed that Czechoslovakia, although alarmed at the German revisionist campaign of the early 1930s, had avoided definite military commitments to either Poland or France. The Bendlerstrasse remained sure that continued Polish-Rumanian military cooperation was trained against aggression from the Soviet Union or the Soviet Union joined by another power, not against Germany itself.[33] Military intelligence corroborated the diplomatic evidence that political and military representatives from Poland and the Little Entente conferred in 1932 without yielding to the French inclination to a military coalition.[34] Finally, Austria appeared for the first time in the Army's operational planning, but as an ally against France, not Poland.[35]

Both the Foreign Office and the Defense Ministry realized that the major assumptions of Germany's eastern policy were being severely tested: an internally weak Poland unable to strengthen its strategic position in eastern Europe; and a Soviet ally willing to bring its foreign policy and military planning to bear against Poland. Yet neither department had the confidence, foresight, nor recklessness to abandon these assumptions and formulate a new *Ostpolitik*.

THE WEST

In 1930 and 1931 the Defense Ministry agreed with Chancellor Brüning and the Foreign Office that economic and mil-

[32] Hammerstein briefing, 27 February, in Vogelsang, "Dokumente," p. 420.

[33] *AA*, documents in file 6188; above, chap. 8, n. 41.

[34] *RWM, Abwehr* report, 27 December, PG 49030. For the military planning of the Little Entente in the early 1930s, see Kiszling, *Vereinbarungen der Kleinen Entente*, pp. 8-10, 16-43, 87-91.

[35] See below. The British military attaché noted the "close and cordial" relations between the German and Austrian Armies, 9 December 1931, *DBFP*, Ser. 2, II, 521. In February 1933, Neurath agreed with Hitler and Blomberg (Defense Minister) that Germany should have a military attaché in Vienna, for "relations between the two Armies [should be] as close as possible." *AA*, Neurath minute, 13 February, 3177/D683467.

itary concessions by the Great Powers were prerequisites for an effective governmental defense against attacks from those who either blamed the republic for signing the *Diktat* of Versailles or who, though not antirepublican, thought that the government should pursue a more aggressive foreign policy. Again like the cabinet and Foreign Office, the Defense Ministry believed that the best course to foreign policy victories was through an understanding with France,[36] and that such an understanding could be achieved by a belligerent style of negotiation if necessary.

The Defense Ministry sought closer relations with the French Army, and in December 1930 Schleicher remarked to French military representatives in Berlin that France and Germany must together revise the eastern borders, for the Polish question posed the greatest threat to world peace.[37] The military leadership did not personally participate in reparations talks, but exerted pressure on the government to hasten revision without conceding anything to the West by way of a reduction of military expenditures, even if such a concession brought quicker economic relief.[38] The Defense Ministry also accepted the Brüning government's disarmament policy. Since the spirit of Locarno had died and France would not voluntarily recognize Germany's rights, Germany should try to isolate France diplomatically by winning the support of the United States, Britain, and Italy for the German demand that other powers disarm to Germany's level. This would, the Germans hoped, force the French to

[36] Vogelsang, *Reichswehr und NSDAP*, pp. 103-105; Schleicher, Hammerstein, and Colonel Ferdinand von Bredow (head of *Abwehr* until he succeeded Schleicher as chief of the *Ministeramt* in 1932) were more enthusiastic proponents of this policy than was Groener.

[37] Castellan, *Réarmement*, pp. 455, 457. In December 1930, Hammerstein toasted the good health of the French Army at a farewell ceremony for the departing French attaché; the Wilhelmstrasse's account of this gesture in *AA*, K6/K000527-30; Franco-German military relations in 1930-31, *ibid.*, K000578ff., 3177/D683382ff. On the deterioration of those relations by the end of 1931, see British military attaché report, 9 December, *DBFP*, Ser. 2, II, 521.

[38] Vogelsang, *Reichswehr und NSDAP*, pp. 110-11; Bennett, *Financial Crisis*, pp. 119, 121, 125.

seek an agreement with Germany on armaments. Meanwhile, Germany should work for Franco-German economic cooperation.[39]

Civil-military accord on disarmament lasted into the early months of 1932.[40] But Schleicher turned against that policy, and, as Defense Minister, challenged the competence of the Foreign Office to a degree unequaled since the time of Seeckt. Schleicher advocated direct negotiations with France. He considered an expansion of the Army absolutely essential to national security and domestic order; this would boost the government's prestige and enable it to incorporate members of paramilitary organizations like the S.A. into the authorized armed force, thereby subduing those groups. Like the great majority of German officers, he had lost faith in the League of Nations and witnessed the dissipation of the spirit of Locarno, both of which had held out some promise of revision (including the restoration of full sovereignty) beyond the changes that had actually been achieved. Because of these domestic and international developments, Schleicher demanded an even more active foreign policy than Brüning's, convinced that France, simultaneously a powerful adversary and colleague, held the key to German revisionism.[41]

At the Foreign Office Bülow and, later, Neurath switched to the idea of direct Franco-German negotiations, since the

[39] *Ministeramt* memorandum, August 1931, in Vogelsang, *Reichswehr und NSDAP*, pp. 426-27.

[40] Groener and Schleicher briefing of senior officers in Berlin, 11-12 January, and Hammerstein briefing, 27 February, in Vogelsang, "Dokumente," pp. 413-14, 419. For evidence that the Defense Ministry had already become restless with the government, however, see Vogelsang, *Reichswehr und NSDAP*, pp. 430-31.

[41] André François-Poncet, *The Fateful Years: Memoirs of a French Ambassador in Berlin, 1931-1938*, trans. J. LeClercq (New York, 1949), pp. 27-28; also Conze, "Sturz Brünings," p. 268; Seeckt, *Wege*, pp. 17-18, 23ff., 32-33. Hammerstein declared that the customs union issue had demonstrated how the Hague Tribunal could decide questions on the basis of power, not right; briefing, 27 February 1932, Aufzeichnungen Generals Curt Liebmann (Befehlshaberbesprechungen), Institut für Zeitgeschichte (Munich).

British and Americans had not deserted France.[42] Although these diplomats agreed with Schleicher on the necessity for bilateral talks, they voiced strong objections to Schleicher's more precipitate proposals: withdrawal from the Disarmament Conference and unilateral abrogation of Part V of the Treaty of Versailles if the conference resolution—to be issued before summer adjournment—did not include a provision for equality of status; bilateral talks with France as a substitute for further multilateral negotiations at Geneva within the framework of the League; and foreign recognition not merely of Germany's equality of status, but of actual figures by which Germany should be granted equality of armaments to match either France or Poland plus Czechoslovakia.

Friction between the two ministries reached its high point in July, when, without notifying or obtaining the authorization of the Foreign Office, Schleicher delivered a radio address calling for a "national" policy for Germany and giving warning that Germany would consider itself free of the military restrictions of the Treaty of Versailles if its demand for equality were not met.[43] That indiscretion aroused French opinion and contributed to the difficulties the Wilhelmstrasse encountered when it tried to persuade the French to begin

[42] The following summary of German disarmament policy in 1932 is based on the accounts in Wilhelm Deist, "Schleicher und die deutsche Abrüstungspolitik im Juni/Juli 1932," *Vierteljahrshefte für Zeitgeschichte*, VII (1959), 163-76; Heineman, "Neurath as Foreign Minister," chap. 5; Vogelsang, *Reichswehr und NSDAP*, pp. 222-25, 294-302. Heineman shows that the Wilhelmstrasse's policy late in 1932 differed from Schleicher's summer program in a number of ways. See also Brüning, *Memoiren*, pp. 552-67; Curtius, *Sechs Jahre*, chap. 14; Eyck, *Weimar Republic*, II, 454ff.; François-Poncet, *Fateful Years*, pp. 31-33; Jordan, *German Problem*, pp. 149-51; Wohlfeil, *Heer und Republik*, pp. 195-98; Arnold Toynbee (ed.), *Survey of International Affairs 1932* (London, 1933), pp. 258-90; John W. Wheeler-Bennett (ed.), *Documents on International Affairs 1932* (London, 1933), pp. 183-234; DBFP, Ser. 2, III, 583-89, and IV, chaps. 2-4; *Foreign Relations of the United States*, 1932, I, 416-528.

[43] Text of the speech (26 July) in Schüddekopf, *Heer und Republik*, pp. 368-73; see also Nadolny, *Mein Beitrag*, p. 126; Vogelsang, *Reichswehr und NSDAP*, pp. 295f.

bilateral talks in search of a compromise; the two countries could then present their agreement to the other participants in the Disarmament Conference for their consent.

As Chancellor in December, however, Schleicher backed Neurath. The Wilhelmstrasse's disarmament policy had become more aggressive since July but had not assumed the extreme proportions of Schleicher's summer demands. A few days after signing the joint resolution of 11 December in Geneva that recognized Germany's equal status, Neurath triumphantly reported to the cabinet that Part V of the peace treaty was no longer valid, and that Germany had not promised not to rearm. But, he added, Germany must for the time being pursue rearmament (that is, equality in a practical, not simply legal sense) through multilateral negotiations in the Disarmament Conference.[44] The December resolution granted Germany "equality of rights in a system which would provide security for all nations." The French viewed the establishment of this system of security as a necessary precondition to Germany's release from the military restrictions of Versailles. But the German cabinet, the diplomats, and the generals celebrated the New Year determined to use equal status to win further concessions from the West in a new disarmament convention.

Both the Defense Ministry and Foreign Office believed that Germany's western policy had improved security against a French attack. The danger of unilateral French military sanctions in the event of a German default in reparations payments had abated in the 1920s as a result of the Ruhr occupation, the Dawes Plan, and the Treaty of Locarno. At the Second Hague Conference to discuss the Young Plan in January 1930, the French conceded that even multilateral sanctions voted by a majority of the creditor nations could not legally be imposed upon Germany. Henceforward,

[44] Heineman, "Neurath as Foreign Minister," pp. 206ff. At the end of the year, Schleicher apparently believed he had obtained tacit French approval for an expansion of the Army; Conze, "Sturz Brünings," p. 268.

charges of German default must be brought before the Permanent Court of International Justice at The Hague, and sanctions imposed only if the court found against Germany. Locarno outlawed unprovoked French aggression and hindered the imposition of French military sanctions, such as reoccupation of the Rhineland, for alleged German infractions of other treaty restrictions (e.g., rearmament, and remilitarization of the Rhineland).[45] For these reasons, and perhaps also because of the defensive emphasis in French military planning, the Defense Ministry considered the danger of French attack small. In 1932 Hammerstein anticipated that, should the Hague Tribunal declare Germany in default, France would not intervene militarily from the west, but engage Poland and Czechoslovakia to employ sanctions from the east. The struggle with France, Hammerstein said, was "diplomatic," not military.[46]

Given the improbability of a one-front conflict with France, the Foreign Office and Defense Ministry were more deeply concerned about whether France would uphold its alliance with Poland and encircle Germany in a two-front war. The two departments received and exchanged conflicting reports about a renewal of the Franco-Polish military convention.[47] The Foreign Office kept the Defense Ministry

[45] On the Young Plan and the question of sanctions, see Eyck, *Weimar Republic,* II, 234-35; Jacobson, *Locarno Diplomacy,* pp. 356-58. Since Locarno was not an alliance, and because all five Locarno states should have been included in any joint staff talks, Anglo-French military planning was unfeasible (the British government opposed holding talks with the French in any case). Thus, France could not count on immediate British military assistance after Britain withdrew its occupation force from the Rhineland and the continent.

[46] Hammerstein briefings, 27 February, 21 May, in Vogelsang, "Dokumente," pp. 420, 425.

[47] Rumors that it would not be renewed were discounted, although apparently no one in either ministry could say with certainty when the convention of 1926 would expire, whether it was in fact renewed, and what its contents were. *AA,* correspondence of 1931-32, K177/ K030400-510, *passim; RWM, Abwehr* report, 19 May 1932, PG

307

informed of rifts in the alliance. Pilsudski wanted to preserve it as an equal, not a vassal; he was confident that Poland was indispensable to France, confident enough to commit sins against the alliance such as forcing the French to withdraw their military and naval missions in 1932; he retained his operational preference for flank attacks (e.g., against East Prussia) rather than a frontal attack toward Berlin; and he interpreted the eager French campaign for nonaggression pacts between Poland and the Soviet Union and Rumania and the Soviet Union as a sign that France wanted to back away from its politico-military commitments to those two allies.[48]

The Foreign Office and Defense Ministry noticed the defensive bias in French military planning. In a study written late in 1930 the French General Staff admitted that the Franco-Polish alliance would not apply if Germany were provoked into a war with Poland, and pointed out how the Treaty of Locarno might also block French intervention.[49] Although the staff's qualifications of French political obligations and freedom of action in the event of a German-Polish conflict rested on legal points, we can also infer from this report the predilection for defensive operations in French military planning. After the evacuation of the Rhineland, the first line of defense for the French system of security (that is, for Poland and Czechoslovakia as well as France) was not the Rhine, but the Franco-German border; there the French intended the Maginot Line to be primarily a defensive shield against German attack.[50]

49031. Colonel Fischer (T3) sent the Foreign Office two different texts of what was alleged to be the renewed convention of 1926; *AA*, Fischer to Foreign Office, 19 December 1931, K177/K030428-38, 443-4.

[48] *AA, ibid.,* K030400-510, *passim* (especially Moltke to Foreign Office, 18 May 1932, 471-4); Rauscher memorandum, 25 October 1930, K190/K036611-13; Rintelen to Foreign Office (Hammerstein read this "with great interest"), 20 February 1931, *ibid.,* K036596-8. See also Laroche, *La Pologne de Pilsudski,* pp. 108-109.

[49] Castellan, *Réarmement,* pp. 469-71.

[50] See above, chap. 4, n. 48. Interdepartmental correspondence

The Foreign Office and Defense Ministry agreed that an understanding with France, combined with Soviet support and the legal and military flaws in the Franco-Polish alliance, offered the multiple advantages of discouraging a Polish attack, constraining Poland to revise its borders peaceably, and restraining France from intervention in a German-Polish war.[51] But interdepartmental differences and conflicts within the Defense Ministry itself jeopardized this strategy of neutralizing the western front. In the late 1920s, Schleicher's adherence to the one-front strategy of preparing for a war with Poland had conformed to his concern for civil-military cooperation in national defense, and to Stresemann's foreign policy. Throughout the years of crisis, Schleicher continued to hope for a Franco-German understanding and a limitation of any future German-Polish war to Germany's eastern front. Yet in the summer and early autumn of 1932, Defense Minister Schleicher pressed for German rearmament in an obstreperous manner that offended both the Foreign Office and France. Schleicher and Blomberg, Germany's chief military representative at the Disarmament Conference, decided that Germany should present a list of specific demands to the conference.[52] This intradepartmental harmony was short-lived, however. As Chancellor and Defense Minister, Schleicher supported Neurath against Blomberg and other officers who urged an abrupt escalation of demands at Geneva.[53]

---

concerning French military planning, *AA*, Bern mission to Foreign Office, 31 December 1929 (transcript to Defense Ministry on 7 January 1930), 5986/E440428-30; T3 to Foreign Office, 24 September 1930, *ibid.*, E440474-512; Bredow (*Abwehr*) to Foreign Office, 10 October, Paris embassy to Foreign Office, 31 October (to Defense Ministry on 11 November), M342/M015365, 399-401.

[51] Breyer, *Deutsche Reich und Polen*, pp. 35-36; Castellan, *Réarmement*, pp. 455, 457-58; Conze, "Sturz Brünings," p. 268; Vogelsang, *Reichswehr und NSDAP*, pp. 102ff. and *passim*.

[52] Heineman, "Neurath as Foreign Minister," pp. 171-72.

[53] *Ibid.*, pp. 213-17. Perhaps differences with Schleicher over disarmament policy contributed to Blomberg's readiness to circumvent and depose Schleicher in January 1933. As in the case of Blomberg's

Blomberg's clash with the Foreign Office in December 1932–January 1933 did not signal a return to the two-front strategy of Seeckt—Soviet support in the rear for a war against France and Poland—although that strategy was implicit in the "war of liberation" that the Nazis, *Stahlhelm*, and some Army officers believed Germany must wage against France. Under Hammerstein and Wilhelm Adam, the Army Command and *Truppenamt* insisted that a defensive war against France—not to mention a two-front conflict—"lay completely outside the realm of military possibility," and continued to base military expansion on the one-front eastern contingency.[54]

Still, the possibility of a two-front war had not been eliminated. It remained the master strategic plan of the Franco-Polish alliance, in spite of the weaknesses of this bond.[55] Officers of Blomberg's politico-military persuasion believed that the prestige of the Army depended on its ability to defend the Reich. They agreed with Hammerstein that if the Army could not resist a Polish-Czechoslovak attack it would lose its right to exist. But they probably regretted more intensely than Schleicher, Hammerstein, or the diplomats the Army Command's verdict that if France invaded Germany the Army would have to abstain from forcible resistance; and they regretted the explanation Hammerstein provided for not resist-

---

removal from the *Truppenamt* in 1929 (see above, chap. 4, n. 61), Prof. Carsten stresses personal animosity and "the rift between the 'office generals' and the 'front.' . . ." *Reichswehr and Politics*, pp. 389-90.

[54] *RWM*, Naval Command paper (Captain Ciliax), February 1936, PG 33965b.

[55] In 1932, a report in the *Abwehr* Department suggested that France, although reluctant to become involved in a conflict with Germany, would probably fight if Germany were taken over by the Hitler movement and tried to regain the Corridor; *RWM*, 10 June, PG 49032. For a contemporary appraisal of the weaknesses yet endurance of the Franco-Polish alliance, see *Wissen und Wehr*, XI (1930), 56-58.

ing, namely, that France was simply too powerful.[56] Blomberg urged that Germany prepare for the most unfavorable contingency, even at the political risk of forcing France into a tougher antirevisionist and pro-Polish stance. Thus, although Schleicher and the Foreign Office had begun to restore ministerial accord over Germany's disarmament policy, they had still not reconciled the two distinct priorities that caused intradepartmental and interdepartmental friction during the periods of both stability and crisis: rapprochement with France, and military preparedness on both fronts.

FORCE AND FOREIGN POLICY: REARMAMENT

In the disarmament negotiations of the early 1930s German Army officers and civilian leaders alike affirmed the right of every nation to adequate military strength for self-defense. They reinforced their case by reminding foreign representatives of the politico-military weaknesses created by the Corridor, the demilitarized zone of the Rhineland, and the limitations on the size and weapons of the standing Army. But the Defense Ministry, again like the Foreign Office, retained those considerations of *Machtpolitik* that had inspired its planning in the 1920s and that justified the use of force for ends that did not conform to the definition of national security as defense against invasion. Without power, Germany could not stand up for its legal and moral rights; human nature had not changed; there would always be wars, and each side in any conflict would always say that it was fighting for its own national defense; Germany could not trust other states to refrain from war and therefore must restore and maintain its politico-military freedom of movement.[57] An increasing

[56] Hammerstein briefing, 27 February 1932, Aufzeichnungen Generals Curt Liebmann (Befehlshaberbesprechungen), Institut für Zeitgeschichte (Munich).

[57] See Friedrich von Cochenhausen, *Wehrgedanken* (Hamburg, 1933), pp. 16-17; Hans von Seeckt, *Landesverteidigung* (Berlin,

311

number of officers considered a "war of liberation" inevitable, and the Nazis won their sympathy by calling a spade a spade: France was Germany's arch-enemy and would respect only force.[58] But every officer, including the military leadership, believed that Germany must prepare for a war with Poland to regain the lost territories.[59]

Adding doctrinal support to this view of the relationship between force and foreign policy, the postwar Clausewitzean

---

1930), especially pp. 17, 27-28. In a speech to the Reichstag on 19 March 1931, Groener admonished the delegates to provide the state with sufficient means of power if they considered power and honor vital to the state; in Bucher, *Reichswehrprozess*, pp. 148-49.

[58] The lieutenants brought to trial at Leipzig in September 1930 proclaimed the *Befreiungskrieg* to be the Army's goal; Carsten, *Reichswehr and Politics*, pp. 315-19.

[59] Not even Groener, perhaps the most discerning *Realpolitiker* in the Defense Ministry, rejected this ultimate solution to the Polish question. In September 1931 he wrote to a friend that a war against Poland to recover the Corridor was " 'a utopia.' " He referred sardonically to those officers who hoped for such a conflict: " 'Unfortunately, strategy is a contagious disease which by preference affects heads which are not exactly filled with wisdom. . . .' " In Craig, *Prussian Army*, p. 441. It is unlikely, however, that Groener, in spite of his strategic wisdom, was immune to the fatalistic conclusion that a war against Poland was inevitable. Having read early in 1931 a study by Captain Almendinger (a member of the Polish division of T3), whose thesis was that Poland would never return the Corridor without war, Groener commented enthusiastically, "that man can amount to something!" ("aus dem Manne kann was werden!!"). Marginal note on message from Schleicher to adjutant of Chief of the Army Command concerning Almendinger's report, 26 January 1931, Nachlass Schleicher, no. 34, Bundesarchiv-Militärarchiv. At most, this is only inferential evidence of Groener's agreeing with Almendinger on this point. But when it is combined with the recollections of General Lanz (who knew Almendinger, a co-worker in T3, and who frequently talked with Groener about the Polish Army), and with Groener's order of 16 April 1930, the following conclusion can be offered: Groener thought that a German-Polish war in 1931 was utopian foolishness, but that it would ultimately be necessary once Germany's military strength and international situation permitted, and if Poland continued to reject peaceful revision.

renaissance in military training and in publications continued after 1929.[60] Moreover, the Army preserved the other principle of Clausewitz that the Foreign Office also accepted, the primacy of the political arm; the Army still defined this political leadership as the government and Foreign Office in documents concerning rearmament and operations. But this desideratum of military subordination to the Foreign Office and cabinet now proved more difficult to observe in practice than it had been during the years of stability. The question of rearmament was the major source of interdepartmental discord.[61] The Defense Ministry pressed for a quicker and more aggressive resolution of the problem that Germany lacked the power to increase its power with relative impunity; the Foreign Office feared that too "active" a campaign for rearmament might injure Germany's chances of obtaining *de jure* concessions from the West.

In January 1931 Prussia finally implemented the "regulations" concerning border and national defense that the cabinet had passed in April 1929. These provisions, their distinction between *Grenzschutz* and *Landesschutz*, and their prohibition of border and national defense in the Rhineland remained in effect, with minor modifications pertaining to the highly secret administration of *Landesschutzarbeiten* (or *L-Arbeiten*) by active and retired officers, and civilian officials. Within this broad national defense program, the Defense Ministry continued to develop the *A-Plan* for the expansion of the standing armed forces in an emergency,[62]

[60] See various articles and reviews in *Wissen und Wehr*, XI-XIII (1930-32).

[61] *Landesschutz* and *Grenzschutz* in the west remained a potentially divisive issue, but appears to have receded as disarmament policy became preeminent in interdepartmental relations. On western defense, see below, n. 94.

[62] On the distinction between those projects actually or nearly in effect (*L-Arbeiten*) and those relating to mobilization, still at the theoretical stage (*A-Arbeiten*), see Rudolf Absolon, *Die Wehrmacht im Dritten Reich*, I (Boppard, 1969), pp. 37-39.

and also drew up the preliminary outlines for a larger peace-time army (*Friedensheer*).

As early as June 1930, the *Truppenamt* had revealed to the Foreign Office its goal of a peacetime force of between two and three hundred thousand regulars and a militia of several hundred thousand, an expansion which, the *Truppenamt* advised, Germany should demand if the Entente powers did not disarm to the level necessary for their national security.[63] Temporarily, the Army concurred with the Foreign Office that Germany lacked the international strength to threaten to rearm.[64] But in 1932 Schleicher publicly demanded more pugnacious tactics. The Foreign Office, which viewed Schleicher as a military man in civilian clothing after he resigned from active service to become Defense Minister, resented his brash intervention and his sway over Papen in this area of foreign policy. The diplomats objected to Schleicher's breach of civil-military discipline when, bypassing the Wilhelmstrasse and its chief representative at the Disarmament Conference, Rudolf Nadolny, the Defense Minister sent instructions directly to Blomberg in Geneva; they rejected Schleicher's most drastic demands.[65]

But the attitudes and actions of Neurath and Bülow reveal at least as much sympathy for military expansion as offense at the intrusion of another department. After Brüning's fall, Schleicher won cabinet approval of an expansion plan that closely resembled the one the *Truppenamt* had recommended in 1930, and on which he, Hammerstein, and Adam agreed. Until the West met Germany's demands for an enlarged standing army and militia, no matter what happened at Geneva, Germany would continue preparations for the *A-Plan*, the second stage of which would begin on 1 April

[63] *AA*, Schlimpert notes, 3 June, K6/K000480; a similar idea for expansion in Seeckt, *Landesverteidigung*, pp. 72-73, 76ff.

[64] Hammerstein briefing of officers in Kassel, 24 April 1931, in Vogelsang, "Dokumente," pp. 409-10; *Ministeramt* memorandum, August 1931, in Vogelsang, *Reichswehr und NSDAP*, pp. 426-27.

[65] See above.

1933.[66] Neurath and Bülow consented to step up Germany's diplomatic offensive to gain international approval for this covert expansion in the form of a disarmament convention, using the euphemistic terms *Umbau* and *Umrüstung* (reorganization) rather than the more blatant *Aufrüstung* (rearmament). And they, like Schleicher, assumed that the multilateral agreement of 11 December would afford Germany legal grounds to declare its freedom to rearm (*Rüstungsfreiheit*) if the Disarmament Conference failed to allow Germany to take the practical military steps necessary for its security and thereby give substance to its equality of rights.[67]

Thus, the community of politico-military interests shared by the Defense Ministry and Foreign Office remained strong, in spite of Schleicher's indelicacy. When the diplomats assented to the reinstitution of military attachés and adopted more aggressive tactics in Geneva, they acted on their own conviction that Germany had the right to increase its military strength and prestige. On the eve of Hitler's takeover, the Foreign Office had reasserted its sole departmental authority for conducting Germany's disarmament policy. Schleicher deferred to the diplomats' expertise at Geneva and to Neurath's assertion that, as a minister, he was directly responsible to the President.[68] Nevertheless, the Defense Ministry and Foreign Office had not eliminated basic interdepartmental differences over the relationship between military planning and foreign policy. Even after Germany had won *de jure* recognition of

[66] *RWM*, Adam, Schleicher, and Hammerstein meeting, 14 July 1932; T2 to T4, 15 July; Hammerstein to various Army departments, 30 August; II H 228. *Truppenamt* memorandum, "Marschbereitschaft des Reichsheeres," 12 December, PG 34095. See also Carsten, *Reichswehr and Politics*, pp. 356-57; Meinck, *Deutsche Aufrüstung*, pp. 6-7; Mueller-Hillebrand, *Das Heer*, pp. 18-20; Völker, *Entwicklung der militärischen Luftfahrt*, pp. 188-89, 192; Vogelsang, *Reichswehr und NSDAP*, pp. 230, 302.

[67] Schleicher briefing of senior officers, 13-15 December 1932, in Vogelsang, "Dokumente," pp. 428-29; also Heineman, "Neurath as Foreign Minister," pp. 203-206, 216.

[68] On Schleicher's support of Neurath, see above.

equal rights in December 1932, the possibility still existed
that the Army might persuade the Chancellor to adopt more
overt *de facto* rearmament, or indeed to authorize the remilitarization of the Rhineland, before the Foreign Office deemed
the international situation favorable.[69]

Plaited together, the tactics, economics, and politics of the
eastern *Grenzschutz* twisted civil-military relations between
the Army and the governments of the Reich and Prussia. The
Army's tactical organization, which antedated the depression
and the rise of the Nazi Party, required the use of local irregulars as the front line of defense.[70] Accordingly, the Army
had begun in 1928 to withdraw garrisons of regular troops
from the border areas of Military Districts I (East Prussia)
and III (which included Silesia). Groener and Heye emphasized the military necessity of these and further relocations
in reply to complaints from diverse sources (the Social Democratic Prussian government, the Nationalists, and the ultra-
revisionist *Deutscher Ostbund*) that withdrawals would injure
local economies and increase the psychological insecurity of
borderland inhabitants.[71]

[69] In January 1933 Blomberg expressed displeasure with the Wilhelmstrasse's continued caution; he urged that Germany submit a set
of military demands to the Disarmament Conference and also raise
the question of the demilitarized status of the Rhineland. Heineman,
"Neurath as Foreign Minister," pp. 214-15.

[70] See above, chap. 5; also interview with General von Ahlfen;
Roos, *Polen und Europa*, p. 41; Bernard Watzdorf, "Die getarnte
Ausbildung von Generalstabsoffizieren der Reichswehr von 1932 bis
1935," *Zeitschrift für Militärgeschichte*, II (1963), 83.

[71] *RK*, correspondence to and from Groener, the Prussian government, and the Reich Chancery, K951/K248764-820. Neither Otto
Braun nor the *Deutscher Ostbund* was convinced by the Bendlerstrasse's tactical arguments. The Prussian Prime Minister wanted to
explain to Groener and other officials "how, under present circumstances as opposed to the accepted opinions before the war, purely
strategic considerations can no longer claim the only decisive importance; that in every case, a compromise must be sought and found
between [strategic] and . . . very important internal political and

In the early 1930s, the economic plight and the feelings of military vulnerability in the eastern provinces became acute as the decline in commerce, caused by the general economic depression and the regional tariff war with Poland, was matched by the rise in tension along the borders.[72] The Defense Ministry then found itself caught in a mesh partly of its own making. Groener and Schleicher displayed growing concern for the economic distress that sapped the strength of the indigenous population, on which the Army relied for border defense.[73] Yet they continued the tactical redisposition, a measure with two consequences: an intensification in the anxiety of borderland civilians at the very moment when the Army wanted to quell the kind of alarmism that might have led to open conflict with Poland; and an increase in the Army's dependence on the paramilitary *Verbände* to man *Grenzschutz* units at a time when military leaders feared that the most militant of these groups, the *S.A.*, might precipitate the dreaded combination of internal civil war and war with Poland.

---

economic points of view." Braun to Chancellor (Müller), 28 July 1928, *ibid.*, K248764-5. Groener had informed the Prussian Minister of the Interior that political and economic considerations mattered "only insofar as important military interests will not be harmed." Groener to Grzesinski, 20 June, *ibid.*, K248769-70.

[72] Brüning attributes the withdrawal of border garrisons from Silesia in the early 1930s to the threat of civil war and Silesia's vulnerability to Polish attack; "Ein Brief," p. 2. But this does not account for withdrawals during the relative calm of the late 1920s.

[73] Schleicher sent members of his staff on inspection tours of the eastern provinces, and Groener wrote felicitous letters to local officials, but the Defense Ministry conceded little—if anything—to Braun or borderland nationalists in the form of a compromise in military tactics. *RK*, correspondence between Groener and Reich Chancery, 18 January 1930, 21 April 1932, K953/K249713, 779-80; also documents in Akten betr. Dienstgebäude, Garnisonen, Festungen (not filmed). Schleicher's "itinerant preacher" was Eugen Ott; Vincenz Müller also toured the border areas. Interview with Ambassador Ott; Müller, *Vaterland*, pp. 326ff.

Instead of reversing the tactical withdrawals, Groener and Schleicher gave their support to the Brüning government's program for eastern aid (*Osthilfe*),[74] a clear sign that they distinguished between the responsibility of the cabinet for the economic and political stability of the borderlands and their own departmental responsibility for military planning there. In making that distinction, the Defense Ministry might be said to have sustained a division of function implicit in civil-military relations. But they respected no such distinction or division when they intervened in Weimar politics in order to safeguard and promote military programs in the unstable domestic climate that their own preoccupation with national security helped to create.[75]

Groener and Schleicher merged national defense and politics to an extent unprecedented since the early years of the republic. The defense of the Reich and the restoration of internal order, they believed, required stripping the various paramilitary organizations of their political trappings. The issue of national defense in a period of mass political dissension was the focal point of tense relations between the Army and the Nazi Party.[76] In December 1928 Hitler had prohib-

[74] Perhaps Müller's report upon returning from his tour (see preceding note) helped convince Schleicher to back *Osthilfe*; see Müller, *Vaterland*, pp. 330-31. On *Osthilfe*, see Bracher, *Auflösung*, pp. 511-17; Eyck, *Weimar Republic*, II, 380-84, 459-63.

[75] Groener and Schleicher moved far beyond the institutional levels of civil-military relations in the belief that the Army should become the nation's educator. In order to train the youth for later service in the regular force or militia, they established the "Reich board of physical training for youth" (*Reichskuratorium für Jugendertüchtigung*). On this program and its close affiliation with the *Stahlhelm, S.A.*, and other *Verbände*, see Berghahn, *Stahlhelm*, pp. 193f., 238; Carsten, *Reichswehr and Politics*, pp. 354-55, 387-88; Conze, "Sturz Brünings," p. 270; Sauer, "Mobilmachung der Gewalt," in Bracher, *Machtergreifung*, pp. 700-701; Vogelsang, *Reichswehr und NSDAP*, pp. 231f.

[76] See especially Carsten, *Reichswehr and Politics*, chaps. 7, 8; Craig, *Prussian Army*, chap. 11; Sauer, "Die Reichswehr," in Bracher,

ited the collaboration of party members with the Army.[77] The Leipzig trial of September 1930 publicized contacts between some officers and the Nazis. The Army preferred right-wing patriotic groups like the *Stahlhelm* to the SPD's *Reichsbanner*, an organization the officers considered untrustworthy for national defense; the Army abhorred Ernst Röhm's vision of turning the *S.A.* into a regular armed force. The Prussian police found incriminating evidence in March 1932 that Silesian *S.A.* leaders would not permit their members to participate in defense against a Polish attack. Groener, now Minister of the Interior as well as Defense Minister, advocated the dissolution of the *S.A.* and *S.S.* (decreed on 12 April 1932), yet admired the patriotism and other "best sentiments" of the less rowdy Nazis. Schleicher initially favored the dissolution, then changed his mind. Subsequently he conspired to oust Groener from the Bendlerstrasse, inspired President Hindenburg's decree of 14 June rescinding the dissolution, supported Papen's July coup d'état in Prussia, maneuvered to save the presidential regime by incorporating the Nazis into it as cabinet colleagues and parliamentary supporters, and finally met his own political demise in January 1933 through the intrigue of Papen, Hitler, and advisers to President Hindenburg.

The war game that Lieutenant Colonel Eugen Ott conducted at the end of November 1932 presents one of the most extreme expressions of the connection drawn in the Bendler-

---

Auflösung, pp. 278-83; Vogelsang, *Reichswehr und NSDAP, passim*; Wohlfeil, *Heer und Republik*, pp. 150-55.

[77] Hitler's order of 3 December 1928 was disobeyed by many *S.A.* men who also belonged to border defense units. Moreover, local military commanders and *S.A.* leaders arranged that, in a defensive emergency, the *S.A. Führer* would hand his entire group over to the Army commander. Interview with Heinrich Bennecke, an *S.A.* leader in Saxony from 1925 to 1933; see his *Die Reichswehr und der "Röhm-Putsch"* (Munich, 1964). In January 1932 the Defense Ministry began to permit Nazis to join the regular Army.

strasse between national defense and politics.[78] Ott (head of the *Wehrmachtsabteilung* in the *Ministeramt*), representatives of military and naval headquarters, and appropriate civilian officials studied the possibility of a state of emergency leading to riots and a general strike; they assumed that the Nazis and Communists would again collaborate in violent acts like the recent strike of the Berlin transport workers. Ott's group concluded that the government lacked sufficient military, police, and emergency civilian resources to restore order and at the same time defend the eastern frontier against the Polish incursions that might ensue if the Poles realized the seriousness of Germany's internal situation. Ott's war game should not be dismissed as a ruse Schleicher employed to attain the chancellorship.[79] Both Ott and Schleicher admitted that they had assumed the worst possible contingency. Moreover, such hypothetical extremes were not uncommon in the Bendlerstrasse in 1932; in February Hammerstein had warned that the Army could not mobilize simultaneously against internal disorder and external attack.[80] The threat of civil war increased with the level of political violence in the interminable procession of presidential, state, and general elections in 1932. The threat of a Polish invasion had abated since the spring, but it could have revived if Polish irregulars had had a German civil war to exploit, or if the Polish government

[78] On Ott's *Kriegsspiel*, see Bracher, *Auflösung*, pp. 673ff.; Carsten, *Reichswehr and Politics*, pp. 378ff.; Dorpalen, *Hindenburg*, pp. 390-94; Ott, "Ein Bild," pp. 367-69; Papen, *Scheitern*, pp. 311-13, also his *Der Wahrheit eine Gasse* (Munich, 1952), pp. 247-50; Kurt Schützle, *Reichswehr wider die Nation* ([East] Berlin, 1963), p. 194 (the Army was not willing to fight fascism); Vogelsang, *Reichswehr und NSDAP*, pp. 333-34, 484-85. Additional information from Ambassador Ott, interview, and his Zeugenschrifttum no. 279, Institut für Zeitgeschichte (Munich).

[79] The author agrees with Hans Herzfeld, "Zur neueren Literatur über das Heeresproblem," pp. 377-78; Vogelsang, "Dokumente," p. 427n.

[80] Hammerstein briefing, 27 February, in Vogelsang, "Dokumente," pp. 421-22.

had decided upon a preventive war before the Nazis could gain power and launch an offensive of their own.[81]

On 2 December Schleicher summoned Ott before the cabinet to deliver the pessimistic verdict reached in the war game; Ott emphasized that the Army would be unable to counteract widespread sabotage and passive resistance. Unlike Schleicher's proposal to seek a parliamentary majority, Papen's plan to strengthen the government envisioned the declaration of a state of emergency and the temporary suspension of parliament if necessary. The cabinet accepted the judgment of Schleicher and Ott that a state of emergency must be avoided, and that reinstating Papen as Chancellor (he had resigned in mid-November, but stayed in the Reich Chancery as head of a caretaker government) was therefore out of the question. With some reluctance, Schleicher accepted the responsibility to form a new government.

FORCE AND FOREIGN POLICY: OPERATIONS

No major changes occurred in the multi-level system of operational studies that the *Truppenamt* had evolved in the 1920s.[82] Collaboration with the Foreign Office continued in some of these exercises, as officials from the Wilhelmstrasse played the parts of German and foreign statesmen, directed the diplomatic phase that preceded the outbreak of hostilities, and explained Germany's international position.[83] The hypothetical situations remained similar, with the conspicuous ex-

[81] In his estimate of the war game, Carsten fails to mention the Polish-Soviet Nonaggression Pact and its strategic implications; *Reichswehr and Politics*, pp. 381, 403.

[82] In 1932 the entire three-year course for General Staff officer candidates was moved to the Defense Ministry, and this *Offizierslehrgänge Berlin* was the forerunner of the *Kriegsakademie* of Hitler's *Wehrmacht*; Erfurth, *Geschichte des Generalstabes*, p. 127.

[83] Manstein, *Soldatenleben*, pp. 131ff.; interviews with Generals Fretter-Pico, Heusinger, Lanz, Nehring, Speidel, Viebahn, and Ambassador Ott.

321

ception that Austria and Italy began to appear as Germany's allies.

In May 1930 the first General Staff tour under the direction of Blomberg's successor at the *Truppenamt*, General Hammerstein, dealt with an imagined Franco-Belgian invasion of Germany.[84] The General Staff tour of the following spring, led by General Adam (he replaced Hammerstein after the latter became Chief of the Army Command), assumed a German-Italian coalition against attacks by France and Yugoslavia. While Italy thwarted the Yugoslav offensive, Germany executed a delaying action against the French thrust toward the Rhine between Mannheim and Koblenz. Austria (*Deutsch/Österreich*) entered the conflict, and combined with Italian forces to overthrow Yugoslavia. Then Austria and Italy, having already sent units to help protect the Germans' southern flank, would send larger forces to southern Germany, whence the three allies would eventually execute a major offensive against the French.[85]

Both of the operational problems assigned General Staff officers in 1932 postulated a German-Polish conflict, as did the transportation exercise which took place in June.[86] The

[84] The French advanced up the Main river valley; the German Army withdrew to the defensive line stretching from the Werra river west of Eisenach to the Czechoslovak border, mobilized, and transferred a few divisions (including one from East Prussia) from the east. *RWM*, *Truppenamt* situation report (no date), II H 605.

[85] *RWM*, II H 606/1. General Adam requested that the Foreign Office send a representative in order to continue close interdepartmental cooperation; Forster apparently attended the exercise. *AA*, Adam to Foreign Office, 20 April 1931; Forster to *Truppenamt*, 9 May; K6/K000617, 620. In a transportation exercise that summer, France and Belgium suddenly attacked Germany and Italy during a (Polish-Soviet) war in eastern Europe; *RWM*, *Truppenamt* situation report, II H 563/1.

[86] *RWM*, Adam to staff officers, 2 January; Adam critique of first operational problem, 7 April; II H 600/2. Adam praised those officers who proposed counterattacks from Silesia and Pomerania rather than a defensive stand at and behind the Oder river; a major Polish advance toward Berlin was assumed. Contrast Adam's critique

western front was the subject of the *Führerreise.* In a situation similar to the General Staff tour of 1931, France declared war on Germany and advanced from Alsace-Lorraine toward the Rhine and valley of the Main; Italy and "German/Austria" joined Germany as allies; and the other countries of Europe stayed neutral (Czechoslovakia and Poland benevolent toward France). The German Army planned to fall back gradually on the rear defensive line (*Rückhalt-Zone*) Fulda-Werra-Thüringer Wald-Frankenwald *Stellung* and thereby protect mobilization in the heart of Germany, leaving some divisions in the east as security against possible Polish intervention. Italian and Austrian units would attack the French southern flank. Meanwhile, the three allies would plan a joint counteroffensive.[87]

The first operational problem of 1933 presumed that German-Polish tension had increased because Germany had expanded its peacetime forces following the annulment of Part V of the Versailles *Diktat* and the agreement in Geneva on a more favorable set of military terms for Germany. War broke out between the two enemies; the League of Nations successfully localized the conflict for the time being, although the Soviet Union and Lithuania partially mobilized and stationed forces along the Polish borders; Czechoslovakia promised strict neutrality.[88]

The Army retained its ambivalent attitude toward the purpose of war games. They were theoretical, and assumed military strengths that did not actually exist in order to train officers in the organization and command of large units.[89] Yet

---

in 1933, below, n. 106. The transportation exercise, file II H 594; on cooperation between the Transport Section and civilian railroad officials, *ibid.,* also II H 563, 570, 572.

[87] *RWM, Truppenamt* situation report (no date), II H 608/1.

[88] *RWM,* Adam to staff officers, 10 January, II H 600/3. The Army would defend East Prussia to the utmost, use the *Grenzschutz* to delay the enemy advance, and mobilize the *A-Heer.*

[89] *RWM,* Adam critique of operational problem, 7 April 1932, II H 600/2; Adam to Chief of the Army Command and sections in the

Hammerstein gave frequent briefings to keep the officer corps informed of the international situation;[90] the *Truppenamt* invited German diplomats to contribute their expertise and lend political reality to the exercises; and on at least one occasion the Chief of the *Truppenamt* informed General Staff officers that, in order to increase the significance of an operational problem, he had closely conformed the military power and operational readiness of Germany and Poland to actual conditions.[91] This ambivalence no doubt continued to puzzle officials in the Wilhelmstrasse;[92] the same ambivalence makes retrospective generalization about patterns in operational planning difficult and tentative.

The major operational exercises mentioned above assumed a French invasion. Why was this the case, when the Army Command did not believe that France would attack Germany as if to repeat the Ruhr invasion of 1923, and furthermore solicited closer relations with the French Army? A number of answers are possible. First, and probably most important, the *Truppenamt* continued to see its duty in preparing for every possible contingency, including French military sanctions, French intervention in a German-Polish war, or a French demand for passage across Germany in a Polish-Soviet conflict.[93] Second, the Army wanted to impress upon

---

Truppenamt, 1 August 1932, II H 600/3; Jodl (T1) situation report for *Führerreise*, 1933 (no date), II H 609/1; interview with General Heusinger.

[90] Vogelsang, "Dokumente," p. 418n.

[91] *RWM*, Adam critique of first operational problem of 1933 (no date), II H 600/3.

[92] The *Truppenamt* asked that a representative from the Foreign Office discuss foreign policy in the General Staff tour of 1930. Yet Herr Schlimpert, the military specialist who attended, reported that, since the game had been based on purely military considerations, the Army had not raised questions of foreign policy or asked him to express his opinions of the exercise. *AA, Truppenamt* to Foreign Office, 19 May; Schlimpert notes, 3 June; K6/K000476, 479.

[93] See the skeptical attitude toward the reliability of diplomatic guarantees against French invasion in *Wissen und Wehr*, XI (1930), 506-11.

Foreign Office officials the necessity for making secret defensive preparations in the west, even at the risk of offending the French, who, the Army could point out, had not renounced the idea of a Franco-German understanding in spite of Germany's illegal rearmament and the unabated participation of *Stahlhelm* members in national defense. Third, officers in the *Truppenamt* might have felt the urge for "liberation" strongly enough to allow it to influence their choice of pressing operational questions. And finally, the evacuation of the Rhineland in the summer of 1930 improved Germany's tactical position in the event of a French attack, and drew attention to western contingency planning. Until then, the mere presence of Allied troops had inhibited clandestine military preparations in the demilitarized zone, and the Rhineland had afforded the French a base of operations, including bridgeheads on the right bank of the Rhine, close to the German Army's rear defensive line. After the evacuation, the Army could take defensive measures west of the Rhine with considerably less danger of detection; the mission of this forward area would be to delay the French advance before it reached the natural barrier of the Rhine.[94]

A number of assumptions persisted from the Army's exercises of the 1920s. Britain, a guarantor of Locarno, would

[94] The transportation exercise of November 1931 included the activation of a border defense in the Schwarzwald and Odenwald (i.e., east of the Rhine); in the demilitarized zone west of the Rhine, civilian authorities awaited orders to obstruct the enemy offensive. *RWM, Truppenamt* situation report (no date), II H 563/2. In the *Führerreise* of May 1933, the *Truppenamt* referred to a front line of defense—*Grenzschutz*, forestry officials, etc.—about 20 kilometers from the Franco-German border; this line would provide security while obstructions already prepared in peacetime were completed. Jodl (T1) situation report (no date), II H 609/1. In spite of the official prohibition against a western *Grenzschutz*, we can infer from the Army's operational studies as well as its contacts with the *Stahlhelm* (under pressure from President Hindenburg in July 1930, the Prussian government lifted its ban of October 1929 against the *Stahlhelm* in the provinces of Rhineland and Westphalia) that border defense in the west had grown past the theoretical stage.

neither prevent France from attacking nor come to the aid of Germany, but would remain neutral, as would the United States.[95] The League could probably not reconcile German-Polish differences that might lead to war, nor deter a Polish attack on Germany, but would try to limit the conflict. Germany could not ignore League opinion; the Army and Foreign Office must be certain that preparatory mobilization and initial operations would not appear aggressive to League members.[96]

Czechoslovakia maintained benevolent neutrality toward France when France invaded Germany, and strict neutrality in a German-Polish conflict.[97] Rumania was not mentioned. The third member of the Little Entente, Yugoslavia, a newcomer in operational exercises, was France's ally against Germany and Italy, a reflection of Franco-Italian and Italo-Yugoslavian animosity. Lithuania concentrated units at the Polish border when war broke out between Germany and Poland.[98] In spite of the Polish-Soviet nonaggression agreement, which, the Army admitted, improved Poland's strategic position against Germany, the *Truppenamt* did not discard the contingency of Soviet assistance against Poland. The Soviet Union could weaken if not destroy Poland in a Polish-Soviet war, or divert Polish forces in a German-Polish conflict.[99]

[95] Britain and the United States are not mentioned in the studies described above, but their neutrality (and Britain's support of Belgian neutrality) is assumed in the *Führerreise* of 1933; *RWM*, Jodl (T1) situation report (no date), II H 609/1.

[96] Manstein, *Soldatenleben*, pp. 131-32; *RWM*, *Truppenamt* directive for a transportation exercise, 9 April 1932, II H 594; Adam to staff officers, 10 January 1933, II H 600/3.

[97] Still, the *Truppenamt* did not ignore the contingency of a Czechoslovak attack; *RWM*, *Truppenamt* situation report for operational problem for General Staff officers, January 1931, II H 600/1.

[98] In December 1930 Lt. Col. Fischer (T3) told naval officers that the Army was " 'preparing an operational study to find out to what extent Russia and Lithuania can play their parts in our plans as allies against Poland.' " Carsten, *Reichswehr and Politics*, p. 284; see above, n. 21, for German-Lithuanian military relations.

[99] See preceding note. The Army considered neither of the Soviet

The notable innovations during the years of crisis were "German/Austria" and Italy as Germany's allies in a war with France. These new hybrids took root in Germany's diplomatic predicament as a result of the customs union project. The Army apparently surmised that Italy's need for allies against France (Mussolini's chief competitor for influence in the Mediterranean, Danube basin, and Balkans, and the ally of Italy's contiguous Balkan opponent, Yugoslavia) would outweigh Italian objections to an Austro-German combination, in these games an alliance, although an economic or political union is implied.[100]

Intradepartmental contradictions in military planning complicate an assessment of the Army's attitude toward a two-front war. The *Truppenamt*, having declared in the late 1920s that a conflict limited to the eastern front was unlikely, criticized the Navy in the early 1930s for basing its planning on the same pessimistic conclusion; yet the *Truppenamt* continued to study *Fall West* in its operational exercises.[101] As

---

nonaggression agreements with France and Poland in the exercises above.

[100] Since Locarno is not mentioned in the Army's theoretical situation reports, it would seem that the hypothesis of Italian support arose from international conditions not directly related to Italy's legal obligations as a guarantor of the security pact. On contacts between the German and Italian Armies in 1931 and T3's reconnaissance of the Franco-Italian border, see British military attaché report, 9 December 1931, *DBFP*, Ser. 2, II, 521; Castellan, *Réarmement*, p. 465.

[101] On the Navy and two fronts, see below. According to Castellan, "the German generals remained prisoners of a conception of Europe" dating back to Bismarck and the elder Moltke, namely, preparation for a war against France; in such a conflict, the Army "could expect . . . by no means negligible material aid from Soviet Russia." *Réarmement*, pp. 487, 494-95. But Castellan's thesis should be amended. In the first place, the Soviet Union might not have substantially supported Germany against France unless simultaneously at war with Poland or threatened by France. Indeed, in the *Führerreise* of May 1933, Germany was presumed to have requested and received Soviet divisions for the defense against France in a Polish-Soviet war; *RWM*, Jodl (T1) situation report (no date), and Adam critique, 1 June,

head of the *Ministeramt* and, later, as Chancellor, Schleicher hesitated to affront France; while Defense Minister under Papen, however, he appeared to ignore his own advice and risked increasing the likelihood of French military sanctions or French intervention in a German-Polish war.

The Army did not contemplate an offensive war.[102] It prepared for the defense of the Reich against external attack, for the emergency mobilization of the *A-Heer*: currently, the *marschbereites Reichsheer*; in the future, the *Feldheer* of 21 divisions. According to the Army Command's timetable for rearmament in five-year stages, Germany could engage in a defensive war against Poland with some prospect of success by 1933, against France by 1938, and by 1943-44 an offensive war against Poland or a two-front defense against France and Poland.[103] But because of domestic disunity, as well as delays and material shortages in fulfilling the *A-Plan*, the *Truppenamt* lacked confidence in the Army's defensive capability to fight even Poland alone.[104]

Nevertheless, as the Groener directive of April 1930 explained, the expanded armed forces might eventually exploit a situation to attain an objective.[105] Implicit in the operational problems that postulated a German-Polish war was the opportunity for Germany to mount a successful counteroffensive

II H 609/1. Second, in spite of overtones of "liberation," contingency planning and defensive preparations in the west were not inconsistent with the Army's alternative strategies to regain the lost eastern territories, an objective the Army hoped to attain without a major conflict in the west.

[102] Reports by British military experts, 1930-32, *DBFP*, Ser. 2, i, 598-603; ii, 515-24; iii, 602-605. See also François-Poncet, *Fateful Years*, p. 28; testimony of Joseph Wirth at Nürnberg, *Trials of War Criminals*, xii, 554-58.

[103] Sauer, "Mobilmachung der Gewalt," in Bracher, *Machtergreifung*, pp. 783-84; Hubatsch, *Admiralstab*, pp. 196-97; E. M. Robertson, *Hitler's Pre-War Policy and Military Plans 1933-1939* (American ed., New York, 1967), p. 21.

[104] Meinck, *Deutsche Aufrüstung*, pp. 7-8, 19; Roos, *Polen und Europa*, p. 7n.; below.

[105] See above, chap. 6.

into Poland to regain the lost territories.[106] The most promising circumstances to exploit would be provided by a Polish-Soviet war, in which Germany might acquire territorial spoils in Poland by blocking French intervention. The *Führerreise* of 1933 hypothesized a situation analogous to that of the winter war game of 1928-29: Germany signed a secret treaty with the Soviet Union, by the terms of which "Germany's old eastern borders should be restored" if Germany became engaged in hostilities by denying the French transit across Germany to help their Polish ally.[107]

The Army acknowledged the importance of joint planning and the ultimate authority of the government to order military resistance in case of Polish aggression.[108] Both departments treated operational planning as a highly secret matter, re-

---

[106] The *Truppenamt* did not overlook the possibility that, rather than seek a "decisive battle of annihilation" by enveloping the enemy, German commanders might have to resort to the more prosaic tactics of pushing back the major Polish attack directed toward Berlin. *RWM*, Adam critique of first operational problem of 1933 (no date), II H 600/3. Most officers had recommended an envelopment or double envelopment from Pomerania and Silesia, but Adam, warning against a blind charge through enemy forces that were dispersed but able to close quickly on the attacker, remarked that "to every Cannae belongs not only a Hannibal, but also a Terentius Varro."

[107] *RWM*, Jodl (T1) situation report (no date), II H 609/1; above, chap. 6.

[108] In a conference with representatives of the Foreign Office and Navy to discuss *Studie "Fall Danzig"* (see below), General Adam declared that the "statesman" would be the one to decide what action to take if Poland attacked Danzig. Groener envisaged the formation of a wartime "Reich defense cabinet" to insure cooperation between the political and military arms. It would be headed by the Chancellor, and would include the Defense Minister, Minister of the Interior, and heads of five or six other departments. Müller, *Vaterland*, p. 334. The Chief of the Army Command would probably have become supreme commander of the armed forces (*Chef der Wehrmacht*), for Groener and Schleicher apparently did not intend to claim control over operations for the Defense Minister; Meinck, *Deutsche Aufrüstung*, p. 113. According to Manstein, however, Groener never "completely renounced having influence on the conduct of operations." *Soldatenleben*, p. 283.

stricted to the executive-departmental sphere, beyond the competence of the Reichstag or the press. But the Foreign Office could not be sure that the Army's "renunciation of romanticism," which the Wilhelmstrasse had observed in the late 1920s, had survived the years of crisis. The operational hypotheses of the early 1930s provide evidence for the Army's awareness of international fluctuations, but also reveal its failure to reconcile theory with reality. German foreign policy during the years of crisis achieved a number of successes, but came nowhere near providing the international prerequisites for some of the Army's war games: the neutrality of Britain, the United States, and Czechoslovakia; the military allegiance of the Soviet Union; and Italian support of Germany (and the Soviet Union) in a European war.[109] The Foreign Office, no matter how impatient with the West and Poland, seems to have been less disillusioned than the Army about Germany's politico-military situation in January 1933, less emotional in its expectations, less romantic in its visions of liberation from the Treaty of Versailles.[110]

THE NAVY

In spite of the shifting international sands, naval planning did not change significantly in the early 1930s. Maritime re-

[109] In the *Führerreise* of 1933, Italy backed the Soviet Union in the League debate over which country had started the Polish-Soviet war, declared that it would withdraw from the League if France mobilized, and partially mobilized its own forces in order to tie down French units along the Franco-Italian border. *RWM*, Jodl (T1) situation report (no date), II H 609/1.

[110] Unlike similar documents of the late 1920s and early 1930s, the situation report for the *Führerreise* of 1933 did not give a dispassionate description of Germany's position; it began with the emotive hypothesis that Germany, "in the struggle for the recovery of its complete freedom, concluded a secret treaty with Russia. . . ." That treaty would restore "Germany's old eastern borders," not merely the Corridor, Danzig, and minor frontier adjustments in Posen and Silesia. *Ibid.* Moreover, in his critique of the game, General Adam affirmed that Germany needed "military freedom [*Wehrfreiheit*] and freedom from the chains of the Treaty of Versailles. . . ." *Ibid.*, 1 June.

covery and the defeat of France remained the Navy's major politico-military objectives. In August 1932 the Operations Section in the Naval Command outlined the international conditions that would afford Germany the most favorable naval position in a future war.[111] The Polish Navy was too small to challenge Germany for command of the Baltic Sea but might use foreign Baltic ports as bases for harassing Germany's Baltic communications. To deny the Poles this opportunity, German policy must make sure that Danzig, the Baltic States, and the Soviet Union maintain strict neutrality.[112] Germany did not require naval support from the Soviet Union; this confident attitude indicated the Naval Command's low regard for the combat effectiveness of the Red Baltic fleet, its unwillingness to jeopardize secret naval activity in Finland by collaborating with the Finns' eastern enemy, and its continuing distrust of the Bolsheviks' intentions in the event of a German-Polish conflict or the internal collapse of the Reich.[113] Because Denmark and Sweden flanked the narrow approaches from the Kattegat to the Baltic Sea, the ideal arrangement for Germany, the Operations Section observed, would allow German vessels free passage through the narrows while preventing that of hostile ships. At least, Germany needed the strict neutrality of the Scandinavian countries to prevent France from establishing bases on their territory.[114]

[111] *RWM, Flottenabteilung* memorandum, early August, PG 33611.

[112] On Poland and the Baltic, also *RWM,* Naval Command papers (Commander Lietzmann), 29 October 1930 and 4 June 1931, PG 33611, 48897, both summarized in Carsten, *Reichswehr and Politics,* pp. 361-62; *Flottenabteilung* paper, 16 December 1930, II M 49.

[113] On German-Soviet naval relations, also *RWM, Flottenabteilung* notes (copy sent to T3 of the *Truppenamt*) of conversation between German and Soviet naval representatives in Berlin, 7 March 1930, PG 33617, condensed in Erickson, *Soviet High Command,* pp. 276-77; Lietzmann papers (see preceding note).

[114] On Scandinavia and the Baltic entrances, also Lietzmann paper, 4 June 1931 (see n. 112 above). After a visit to Copenhagen in November 1932, Lietzmann reported that Danish naval leaders had assured him that they held "no naval agreement of any kind with France"; they thought it "absurd" to imagine that Denmark was in

The Naval Command usually assumed that the next war would be fought on Germany's two fronts, since the League and the Treaty of Locarno were ambiguous deterrents to French intervention even in a conflict in which Poland was clearly the aggressor. The *Reichsmarine* asserted Germany's "absolute dependence" on overseas trade through the North Sea in a two-front war, and, obsessed with Britain's geographic position and naval power, avowed British neutrality (preferably benevolent) to be a critical objective of German policy. Farther around the continental periphery, Germany should encourage Italian opposition to France in the Mediterranean; the more naval pressure on France there, the less likely the French Navy would be to commit large forces to the North Sea or the Baltic.[115]

The launching of the first battle cruiser, *Deutschland*, in May 1931 and the beginning of construction on *Panzerschiff B* encouraged the Navy not only to study the strategic implications of a conflict with France, but to practice "group tactics" designed for a *Handelskrieg* in the North Sea.[116] Moreover, because of the surge of frustrated national pride during the years of crisis, references to maritime security and pres-

---

tow of France, for Danish policy was based upon defense of Danish neutrality. *RWM*, Naval Command minute, late November, PG 48898.

[115] *RWM*, *Flottenabteilung* memorandum, early August 1931, PG 33611; Lietzmann papers and *Flottenabteilung* paper (see n. 112 above).

[116] *RWM*, Raeder report on autumn maneuver 1932, 22 December, II M 100/23; on the launching of the *Deutschland*, see Assmann, *Deutsche Seestrategie*, p. 112. The French had already begun construction of the "Dunkerque" class ship, stronger and faster than the German battle cruiser, and exceeding the limits for cruisers upon which Britain, the United States, and Japan had agreed at the London Naval Conference of 1930; Northedge, *Troubled Giant*, pp. 342-45; Wacker, *Bau des Panzerschiffes*, pp. 56-57. Nevertheless, the Naval Command continued its program to build more battle cruisers, hoping that superiority in numbers, gunnery, and tactics would give the German ships the edge in North Sea operations; *RWM*, Naval Command paper (Treue), 1939, PG 31871.

tige became shriller than in the late 1920s, and the connection between power and freedom more readily assumed. Captain Karl Schuster, head of the Fleet Department, defined policy as " 'the expression of the state's power.' " In Germany's current weak and landlocked position, it could only "vegetate." Germany must build a strong navy if it wanted to live, to breathe, to force open "the gateway to the world" and keep it open, to be free. Only with a powerful navy would Germany command the prestige (both *Seegeltung* and *Weltgeltung*) to defend the Reich and conduct a global policy.[117]

On a less passionate level, Groener's directive of 16 April 1930 and the subsequent consultation between the Naval Command and the office of the Defense Minister established the guidelines for naval planning in the event of an emergency. Different levels of naval force might be employed, analogous to the Army's preparations: the "navy ready for action" (*verwendungsbereite Reichsmarine*); the "reinforced navy" (*verstärkte Reichsmarine*, or *v.R.M.*), prepared for combat within seventy-two hours; and the "mobilized navy" (*aufgestellte Marine*, or *A-Marine*), requiring an additional ten days beyond the period needed to ready the "reinforced navy."[118]

If Poland should attack (*V-Fall Ost*), the Navy was by 1932 ready to execute *Studie Ost* (known as *Studie Gdingen* in the late 1920s), an operation plan designed to employ the "reinforced navy" against Polish naval forces, sea communications, and Gdingen.[119] *Studie Ost* presupposed that no

[117] *RWM*, Schuster papers, presented to *Führergehilfen* of both services, 4 and 11 March 1932, II M 57/41, 57/53; 9 and 18 January 1933, II M 59/1. The definition of policy is that of Wegener, whom Schuster quoted approvingly; see above, chap. 7, n. 22 and, for the terms *Seegeltung* and *Weltgeltung*, n. 12.

[118] *RWM*, Groener to Chiefs of Army and Naval Commands, "Die Aufgaben der Wehrmacht," PG 34072; Raeder directive, September 1930, PG 33442.

[119] *RWM*, directive written by Schuster for Raeder, "Operative Weisungen des Chefs der Marineleitung für den Einsatz der 'verstärkten Reichsmarine' im V-Fall 'Ost,' " 11 April 1931, PG 33306a;

French naval units had entered the Baltic. Other plans in preparation, as well as the Navy's operational exercises, examined the broader strategic hypothesis of a two-front war.[120] In these, the Navy retained its penchant for North Sea operations, already evident in naval planning in the late 1920s. German commerce would "stand or fall with the neutrality of the two Anglo-Saxon Great Powers." Franco-Italian tension, and the necessity for France to protect troop transports from its North African colonies, should preoccupy the French Navy in the Mediterranean.[121] Under these favorable circum-

---

Chief of Staff of Fleet Command to Chief of the Naval Command concerning revised orders for execution of *Studie Ost*, 23 November 1932, PG 34118; tactical preparations and modifications in files PG 34102, 34118, 33965b. See the allusion to *Studie Ost* in evidence presented at Nürnberg, *Trial of the Major War Criminals before the International Military Tribunal* (42 vols.; Nuremberg, 1947-49), xxxiv, 471-77 (document 135-C).

[120] The Navy's four "operational studies": I, *Studie Ost*; II, *Studie Ostseeverteidigung* (see above, chap. 7, n. 15); III, *Studie Zufuhr-Schutz*; IV, *Erweiterte Studie Ost*. The Naval Command had completed the first of these on paper by November 1930; anticipated finishing the second and third by summer 1931; and probably early in 1932 began the fourth, a study that included the contingency of a Polish occupation of Danzig and other Baltic ports (see below for *Studie "Fall Danzig,"* apparently a part of *Erweiterte Studie Ost*). *RWM*, Boehm briefing of senior officers at commanders' conference (*Führerbesprechung*) in Kiel, 26-27 November 1930, PG 34066; *Studie* III, summer 1931, PG 33444. *Studie* III considered measures to defend German communications in the North Sea, assuming that the United States and Britain would remain neutral if not allied with Germany. The Navy incorporated its *Studien* into theoretical war games, but intended each of them to become an actual plan of operation. The Navy issued directives for the possible execution of *Studie Ost* (see preceding note), and *Studie Ost* can properly be called an operation plan, probably the only one in existence in either service by 1933.

[121] *RWM*, notes for Raeder critique of autumn maneuver 1930, 12 September, and Raeder's final report on the game, 7 March 1931, PG 34051; *AA*, Naval Command to Foreign Office, situation reports for *Führerkriegsspiel*, 8 January 1932, K6/K000641-53; *RWM*,

stances the German Navy could hope to contend with France for command of the North Sea.[122] Raeder urged naval officers not to forget this, their long-range assignment to protect Germany's North Sea communications. And Commander Karl Dönitz, observing that the loss of East Prussia would "never decide the outcome of a war," concluded that the decisive land and sea actions in a two-front war would be fought in the west.[123]

The Navy stayed on the periphery of civil-military relations during the years of crisis. Although Admiral Raeder advised against outlawing the *S.A.* and *S.S.* without simultaneously dissolving the *Reichsbanner*, he refused to act as Schleicher's accomplice in the political maneuvering against Groener.[124] The political bias toward National Socialism among junior naval officers increased sharply in the early 1930s as the Nazis poured scorn over the republic and over the Social Democrats' allegedly unpatriotic opposition to the Navy's construction program.[125] But Raeder and most of the officer corps abhorred Nazi extremism and preferred the eclipse of an inept Reichstag by an authoritarian presidential system.

Raeder report on autumn maneuver 1932, 22 December, II M 100/23; also Gemzell, *Raeder, Hitler und Skandinavien*, pp. 36-43.

[122] *RWM*, Lietzmann paper, 4 June 1931, PG 48897. Gemzell maintains that the Navy's change to the maritime strategy coincided with the publication of Wegener's book in 1929 (above, chap. 7, n. 22), but he does not account for the persistence of the battle strategy alongside the new school in the 1930s; *Raeder, Hitler und Skandinavien*, pp. 36-41.

[123] *RWM*, Raeder briefing at commanders' conference in Kiel, 26-27 November 1930, PG 34066; Dönitz paper, 1932, II M 57/51; Schuster papers (see n. 117 above); Hubatsch, *Generalstab*, pp. 194-95.

[124] Carsten, *Reichswehr and Politics*, pp. 341-51, *passim*; Raeder, *My Life*, pp. 159-61.

[125] Karl Heinz Abshagen, *Canaris*, trans. Alan H. Brodrick (London, 1956), pp. 61, 64f.; Carsten, *Reichswehr and Politics*, p. 314; Admiral Leopold Bürkner, Zeugenschrifttum no. 364, Institut für Zeitgeschichte (Munich).

The Navy was more impatient than the Foreign Office to restore naval attachés,[126] and readier to accelerate the pace toward Germany's freedom to rearm.[127] Still, the Naval Command encouraged cooperation with the Foreign Office because of the interdependence of military planning and foreign policy. In January 1931, on the invitation of the Fleet Department, Ernst von Weizsäcker addressed naval *Führergehilfen* on the subject, "Policy and National Defense." Citing the German invasion of Belgium in 1914 as an example of what could happen if the armed forces and Foreign Office did not collaborate, this former officer of the Imperial Navy charged his audience to recognize the connection between policy and defense planning during both peace and war, and to help implement that principle at the departmental level.[128] Captain Schuster returned to this theme a year later, asserting that Clausewitz applied to naval as well as land warfare; naval strategy depends on the political objective, which must not exceed military competence.[129] On the Baltic, in a two-front war or a conflict with Poland alone, Germany had to be especially observant of the complex legal and political impli-

[126] Kehrig, *Wiedereinrichtung*, pp. 123-24, 132-41; *AA*, Bülow to Neurath concerning future naval attachés to London, Paris, Rome, Washington, Tokyo, and Stockholm, as well as a naval assistant for the military attaché to Moscow, 9 January 1933, 3177/D683463-4.

[127] On the Navy's *Umbauplan*, which Schleicher approved in November 1932, see Assmann, *Deutsche Seestrategie*, p. 115; Hubatsch, *Admiralstab*, p. 197; Raeder, *My Life*, p. 162; also *RWM*, Naval Command notes for use at the Disarmament Conference, 15 January 1932, PG 31783; Naval Command paper (Treue), 1939, PG 31871, including Naval Command memorandum of 29 July 1932 on German naval aims in disarmament negotiations.

[128] *AA*, Flottenabteilung to Foreign Office, 5 July 1930; Bülow to *Flottenabteilung*, 27 September; K6/K000495, 522; text of Weizsäcker's lecture, *ibid.*, K000557-75; the *Flottenabteilung* thanked the Foreign Office for Weizsäcker's address, as well as a similar talk by Forster (date and exact subject unknown), *ibid.*, K000556.

[129] *RWM*, Schuster paper before Army and Navy *Führergehilfen*, 4 March 1932, II M 57/41. Quoting Wegener on *Weltpolitik*, Schuster supposed that the Foreign Office would be the Navy's " 'twin-brother' " in pursuing a policy of sea power.

336

cations of naval operations, since Germany lacked the *Macht* to pressure Denmark and Sweden, or to risk the disapprobation of the League. Therefore the Navy must cooperate with the Foreign Office during peacetime, to insure that Germany's international situation would be as favorable as possible in the event of war.[130]

Studie Ost and *Studie "Fall Danzig"* marked the high point of joint planning between the Navy and Foreign Office during the Weimar period.[131] In January 1930 the Naval Command described the politico-military foundations of *Studie Ost*.[132] Weak and surrounded by military alliances, Germany could not conceivably fight even a limited war with a small state; nor could it count on a mobilization period (*Anlaufzeit*) before the outbreak of hostilities, for open signs of rearmament while it was still at peace would give the enemy political justification for immediate attack. Nevertheless, Germany should be prepared to counter an enemy attack with available and quickly mobilized auxiliary forces. If the government should order armed self-defense against an attempted Polish *fait accompli*, the Navy would recommend the execution of *Studie Ost* to demonstrate Germany's determination to resist, to neutralize Gdingen before Poland could secure it indefinitely as a base of operations against German communications with East Prussia, and to discourage other powers— notably France—from intervening on the side of Poland by eliminating Poland's seaport. The Naval Command wanted the benefit of the Wilhelmstrasse's opinion of *Studie Ost*, the use of prohibited weapons in executing it, and the efficacy of

[130] *RWM*, Lietzmann paper, 4 June 1931, PG 48897; Naval Command memorandum, 3 August, II M 48; Schuster paper, 11 March 1932, II M 57/53; *Flottenabteilung* memorandum, early August 1932, PG 33611; Naval Command minute on Lietzmann's visit to Copenhagen (see n. 114 above).

[131] Although the Chancellors in the early 1930s approved the preparation of secret contingency plans for naval action against Poland, they usually delegated the Foreign Office to represent the political point of view in joint planning.

[132] *AA*, Naval Command to Foreign Office, 16 January, K7/ K000669-77.

diplomatic steps in preventing unfavorable foreign reactions to Germany's emergency measures. Further, the *Marineleitung* asked, what diplomatic moves might deny Poland the use of Danzig as a naval base, and, should these fail, at what point could Germany justifiably begin operations against Polish forces in Danzig without showing consideration for the city's neutrality?

Foreign Office officials replied in a conference with representatives of the Naval Command on 26 June.[133] The Wilhelmstrasse's attitude toward such an attack would depend "on the general political situation at the outbreak of a conflict with Poland." In order to prevent Germany from being labeled the "aggressor" by international opinion, the Foreign Office would make every effort to settle the dispute peacefully or, failing that, to contain the conflict through the action of the League Council. The diplomats would not object to the use of forbidden weapons (mines and airplanes) in the Baltic if the government declared the assault politically permissible.

The political justification the Foreign Office might adduce for emergency defensive measures would also depend on the nature of the German-Polish struggle and the international situation, but the diplomats would probably implore the League to take the fastest possible action, and point out that Germany had signed the Kellogg Pact. Finally, the Foreign Office saw that Poland might seize Danzig in a war with Germany; the diplomats were examining the possible diplomatic means by which Germany could help Danzig to force Poland to remove its munitions depot from the Westerplatte and prevent Polish exploitation of Danzig as a naval base. The Foreign Office might also request a neutral power (Britain or Italy) to occupy Danzig and guarantee its neutrality. If all these measures failed to deter the Poles, then Germany would have the right to attack enemy forces in the Free City, since they threatened East Prussia and German sea communica-

---

[133] *AA*, joint protocol of meeting, *ibid.*, K000683-8; also Foreign Office memoranda of May and June on Poland's legal rights in Danzig in the event of war, *ibid.*, K000681-2, 690-1, 698-718.

tions. The joint protocol of the meeting concluded with the strong statement that only the political leadership, having abandoned hope of ending the hostilities through diplomatic channels, could order an attack against either Gdingen or Danzig.[134]

In 1932 the Naval Command conferred with Brüning and representatives of the Foreign Office and Army Command about the contingency of a Polish seizure of Danzig, in this case (unlike *Studie Ost*) while Germany and Poland were not at war. On 6 May, with tension abnormally high on the German-Polish border, Brüning told Raeder that, although Poland would probably not move against Danzig so long as Pilsudski remained in power, he still wanted the Defense Ministry and Foreign Office to plan retaliatory measures.[135] Brüning therewith gave the government's imprimatur to the Navy's preparation of *Studie "Fall Danzig."* The Naval Command feared that the government's failure to act would cause internal unrest and the loss of international prestige. In the Wilhelmstrasse Bülow concurred, and he supported the recommendation of Admiral Groos (Chief of the Naval Command Office): if Polish regular or irregular forces attacked Danzig, Germany should send a warship to the Free City. But the Naval Command soon retracted this counsel, anxious lest the ship provide the Poles with both an excuse and easy prey should they intend to launch hostilities against the Reich after occupying Danzig. The Navy acknowledged its subordination

[134] In subsequent correspondence and operational exercises, the Naval Command adhered to this principle of subordination to the "politische Führung" for the order to prepare the "reinforced Navy" for action and to execute *Studie Ost*: *RWM*, Naval Command notes of commanders' conference in Kiel, 26-27 November 1930, PG 34066; *AA*, Naval Command to Foreign Office, 9 December, K7/ K000728-30; Forster minutes of 9 and 21 May 1931, *ibid.*, K000731-3 (Forster probably represented the Foreign Office at the Navy's conference in Kiel in November 1930; *Flottenabteilung* to Foreign Office, 8 November, K6/K000523).

[135] *RWM*, Naval Command minute, 6 May, PG 34089. The Naval Command seems to have proposed this meeting with the Chancellor; *Flottenabteilung* memorandum, 4 May, *ibid.*

to orders from the government, however, adding the unnecessary reminder that the political leadership, should it decide on political grounds to send a warship, would "bear the full responsibility for the consequences."[136]

Although the Navy subordinated its Baltic contingency plans to foreign policy considerations and the control of the political arm, it did not do the same with its broader strategic assumption of a war against France. Perhaps some naval officers saw a reassuring confirmation of that assumption in the more hostile policy of the French and in the more "active" policy of German civilian leaders, who attempted to win the support of the United States, Britain, and Italy against France in reparations and disarmament negotiations. Perhaps also some diplomats reinforced the Navy's western expectations on a number of occasions: when they addressed the question of neutrals' rights in a future *Handelskrieg* with France instead of rejecting the contingency of a Franco-German conflict as politically improbable and militarily hopeless;[137] when a Foreign Office official asserted that the world would gradually have to "accustom itself again to the German flag as a factor in international politics";[138] and when the diplomats failed to demand clarification of the relationship between hypothesis and reality in the Navy's operational exercises— Raeder's situation report for the *Führerkriegsspiel* of 1932 explicitly stated that the game would study North Sea operations against France, using battle cruisers.[139] Nevertheless,

---

[136] *RWM*, Naval Command notes of conference among Groos, Bülow, Meyer, Hey (in the Eastern Department), and, representing the Army, General Adam and Colonel Fischer, 26 August 1932, PG 34117; various naval documents, December 1932 and January 1933, *ibid.*

[137] *AA*, Foreign Office correspondence with Naval Command relating to *Führerkriegsspiel* 1932, K6/K000640-60, especially Martius notes of his remarks at the exercise, held in Kiel at the end of January, K000654-5.

[138] *AA*, Weizsäcker address before naval *Führergehilfen*, 8 January 1931, *ibid.*, K000559.

[139] *AA*, 8 January 1932, *ibid.*, K000648; Raeder also referred to the Navy's *Studie* III (see n. 120 above).

in spite of its diplomatic travails during the years of crisis, the Foreign Office had neither concluded that a "war of liberation" against France was inevitable nor inferred from the international situation that Germany could rely upon the neutrality of Britain and the United States and the support of Italy in the Mediterranean.[140] Had the collaboration between the Foreign Office and Naval Command in operational exercises been less superficial, the diplomats might have grown more aware and critical of the essential continuity in naval planning. Moreover, naval officers might have moderated their enthusiasm for *Handelskrieg* in the North Sea in view of the uncertainty of the international barometer measuring freedom of movement in a future war. And both professions might have achieved in practice Schuster's application of Clausewitzean theory to foreign policy and naval planning.

The ideal of cooperation between the two services also fell short of realization in practice. Under the existing command system in the armed services, the Navy enjoyed a certain amount of freedom; no joint staff existed to coordinate planning, an institutional innovation that would probably have reinforced the dominance of the Army in national defense.[141] The Navy's construction program benefited from the support of Groener and Schleicher, yet the Naval Command was not forced to disown the western strategy for which the cruisers were designed. And the Navy could follow the general guidelines in Groener's directive of April 1930 without having to conform to the same set of operational priorities as the Army in *A-Plan* preparations.[142]

---

[140] *RWM, Flottenabteilung* situation reports for war game, April 1933, PG 34076.

[141] The Naval Command continued to fear that its material needs and strategic ideas might be ignored in a joint command which institutionalized the preponderance of the Army in defense planning; Meinck, *Deutsche Aufrüstung*, pp. 111-13, 219n.

[142] The *Flottenabteilung* would "clarify the strategic and tactical inferences" drawn from the general directives of the Defense Minister insofar as these pertained to the Navy; *RWM*, Raeder memorandum, 14 January 1930, PG 33442.

341

In 1932 the Army declared that it was "in no position to wage war."[143] If a German-Polish conflict did erupt, the *Truppenamt* would not have a fixed plan of operations, but would base its movements on the enemy's. Should the Army counterattack from Pomerania, it expected the Navy's cooperation; the *Truppenamt* would not consider supporting *Studie Ost* from Pomerania or East Prussia until much larger land forces were available.[144] Moreover, in conversations concerning *Studie "Fall Danzig,"* the *Truppenamt* flatly rejected the Navy's condition for sending a warship to the Free City; the Army would not think of ordering East Prussian units (regular or irregular) to march on Danzig if the Poles threatened the German vessel.[145]

The Army's *A-Plan* also did not mesh with the Navy's in terms of Germany's broad strategic capabilities. Certainly the Navy did not ignore the possibility that the Soviet threat might divert Polish troops; nor did the Army disregard the contingency of Italian support against France. For the Navy, however, the bearing of the "Anglo-Saxon" naval powers and Scandinavian states counted far more than the posture of the Soviet Union; in the Army's exercises, Italy had only recently appeared as a reflection of changing international circumstances, not a virtual *sine qua non* of a war with France. The Navy consistently treated the Polish question as a minor consideration in the two-front war to free Germany from the chains of Versailles. Although Army officers were not immune to the "utopian" idea of a "war of liberation," the *Truppenamt* declared that the Army would not even be able to consider a two-front defensive war until 1944. Meanwhile, the *Truppenamt* affirmed, the armed forces must cooperate

[143] *RWM*, Manstein (T1) at conference with naval representatives to discuss *Studie "Fall Danzig,"* early August, PG 34117.

[144] *RWM*, Naval Command memorandum, 2 July 1932, and *Truppenamt* to Naval Command, 17 October, PG 34095; also documents in files PG 34102, 34118.

[145] See above, n. 136; also *RWM*, Naval Command notes of conference with Manstein (T1) and Fischer (T3), early August 1932, PG 34117.

in preparing for *Fall Ost*, and neither service should base its rearmament and operational planning on *Fall West*. In any conflict, on one or two fronts, the Army would determine the pace and objectives of operations. In reply, out of step with policy in the Foreign Office and planning in the Army Command, the Naval Command persevered; even in case of a conflict restricted to the eastern front, Germany must be prepared to ward off French intervention; building a strong Navy to defend Germany's "freedom to the west" required foresight and time.[146]

[146] *RWM*, Schuster papers, 4 March 1932 and 9 January 1933 (see n. 117 above); Naval Command memorandum, 7 April 1933, PG 34095; Naval Command paper (Captain Ciliax), February 1936, PG 33965b; Gerhard Bidlingmaier, "Die strategischen und operative Überlegungen der Marine 1932-1942," *Wehrwissenschaftliche Rundschau*, XIII (1963), 313, *passim*; Hubatsch, *Admiralstab*, pp. 196-97.

Conclusion

DURING the years of stability, 1924-29, Gustav Stresemann served as both party leader and Foreign Minister; responsible to the Reichstag, expert in articulating national objectives and negotiating them, Stresemann combined the parliamentary and bureaucratic interests in his conduct of foreign policy. Under his guidance, the Foreign Office pursued interrelated goals—sovereignty, security, and territorial revision—in a peaceful and conciliatory fashion. The diplomats believed that Rapallo and Locarno would be instrumental in regaining the lost eastern territories without war, for such agreements improved Germany's leverage over Poland in negotiations concerning international trade, the minority question, and revision of the Treaty of Versailles. But the Wilhelmstrasse also used its eastern and western policies to strengthen Germany's strategic position by surrounding Poland with a potential German-Soviet alliance, weakening the Franco-Polish alliance, and maintaining illegal rearmament on Soviet as well as German soil.

Military leaders discovered that the diplomats were aware of the relationship between foreign policy and military planning. Indeed, Gessler, Groener, Schleicher, Heye, the *Truppenamt*, Zenker, Raeder, and the *Flottenabteilung* shared with the diplomats the following politico-military axioms: Germany's international situation was unfavorable and its military power inadequate to risk war (especially a two-front war); Germany must rearm and might become engaged in a future war, not because of strictly defensive necessity, but from a willingness to use force to take back the lost eastern territories if peaceful means failed; the military leadership should promote the military point of view energetically, but, in the manner of Clausewitz, military planning should be co-ordinated with and be subordinate to foreign policy, and the military arm should subserve the political leadership, of which the Foreign Office was a departmental segment.

Because of these common assumptions and the conscientious efforts of civilian and military leaders to apply them in practice, foreign policy became closely interwoven with military planning in the Weimar system of civil-military relations. Interdepartmental cooperation between the Foreign Office and Defense Ministry, the foundation of the Weimar system, increased after Seeckt's dismissal in October 1926 and the withdrawal of the Inter-Allied Military Control Commission in January 1927. From joint planning at the departmental level came the evaluations of Germany's power relative to foreign armed forces and of Germany's position with respect to foreign alignments and treaty obligations; joint planning encompassed the organization, expansion, and mobilization of the Reichswehr for national defense; and joint planning extended into operational studies for the employment of the armed forces, either in self-defense or for the "exploitation of a favorable political situation" such as a Polish-Soviet war.

In joint planning differences came to the surface. The Foreign Office gained authority over the Army's activities in the Soviet Union, but the diplomats continued to weigh the actual usefulness and strategic advantages of this military collaboration cautiously against its possible damage to Germany's western policy. The *Truppenamt* agreed with the Wilhelmstrasse that rapprochement with France might help prevent the escalation of a German-Polish conflict into a dreaded two-front war; yet the *Truppenamt*, concerned with security on both fronts, advocated a western *Grenzschutz* in implicit defiance of Stresemann's western policy of understanding and the Defense Minister's consequent prohibition of defensive measures in the demilitarized Rhineland. The *Truppenamt* resented the waves made by Schleicher's *Ministeramt* in both the organizational and operational waters of military planning. The Foreign Office could not trust the Army or Navy to define the relationship between theoretical operational exercises and the actual international situation carefully and consistently. In the inter-service conflict between the continental anti-Polish strategy of the Army and the maritime anti-French strategy of the Navy, the Wilhelmstrasse clearly backed the former, assigning the Navy a minor role in national defense.

In spite of these differences, the Foreign Office and Defense Ministry were united in the conviction that political or civilian primacy over politico-military activity should be restricted to the executive and its departments, not portioned out to the Reichstag or the Prussian government. This persuasion developed partly in response to the need for secrecy in advancing illegal *Landesschutz* and mobilization plans; it also reflected the departments' and the executive's strong preference for bureaucratic expertise and efficiency in defense planning, competences jeopardized by party politics in the Reichstag and obstructed by the Social Democratic government of Prussia.

The principles of executive-departmental control and interdepartmental collaboration which undergirded the Weimar system of civil-military relations neither explicitly violated the constitution nor completely settled the civil-military conflicts inherent in the constitution and conspicuous in practice during the years of stability. Indeed, to some degree the Weimar system—and the governments of the late 1920s—anticipated the characteristics of civil-military relations and the *Präsidialstaat* of the years of crisis, 1930-33: presidential interference, personal bickering and scheming, nonparty experts as ministers, ministerial responsibility to the President rather than the Reichstag, interdepartmental and intradepartmental disagreements, military interference in political affairs, tension between the Reich and Prussia, and inter-service rivalry. But by and large, the environment of relative international and domestic stability and the definition of political primacy, in which the political and military leadership coincided, combined to provide the atropine necessary to control institutional spasms in civil-military relations. Had such circumstances endured, the Weimar system would probably have survived with its authoritarian profile, excluding the Reichstag from important politico-military decisions, consolidating itself at the departmental level without emergency executive decrees or excessive intervention from the President and Chancellor, and trying to answer looming constitutional questions within the executive-departmental sphere without resorting to drastic institutional change.

The crisis of the early 1930s affected both the institutional bases and the methods of German foreign policy. Curtius was the last Weimar party minister in the Wilhelmstrasse; his resignation in October 1931 signalled the surging pressure of public criticism and the drift toward greater departmental separation from the party conflict in the Reichstag. Brüning, Papen, and Schleicher, Curtius, Neurath, and Bülow all regarded revision of Versailles as an immediate domestic necessity as well as the foreign policy objective that Stresemann had not fully achieved. In search of instant revisionist victories, they pursued a more "active" policy toward the West, abandoning Stresemann's conciliatory manner to test a more contentious style of negotiation. But western concessions over reparations and disarmament did not stabilize German politics, nor permit a German-Austrian customs union, nor give Germany sufficient diplomatic and strategic advantage to press for a resolution of the Polish question. Germany's *Ostpolitik* retained the general contours it had been given during the Stresemann era, in spite of Papen's inclination toward forming an anti-Soviet bloc with Poland and France, and even after the Soviet Union had signed nonaggression agreements with France and Poland in 1932. Reluctant to discard its eastern policy in reply to changing international circumstances, Berlin continued to postpone revision of the German-Polish border, avoiding in the meantime any compromise settlement or reconciliation with Poland that implied recognition of the borders, and preserving the Rapallo tie as a strategic counterbalance to Poland.

The Defense Ministry and Foreign Office maintained joint planning; they cooperated in the reinstitution of military and naval attachés, the evaluation of Germany's strategic situation, the implementation of unlawful national defense programs, the campaign for revision of the military clauses of the Treaty of Versailles, the study of operational contingencies, and the preparation of the Navy's *Studie Ost* and *Studie "Fall Danzig"* with respect to a clash with Poland. The differences that had emerged at this departmental level during the 1920s persisted. The Wilhelmstrasse feared that secret military collaboration with the Red Army might harm Germany's relations with the West. The Army agreed with the Foreign Office that the Allied evacuation of the Rhineland in 1930 weakened the Franco-Polish alliance further, that Germany must not risk a two-front war by alarming France, and that *Landesschutz* should be based on the one-front strategy of a war with Poland. Yet the *Truppenamt* studied *Fall West* (defense against French attack); Defense Minister Schleicher startled the French with bellicose statements about Germany's political and military rights in the summer of 1932; and Blomberg recommended an escalation of Germany's revisionist demands, including remilitarization of the Rhineland, shortly after the West had recognized Germany's equality of rights at the Geneva Disarmament Conference in December 1932. The intervention of Groener and Schleicher in domestic politics increased along with the Nazi extremism which they hoped to control by absorbing the *S.A.* within an expanded standing army and militia; although the Army officer corps shared the Bendlerstrasse's fear of civil war and nervous disdain for the *S.A.*'s military self-image, many officers were growing more and more irritated with the *Ministeramt*'s politics and power over military affairs. The Navy opposed the organization of a joint inter-service command that would have been dominated by the Army, regretted the Army's refusal to commit troops to *Studie Ost* and *Studie "Fall Danzig,"* and insisted that military planning be based on the contingency of a two-front war since France remained Germany's arch-enemy. In spite of the Army's failure to reconcile hypothetical operational contingencies (in which Austria and Italy now figured at Germany's side) with Germany's actual strategic situation, the Foreign Office and Army together were essentially committed to the one-front eastern strategy.

The crisis did not cause this politico-military inconsonance, but it convulsed the central political nervous system in which foreign policy and military planning functioned, magnifying those institutional pressures that had been kept under control in the preceding years and weakening the mutual accord on the principle of political primacy. At the federal level, in July 1932 the Papen government decided to resolve Reich-Prussian dualism once and for all. Alleging that the Prussian government could no longer maintain law and order, Papen persuaded Hindenburg to sign a presidential decree appointing the Chancellor Reich Commissioner of Prussia. Papen's Prussian coup of 20 July was applauded by Neurath and Schleicher, the officer corps, and the bureaucracy, all of whom had grown convinced that the consequences of dualism and Social Democrats in high Prussian offices would be continued political embarrassment and military insecurity for the Reich. Neither the ambivalent Supreme Court ruling in October nor Papen's subsequent consolidation of Reich authority by taking over the Prussian administration resolved this dualism completely in favor of the central government, and remnants of the Braun-Severing regime survived into the first week of Hitler's chancellorship.[1] Still, the Reich-Prussian relationship had changed radically; the central authorities were in a better position to execute national defense policy, legal or illegal, in the largest *Land*.

[1] On the coup and Reich-Prussian relations in the early 1930s, see Beck, *Prussian Republic*, chaps. 4, 5; Bracher, *Auflösung*, pp. 565-600; Carsten, *Reichswehr and Politics*, pp. 339-40, 368-70, 376; Dorpalen, *Hindenburg*, pp. 342-45, 368-70; Eyck, *Weimar Republic*, II, 410-25; Liang, *Berlin Police Force*, pp. 152-61; Vogelsang, *Reichswehr und NSDAP*, pp. 235-50, 466-75, 480, 486.

In the executive-departmental sphere, the President, Chancellors, bureaucrats, and generals still agreed that the Reichstag should not control matters of national defense, but simply provide stable and patriotic support for military budgets and other policies emanating from them. But within this sphere, personal maneuvering and the encroachment of some officials on the responsibilities of others colored the practices of the *Präsidialstaat* and undermined the institutional foundations recently laid by the Weimar system. Brüning required the aid of a presidential decree to ban the *S.A.* and *S.S.*; Papen needed a decree to subvert the Prussian government. Brüning, Groener, and Schleicher combined cabinet portfolios, concentrating greater power in the Reich Chancery and Defense Ministry. Papen and Schleicher pursued foreign policies without and against the advice of the Foreign Office. Papen and Schleicher themselves diverged over how the executive should deal with the Reichstag. Papen would have risked civil war by temporarily suspending the Reichstag, a violation of the constitution. Schleicher believed that the nonparty cabinet of barons he inherited from Papen must be reshuffled to include a few party ministers; in this way, the government might secure a parliamentary majority for a program of public works and social reform. Neurath and other bureaucrats viewed Schleicher's plan as a repudiation of the presidential cabinet and return to the party cabinet, a reversal they considered antithetical to sound government.[2] Neurath resented the intrusion of Papen and Schleicher into foreign policy in the summer of 1932, and consulted only President Hindenburg—not the Chancellor or the cabinet—before leaving for Geneva early in December.

Schleicher's political adventurism as Defense Minister in 1932 marked the culmination of Seeckt's peculiar application of Clausewitz to the Weimar Republic: the conditional definition of "political leadership," and the military's selective

[2] Heineman, "Neurath as Foreign Minister," pp. 124-25, 217-19; Vogelsang, *Reichswehr und NSDAP*, p. 487.

obedience to that leadership. Schleicher would obey the President, not the Chancellor. He would cooperate with the Foreign Office at the departmental level only if its policy agreed with his. His intervention went far beyond giving advice, which would have been consistent with interdepartmental collaboration according to Clausewitz and the Weimar system. The position of the Foreign Office became stronger between July 1932 and January 1933, but Defense Minister Schleicher had jolted interdepartmental relations in a manner that suggests that he might have done so again as Chancellor and Defense Minister, after stabilizing domestic politics and finding more space on his docket for foreign affairs.

Because of these disputes and concomitant pressures, by January 1933 the center of gravity in German foreign policy and military planning had shifted from interdepartmental to executive-departmental relations. The *Präsidialstaat* and crisis system of civil-military relations left the major problems within the executive-departmental sphere acute: the degree of presidential interference and the relationship between the President and Chancellor; the Chancellor's readiness to assume or defy the competence of bureaucratic departments; and the relative influence of the Foreign Minister and Defense Minister. The future institutional profile of the executive-departmental sphere would determine the authority of the Foreign Office and Defense Ministry over foreign policy and military planning, the conduct of joint planning at the departmental level, the choice of strategies for national defense and territorial revision, and the further evolution of civil-military relations.

The Weimar system of civil-military relations had fostered a high degree of departmental authority in the formulation and implementation of national policy. The crisis system had threatened this departmental dominion by increasing the Chancellor's power relative to that of the departments; but under this system the extraparliamentary administration of state affairs by departmental experts had also increased. Both of these Weimar experiences helped to persuade the Foreign

Office and Defense Ministry that each would enjoy a privileged position and exercise considerable political power under the Hitler regime, especially since Neurath and Blomberg—one a professional diplomat, the other a professional soldier who remained on the active list as Defense Minister—had received the personal blessing of President Hindenburg. Hitler acceded to the chancellorship on 30 January 1933 with the assistance of Blomberg (who disregarded an order from the Bendlerstrasse when called by the President to accept the position of Defense Minister), the enthusiastic approval of those officers and bureaucrats who believed in the "national revolution" promised by Hitler, and the willing indulgence of other civilian and military officials (including Schleicher and Hammerstein) who assumed that the new Chancellor and his mass following could be controlled by a cabinet dominated by conservatives and supported by a Reichstag majority amenable to conservative authoritarian rule.

Within a few months, however, Hitler had armed himself with emergency powers not subject to presidential constraint, "coordinated" the civil service, state governments, and other institutions, and abolished all political parties except his own. The process of *Gleichschaltung* and the swift realization of the Nazi dictatorship changed the institutional configuration of German civil-military relations. Like its predecessors in the Weimar Republic, the Nazi system of civil-military relations claimed to be "legal" or legitimate as well as efficient, and adjusted the principle of civilian control to conform with a new set of political assumptions and circumstances. First, Hitler eliminated the parliamentary and federal levels; then, resolved to be dictator, Hitler transformed the decision-making process in the executive-departmental sphere. After Hindenburg's death in August 1934, Hitler ended the duality and rivalry between the President and Chancellor—largely a fiction since the Enabling Act of 23 March 1933, although a reality in the republic—by assuming the title of "Führer and Reich Chancellor." Hitler mistrusted and disdained career bureaucrats and aristocratic officers as much as he needed

353

their obedience and administrative talents. Consequently he did not allow the Nazi Party to assimilate these departmental pillars of the Reich; he shrewdly flattered the professionals' faith in their own administrative expertise; and he reduced and ultimately ended the authority the departments had established in policy-making in the 1920s and had defended against encroachment by the Chancellor during the years of crisis.

Although Neurath lost influence over the determination of foreign policy goals and means, he and the great majority of German diplomats stayed on. They accepted their declining status in policy-making; they successfully guarded their remaining departmental prerogatives against eclipse by party agencies and individuals competing with the Wilhelmstrasse and with each other in the field of foreign policy; the diplomats reorganized the Foreign Office along pre-Weimar lines, reviving the old "Political Department"; they embraced the *Führerprinzip* as a guarantee of decisive executive action above a maze of overlapping jurisdictions among state and party agencies; finally, they assiduously contributed their professional skill to the implementation of Hitler's foreign policy moves.[3]

By restoring order, purging the *S.A.*, and rearming Germany, Hitler began to fulfill the alluring promises which he had made to the armed forces: they would not be burdened with internal police duties, a distasteful task during the Weimar Republic; they would be the state's "sole bearer of arms" for national defense; they would have to expand if Germany ever hoped to defend itself, cast off the chains of Versailles, and return to continental stature. In 1933 the military welcomed a stronger executive, assuming that the role of the military arm as counsel and colleague would remain both important and compatible with the principle of civilian primacy.

[3] See Heineman, "Neurath as Foreign Minister"; Hill, "Wilhelmstrasse in the Nazi Era"; Jacobsen, *Nationalsozialistische Aussenpolitik*; Gerhard L. Weinberg, *The Foreign Policy of Hitler's Germany: Diplomatic Revolution in Europe 1933-36* (Chicago, 1970).

354

But Hitler feared a recurrence of the kind of selective obedience to political authority that Seeckt and Schleicher had exemplified. By means of the loyalty oath (August 1934) and successive changes in the structure and personnel of the military command, Hitler made sure that the armed forces would not challenge his notion of absolute civilian control: political leadership rests unequivocally in the hands of the Führer, whose will is binding on all departments in the "total state." In spite of this unanticipated and uncomfortable evolution in the structure and philosophy of military command, which reduced military leaders to subaltern status, the vast majority of officers in the *Wehrmacht* remained loyal to the regime and, like the diplomats, lent their expert knowledge to Hitler's politico-military planning.

Most diplomats and generals did not subscribe to the territorial or racial extremes embodied in Hitler's idea of *Lebensraum*, but by and large they shared his view of Germany's broad objectives in continental power politics: sovereignty, security, and territorial revision.[4] The means Hitler used, however, were both more flexible and more belligerent than those of Weimar policy. Hitler adopted a new *Ostpolitik*, concluding the German-Polish Nonaggression Pact in January 1934 and loosening Germany's political and military ties with the Soviet Union; the Foreign Office and Defense (War) Ministry reluctantly but dutifully adjusted to this bold departure from the ossified eastern policy of Weimar. Toward the West, on the other hand, Hitler's policy retained the same outline evidenced in the Foreign Office and Defense Ministry during the years of crisis: try to win British and Italian support against France while threatening to abrogate the Treaty

[4] In the continuing debate over the significance of ideology in Hitler's foreign policy, Jacobsen and Weinberg (see preceding note) offer two of the most recent and well-documented analyses and give ideology an important causal role. On the Army and military planning under Hitler, see especially Meinck, *Deutsche Aufrüstung*; Müller, *Heer und Hitler*; Robert J. O'Neill, *The German Army and the Nazi Party, 1933-1939* (London, 1966); Robertson, *Hitler's Pre-War Policy and Military Plans*.

of Versailles. In collaboration with Hitler and with each other, the Wilhelmstrasse and the Bendlerstrasse made careful diplomatic and military preparations for Germany's withdrawal from the League and the Disarmament Conference in October 1933, for the remilitarization of the Rhineland in March 1936, and for the conquest of Austria and Czechoslovakia in 1938-39 without serious western intervention.[5]

The men in the Foreign Office and War Ministry were not averse in principle to the use of force or threats of force for exploiting a favorable political situation to revise Versailles and regain Germany's "freedom." But they were more cautious than Hitler about the risks involved in employing this instrument of national policy. On 25 October 1933, Blomberg issued a directive to the service chiefs that stands in sharp contrast to military planning in the Weimar Republic: "Irrespective of the prospects of military success, the Reich government is determined to resist by force of arms" any violation of German territory (or air space or territorial waters) by states imposing sanctions because of Germany's withdrawal from Geneva on 14 October.[6] Through this directive and in his subsequent foreign policy coups, Hitler set the tenor of politico-military activity up to the outbreak of war in September 1939. The political leadership would decide the acceptability of risk, and would not be deterred as much as Weimar Chancellors, Foreign Ministers, or Defense Ministers had been by Germany's evident military weakness relative to its adversaries.

Hitler would also choose the strategies in the event of war.

[5] On the interdepartmental planning of defensive measures in the Rhineland from 1933 to 1936, see Donald C. Watt, "German Plans for the Reoccupation of the Rhineland: A Note," *Journal of Contemporary History*, I (1966), 193-99. While joint politico-military planning continued, the collegial spirit that had animated it before 1933 was dampened: the informal evening meetings among junior men from both ministries ceased; Blomberg ordered Beck to end his contacts with Bülow; the *Führerprinzip* demanded vertical obedience detrimental to interdepartmental fraternization.

[6] *RWM*, PG 33306a.

356

The Army's defensive priorities and operational contingencies continued to evince the Weimar ambivalence toward France and the dread of a two-front war: Germany must prepare for, yet not risk, a war with France, a nation that denied Germany its freedom and remained Poland's ally;[7] Germany must be certain of British neutrality in any future conflict on the continent. The Navy, buoyed up because Hitler showed a keener interest in maritime power than any Weimar civilian leader ever had, continued to plan for North Sea operations against France and, in the late 1930s, against Britain as well. By 1937-38, however, some diplomats and military leaders—notably General Ludwig Beck, Chief of the General Staff—had concluded that Hitler was willing to engage in an offensive war for territory and "freedom" whose empirical limits and intangible implications transcended those of Weimar. The *Führerprinzip*, the ideological and strategic dimensions of Hitler's plans for eastern expansion, the possibility of a war against Britain, the political leadership's eagerness to take risks that defied military advice and outdistanced military preparedness: these mark basic departures from Weimar institutions and strategies.

The Nazi system of civil-military relations inherited tensions that had troubled the Weimar Republic. The Foreign Office and War Ministry sometimes disagreed over the timing and tactics of unilateral revision. Friction increased between the Chief of the General Staff and the War Minister and his staff; the latter, an aggressive descendant of the *Ministeramt*, openly staked its claim to both the organizational and operational spheres of military planning and became Hitler's own military staff (the *O.K.W.*) in 1938. The attempts to centralize the military command structure neither completely subordinated the services (three in number after the establishment of a separate air arm) to one joint operations com-

[7] See above, chap. 9, n. 101. In spite of Hitler's Soviet policy (and inconsistent with the Führer's flirtation with the idea of a German-Polish alliance against the Soviet Union), the Army still clung to the hope of Soviet help in a war against Poland, a major strategic legacy from Weimar planning.

mand nor resolved the conflict between the continental and maritime strategies of the Army and Navy. To settle or control such differences at the departmental level, the Weimar system had relied upon departmental responsibility and close interdepartmental collaboration, with minimum executive interference. The crisis system had upset this pattern by increasing both the interference and the power of the executive, and by allowing competing interests to define the political leadership so as to circumvent the Chancellor or the cabinet or individual departments, whichever and whenever desirable. The Nazi system strictly subordinated departmental planning and interdepartmental relations to a single unchallenged and unchecked civilian authority.

The Weimar system is both a landmark and an anomaly in modern civil-military relations. On the one hand, it provides a model for the virtual exclusion of the parliamentary or legislative level from politico-military activity in a representative system of government. On the other hand, the degree of departmental authority and style of interdepartmental relations in the Weimar system could not survive the pressures of emergency executive rule. At least since the Great Depression, European and American governments have tended to view politics—both domestic and international—as a perpetual emergency. The chief executive (with his non-departmental advisers) has increased his power over foreign policy and military planning, with the frequent result that executive fiat has overruled departmental advice, discouraged harmonious interdepartmental collaboration, and overcome interdepartmental differences. Still somewhat insecure in the adolescent Weimar system, reacting defensively to the instability of the early 1930s, Weimar diplomats and military leaders supported and acquiesced in the Nazi form of executive power; they were willing to eliminate even the vestiges of parliamentary and Prussian interference and to allow the *Führerprinzip* to engulf the executive-departmental sphere in the common national interests of unity and politico-military goals.

358

Bibliography

A. UNPUBLISHED SOURCES

1. Documents of the German Foreign Office (*AA*).
   The files cited in this study were read in the original at the Politisches Archiv of the German Foreign Office, Bonn, and in photocopy at the Library of the British Foreign Office, London. Microfilms of these files are on deposit in the National Archives, Washington, D.C. The following list is arranged according to department or category and, in each section, numerically by microfilm serial number. These serial numbers are preserved in the German documents currently being published, *Akten zur deutschen auswärtigen Politik, 1918-1945, aus dem Archiv des Auswärtigen Amts*, Series B, 1925-1933 (Göttingen, 1966 and continuing).

   a. Büro des Reichsministers
      2860 Russland
      2945 Polen
      3170 Entwaffnung und Interallierte Kommissionen und Ostfestungen
      3177 Militärwesen
      3241 Politische Schriftstücke aus dem Nachlass des Reichskanzlers bezw. Reichsministers Stresemann
   b. Büro Staatssekretär
      4506 Arnold Rechberg und ähnliche illegale Aktionen zur Herbeiführung einer deutsch-französischen Militärallianz
      4530 Interallierte Militärkontrolle
      4556 Ostprobleme: Russland-Polen-Randstaaten

4562 Deutsch-Russische Beziehungen
4564 Militärische Angelegenheiten mit Russland
4569 Polnische Angelegenheiten
c. Abteilung IVPo
L558 Politische Beziehungen Polens zu Deutschland
L575 Revision der Ostgrenze; Korridorproblem
L678 Militärangelegenheiten
d. Geheimakten
5964 Politische Beziehungen zwischen Frankreich und Polen
5986 Militärangelegenheiten (Frankreich)
6176 Deutsch-polnische Grenzproblem
6188 Politische Beziehungen zwischen Polen und Rumanien
6190 Politische Beziehungen zwischen Polen und Tschechoslowakei
6192 Zwischenstaatliche aussenpolitische Probleme: Kleine Entente
6601 Politische Beziehungen Danzig-Polen
6698 Reichswehr und Russland
9182 Deutscher Militär-Attaché in Polen
9524 Militärangelegenheiten (Russland)
K6 Militärpolitik
K7 Besprechungen mit der Marineleitung über Danzig (Studie Ost)
K16 Politische Beziehungen zwischen Frankreich und Tschechoslowakei
K94 Militärangelegenheiten (Tschechoslowakei)
K154 Neutralisierung der Ostsee
K170 Politische Beziehungen Polens zu Deutschland
K177 Politische Beziehungen zwischen Frankreich und Polen
K178 Politische Beziehungen zwischen Polen und Rumanien
K179 Politische Beziehungen zwischen Polen und Russland

K182   Sicherheitspakt
K190   Militärangelegenheiten (Polen)
K191   Marineangelegenheiten
K290   Nichtangriffspakt Verhandlungen (Russlands)
        mit Frankreich, Polen, und anderen Staaten
K299   Marineangelegenheiten (Russland)
K1949   Politische Beziehungen Polens zu Deutschland
M342   Militärische Nachrichten
e. Nachlass Stresemann
   Politische Akten

7114	7131
7115	7133
7118	7143
7123	7147
7127	7149
7128	7150
7129	7155

   Allgemeine Akten

7318	7370
7332	7371
7333	7372
7338	7375
7346	

   Aus dem Nachlass Stresemann von Konsul Bernhard
   dem Auswärtigen Amt übergebene Schriftstücke
       7414
f. Direktoren: Handakten
   5265 Wallroth: Polen, Politik
   5462 Dirksen: Korridorgespräche
   5551 Trautmann: Polen, Groener Denkschrift (1929)
   9480 Dirksen: Russische Militär-Angelegenheiten
        (1928-31)
   9481 Dirksen: Russische Militär-Angelegenheiten
        (1926-28)
g. Files containing documents cited but not filmed
   Abteilung IVPo, Akten betr. Politische Beziehungen
   Polens zu Deutschland, Bände 24, 36

Abteilung IVPo, Akten betr. Militärangelegenheiten, Band 8

2. Documents of the German Reich Chancery (*RK*), on deposit in the Bundesarchiv, Koblenz.

  a. Filmed

    3543 Alte Reichskanzlei. Kabinettsprotokolle (1925-27)

    3575 Alte Reichskanzlei. Kabinettsprotokolle (1928-31)

    K951 Alte Reichskanzlei. Reichswehr, Volkswehr, und Wehrpflicht

    K953 Alte Reichskanzlei. Landesverteidigung

    K955 Alte Reichskanzlei. Reichsmarine-Schiffsbau

    K1947 Alte Reichskanzlei. Polen

  b. Files containing documents cited but not filmed

    Alte Reichskanzlei. Akten betr. Dienstgebäude, Garnisonen, Festungen

    Alte Reichskanzlei. Akten betr. Polen, Bände 8-10

    Alte Reichskanzlei. Akten betr. Reichsmarine, Band 2

    Alte Reichskanzlei. Akten betr. Reichswehr, Volkswehr, und Wehrpflicht, Band 5

3. Documents of the German Defense Ministry (*RWM*).

The Army files and the Navy documents designated "II M" and "Fach" were read in the original at the Militärgeschichtliches Forschungsamt, Freiburg. The Navy files marked "PG"—microfilm serial numbers—are part of a complete set of filmed German naval records deposited with the Naval Historical Branch, Ministry of Defence, London. (Note: since the completion of the documentary research for this study, the Bundesarchiv-Militärarchiv, formerly in Koblenz, has moved to Freiburg and taken over the document section of the Militärgeschichtliches Forschungsamt. In the resultant recataloguing, the files listed below have been given new serial numbers.)

a. Army

II H 135/2	Truppenamt. Organisation und Ausrüstung
II H 221	Truppenamt. Geheim Allgemeines
II H 228	Truppenamt. Neues Friedensheer
II H 249	Truppenamt. Nachschub, Truppentransporte, Benutzung der Eisenbahn
II H 518	Truppenamt, Heeresabteilung (T1). Rückwärtige Widerstands-Zonen Osten
II H 524/2	Truppenamt, T1. Landesverteidigung (organisatorisch), Pommern-Stellung
II H 525	Truppenamt, T1. Oderausbau
II H 560	Truppenamt, T1. Unterlagen und Schlussbesprechungen von Transportübungsreisen, Winteraufgaben, Allgemeines
II H 561	Truppenamt, T1. Transport-übungsreisen, Winteraufgaben, Allgemeines
II H 562	Truppenamt, T1. Blumenstrauss/Ost 1927/28
II H 563/1	Truppenamt, T1. Transport-übungsreise 1931
II H 563/2	Truppenamt, T1. Transportübungsaufgabe 1932
II H 570	Truppenamt, T1. Strategischer Ausbau d. Eisenbahnen im Reiche
II H 572	Truppenamt, T1. "Weisungen," Marschbereitschaft, A-Vorbereitungen
II H 594	Truppenamt, T1. Transport-übungsreise 1932
II H 597	Truppenamt, T1. Folgerungen aus den Studien des T.A. 27/28 und 28/29
II H 600/1	Truppenamt, T1. Operative Aufgabe 1931
II H 600/2	Truppenamt, T1. Operative Aufgaben 1932

II H 600/3	Truppenamt, T1. Operative Aufgaben 1933
II H 605	Truppenamt, T1. Truppenamtsreise 1930
II H 606/1	Truppenamt, T1. Truppenamtsreise 1931
II H 608/1	Truppenamt, T1. Führer-Reise 1932
II H 609/1	Truppenamt, T1. Führer-Reise 1933

b. Navy

II M 2	Marineleitung. Spitzenorganisation
II M 48	Chef der Marineleitung. Kriegsrechtliche Stellung der Ostsee-Eingänge
II M 49	Marineleitung, Flottenabteilung. Die Marine der Ostseemächte, völkerrechtliche und seestrategische Fragen der Ostsee
II M 57/5	Marineakademie, Flottenabteilung. Vortrag Nr. 5—Schenk (1922)
II M 57/32	Marineakademie, Flottenabteilung. Vortrag Nr. 32—von Ditten (1924)
II M 57/41	Marineakademie, Flottenabteilung. Vortrag Nr. 41—Schuster, "Grundlagen des Seekrieges" (1932)
II M 57/46	Marineakademie, Flottenabteilung. Vortrag Nr. 46—Marwitz (1929)
II M 57/51	Marineakademie, Flottenabteilung. Vortrag Nr. 51—Dönitz (1932)
II M 57/53	Marineakademie, Flottenabteilung. Vortrag Nr. 53—Schuster, "Kriegsaufgaben der Reichsmarine" (1932)
II M 57/57	Marineakademie, Flottenabteilung. Vortrag Nr. 57—Bonin (1928)
II M 57/58	Marineakademie, Flottenabteilung. Vortrag Nr. 58—Boehm, "Kriegsaufgaben der Marine" (1929)
II M 57/60	Marineakademie, Flottenabteilung. Vortrag Nr. 60—Groener (1928)

II M 59/1   Marineakademie. Vortrag 1—Schuster, "Unsere seestrategische Lage" (1933)

II M 62/1   Marineleitung. MI; Verschiedenes

II M 66/1   Marineleitung. Marine - Ausbildungs-pläne, Reise, Übungen

II M 69/1   Marineleitung. Denkschrift über Panzerschiff "A"

II M 100/1 Marineleitung, Flottenabteilung. Allgemeines

II M 100/14 Marineleitung, Flottenabteilung. Führerkriegsspiel Dezember 1927

II M 100/17 Marineleitung, Flottenabteilung. Führerreise 1928

II M 100/18 Marineleitung, Flottenabteilung. Führerreise 1928

II M 100/23 Marineleitung, Flottenabteilung. Herbstmanöver 1932

Fach 7896   Marineleitung, Flottenabteilung. Zusammenarbeit mit Heer

PG 26648   Marineleitung. Schuster, "Der Kampf der Marine gegen Versailles 1919-1935" (1937)

PG 31039   Marineleitung. "Die marinepolitische Entwicklung, die operativen und taktischen Grundüberlegungen der Kriegsmarine . . . von 1919 bis Kriegsbeginn 1939"

PG 31783   Marineleitung. Marinepolitik-Abrüstung

PG 31871   Marineleitung. Dr. Treue, "Aufbau der Kriegsmarine 1926-1939" (1939)

PG 33306a   Marineleitung. Überholte operative Weisungen und Befehle

PG 33442   Marineleitung. Rüstungsplan

PG 33444   Marineleitung. Studie III: Zufuhrschutz

PG 33611   Marineleitung. Marinepolitische Angelegenheiten

PG 33617	Marineleitung. Russland
PG 33965b	Marineleitung. Ciliax, "Die militär-politische und seestrategische Lage Deutschlands" (1936)
PG 34048/3	Marineleitung, Flottenabteilung. Herbstmanöver 1928; Gefechtsübung 1929
PG 34051	Marineleitung, Flottenabteilung. Manöver
PG 34061	Marineleitung, Flottenabteilung. Admiralstabfragen
PG 34065	Marineleitung, Flottenabteilung. Kriegsaufgaben
PG 34066	Marineleitung, Flottenabteilung. Kriegsaufgaben
PG 34072	Marineleitung, Flottenabteilung. Verwendung der Marine im Kriegsfalle
PG 34073	Marineleitung, Flottenabteilung. Kriegsspiele
PG 34073/1	Marineleitung, Flottenabteilung. Kriegsspiele
PG 34076	Marineleitung, Flottenabteilung. Kriegsspiele
PG 34089	Marineleitung, Flottenabteilung. Ostseeverteidigung-Pillau
PG 34095	Marineleitung, Flottenabteilung. Heeresangelegenheiten
PG 34101	Marineleitung, Flottenabteilung. Studie "Gdingen"
PG 34102	Marineleitung, Flottenabteilung. Studie "Gdingen"
PG 34117	Marineleitung, Flottenabteilung. Studie "Fall Danzig"
PG 34118	Marineleitung, Flottenabteilung. Studie Ost
PG 34168/1	Marineleitung. Sammlung von Besprechungsniederschriften

PG 34177	Marineleitung. Vorträge
PG 34463	Flottenkommando. Politisches
PG 48897	Marineleitung. Attaché- Verwaltungs- und Personalangelegenheiten
PG 48898	Marineleitung. Auslands- Berichte
PG 49029	Archiv der Marine. Osten
PG 49030	Archiv der Marine. Südosten
PG 49031	Archiv der Marine. Polen
PG 49032	Archiv der Marine. Westen

4. Private Papers

Admiral a.D. Leopold Bürkner, Zeugenschrifttum no. 364, Institut für Zeitgeschichte, Munich

General der Infanterie a.D. Hermann Foertsch, Zeugenschrifttum no. 37, Institut für Zeitgeschichte, Munich

Nachlass Otto Gessler, no. 55, Bundesarchiv, Koblenz

Nachlass Wilhelm Groener, nos. 39, 149, 165, Bundesarchiv-Militärarchiv, Freiburg

Generaloberst a.D. Gotthard Heinrici, Zeugenschrifttum no. 66 II, Institut für Zeitgeschichte, Munich

Aufzeichnungen Generals Curt Liebmann (Befehlshaberbesprechungen), Institut für Zeitgeschichte, Munich

Botschafter a.D. Eugen Ott, Zeugenschrifttum no. 279, Institut für Zeitgeschichte, Munich

Nachlass Kurt von Schleicher, nos. 34, 35, 44, Bundesarchiv-Militärarchiv, Freiburg

Seeckt Papers, rolls 19 and 20 (microfilm), Hoover Institution, Stanford, Calif.

5. Interviews and Correspondence

The following persons provided information through interviews and letters, during the spring and early summer of 1966.

Generalmajor a.D. Hans von Ahlfen

Dr. Heinrich Bennecke

General der Infanterie a.D. Kurt Brennecke

General der Infanterie a.D. Theodor Busse

Grossadmiral a.D. Karl Dönitz

Generalleutnant a.D. Hans von Donat

Generalleutnant a.D. Hermann Flörke

General der Artillerie a.D. Maximilian Fretter-Pico

Generaloberst a.D. Franz Halder (correspondence only)

General der Artillerie a.D. Friedrich Wilhelm Hauck

Generaloberst a.D. Paul Hausser

Generaloberst a.D. Gotthard Heinrici

General a.D. Adolf Heusinger

Generalleutnant a.D. Fritz Kühne

General der Gebirgstruppe a.D. Hubert Lanz

Generalfeldmarschall a.D. Erich von Manstein
  (correspondence only)

General der Panzertruppe a.D. Walther Nehring

Botschafter a.D. Eugen Ott

Dr. Jürgen Rohwer

General a.D. Dr. Hans Speidel

General der Infanterie a.D. Max von Viebahn

Vizeadmiral a.D. Gerhard Wagner

B. PUBLISHED SOURCES

Anschütz, Gerhard. *Die Verfassung des Deutschen Reichs vom 11. August 1919*. Rev. ed. Berlin, 1926.

Becker, Josef. "Zur Politik der Wehrmachtabteilung in der Regierungskrise 1926/27," *Vierteljahrshefte für Zeitgeschichte*, XIV (1966).

Carsten, F. L. "Reports by Two German Officers on the Red Army," *The Slavonic and East European Review,* XLI (1962).

Conze, Werner, "Zum Sturz Brünings," *Vierteljahrshefte für Zeitgeschichte*, I (1953).

Craig, Gordon A. "Quellen zur neuesten Geschichte: ii. Briefe Schleichers an Groener," *Die Welt als Geschichte,* XI (1951).

Documents on British Foreign Policy 1919-1939. Edited by E. L. Woodward and Rohan Butler. London, 1946 and continuing.

Goerner, E. A. (ed.) *The Constitutions of Europe.* Chicago, 1967.

Horak, Stephen. *Poland's International Affairs 1919-1960.* Bloomington, Ind., 1964.

Nauticus. "New Germany's New Navy," *The Review of Reviews,* LXXVIII (1929).

Nazi Conspiracy and Aggression. 8 vols. and 2 supplements. Washington, D. C., 1946ff.

Papers Relating to the Foreign Relations of the United States. Washington, D. C.

Phelps, Reginald H. "Aus den Groener Dokumenten," *Deutsche Rundschau,* LXXVI (1950).

————. "Aus den Seeckt Dokumenten," *Deutsche Rundschau,* LXXVIII (1952).

Rothfels, Hans. "Ausgewählte Briefe von Generalmajor Helmuth Stieff," *Vierteljahrshefte für Zeitgeschichte,* II (1954).

Schüddekopf, Otto-Ernst. *Das Heer und die Republik: Quellen zur Politik der Reichswehrführung, 1918 bis 1933.* Hanover & Frankfurt, 1955.

Trial of the Major War Criminals before the International Military Tribunal. 42 vols. Nuremberg, 1947-49.

Trials of War Criminals before the Nuernberg Military Tribunals under Control Council Law No. 10. 15 vols. Washington, D. C., 1949ff.

Turner, Henry Ashby Jr. "Eine Rede Stresemanns über seine Locarnopolitik," *Vierteljahrshefte für Zeitgeschichte,* XV (1967).

Völker, Karl-Heinz. *Dokumente und Dokumentarfotos zur Geschichte der deutschen Luftwaffe.* Stuttgart, 1968.

Vogelsang, Thilo. "Neue Dokumente zur Geschichte der Reichswehr 1930-1933," *Vierteljahrshefte für Zeitgeschichte,* II (1954).

Wheeler-Bennett, John W. (ed.) *Documents on International Affairs 1932.* London, 1933.

C. MEMOIRS AND DIARIES

Beck, Jozef. *Final Report.* New York, 1957.

Bismarck, Otto von. *Die gesammelten Werke.* 15 vols. in 19. Berlin, 1924ff.

Braun, Otto. *Von Weimar zu Hitler.* 2d ed. New York, 1940.

Brecht, Arnold. *Mit der Kraft des Geistes: Lebenserinnerungen, 1927-1967.* Stuttgart, 1967.

Brüning, Heinrich. *Memoiren 1918-1934.* Stuttgart, 1970.

————. *Reden und Aufsätze eines deutschen Staatsmanns.* Edited by W. Vernekohl. Münster, 1968.

Curtius, Julius. *Sechs Jahre Minister der Deutschen Republik.* Heidelberg, 1948.

D'Abernon, Lord. *Lord D'Abernon's Diary.* 3 vols. London, 1929-30.

Dirksen, Herbert von. *Moscow, Tokyo, London: Twenty Years of German Foreign Policy.* Norman, Okla., 1952.

Dönitz, Karl. *Mein wechselvolles Leben.* Göttingen, 1968.

Foerster, Wolfgang. *Generaloberst Ludwig Beck: Sein Kampf gegen den Krieg.* Munich, 1953.

François-Poncet, André. *The Fateful Years: Memoirs of a French Ambassador in Berlin, 1931-1938.* Translated by Jacques LeClercq. New York, 1949.

Gamelin, Maurice. *Servir.* 3 vols. Paris, 1946-47.

Gessler, Otto. *Reichswehrpolitik in der Weimarer Zeit.* Edited by Kurt Sendtner. Stuttgart, 1958.

Geyr von Schweppenburg, Leo Freiherr. *Erinnerungen eines Militärattachés.* Stuttgart, 1949.

Groener, Wilhelm. *Lebenserinnerungen.* Edited by Freiherr Hiller von Gaertringen. Göttingen, 1957.

Hoffmann, Max. *War Diaries and Other Papers.* Translated by Eric Sutton. 2 vols. London, 1929.

Köstring, August-Ernst. *General Ernst Köstring: Der militärische Mittler zwischen dem Deutschen Reich und der Sowjetunion 1921-1941.* Edited by Hermann Teske. Frankfurt am Main, 1966.

Kordt, Erich. *Nicht aus den Akten*. Stuttgart, 1950.

Laroche, Jules. *La Pologne de Pilsudski: Souvenirs d'une ambassade, 1926-1935*. Paris, 1953.

Lipski, Josef. *Diplomat in Berlin*. Edited by W. Jedrzejewicz. New York, 1968.

Manstein, Erich von. *Aus einem Soldatenleben, 1887-1939*. Bonn, 1958.

Meissner, Otto. *Staatssekretär unter Ebert-Hindenburg-Hitler*. Hamburg, 1950.

Müller, Vincenz. *Ich fand das wahre Vaterland*. Edited by Klaus Mammach. [East Berlin], 1963.

Nadolny, Rudolf. *Mein Beitrag*. Wiesbaden, 1955.

Papen, Franz von. *Vom Scheitern einer Demokratie 1930-1933*. Mainz, 1968.

————. *Der Wahrheit eine Gasse*. Munich, 1952.

Rabenau, Friedrich von. *Seeckt: Aus seinem Leben, 1918-1936*. Leipzig, 1940.

Raeder, Erich. *My Life*. Translated by Henry W. Drexel. Annapolis, Md., 1960.

Sahm, Heinrich, *Erinnerungen aus meinen Danziger Jahren, 1919-1930*. Marburg, 1955.

Schellenberg, Walter. *The Labyrinth: Memoirs of Walter Schellenberg*. Translated by Louis Hagen. New York, 1956.

Schmidt, Paul. *Statist auf diplomatischer Bühne 1923-45*. Bonn, 1949.

Schwerin von Krosigk, Lutz Graf. *Es Geschah in Deutschland*. Tübingen & Stuttgart, 1951.

Severing, Carl. *Mein Lebensweg*. 2 vols. Cologne, 1950.

Stresemann, Gustav. *Vermächtnis*. Edited by Henry Bernhard. 3 vols. Berlin, 1932-33.

Weizsäcker, Ernst von. *Memoirs of Ernst von Weizsäcker*. Translated by John Andrews. Chicago, 1951.

Ziehm, Ernst. *Aus meiner politischen Arbeit in Danzig, 1914-1939*. Marburg, 1957.

D. Secondary Works

Abshagen, Karl Heinz. *Canaris.* Translated by Alan H. Brodrick. London, 1956.

Absolon, Rudolf. *Die Wehrmacht im Dritten Reich,* i. Boppard, 1969.

Albord, Tony. *La défense nationale.* Paris, 1958.

Aron, Raymond. *Peace and War: A Theory of International Relations.* Translated by R. Howard and A. B. Fox. New York, 1966.

Assmann, Kurt. *Deutsche Seestrategie in zwei Weltkriegen.* Heidelberg, 1957.

Bankwitz, Philip C. F. *Maxime Weygand and Civil-Military Relations in Modern France.* Cambridge, Mass., 1967.

Bariéty, Jacques, and Bloch, Charles. "Une tentative de réconciliation franco-allemande et son échec (1932-1933)," *Revue d'histoire moderne et contemporaine,* xv (1968).

Beck, Earl R. *The Death of the Prussian Republic: A Study of Reich-Prussian Relations, 1932-1934.* Tallahassee, Fla., 1959.

Beck, Ludwig. *Studien.* Edited by Hans Speidel. Stuttgart, 1955.

Bennecke, Heinrich. *Die Reichswehr und der "Röhm-Putsch."* Munich, 1964.

Bennett, Edward W. *Germany and the Diplomacy of the Financial Crisis, 1931.* Cambridge, Mass., 1962.

Benoist-Méchin, Jacques. *Histoire de l'armée allemande.* 6 vols. Michel ed. Paris, 1964-66.

Bensel, Rolf. *Die deutsche Flottenpolitik von 1933 bis 1939: Eine Studie über die Rolle des Flottenbaus in Hitlers Aussenpolitik.* Frankfurt am Main, 1958.

Berghahn, Volker R. *Der Stahlhelm: Bund der Frontsoldaten 1918-1935.* Düsseldorf, 1966.

Berndorff, H. R. *General zwischen Ost und West.* Hamburg, 1951.

Bidlingmaier, Gerhard. *Seegeltung in der deutschen Geschichte*. Darmstadt, 1967.

——. "Die strategischen und operative Überlegungen der Marine 1932-1942," *Wehrwissenschaftliche Rundschau,* XIII (1963).

Bonnefous, Édouard. *Histoire politique de la Troisième République*. 7 vols. Paris, 1956ff.

Bracher, Karl Dietrich. *Die Auflösung der Weimarer Republik*. 2d ed. Stuttgart & Düsseldorf, 1957.

——, Wolfgang Sauer, and Gerhard Schulz. *Die nationalsozialistische Machtergreifung*. 2d ed. Cologne & Opladen, 1962.

Bretton, Henry L. *Stresemann and the Revision of Versailles*. Stanford, Calif., 1953.

Breyer, Richard. *Das Deutsche Reich und Polen 1932-1937: Aussenpolitik und Volksgruppenfragen*. Würzburg, 1955.

Broszat, Martin. *Zweihundert Jahre deutsche Polenpolitik*. Munich, 1963.

Brüning, Heinrich. "Ein Brief," *Deutsche Rundschau,* LXX (1947).

Bucher, Peter. *Der Reichswehrprozess: Der Hochverrat der Ulmer Reichswehroffiziere 1929/30*. Boppard, 1967.

Buchheit, Gert. *Der deutsche Geheimdienst*. Munich, 1966.

Carr, Edward Hallett. *German-Soviet Relations between the Two World Wars, 1919-1939*. Baltimore, 1951.

——. *A History of Soviet Russia: Socialism in One Country 1924-1926*. 3 vols. New York, 1950-64.

——. *The Twenty Years' Crisis, 1919-1939: An Introduction to the Study of International Relations*. 2d ed. New York, 1946.

Carsten, F. L. *The Reichswehr and Politics, 1918 to 1933*. Oxford, 1966.

Caspar, Gustav Adolf. *Die sozialdemokratische Partei und das deutsche Wehrproblem in den Jahren der Weimarer Republik*. Frankfurt am Main, 1959.

Castellan, Georges. *Le réarmement clandestin du Reich, 1930-1935*. Paris, 1954.

Challener, Richard D. *The French Theory of the Nation in Arms, 1866-1939.* New York, 1955.

Chastenet, Jacques. *Histoire de la Troisième République.* 7 vols. Paris, 1952-63.

Clausewitz, Carl von. *On War.* Translated by Colonel J. J. Graham. 3 vols. Rev. ed. London, 1940.

Cochenhausen, Friedrich von. *Kriegsspiel-Fibel.* Berlin, 1930(?).

———. *Wehrgedanken.* Hamburg, 1933.

Conze, Werner. "Brünings Politik unter dem Druck der Grossen Krise," *Historische Zeitschrift,* cxcix (1964).

———, and Raupach, Hans. (eds.) *Die Staats- und Wirtschaftskrise des Deutschen Reichs 1929/33.* Stuttgart, 1967.

Craig, Gordon A. *From Bismarck to Adenauer: Aspects of German Statecraft.* Baltimore, 1958.

———. *The Politics of the Prussian Army, 1640-1945.* New York, 1956.

———, and Gilbert, Felix. (eds.) *The Diplomats 1919-1939.* Princeton, N. J., 1953.

Das 12. Infanterie-Regiment der Deutschen Reichswehr, 1.1.1921 bis 1.10.1934. Berlin & Osterwieck/Harz, 1939.

Debicki, Roman. *Foreign Policy of Poland 1919-39: From the Rebirth of the Polish Republic to World War II.* New York, 1962.

Deist, Wilhelm. "Schleicher und die deutsche Abrüstungspolitik im Juni/Juli 1932," *Vierteljahrshefte für Zeitgeschichte,* vii (1959).

Demeter, Karl. *Das deutsche Offizierkorps in Gesellschaft und Staat, 1650-1945.* Frankfurt am Main, 1962.

Deutsche Einheit, Deutsche Freiheit: Gedenkbuch der Reichsregierung zum 10. Verfassungstag, 11. August 1929. Berlin, 1929.

Dorpalen, Andreas. *Hindenburg and the Weimar Republic.* Princeton, N. J., 1964.

Duroselle, Jean-Baptiste. *Histoire diplomatique de 1919 à nos jours.* Paris, 1953.

Dyck, Harvey Leonard. *Weimar Germany and Soviet Russia, 1926-1933: A Study in Diplomatic Instability.* New York, 1966.

Earle, Edward Mead. (ed.) *Makers of Modern Strategy: Military Thought from Machiavelli to Hitler.* Princeton, N. J., 1943.

Easum, Chester V. *Half-Century of Conflict.* New York, 1952.

Ebeling, Hans. *The Caste: The Political Role of the German General Staff between 1918 and 1938.* London, 1945.

Erdmann, Karl Dietrich. "Deutschland, Rapallo und der Westen," *Vierteljahrshefte für Zeitgeschichte,* xi (1963).

————. "Das Problem der Ost- oder Westorientierung in der Locarno-Politik Stresemanns," *Geschichte in Wissenschaft und Unterricht,* vi (1955).

Erfurth, Waldemar. *Die Geschichte des deutschen Generalstabes von 1918 bis 1945.* Göttingen, 1957.

Erickson, John. *The Soviet High Command: A Military-Political History, 1918-1941.* London, 1962.

Eschenburg, Theodor. *Die improvisierte Demokratie: Gesammelte Aufsätze zur Weimarer Republik.* Munich, 1963.

Eyck, Erich. *A History of the Weimar Republic.* Translated by H. P. Hanson and R.G.L. Waite. 2 vols. New York, 1962-63.

Ferrell, Robert H. *Peace in their Time: The Origins of the Kellogg-Briand Pact.* New Haven, Conn., 1952.

Frankel, Joseph. *The Making of Foreign Policy: An Analysis of Decision-Making.* London, 1963.

————. *National Interest.* London, 1970.

Frantz, Gunther. *Die Vernichtungsschlacht in kriegsgeschichtlichen Beispielen.* Berlin, 1928.

Freund, Gerald. *Unholy Alliance: Russian-German Relations from the Treaty of Brest-Litovsk to the Treaty of Berlin.* New York, 1957.

Gasiorowski, Zygmunt. "Did Pilsudski Attempt to Initiate a Preventive War in 1933?," *Journal of Modern History,* xxvii (1955).

Gasiorowski, Zygmunt. "The Russian Overture to Germany of December 1924," *Journal of Modern History,* XXX (1958).

———. "Stresemann and Poland after Locarno," *Journal of Central European Affairs,* XVIII (1958-59).

———. "Stresemann and Poland before Locarno," *Journal of Central European Affairs,* XVIII (1958-59).

Gathorne-Hardy, G. M. *A Short History of International Affairs, 1920-1939.* 4th ed. London, 1950.

Gatzke, Hans W. "Von Rapallo nach Berlin: Stresemann und die deutsche Russlandpolitik," *Vierteljahrshefte für Zeitgeschichte,* IV (1956).

———. "Russo-German Military Collaboration during the Weimar Republic," *American Historical Review,* LXIII (1958).

———. "The Stresemann Papers," *Journal of Modern History,* XXVI (1954).

———. *Stresemann and the Rearmament of Germany.* Baltimore, 1954.

Gemzell, Carl-Axel. *Raeder, Hitler und Skandinavien: Der Kamp für einen Maritimen Operationsplan.* Lund, 1965.

Gibson, Irving M. "The Maginot Line," *Journal of Modern History,* XVII (1945).

Giese, Fritz E. *Die Deutsche Marine 1920 bis 1945.* Frankfurt am Main, 1956.

Göhring, Martin. *Stresemann: Mensch, Staatsmann, Europäer.* Wiesbaden, 1956.

Görlitz, Walter. *Gustav Stresemann.* Heidelberg, 1947.

———. *History of the German General Staff, 1657-1945.* New York, 1953.

Gordon, Harold J. Jr. *The Reichswehr and the German Republic, 1919-1926.* Princeton, N. J., 1957.

Gottwald, Robert. *Die deutsch-amerikanischen Beziehungen in der Ära Stresemann.* Berlin-Dahlem, 1965.

Groener-Geyer, Dorothea. *General Groener, Soldat und Staatsmann.* Frankfurt am Main, 1955.

Grün, George A. "Locarno: Idea and Reality," *International Affairs,* XXXI (1955).

Guske, Claus. *Das politische Denken des Generals von Seeckt: Ein Beitrag zur Diskussion des Verhältnisses Seeckt-Reichswehr-Republik.* Lübeck, 1971.

Haeussler, Helmut. *General William Groener and the Imperial German Army.* Madison, Wisc., 1962.

Hallgarten, George W. F. "General Hans von Seeckt and Russia, 1920-1922," *Journal of Modern History,* XXI (1949).

Haungs, Peter. *Reichspräsident und parlamentarische Kabinettsregierung: Eine Studie zum Regierungssystem der Weimarer Republik in den Jahren 1924 bis 1929.* Cologne & Opladen, 1968.

Heineman, John L. "Constantin Freiherr von Neurath as Foreign Minister, 1932-1935." Unpublished Ph.D. dissertation, Cornell University, 1965.

Helbich, Wolfgang J. "Between Stresemann and Hitler: The Foreign Policy of the Brüning Government," *World Politics,* XII (1959).

Helbig, Herbert. "Die Moskauer Mission des Grafen Brockdorff-Rantzau," *Forschungen zur Osteuropäischen Geschichte,* II. Berlin, 1955.

————. *Die Träger der Rapallo-Politik.* Göttingen, 1958.

Herzfeld, Hans. "Zur neueren Literatur über das Heeresproblem in der deutschen Geschichte," *Vierteljahrshefte für Zeitgeschichte,* IV (1956).

————. *Das Problem des Deutschen Heeres 1919-1945.* Laupheim, 1950(?).

Hilger, Gustav, and Meyer, Alfred G. *The Incompatible Allies: A Memoir-History of German-Soviet Relations, 1918-1941.* New York, 1953.

Hill, Leonidas E. "The Wilhelmstrasse in the Nazi Era," *Political Science Quarterly,* LXXXII (1967).

Höltje, Christian. *Die Weimarer Republik und das Ostlocarno-Problem 1919-1934.* Würzburg, 1958.

Hoffmann, Stanley. *The State of War: Essays on the Theory and Practice of International Politics.* New York, 1965.

Hollweg, Admiral (Ret.). "Das Versailler Diktat und die deutschen Seeinteressen," *Nauticus,* XVII (1923).

Hossbach, Friedrich. *Die Entwicklung des Oberbefehls über das Heer in Brandenburg, Preussen und im Deutschen Reich von 1655-1945.* Würzburg, 1957.

Howard, Michael. (ed.) *Soldiers and Governments: Nine Studies in Civil-Military Relations.* London, 1957.

————. (ed.) *The Theory and Practice of War: Essays Presented to Captain B. H. Liddell Hart on His Seventieth Birthday.* London, 1965.

Hubatsch, Walther. *Der Admiralstab und die obersten Marinebehörden in Deutschland 1848-1945.* Frankfurt am Main, 1958.

Huntington, Samuel P. (ed.) *Changing Patterns of Military Politics.* New York, 1962.

————. *The Soldier and the State: The Theory and Politics of Civil-Military Relations.* Cambridge, Mass., 1957.

Jacobsen, Hans-Adolf. *Nationalsozialistische Aussenpolitik 1933-1938.* Frankfurt am Main, 1968.

Jacobson, Jon S. *Locarno Diplomacy: Germany and the West, 1925-1929.* Princeton, N. J., 1972.

Janowitz, Morris. *The Professional Soldier: A Social and Political Portrait.* Glencoe, Ill., 1960.

Jervis, Robert. *The Logic of Images in International Relations.* Princeton, N. J., 1970.

Jordan, W. M. *Great Britain, France and the German Problem 1918-1939.* London, 1943.

Kehr, Eckart. *Der Primat der Innenpolitik.* Edited by Hans-Ulrich Wehler. Berlin, 1965.

Kehrig, Manfred. *Die Wiedereinrichtung des deutschen militärischen Attachédienstes nach dem Ersten Weltkrieg (1919-1933).* Boppard, 1966.

Kennan, George. *Russia and the West under Lenin and Stalin.* Boston, 1960.

Kimmich, Christoph M. *The Free City: Danzig and German Foreign Policy, 1919-1934*. New Haven, Conn., 1968.

Kiszling, Rudolf. *Die militärischen Vereinbarungen der Kleinen Entente 1929-1937*. Munich, 1959.

Klein, Fritz. *Die Diplomatischen Beziehungen Deutschlands zur Sowjetunion, 1917-1932*. Berlin, 1952.

Kluke, Paul. "Deutschland und Russland zwischen den Weltkriegen," *Historische Zeitschrift*, CLXXI (1951).

Knauss, Bernhard, "Politik ohne Waffen. Dargestellt an der Diplomatie Stresemanns," *Zeitschrift für Politik*, X (New Series, 1963).

Kochan, Lionel. *Russia and the Weimar Republic*. Cambridge, 1954.

Köttgen, Arnold. *Das deutsche Berufsbeamtentum und die parlamentarische Demokratie*. Berlin & Leipzig, 1928.

Korbel, Josef. *Poland between East and West: Soviet and German Diplomacy toward Poland, 1919-1933*. Princeton, N. J., 1963.

Kraehe, Enno. "The Motives behind the Maginot Line," *Military Affairs*, VIII (1944).

Kruszewski, Charles. "The German-Polish Tariff War (1925-1934) and Its Aftermath," *Journal of Central European Affairs*, III (1943).

La Gorce, Paul-Marie de. *The French Army: A Military-Political History*. Translated by Kenneth Douglas. New York, 1963.

Liang, Hsi-Huey. *The Berlin Police Force in the Weimar Republic*. Berkeley, Calif., 1970.

Liddell Hart, B. H. *The German Generals Talk*. New York, 1948.

Lutz, Ralph H. (ed.) *Fall of the German Empire 1914-1918*. 2 vols. Stanford, Calif., 1932.

Matthias, Erich. *Die deutsche Sozialdemokratie und der Osten 1914-1945*. Tübingen, 1954.

———, and Morsey, Rudolf. (eds.) *Das Ende der Parteien 1933*. Düsseldorf, 1960.

Mayer, Arno J. "Internal Causes and Purposes of War in Europe, 1870-1956: A Research Assignment," *Journal of Modern History*, XLI (1969).

————. *Political Origins of the New Diplomacy, 1917-1918.* New Haven, Conn., 1959.

Meier-Welcker, Hans. *Seeckt.* Frankfurt am Main, 1967.

Meinck, Gerhard. *Hitler und die Deutsche Aufrüstung, 1933-1937.* Wiesbaden, 1959.

Mertens, Carl. *Reichswehr oder Landesverteidigung?* Wiesbaden, 1927.

Meyer, Henry Cord. *"Mitteleuropa" in German Thought and Action 1815-1945.* The Hague, 1955.

Morgan, J. H. *Assize of Arms: The Disarmament of Germany and Her Rearmament, 1919-1939.* New York, 1946.

Moser, Otto von. *Das militärisch und politisch Wichtigste vom Weltkriege.* Stuttgart, 1926.

————. *Die obersten Gewalten im Weltkrieg.* Stuttgart, 1931.

Müller, Klaus-Jürgen. *Das Heer und Hitler: Armee und nationalsozialistisches Regime 1933-1940.* Stuttgart, 1969.

Mueller-Hillebrand, Burkhart. *Das Heer 1933-1945.* Vol. I: *Das Heer bis zum Kriegsbeginn.* Darmstadt, 1954.

Newman, William J. *The Balance of Power in the Interwar Years, 1919-1939.* New York, 1968.

Nicolson, Harold. *Diplomacy.* 3d ed. London, 1963.

Nobécourt, Jacques. *Une Histoire politique de l'armée.* 2 vols. Paris, 1967.

Northedge, F. S. *The Troubled Giant: Britain Among the Great Powers 1916-1939.* New York, 1966.

O'Neill, Robert J. *The German Army and the Nazi Party, 1933-1939.* London, 1966.

Ott, Eugen. "Ein Bild des Generals Kurt von Schleicher; aus den Erfahrungen seiner Mitarbeiter dargestellt," *Politische Studien,* X (1959).

Puchert, Berthold. *Der Wirtschaftskrieg des deutschen Imperialismus gegen Polen 1925-1934.* [East] Berlin, 1963.

Rangliste des Deutschen Reichsheeres. Berlin, 1924-32.

Rangliste der Deutschen Reichsmarine. Berlin, 1924-32.

Renouvin, Pierre, and Duroselle, Jean-Baptiste. *Introduction to the History of International Relations.* Translated by Mary Ilford. New York, 1967.

Rheinbaben, Werner Freiherr von. "Deutschland und Polen," *Europäische Gespräche,* VI (1928).

————. "Deutschland und Polen; zwölf Thesen zur Revisionspolitik," *Europäische Gespräche,* IX (1931).

Ritter, Gerhard. "Das Problem des Militarismus in Deutschland," *Historische Zeitschrift,* CLXXVII (1954).

————. *Staatskunst und Kriegshandwerk.* 4 vols. Munich, 1954-68.

Robertson, E. M. *Hitler's Pre-War Policy and Military Plans 1933-1939.* American ed. New York, 1967.

Rössler, Hellmuth. (ed.) *Locarno und die Weltpolitik 1924-1932.* Göttingen, 1969.

Roos, Hans. *Polen und Europa: Studien zur polnischen Aussenpolitik 1931-1939.* Tübingen, 1957.

Rosenbaum, Kurt. *Community of Fate: German-Soviet Diplomatic Relations 1922-1928.* Syracuse, N. Y., 1965.

Rosinski, Herbert. *The German Army.* Edited by Gordon A. Craig. New York, 1966.

Ruge, Wolfgang. *Stresemann: Ein Lebensbild.* [East] Berlin, 1965.

Salewski, Michael. *Entwaffnung und Militärkontrolle in Deutschland 1919-1927.* Munich, 1966.

Schieder, Theodor. *Die Probleme des Rapallo-Vertrags: Eine Studie über die deutsch-russische Beziehungen 1922-1926.* Cologne, 1956.

Schmädeke, Jürgen. *Militärische Kommandogewalt und parlamentarische Demokratie.* Lübeck & Hamburg, 1966.

Schmidt-Richberg, Wiegand. *Die Generalstäbe in Deutschland 1871-1945: Aufgaben in der Armee und Stellung im Staate.* In *Beiträge zur Militär- und Kriegsgeschichte.* Vol. III. Stuttgart, 1962.

Schmitt, Bernadotte. (ed.) *Poland.* Berkeley, Calif., 1945.

Schramm, Wilhelm Ritter von. "Wege und Umwege der deutschen Kriegstheorie," *Revue militaire générale,* nos. 8 and 10 (1960).

Schüssler, Wilhelm. (ed.) *Weltmachtstreben und Flottenbau.* Witten, 1956.

Schützle, Kurt. *Reichswehr wider die Nation: Zur Rolle der Reichswehr bei der Vorbereitung und Errichtung der faschistischen Diktatur in Deutschland (1929-1933).* [East] Berlin, 1963.

Schulz, Gerhard. *Zwischen Demokratie und Diktatur: Verfassungspolitik und Reichsreform in der Weimarer Republik,* I. Berlin, 1963.

Seabury, Paul. *The Wilhelmstrasse: A Study of German Diplomats under the Nazi Regime.* Berkeley, Calif., 1954.

Seeckt, Hans von. *Bemerkungen . . . bei Besichtigungen und Manövern aus den Jahren 1920 bis 1926.* Berlin, 1927.

————. *Gedanken eines Soldaten.* Berlin, 1929.

————. *Landesverteidigung.* Berlin, 1930.

————. *Wege deutscher Aussenpolitik.* Leipzig, 1931.

Speidel, Hans. "1813/1924: Eine militärpolitische Untersuchung." Unpublished Ph.D. dissertation, University of Tübingen, 1925.

Speidel, Helm. "Reichswehr und Rote Armee," *Vierteljahrshefte für Zeitgeschichte,* I (1953).

Spenz, Jürgen. *Die diplomatische Vorgeschichte des Beitritts Deutschlands zum Völkerbund 1924-1926.* Göttingen, 1966.

Stambrook, F. G. "The German-Austrian Customs Union Project of 1931: A Study of German Methods and Motives," *Journal of Central European Affairs,* XXI (1961).

————. " 'Das Kind'—Lord D'Abernon and the Origins of the Locarno Pact," *Central European History,* I (1968).

Stein, George H. "Russo-German Military Collaboration: The Last Phase, 1933," *Political Science Quarterly,* LXXVII (1962).

Szczepanski, Max von. *Politik als Kriegführung.* Berlin, 1926.

Taylor, Telford. *Sword and Swastika: Generals and Nazis in the Third Reich.* New York, 1952.

Temperley, H.W.V. (ed.) *A History of the Peace Conference of Paris.* 6 vols. London, 1920-24.

Thimme, Annelise. *Gustav Stresemann.* Hanover & Frankfurt, 1957.

————. "Die Locarnopolitik im Lichte des Stresemann-Nachlasses," *Zeitschrift für Politik,* III (New Series, 1956).

Thomas, Georg. *Geschichte der deutschen Wehr- und Rüstungswirtschaft (1918-1943/45).* Edited by Wolfgang Birkenfeld. Boppard, 1966.

Thomée, Gerhard. *Der Wiederaufsteig des deutschen Heeres 1918-38.* Berlin, 1939.

Tournoux, Paul-Émile. *Haut commandement, gouvernement et défense des frontières du nord et de l'est, 1919-1939.* Paris, 1960.

Toynbee, Arnold J. (ed.) *Survey of International Affairs 1932.* London, 1933.

Tschischwitz, Erich von. *Manöver und grössere Truppenübungen.* Berlin, 1930.

Turner, Henry Ashby Jr. *Stresemann and the Politics of the Weimar Republic.* Princeton, N. J., 1963.

Ushakov, V. B. *Deutschlands Aussenpolitik 1917-1945.* Translated by E. Wurl. [East] Berlin, 1964.

Vagts, Alfred. *Defense and Diplomacy: The Soldier and the Conduct of Foreign Relations.* New York, 1956.

————. *A History of Militarism: Civilian and Military.* Rev. ed. New York, 1959.

Vietsch, Eberhard von. *Arnold Rechberg und das Problem der West-Orientierung Deutschlands nach dem 1. Weltkrieg.* Koblenz, 1958.

Völker, Karl-Heinz. *Die Entwicklung der militärischen Luftfahrt in Deutschland 1920-1933.* In *Beiträge zur Militär- und Kriegsgeschichte.* Vol. III. Stuttgart, 1962.

Vogelsang, Thilo. *Reichswehr, Staat und NSDAP.* Stuttgart, 1962.

Von Riekhoff, Harald. *German-Polish Relations, 1918-1933.* Baltimore, 1971.

Wacker, Wolfgang. *Der Bau des Panzerschiffes 'A' und der Reichstag.* Tübingen, 1959.

Wagner, Siegfried. *Die Polnische Gefahr.* Berlin, 1930.

Wallach, Jehuda L. *Das Dogma der Vernichtungsschlacht: Die Lehren von Clausewitz und Schlieffen und ihre Wirkungen in zwei Weltkriegen.* Frankfurt am Main, 1967.

Wandycz, Piotr S. *France and Her Eastern Allies, 1919-1925: French-Czechoslovak-Polish Relations from the Paris Peace Conference to Locarno.* Minneapolis, Minn., 1962.

Watt, Donald C. "German Plans for the Reoccupation of the Rhineland: A Note," *Journal of Contemporary History,* I (1966).

――――. *Personalities and Policies: Studies in the Formulation of British Foreign Policy in the Twentieth Century.* Notre Dame, Ind., 1965.

Watzdorf, Bernard. "Die getarnte Ausbildung von Generalstabsoffizieren der Reichswehr von 1932 bis 1935," *Zeitschrift für Militärgeschichte,* II (1963).

Weinberg, Gerhard L. *The Foreign Policy of Hitler's Germany: Diplomatic Revolution in Europe 1933-36.* Chicago, 1970.

Wheeler-Bennett, John W. *The Nemesis of Power: The German Army in Politics, 1918-1945.* London, 1953.

Wissen und Wehr. Berlin, 1927-32.

Wohlfeil, Rainer. *Heer und Republik.* In *Handbuch zur deutschen Militärgeschichte.* Vol. VI: *Reichswehr und Republik (1918-1933).* Frankfurt am Main, 1970.

Wolfers, Arnold. *Britain and France between Two Wars: Conflicting Strategies of Peace from Versailles to World War II.* New York, 1940.

――――. *Discord and Collaboration: Essays on International Politics.* Baltimore, 1962.

Wright, Quincy. *A Study of War*. Abridged ed. Chicago, 1964.

Wünsche, Wolfgang. *Strategie der Niederlage*. [East] Berlin, 1961.

Zimmermann, Ludwig. *Deutsche Aussenpolitik in der Ära der Weimarer Republik*. Göttingen, 1958.

Index

Adam, Wilhelm, 310, 314, 322, 329n, 330n
Almendinger, 312n
Alsace-Lorraine, 135-36
Alvensleben, Werner von, 299n
Anglo-French Entente, *see* Britain, France
Anschluss, 53, 282-84, 287-88
Arbeitskommandos, 177
Army: and Austria, 132, 302, 322-23, 327, 350; and Britain, 122, 133-38, 140, 214-25 *passim,* 301, 303, 325-26, 330; and Clausewitz, 8-9, 167-73, 176, 237, 312-13; and Czechoslovakia, 129-32, 204, 222, 301-2, 307, 310, 323, 326, 330; force and foreign policy, 8-9, 72n, 100, 107, 135, 155, 159, 164-67, 229, 231-34, 236-37, 295, 311-12, 328-29, 330n, 345; and France, 122, 129-30, 133-38, 140, 143-48, 150-51, 154-57, 167, 174, 204, 210-25 *passim,* 229, 231, 236, 259-62, 301-11, 322-29, 342-43, 346, 349; and Franco-Polish alliance, 103-4, 107, 109, 147-48, 150, 152, 155-56, 158, 204, 208, 210-25 *passim,* 234, 307-10, 323-24, 329, 349; general mission, 8, 87, 133, 159-60, 232-33, 292, 354; High Command (First World War), 5, 168; and Italy, 131-32, 224, 303, 322-23, 326-27,

330, 342; and League of Nations, 136-37, 209-10, 213-15, 221-22, 231, 304, 323, 326, 330n; and Lithuania, 100, 108-10, 210, 216, 222, 298-99, 323, 326; and Locarno, 97n, 125-26, 140-41, 147, 150, 151-52n, 153, 156, 174, 220, 231, 303-4; in Nazi Germany, 352-58; operations, 8, 100, 123, 124n, 150, 152, 174, 194, 196, 203-34, 236-37, 259-62, 321-30, 341-43, 346-47, 349-50; politics, 9, 88-89, 92, 96, 153, 157, 177, 186-88, 200-201, 291-93, 298, 316-21, 347, 349; railroads, 100, 121, 195n, 207n, 231, 323n; and Rumania, 131, 213-14, 222, 302, 326; tactics, 196-97, 207, 222, 230-31, 316-18, 329n; two-front war, 8, 96, 150-56, 203-4, 208, 215, 224-25, 231, 236, 262, 310-11, 327-28, 342-43, 345-46, 349-50; and United States, 134n, 210, 215, 220-21, 303, 326, 330; "war of liberation," 8, 125, 150, 165-67, 218, 234, 310, 312, 325, 328n, 330, 342;

and Poland: German borders and lost territories, 98-100, 122n, 132, 145-46, 165, 167, 231, 234, 236-37, 295, 297n, 312, 328-29, 330n, 345

Hindenburg, Paul von, 5, 18, 46n,
75n, 92, 93-94n, 95, 108, 168,
190, 267, 291, 300n, 319, 325n,
350, 353
Hitler, Adolf, 187, 229, 268n,
271, 293n, 302n, 310n, 315,
318-19, 350, 353-58
Hoesch, Leopold von, 28, 56, 59,
78, 144, 286, 290n
Hoffmann, Max, 108, 144
Hoover Moratorium, 283
Hungary, 54, 57, 131, 212

Inter-Allied Military Control
Commission, 71, 88, 182, 184,
209, 346. *See also* military
surveillance
interdepartmental relations
(Foreign Office and Defense
Ministry), 3, 6-9, 84, 88-93,
95-97, 125, 156, 168-76,
189-93, 202, 227-28, 234,
237-38, 262, 290, 293-95, 313,
345-52: attachés, 97, 104-5,
294, 315, 349; border and national defense, 153-54, 176,
178, 181-89, 192, 196-97n,
219-20, 225, 237-38, 311,
313n, 325, 346-47, 349; foreign
alignments and armies, 101-58
passim, 236-37, 295-311 *passim*, 345-47, 349-50; mobilization, 201-2, 237, 347; operations, 31, 174-75, 204, 209-28,
236-37, 321-22, 324, 329-30,
346-47, 349-50. *See also* Navy,
Foreign Office
inter-service relations (Army and
Navy): operations, 8, 219n,
257-62, 327, 339, 341-43, 347,
349-50; organization and
command, 8, 256-57, 341, 349;
rearmament, 257-58, 333,
341, 343

Italy, 58, 285, 287-88, 326-27:
guarantor of Locarno, 65, 146,
224, 243n, 287

Japan, 272, 275, 300
Junkers firm, 117, 120

Kapp *Putsch*, 87n, 88, 177, 249
Kazan, 120-21
Kellogg-Briand Pact, 81, 164, 338
Kleefeld, Kurt von, 143n
Klönne, Moritz, 144, 145n
Köpke, Gerhard, 104n, 114,
182n, 226
Köster, Roland, 78, 79n, 97
Köstring, August-Ernst, 300n
Korfanty, W., 77
Krestinski, Nicolai, 57n, 70, 98n,
122n
Krupp firm, 143
Kühlenthal, 105, 126-27, 226n
Küstrin, 178, 197, 230

Lanz, Hubert, 103-5, 107, 312n
Latvia, 38, 109
Lausanne Conference, 284, 288
League of Nations, 13, 64, 69-70,
77, 84, 162
Leipzig trial, 292-93, 312n, 319
Lenin, V. I., 124n
Lieth-Thomsen, von der, 112
Lietzmann, 331n
Lipetsk, 114, 120
Lippe, Georg von der, 144-45,
146n
Lithuania, 38, 40, 77, 108, 274,
299. *See also* Poland, Lith-
uania
Little Entente, 57-58, 131-32,
148, 279, 302
Litvinov, Maxim, 48, 118n, 120,
251, 277
Litvinov Protocol, 52
Lloyd George, David, 5

DATE DUE
